Toward a Just Social Order

TOWARD
A JUST SOCIAL
ORDER

Derek L. Phillips

PRINCETON UNIVERSITY PRESS

PRINCETON, NEW JERSEY

Again, for Klaske

CONTENTS

PREFACE AND ACKNOWLEDGMENTS

POVERTY amidst affluence, chronic unemployment, political apathy and cynicism, crime and corruption, sexism, racism, and a moral climate of widespread hedonism—these are evils familiar to all of us. Our societies are so arranged that many men, women, and children suffer from insufficient food, unsafe dwellings, a low-level education, and inadequate health care. The order of things is such that large numbers of people are subject to danger, extreme dependence, and violations of their human rights. They feel afraid, manipulated, abused, cheated, and often alienated and powerless as well.

Not surprisingly, many persons today have lost consciousness of the very possibility of a decent and humane society. Still, some among us retain the conviction that there must be something better than what now exists. One version of this "something better" is what I call a *just social order*: a society characterized by both stability and justice. A major aim of this book is to specify what I mean by a just social order, and to indicate why such a notion deserves serious attention. Rather than providing a critique of the existing social order—whose ills seem to me rather evident—my focus is on offering a broad outline and a credible version of a new society.

As things now stand, various "solutions" to the problems of advanced societies reflect the outcome of power conflicts, interest-group struggles, and the taken-for-granted commitments and allegiances of bureaucrats and policy-makers. It might be thought that a concern with the practical problems of the world is one of the responsibilities of the social scientist. But most social scientists would deny this. According to the dominant position in the social sciences, normative questions about whether a particular institutional arrangement or pattern of conduct is just or appropriate for human freedom and well-being are beyond systematic discourse.

But, as I will show, these kinds of normative questions are in principle no less objective and decidable than questions of an empirical nature. Contrary to what most social scientists seem to believe, normative theories do not have an inferior logical or epistemological status to that enjoyed by explanatory theories. Hence, there ought not to be prohibitions against the social theorist pro-

ix

posing alternative institutional arrangements and modes of social organization that transcend those of present-day society.

What we require is an increased willingness on the part of social scientists not only to describe and explain but also to advance and defend normative arguments concerning the just social organization of society. In fact, normative issues belong at the head of our agenda. To deny this is to risk self-delusion and an uncritical acceptance of the status quo. I have tried my best to avoid both.

I owe a great debt to several persons whose help I received in writing this book. My first acknowledgment is to John Alt, who provided detailed comments on successive drafts of the complete manuscript. His keen eye and analytical skills forced me both to clarify some of my arguments and to pay attention to important issues I might otherwise have ignored. Next, I want to thank Karol Edward Sołtan for useful suggestions about earlier versions of several chapters. In addition, discussions with Jos de Beus, Hans Daudt, Percy Lehning, and Robert van der Veen concerning the materials in Part IV were extremely stimulating and helpful. Further, I am grateful to Eliot Freidson, Irwin Goffman, and Richard Miller who commented on individual chapters. Finally, I want to express appreciation to Charles Lemert as well as to an anonymous individual who read the manuscript for Princeton University Press. I am especially indebted to Charles Lemert for reading the whole manuscript twice, and for being very specific about its strengths and weaknesses.

The staff of the Press have been consistently helpful, and their skill has done much to help make the book what it is. Klaske Muizelaar's gentle understanding and sense of justice have sustained me throughout. I dedicate this book to her.

April 1985

Toward a Just Social Order

INTRODUCTION

THIS book is an exploration in social theory. More specifically, it is about justice and social order. It tries to use theoretical ideas from two somewhat alien disciplines—sociology and philosophy—to locate and defend the justifiable principles required for regulating what I call a "just social order."

I begin with the recognition that whenever and wherever individuals live together, they need social order. People require a stable and coherent social environment in which to interact with one another, plan securely, carry on various sorts of transactions, and work to attain their purposes. At the individual level, it is obvious that infants and small children cannot long survive in the absence of agreed-upon rules and norms concerning who will see to their upbringing. From the cradle to the grave, in fact, most persons are caught up in a web of patterned relationships. At the societal level, stability and survival depend upon regularities and uniformities among the distinct individuals and groups who constitute society. Whatever the differences may be in their concrete form in one place and time or another, each and every society has distinct social arrangements for dealing with births, deaths, sexual relations, socialization, the allocation of goods and services, and the like. These regularities and uniformities of human conduct—sometimes spoken of as social institutions—provide the order that is the necessary matrix of social life.

The point is clear; a general context of social order protects and extends the well-being of individuals and helps assure the stability of the wider society in which they find themselves. In focusing on social order, then, I am acknowledging the human requirement for coordinated social relationships and institutionalized arrangements, which allow for continuity and predictability in everyday life.

The remarks above relate to what has long been termed the social order question. Essentially, that question asks: What makes society possible? In the face of a wide variety of individual desires and ends and the potentiality of a "war of all against all," how is social order possible? In directing my attention to the social order question, I am interested in explaining how a plurality of individual

3

acts become interrelated and ordered. This, in short, is the *explanatory* component of my project.

There is, however, a second component in my study: an emphasis on the *normative*. In considering the normative component, I am taking a step usually avoided by social scientists. This step involves the specification and justification of the particular mechanisms that should—normatively speaking—provide for social order. There are several normative questions at issue here. They are considered at some length later, so I will only briefly mention them now.

Since social order can be achieved and maintained in a wide variety of ways, is there any rational justification for one set of mechanisms in preference to another? After all, we know that social order can be the result of compulsion, coercion, manipulation, and the like, as well as of consensus about certain codes of social conduct. Doesn't it make a difference, then, how social order comes about? In the Soviet Union, for example, a high degree of social order may exist as a consequence of widespread agreement about particular moral values and standards. This is one explanation for social order. An alternative explanation is that the social order is the result of such mechanisms as requiring citizens to inform on people who engage in "deviant" actions or having the government provide excursions to Siberia for certain dissidents. In this case, social order is seen as being maintained by fear and coercion. One of my intentions here is to consider whether there are compelling arguments for the normative superiority (or inferiority) of "internal" compared with "external" sources of social order.

Further, I am interested in the normative dimension in situations where perhaps the vast majority of citizens accepts the moral values and standards espoused by those in power, while a small minority argues for a completely different set of values and standards. Although many sociologists emphasize the extent to which social order is maintained by general consensus about values and standards, few give any attention to the status of those moral values and standards that undergird the social order. In a very real sense, they lack a deep concern about moral elements in social life. Such moral elements are, however, of concern to me. Given the existence of competing sets of moral principles, is it possible to rationally justify one set as superior to the others?

Although attention will be given to the above questions, my most ambitious normative quest is the specification and justification of those particular moral principles and values which *ought* to provide for social order. This involves an entirely different sort of inquiry than that involved in *explaining* social order. The normative question is, essentially, what *ought* to make organized social life possible? What *ought* to hold society together? What *ought* to be the source of social cohesion and integration in a society?

In pursuing this general normative question, I am aware of violating a widely held methodological canon. According to the dominant view in the social sciences (in fact, in science more generally), one must strive for value-neutrality and try to avoid all value-judgments. Conflicts over values, or disagreements about right and wrong or justice and injustice, are not to be settled by science. There is no way that particular moral values or value-judgments can be objectively shown to be true or correct. No rational justificaton of values can ever be given. From this standpoint, value-judgments are only individual, subjective preferences outside the realm of rational inquiry.

Thus, it is considered illegitimate for the sociologist to move from explanation to evaluation. In fact, evaluation is not only viewed as "off limits" for the sociological theorist but evaluation itself is often viewed as an inferior sort of intellectual endeavor. The theorist must, then, focus only on the way things are—not on the way they ought to be.

The dichotomy between the "is" and the "ought," the argument goes, must be maintained. Sociology is to be either analytic or empirical and descriptive, not moral and prescriptive. Normative claims about what is right or just, about moral preferences, or about the normative standing of our own or other people's values do not belong in a mature social science. We can, in our own private lives, choose to accept or reject one or another set of moral values or principles, but there is no ultimate rational justification for such choices. Value-judgments and normative claims are not, therefore, the concern of a science characterized by an emphasis on value-neutrality. The sociologist must behave as if he or she were a moral skeptic, uncommitted to any moral viewpoint. It is not for him or her to assess the justice of an institution or the moral rightness of an act. Questions about morality belong in the realm of philosophy, not sociology. After all, the social sciences have successfully freed themselves from philosophy by becoming value-free and adopting the scientific method. Genuine science, in short, can give no guidance as to right and wrong or the justice or injustice of a particular institutional arrangement.

It is probably not surprising that most social scientists hold such views about value-judgments and normative theorizing. There was a long period during which philosophers in the dominant analytic tradition insisted that the normative must be rigidly segregated from the properly philosophical. Ethics, on this reading, was the logical study of the language of morals. The professional philosopher was seen as having no special competence that would allow him or her to make assessments about the justice of a particular institutional arrangement or to give advice about what people ought to do with their lives. As was (and is) the case in sociology, fact and value, description and prescription, were to be strictly separated. Adherence to this rigid dichotomy in philosophy meant, of course, that analytical philosophers were constrained from saying anything at all about concrete moral, social, or political issues. Just as in the social sciences, there was a strong commitment to detachment and value-neutrality.

But this earlier agreement between social scientists and analytical philosophers is now largely something of the past. Certainly since the appearance of John Rawls's *A Theory of Justice* in 1971 and Robert Nozick's *Anarchy, State, and Utopia* three years later, there has been an increasing number of publications in normative ethics. Rejecting value-neutrality and the dictates of positivism and cultural relativism, many contemporary moral and political philosophers engage in theorizing that is openly normative in character. To a large extent, these theorists are concerned with providing an adequate justification for specified moral principles that can then be used to assess the moral rightness of an act or the justice of an institution. Among sociologists, by contrast, detachment and value-neutrality continue to reign supreme.

Much of current moral and political philosophy is directed at finding a nonrelativist foundation for ethics, at justifying principles that ought to govern the ways that people treat one another, and at specifying the kinds of social, political, and economic arrangements that justice requires. A common aim in the work of these theorists is to provide a vision of a better society: a society that is more just, more legitimate, more authentic for the lives of human beings. To a large extent, I share their aims. Like them, I want to specify and defend those moral principles by which social relationships and institutions ought to be guided or regulated. In this regard, my study is clearly normative in character.

As already noted, however, I am also concerned with describing and explaining social phenomena. This twin concern with both explanatory and normative theorizing is reflected in the notion of a "just social order." In exploring this idea, I intend to do two things: first, to devote attention to the social order problem that has long preoccupied social theorists; and, second, to distinguish a "just" social order from a social order that rests on coercion, fear, ignorance, or on other factors that can be viewed as undercutting its moral justifiability. More specifically, I attempt to provide answers to two different types of questions. One question, which arises from what might be termed the sociology of moral values, asks how moral values influence social actions and relationships and help assure social order; the other, which involves issues of normative ethics, asks about the particular moral values or principles that ought to help assure social order.

In Part I, I begin by briefly reviewing several approaches to the social order problem. This is followed by a discussion of the status of normative theorizing and the possibility of providing a rational justification for specific moral principles. In Chapter 2, the longest section of Part I, systematic attention is devoted to a critical examination of the viewpoints of four leading theorists whose work is explicitly normative in character. These theories are directed at locating moral principles that can provide the foundation for a just society and that will allow for the evaluation of particular laws and institutions. On the basis of this exploration, I arrive at the specification of moral "first principles" that should—normatively speaking—regulate the just social order. Most importantly, perhaps, I show why a just social order *is* regulated by those first principles and by the institutional arrangements to which they give rise.

Since I agree with most other sociologists that individuals must be motivated to act in conformity with normative standards, and that it is the internalization of these standards that provides much of the restraining control necessary for social order, I give considerable attention to the general mechanism of socialization. In Part II, I compare and contrast two different theories, which explain how socialization helps assure that children incorporate the relevant social values and normative standards into their personalities. My main concern in this respect is with what is sociologically and psychologically feasible as regards the moral development of the young. But in addition to this explanatory interest, there is a normative concern as well. Specifically, I consider whether there are limits to what is morally acceptable for parents or other child-rearers in socializing their children. Then, in Chapter 5, I specify what ought to be involved in socialization for a just social order.

In Part III, I focus on the law as a mechanism of social control necessary for preventing the violation of social norms and standards, on the one hand, and for containing and controlling deviant actions, on the other. Although I consider the various demands that a legal system must meet in contemporary Western societies, my major concern is with the normative or prescriptive character of law and morality, especially as this involves the legitimate authority of a legal system and the moral obligations of citizens to obey its dictates.

Finally, in Part IV, I devote attention to the kinds of economic arrangements that are best able to assure both social order and justice. Various views of economic justice are systematically examined, alternative productive arrangements are briefly considered, some general principles of distribution and redistribution are set forth, and a number of specific social policies and programs are discussed and defended.

Throughout this book, I emphasize that—both individually and collectively—human beings require order *and* justice. Whatever degree of social order may be achieved, however, it must be subordinate to those moral principles that transcend it and provide the terms by which it must be judged. My aspiration, the goal toward which this book is directed, then, is the specification of the kind of society that is sociologically and morally required: what I term a *just social order*.

I

Explanation and Evaluation

ONE

Toward a Just Social Order

THE problem of social order has long been at the center of philosophical and sociological inquiry. Aristotle, Hobbes, Locke, Rousseau, Comte, Durkheim, and Parsons are only a few among the many who have wrestled with the social order question. As already noted, that question asks: Why have human societies not been characterized by the "war of all against all"? What holds society together? What are the sources of social cohesion and integration in a society? What is it in social relations that makes organized group life possible?[1]

Numerous answers have been offered to one or another variation of these questions, and there are several contemporary sociological approaches that provide competing accounts of what makes social order possible. In the first part of this chapter, I begin by examining the four dominant theoretical approaches to the social order problem: the private interest doctrine, situational analysis, the consensus doctrine, and the conflict approach. The first two take the form of micro-sociological theories, while the latter two are more macro in character. I then turn to a consideration of the answers to the social order problem provided by two of today's leading social theorists, Jeffrey Alexander and Anthony Giddens. It is not my intention to provide a detailed description and analysis of their various approaches. Rather, I want mainly to indicate how they account for social order and how they conceive of morality or moral values in their theories. In the second half of this chapter, I discuss the status of normative theorizing and the rational justification of specific moral principles.

I

The Private Interest Doctrine

The doctrine of private interest assumes that individuals are guided entirely by considerations of self-interest and, so far as

---

[1] As Parsons points out, some social theorists have wondered whether social order was possible at all and have even denied its possibility. Others assume that

11

possible, act to choose the most efficient means for achieving their own private ends or aims. Under the most extreme form of this theory, every individual's ends are independent of every other individual's ends—even though they are, of course, influenced by the ends that others pursue and by the means chosen to achieve them. Although Herbert Spencer believed that the pursuit of individual interests formed a self-regulating mechanism in society,[2] most private interest theorists emphasize the inevitability of conflict, arising either because people desire different things or because they must compete for scarce resources. Hobbes, for instance, posited war as inherent in human nature, which must therefore become subject to a social order represented by the absolute power of the sovereign.[3]

Whatever the actual sources of conflict, private interest theorists see rules and laws emerging as a necessary condition for social order among persons with conflicting desires and objectives. Further, they stress that individuals will voluntarily comply with these rules or laws only to the extent that they believe compliance better serves their self-interest than does noncompliance. Max Weber was one of the theorists who viewed social life as characterized by competitive struggles among individuals and groups of individuals as each seeks to realize its own interests. But these competitive struggles, according to Weber, often generate social regularities or social order. He observes that "many of the especially notable uniformities in the course of social action . . . rest . . . entirely on the fact that the corresponding type of social action is in the nature of the case best adapted to the normal interests of the actors as they themselves are aware of them."[4] With regard to social order in the marketplace, for example, he says that "all economic activity in a market economy is undertaken and carried through by individuals acting to provide for their own ideals or material interests."[5] Thus, for Weber, social order is frequently—though not always—created and maintained by the actions of people mutually pursuing their individual interests.

---

social order in fact *exists*, however imperfectly, and proceed to ask under what conditions this fact of its existence can be explained. Talcott Parsons, *Social Systems and the Evolution of Action Theory* (New York: Free Press, 1977), p. 69.

[2] Herbert Spencer, *The Man Versus the State* (Ohio: Caxton, 1960).

[3] Thomas Hobbes, *Leviathan* (London: Dent, 1928).

[4] Max Weber, *Economy and Society*, trans. Guenther Roth and Claus Wittich, 3 vols. (New York: Bedminster Press, 1968), p. 30.

[5] Ibid., p. 202.

Among contemporary sociologists, George Homans is the best known exponent of a private interest approach.[6] Working with an exchange model based on principles of the free market, Homans attempts to get beneath existing norms and values to locate an abiding substructure upon which organized social interaction (social order) depends. To attain various goals (prestige, wealth, social approval), Homans argues, individuals engage in exchange processes. Social interaction consists of exchange involving such rewards as esteem, admiration, and respect, and certain costs like boredom, embarrassment, expenditures of time, and the like. According to Homans, it is the informal rules governing these exchanges that provide for social order.

The weaknesses of the logic of private interest are well known. It is unable to explain how there could have been sufficient similarity among individuals and enough continuity over time to have created what are widely recognized as organized societies. Further, and contrary to what the private interest theorists claim, not all adherence to rules and laws is explainable by people's calculations that they benefit from them or by their fear of punishment if these rules and laws are disobeyed. That is, the private interest doctrine almost totally ignores the existence of shared normative standards. Most importantly for my concerns here, private interest theories, taken to the extreme, appear to have no room (have no need) for moral notions like "wrong," "bad," or "immoral." Since social action is viewed as reducible to individual desires or to a calculation of means and ends, *moral* discourse is not even possible.

In its pure form, the doctrine of private interest is not really concerned with moral considerations at all. This is not to say, however, that moral rhetoric is missing from the language of those emphasizing an instrumental explanation for social order. Homans speaks, for example, of "distributive justice," describing it as follows: "A man in an exchange of relation with another will expect that the rewards of each man be proportional to his costs—the greater the rewards, the greater the costs—and the net rewards, or profits, of each man be proportional to his investments—the greater the investment, the greater the profit."[7] But Homans never provides any justification for this conception of distributive justice. Nor does he give any independent arguments to defend it as a

[6] George Homans, *Social Behavior: Its Elementary Forms* (New York: Harcourt, Brace & World, 1961).
[7] Ibid., p. 75.

moral notion. Since morality concerns human beings who are able to distinguish what they *ought* to do from what they want to do, the private doctrine theory makes it impossible for individuals to treat one another as moral persons. A theory of social order based entirely on considerations of private interest omits totally the moral dimension in human relations.

Situational Analysis

Somewhat like Homans, Erving Goffman sees people as narrowly self-interested beings who are almost exclusively concerned with their own particular goals or ends.[8] Men and women are viewed as "actors" playing their parts with different styles and varying degrees of skill. In Goffman's world, the characters are played by actors who treat their roles as public means to private ends. For him, society is a pseudo-moral system in which everyone is busily involved in the exchange of impressions.

But in contrast to Homans, Goffman focuses on the pre-existing rules—which are themselves largely situationally dependent—that help sustain orderly social relations. While Homans's subjects are consciously aware of what they are doing and why they are doing it, Goffman's actors utilize tacit rules and resources in their social encounters. Instead of emphasizing the particular attributes that individual actors bring to a social situation (prestige, power, and the like), Goffman stresses the importance of the properties and structures of the situations themselves in influencing social conduct.

Nevertheless, Goffman does—like Homans—see people's actions as being determined largely by a concern with strategic conduct. Much of the activity occurring during a social encounter, he says, "can be understood as an effort on everyone's part to get through the occasion and all the unanticipated and unintended events that can cast participants in an undesirable light, without disrupting the relationships of the participants."[9] There are, he emphasizes, frequently taken-for-granted norms that participants in a social situation draw upon in cooperating to sustain one another's presentations of self. Social encounters are characterized

[8] Erving Goffman, *The Presentation of Self in Everyday Life* (Garden City: Doubleday Anchor, 1959); Erving Goffman, *Interaction Ritual* (Garden City: Doubleday Anchor, 1967); Erving Goffman, *Strategic Interaction* (Philadelphia: University of Pennsylvania Press, 1969).

[9] Goffman, *Interaction Ritual*, p. 41.

14

by a tacit recognition that everyone is engaged in "face-work," and a tacit agreement to help each other perform such face-work. Thus,

> when an individual projects a definition of the situation and thereby makes an implicit or explicit claim to be a person of a particular kind, he automatically exerts a *moral* demand upon the others, obligating them to value and treat him in the manner that persons of his kind have a right to expect.[10]

While, undoubtedly, people often do exert a "moral" demand on others to honor their presentation of self, for Goffman there are no independent "moral" reasons for accepting or rejecting such demands. Furthermore, there appear to be no situations where moral agents who possess an identity and are capable of exercising choice even exist. In fact, Goffman's whole notion of actors and performances is rather unsatisfactory. If, as he argues, we are all involved in performing, then obviously there must be a legitimate sense in which we can speak of people as *not* being involved in performing. Since performances involve dissembling, i.e., playing a role that one does not normally play, there must be some notion of one's usual or normal role. Put another way, play-acting can have explanatory force only if there are many other instances of people not engaged in play-acting. What is missing in Goffman's account is a serious notion of human beings as creatures with a sense of personal identity. If Goffman's actors are not simply and always "actors" in the theatrical sense, then we require some notion of autonomous human beings who can choose and take responsibility for their activities.

Thus, Goffman's actors lack a sense of personal identity as well as a commitment to moral standards and principles other than those found in one or another social situation. "The general capacity to be bound by moral rules may well belong to the individual," he says, "but the particular set of rules which transforms him into a human being derives from requirements established in the ritual organization of social encounters."[11] In some unspecified sense, then, it is moral rules that transform an individual into a human being. It is apparently the binding nature of the moral rules required for maintaining social order in face-to-face situations that makes one a human being. Aside from questions about the adequacy of this notion of what it is to be a human being, there is also

---

[10] Goffman, *Presentation of Self*, p. 13. Italics added.
[11] Goffman, *Interaction Ritual*, p. 45.

15

the serious problem that what is right or wrong, good or bad, just or unjust, is to be established entirely by reference to what is required to sustain orderly social relations. There are for Goffman, then, no rational standards and principles of morality that might sometimes impose a requirement on human beings *not* to be bound by the moral rules dominant in one or another social situation. Insofar as there is any emphasis on morality in Goffman's work, it is entirely a situational morality.

While Goffman accounts for social order on the basis of social actors in face-to-face situations sharing the same symbolic order of meanings, definitions, and implicit rules, ethnomethodologists renouce an interest in explaining social order.[12] Instead, their concern is with understanding how social actors manage to produce and sustain a sense of orderliness and coherence. Garfinkel, who is widely regarded as the principal progenitor of this approach, states that ethnomethodology is

> directed to the tasks of learning how members' ordinary ac-
> tivities consist of methods to make practical actions, practical
> circumstances, common-sense knowledge of social structures,
> and practical sociological reasoning analyzable; and of discov-
> ering the formal properties of common-place, practical actions,
> "from within" actual settings, as ongoing accomplishments of
> those settings.[13]

The concern of ethnomethodologists is not, then, with discovering pre-existing sets of rules or norms that constrain actions and assure social order. Their focus is on learning how actors in face-to-face situations manage to impute and sustain a sense of orderliness.

But despite their difference from Goffman and other theorists (e.g., symbolic interactionists) to social interaction, ethnomethodologists, too, largely ignore moral considerations in their work. Consider, for example, Garfinkel's criticism of those sociologists who explain social order as the product of certain shared rules and norms that ensure constraint. He accuses these persons of seeing man as a "cultural dope" who "produces the stable features of the society by acting in compliance with pre-established and legitimate

---

[12] See, for example, Harold Garfinkel, *Studies in Ethnomethodology* (Englewood Cliffs, N.J.: Prentice Hall, 1967); Aaron Cicourel, *Cognitive Sociology* (Harmondsworth: Penguin, 1973); D. H. Zimmerman and D. L. Wieder, "Ethnomethodology and the Problem of Order," in Jack Douglas, ed., *Understanding Everyday Life* (London: Routledge & Kegan Paul, 1972).

[13] Garfinkel, *Studies in Ethnomethodology*, pp. vii–viii.

alternatives of action that the common culture provides."[14] But it seems to me that Garfinkel's conception is subject to a similar criticism. Whereas he rejects the view that individuals simply accept those action-guiding alternatives provided by the common culture, he replaces it with the view that the actor has no agency except in the actual presence (face-to-face interaction) of others. As with Goffman's conception of human actors, they have no moral agency. Totally absent in the writings of Garfinkel and others who focus on social order by way of situational analysis is a conception of man as a being who is responsible for his actions. Missing is a conception of men and women as moral agents who are capable of choosing how they should act, of determining what they *ought* to do, and taking responsibility for their choices. No more than in the writings of Homans and Goffman, does one find a conception of human beings who manifest their moral autonomy through the exercise of freedom and responsibility. Garfinkel has replaced the view of man as a "cultural dope" with an equally unappealing conception: man as a "moral dope."

The Consensus Doctrine

Social scientists (Durkheim, Parsons, and probably the vast majority of sociologists) who advocate the doctrine of consensus start from an entirely different position from either those emphasizing private interests or those involved in situational analysis. Rather than beginning with the individual busily calculating ends, means, and the rewards and punishments for observing or disobeying various rules and laws, or with the norms and values operative in face-to-face relations, the consensus theorists begin with the group or society—entities characterized by *shared* values, meanings, and understandings. Social order (organized social life) is made possible, they argue, by consensus about these values and meanings. When the individual is born, he or she immediately encounters, and may eventually internalize, these shared social values and meanings. The various rules and laws, then, are viewed as totally a manifestation of a society's shared values. Thus Parsons defines "institutions or institutionalized patterns" as being "*normative* patterns, which define what are felt to be, in the given society, proper, legitimate, or expected modes of action or of social relationship. . . . They are patterns supported by common moral sentiments."[15]

---

[14] Ibid., p. 68.

[15] Talcott Parsons, *Essays in Sociological Theory: Pure and Applied* (Glencoe, Ill.: Free Press, 1949), p. 203.

And Durkheim explained social order in terms of the constraints provided by the moral rules embodied in the state, occupational associations, religion, and in society as a whole.

According to consensus theorists like Durkheim and Parsons, individuals come to be motivated to act in conformity with normative standards, thereby themselves providing the restraining control necessary for social order. Parsons says that motivation is kept at the level and in the direction necessary for the continuing operation of the social system through the mechanisms of *socialization* and *social control*.[16] The mechanism of socialization is the process by which individuals are motivated to "meet the exigencies imposed on them by the imperatives of their culture and society,"[17] i.e., to incorporate the normative standards of the society into their personalities. The mechanism of social control is concerned with regulating the behavior of people who have undergone socialization yet are not motivated to conformity.[18] As Parsons himself points out, it is not always possible to draw a rigid line between socialization and social control mechanisms. But it is clear that mechanisms of social control come into play when social systems fail to achieve integration through socialization.

Once social norms are internalized, they may be seen (as Durkheim saw them) as "society living in us." When these norms are inculcated in early childhood, they become part of the personality structure itself. This is not to say, however, that an individual may not violate those norms and value standards that he or she has internalized. In such instances, Parsons says:

> Here the relation to the internal integration of personality, on the one hand, and the situational objects, on the other, is significant. Such a dysphoric feeling directed toward ego's own internalized standards, in such a way that he himself is the judge, may be called *guilt*. If, on the other hand, the orientation is towards alter's reaction, according to what are interpreted to be his standards of approval or esteem, it may be called *shame*. If finally it is concerned *only* with *overt* consequences which will be injurious to ego, it is *fear*.[19]

[16] Talcott Parsons and Edward Shils, eds., *Toward a General Theory of Action* (Cambridge, Mass.: Harvard University Press, 1951), p. 227.

[17] Parsons, *Social Systems*, p. 98.

[18] Parsons and Shils, *Toward a General Theory*, pp. 227–30.

[19] Ibid., p. 142.

Although Parsons mentions guilt, shame, and fear as three reactions (feelings) that one may experience when he or she violates (or contemplates violating) internalized norms and values, it is the first two of these that Parsons views as crucially important in providing the internal control necessary for the maintenance of social order. Since the individual's failure to live up to his own and others' expectations results in his experiencing the negative sanctions of guilt and shame, he is motivated to conform in order to avoid these painful emotions. An individual, Parsons writes, "either has a rather high degree of 'self-respect' or in some sense or other feels 'guilt' or 'shame.' "[20]

In short, social order is made possible by consensus within a social system as to normative standards. Motivation to observe and honor these normative standards is assured through the mechanisms of socialization and social control, and through the feelings of self-respect, guilt, and shame, which result from the process of internalization.

Just as there are weaknesses in the other theories considered above, there are also serious problems with a theory that tries to explain social order entirely in terms of consensus and social solidarity. First, the model is unable to account for the existence of social conflict. So long as there is a basic social consensus as to the central societal values and goals, there is both social harmony and stability. With consensus about existing rules and laws—which are seen as totally a manifestation of shared values within the group or society—there is no room for the existence of conflict. In fact, however, the very emphasis on "rules" among consensus theorists is a bit strange. If, indeed, there is agreement concerning the norms that regulate people's interactions and relationships with one another, then there is no need for explicit rules at all. The creation of rules and laws appears, after all, to occur as an answer to the need for external reminders and sanctions concerning standards of conduct and behavior about which consensus is lacking. In other words, the very existence of rules—which concensus theorists claim are the expression of shared values—is explainable only if one assumes that conflict is at least implicit. Consensus theorists do, then, recognize the existence of social conflict—even though it is left unexplained by the doctrine of consensus.

A second criticism leveled against those in the consensus tradition is that they have made too much of control mechanisms and

---

[20] Parsons, *Essays*, p. 168.

too little of human spontaneity and inner conflict. With regard to the internalization of social norms, Freud's theory of the superego is the source and the model in the writings of Parsons and many other consensus theorists. But, as Wrong points out: "The whole stress on inner conflict, on the tension between powerful impulses and super-ego control, the behavioral outcome of which cannot be prejudged, drops out of the picture."[21] In Freud's view, to say that a norm has been internalized is not to say that an individual will, in fact, live up to it. It is only to say that he may suffer guilt feelings if he does not do so. As to the emphasis on "self-respect" among the consensus theorists, where individuls are seen as motivated by the desire to achieve a positive self-image by gaining the approval or acceptance of others, this too has been heavily criticized. The view that individuals mutually seek approval from one another by conforming to shared values ignores such possible motivating factors as sexual drives, the quest for power, the desire for material satisfaction, and the need to maintain individual integrity. By overemphasizing the extent to which the internalization of norms and the need for self-respect contribute to the stability and integration of society, as the consensus theorists do, we end up with "the disembodied, conscience-driven, status-seeking phantom of current theory."[22]

A third weakness in consensus theory, and the one of most concern to me here, is given considerable attention by Alvin Gouldner. "While stressing the importance of the ends and values that men pursue," Gouldner points out, "Parsons never asks *whose* ends and values they are. Are they pursuing their own ends or those imposed upon them by others?"[23] In point of fact, Gouldner argues, Parsons and other consensus theorists emphasize the moral ends and values that are compatible with the maintenance of the established form of industrialization in which their own work takes place. The overcommitment to social order by those in the consensus tradition, says Gouldner, "is a tacit commitment to resist any change that threatens the order of the status quo."[24]

While I agree with Gouldner that many consensus theorists may

---

[21] Dennis Wrong, "The Oversocialized Conception of Man in Modern Sociology," reprinted in Lewis A. Coser and Bernard Rosenberg, eds., *Sociological Theory*, 4th ed. (New York: Macmillan, 1976), p. 106.

[22] Ibid., p. 112.

[23] Alvin W. Gouldner, *The Coming Crisis of Western Sociology* (New York: Basic Books, 1970), p. 193.

[24] Ibid., p. 252.

indeed be committed to the maintenance of the status quo, I do not see this as a necessary consequence of their concern with social order. After all, there is no reason that one cannot be committed to a social order (what I term a "just social order") different from the one existing in the here and now. That is, while the consensus theorists' commitment to the existing social order might be a reason for criticism, this does not mean that there may not be other possible social orders, which even the critics of the consensus theorists might see as worth defending.

Much more important are Gouldner's remarks concerning the stress on *moral values* by consensus theorists. "The commitment of those obsessed with order is not to morality as such," Gouldner asserts, "but only to *a* moral system that yields order."[25] This raises the crucial question of whether there is anything to be said (normatively speaking) about the moral status of a particular society— either absolutely, in terms of some posited set of moral principles, or in comparison with other societies. Does the fact that there may have been "normative consensus" in Nazi Germany, Stalinist Russia, and South Africa, or in support of the Vietnam War in the United States, or that there is today perhaps normative consensus in Sweden or Cuba, mean that the social orders in these different societies all have the same identical moral status? If the moral authority of "society," as an agency of constraint and control of the individual's actions, is internalized in the personality of the individual, thus helping assure social order, does this not imply that any "well-ordered" society is intrinsically (and equally) moral?

According to the consensus view, the morally praiseworthy individual is he or she who fully internalizes the normative standards of the society—whatever these might be. This, Gouldner points out, is an ethics of conformity.[26] But, in a deeper sense, it is a

---

[25] Ibid., p. 231.

[26] Ibid. In his more recent writings, Parsons responds to charges concerning his ethics of conformity. He now extends his use of the term *moral* somewhat, while continuing to ignore any questions about the comparative status of various moral values. Parsons, *Social Systems*, p. 253. Italics added: "[M]odern society has been moving in the direction of greatly increased associational pluralism, with the possibility of moral justification for increasingly broad ranges of acceptable choices. This view casts serious doubt on the allegation that functional analysis of social systems implies an imperative of conformity. We must keep in mind that we are here speaking of the general action level, and that *the term 'moral' refers to any culturally grounded justification of selection among alternatives for action*, whether they be for sustaining a given social system, or for its revolutionary overturn, or for any of the wide variety of withdrawing or otherwise deviant modes of association." But

mistake to refer to it as an "ethics" of conformity, or of anything else, because it leaves no room at all for the moral point of view. There are, for consensus theorists, no relevant standards of "right" or "wrong" (good or bad, justice or injustice) other than those prevalent in a given group or society. The well-integrated group or society is one in which everyone shares (i.e., has internalized) exactly the same norms and values.

Durkheim insists that the moral system of a society is a function of its social organization. "History has established that except in abnormal cases, each society has in the main a morality suited to it," says Durkheim, "and that any other would not only be impossible but also fatal to the society which attempted to follow it."[27] And elsewhere, he writes that "there is no one unique morality and we dare not condemn as immoral the moral systems that preceded ours, for the ideal that they represent was valid for the society in which they were established."[28]

Since society is, for Durkheim, coterminous with morality, an individual can be moral only by obeying the normative demands of the society in which he finds himself. Within the Durkheimian logic, statements like "Society X is morally superior to society Y" or "This is a bad society" are not even expressible. Societies may differ in their degree of efficiency, in their extent of organization, or in the amount of "anomie," and the sociologist is fully capable of delivering judgments about such differences. But since the only sources and measures of judgments about morality are those of a given society, there are (logically) no detached, independent, standards by which the morality sanctioned by a particular society can be judged and evaluated. Thus questions about the moral status of a society, or of its political order and institutions, cannot even be raised. Whatever normative patterns exist reflect the "needs" of the social whole; they are the moral requirements that must be met if society is to survive. "If there is one fact that history has irrefutably demonstrated," writes Durkheim, "it is that the morality

what is accomplished by extending the term *moral* from that which assures social order to now include "any culturally grounded justification of selection among alternatives for action"? Does Parsons really mean that whatever the justification for one or another alternative for action—a particular religious practice or discrimination against blacks—it deserves the term *moral*? Surely, this is not what he intends.

[27] Émile Durkheim, *Sociology and Philosophy*, trans. D. F. Pocock (Glencoe, Ill.: Free Press, 1953), p. 56.

[28] Émile Durkheim, "Pragmatism and Sociology," in Kurt H. Wolff, ed., *Essays on Sociology and Philosophy* (New York: Harper Torchbooks, 1964), p. 433.

of each people is directly related to the social structure of the people practicing it."[29]

Parsons shares Durkheim's views and is, in fact, explicit about the relativity of moral values. Moral value standards, he says, are "the court of last appeal."[30] And he goes on to state: "Any specific system of morals is adapted to the specific integrative problems confronted by the action-system which it, in one sense, controls. Morals, in this sense, are relative."[31] The appropriateness of any particular system of morals is determined entirely by its consequences for a system of action.[32]

Durkheim, Parsons, and other consensus theorists claim, then, that it is meaningless to say that the moral standards of one group or society are better or worse than those of another group or society (or of a previous age). This position allows them to speak of differences in the extent of social order existing in various societies and groups, but they are mute so far as the moral standards upon which that social order rests are concerned.

The point is clear; when the primary emphasis is on social order, then everything that produces consensus, restraint, and stability is on the same moral footing. So long as there is consensus within a society about certain normative standards, so long as people internalize these standards, so long as social control mechanisms take up the slack for faulty socialization, so long as the "needs" of the social system are met, so long as all of these requirements are fulfilled, a society is intrinsically "well functioning." There is, then, no vantage point from which anything can be said about the *moral* status of these (or other) "normative" standards. Nor, as already noted, is it possible to say anything about the moral status of one particular institutional arrangement or of one society as compared with another.

The Conflict Approach

As I observed earlier, Gouldner has been highly critical of the doctrine of consensus. Much of his work, as well as that of such theorists as Coser and Collins, represents a conflict approach to

[29] Émile Durkheim, *Moral Education*, trans. Everett K. Wilson and Herman Schnurer (New York: Free Press of Glencoe, 1961), p. 87.
[30] Parsons and Shils, *Toward a General Theory*, p. 74.
[31] Ibid.
[32] Ibid.

the study of social order.[33] For these writers, there is a strong emphasis on power relationships, coercion, competition, and the mechanisms of political allocation. They point to the many ways in which social order—if it is maintained at all—is maintained not by consensus but by constraint, not by shared values but by conflict over values and by the coercion of some by others. Whereas consensus theorists give predominance to stability, harmony, and consensus, conflict theorists lay heavy stress on change, conflict, and constraint.

Sociologists like Durkheim and Parsons argue that consensus about values and norms helps provide social cohesion and thus assures social order. Lewis Coser, on the other hand, suggests that conflict about values, goals, and interests may also be a precondition for the orderly functioning of society. In his book, *The Functions of Social Conflict*, he describes conflict as arising in a struggle for such scarce goods as status, power, and resources, or through adherence to conflicting values.[34] Such conflict, he argues, serves not only to divide people but often to unify them as well. He writes:

> Once groups and associations have been formed through conflict with other groups, such conflict may further serve to maintain boundary lines between them and the surrounding social environment. In this way, social conflict helps to structure the larger social environment by assigning positions to the various subgroups within the system and by helping to define the power relations between them.[35]

Coser's major sociological focus, he says, is on "those consequences of social conflict which make for an increase rather than a decrease in the adaptation or adjustment of particular relationships or groups."[36] At the societal level, Coser observes, conflict may function as an important stabilizing mechanism for society.[37] The "integrative" function of conflict, therefore, is to provide for social order. But just as with the consensus theorists, Coser's concern is mainly with "adaptation or adjustment" to the larger society. In other words, he demonstrates a conservative bias by view-

---

[33] Gouldner, *Coming Crisis*; Lewis A. Coser, *The Functions of Social Conflict* (New York: Free Press, 1956); and Randall Collins, *Conflict Sociology: Toward an Explanatory Science* (New York: Academic Press, 1975).

[34] Coser, *The Functions*.

[35] Ibid., p. 155.

[36] Ibid., p. 8.

[37] Ibid., p. 155.

ing conflict as functional for society *as it is*. As I indicated in my criticisms of those in the consensus tradition, what is functional for a society may not be what morality demands for its citizens.

A sharp contrast to Coser's functional theory of conflict is presented by Randall Collins in his book, *Conflict Theory*.[38] To a large extent, he attempts to reconstruct macro-sociology from a micro-sociological perspective. The basis of social order, in his view, is to be found in those sorts of micro-situations examined by Homans, Goffman, Garfinkel, and various phenomenologists. These micro-situations are viewed as having something of a ritual quality, for they are constructed by shared beliefs and understandings. Social life—on both the micro and macro level—is seen by Collins as mainly a fight over the control of resources. When the balance of resources—status, power, means of communication, tools, knowledge, and the like—changes, there will ensue changes in the rituals and the realities that people experience. This occurs, says Collins, because those with the greater resources will always utilize these resources to redefine and control the situation.

For Collins, all social reality is micro-experience involving people's cognitions in their concrete, everyday situations. Based on what he assumes we know about micro-situations, Collins formulates various principles that have consequences for macro-sociological theory. The basis of social order at the societal level, then, is to be found in the aggregation of many micro-episodes.

Collins's particular brand of conflict theory rests on the basic premise that individuals pursue advantage on the basis of their available resources, and that social structures are nothing more than people interacting with one another in a variety of micro-situations. That is, the "structural" qualities of social systems are mainly the results of conduct in micro-situations. Collins sets forth the following as one of his "first principles" of conflict analysis: "Think of people as animals maneuvering for advantage, susceptible to emotional appeals, but steering a self-interested course toward satisfaction and away from dissatisfaction."[39] Another of his first principles states that "Ideals and beliefs likewise are to be explained in terms of the interests which have the resources to make their viewpoint prevail."[40] Collins presents approximately

[38] Collins, *Conflict Sociology*.
[39] Ibid., p. 69.
[40] Ibid., p. 61.

three hundred such propositions and subpropositions designed as an interconnected series of causal explanations.

Self-interest, maneuvering for advantage, and a concern with making one's own viewpoint prevail are all central to Collins's conflict approach. Above all, his theory advises us to be tough-minded and realistic. "Theoretical and explanatory developments in the social sciences," he writes, "can have the greatest impact in making us aware of the plurality of realities, the multiplicity of interests, and the tricks used to impose one reality upon others."[41]

Rather than endorsing the view of those sociologists who argue that shared moral values or beliefs may serve to influence and even help explain people's actions, Collins suggests that we turn the (presumed) relationship around. What ought to concern us, says Collins, is how various factors of power, coercion, control of resources, and the like, produced particular moral values or beliefs in the first place. In other words, he seems to be claiming that moral values, beliefs, norms, principles, and standards are purely epiphenomenal, explained totally by their use in economic and political conflict, and without any autonomy of their own.

Nevertheless, the field of ethics "cannot but benefit from the development of social science."[42] The reason that ethics can benefit, Collins states, is as follows:

> Ethics is always an area of the ultimately arbitrary, but concerns itself with drawing out the consequences from those choice points, or tracing action back to them. With the aid of social science, ethics can move beyond its conventional middle-class Christian biases built into some notion of rationality, interest, or the concept of "good" itself, to a far more sophisticated view of the choices that confront us.[43]

But this view of ethics is, of course, one-sided and vulgar in the extreme. Resting as it does on various assumptions about self-interest, impression management, and the inevitability of coercion, this is not at all surprising. Rather than seeing ethics as being concerned with those fundamental principles that ought to help regulate human conduct, Collins views ethics as simply another device for imposing one's own standpoint and dominating others. Further, of course, ethics is seen as "ultimately arbitrary."

[41] Ibid., p. 548.
[42] Ibid., p. 547.
[43] Ibid.

26

Given Collins's own views about reality construction and his assumptions about the motivations of human actors, one might choose to regard Collins's book as itself a purely arbitrary piece of reality construction. Be that as it may, he assumes that moral principles or standards have only an instrumental value in serving the interests of one or another individual or group. Apart from their utility in those everyday struggles Collins sees as constituting the human condition, such principles and standards are completely arbitrary and unjustifiable. In common with Homans's doctrine of private interest, then, Collins's theory makes it impossible for individuals to treat one another as moral beings.

Perhaps more than any other contemporary sociologist, Alvin Gouldner has explicitly considered social order and moral values from a conflict perspective. Most especially in his monumental *The Coming Crisis of Western Sociology*, he has himself been deeply involved in moral evaluation and critique.[44] And while his major focus was never on social order *per se*, he has subjected the consensus theorists, and especially Parsons, to careful scrutiny. For these reasons, his views deserve brief examination.

In his critique of Talcott Parsons and sociological functionalists, Gouldner attacks their claim to nonpartisanship and a value-free theory. "Functionalism's concern with social 'order,' " he writes, "has served to project an image of itself as being committed only to the common needs of *all* elements of modern society, and as, presumably, nonpartisan."[45] Yet this concern with social order, Gouldner argues, is highly conservative in that it treats existing institutional arrangements as given and essentially unchangeable. It is the refusal of Parsons and other functionalists to acknowledge their own normative commitment to the maintenance of the status quo that draws Gouldner's fire.

But beyond the value-commitment concealed in functionalist analyses of social order, there is, for Gouldner, also something highly questionable in the very emphasis on social order itself and on the relationship between social order and morality. With regard to the supposed need for social order, he asserts that: "The overt commitment to social order is a tacit commitment to resist any change that threatens the order of the status quo, even when that change is sought in the name of the highest values: freedom, equal-

[44] Gouldner, *Coming Crisis*.
[45] Ibid., p. 331.

ity, justice."[46] As I already noted, however, there is no logical necessity for a commitment to the desirability of social order to commit one to the maintenance of the status quo. Similarly with Gouldner's rejection of the linkage between morality and social order; he seems to consider the very emphasis on moral consensus as itself repugnant. It is his view that "concern to maintain social order *through* a reliance upon *morality* requires a distinctive kind of morality, one that maintains the existent patterns of life chances and the institutions through which they are allocated."[47] Again, I see no reason that this should necessarily be the case.

Gouldner's real target, I believe, is not morality as such but rather the functionalists' commitment to what he terms the "quiet values": temperance, wisdom, knowledge, goodness, cooperation, or a trust and faith in the goodness of God.[48] But there are other spiritual values——Gouldner mentions freedom and equality—to which the functionalist advocates are not committed. In comparing Platonism and sociological functionalism, Gouldner attacks both for their central moral value, a concern with social order. He says that "A key concern of Functionalists, no less than Plato, is that social systems should be orderly—not free, not equal, not happy—and both largely believe that this depends on men's conformity with their society's shared values."[49] Once again, I see no compelling reason why a social system should not be characterized by an emphasis on both order and freedom or equality.

Gouldner himself several times mentions freedom and equality as if these were the paramount moral values to which we ought to be committed. And yet nowhere does he attempt to specify what he means by these concepts or to justify his preference for these as against other moral values. Very much like those whom he so severely criticizes, Gouldner never systematically formulates and defends his own value-preferences. Although he does give considerable attention to explicating his own value-commitments, he never openly specifies the moral grounds of his own critiques. Further, and not surprisingly, Gouldner appears not to have even considered the possibility of there being moral values and principles that might be rationally justifiable. But perhaps he cannot, since he claims that the centrality of moral values in the writings

---

[46] Ibid., p. 252.
[47] Ibid., p. 253.
[48] Ibid.
[49] Ibid., p. 422.

28

of Durkheim and Weber constituted, in his words, an emphasis on "the *non-rational* in men."[50]

Alexander's Approach

In his first volume of *Theoretical Logic in Sociology*, Alexander sets forth the idea of a theoretical logic of presuppositions independent of and prior to any substantive sociology. There are, he argues, two main axes of such a logic: the rationality of action and the nature of social order.[51] Various problems concerning action and order are seen as constituting the residual categories of contemporary theoretical debate. In Alexander's words:

> Action and order represent the true presuppositions of sociological debate; they establish a general framework that cannot be subsumed under other kinds of theoretical dispute and, at the same time, they manifest properties that decisively affect sociological thought at every level of the intellectual continuum.[52]

For the sociological investigator, says Alexander, decisions must always be made about both action and order. Further, such decisions can be independent of each other. With regard to action, Alexander emphasizes, there will be a commitment to either rational or nonrational action. With a decision about social order, the choice will be for either the individual or the collective level of analysis.[53]

Based on his two conceptual distinctions concerning action and order, Alexander indicates that social theories can be located in terms of their position on action (rational or nonrational) and order (individual or collective). The two "rational" categories emphasize either an instrumental (individual) or a material (collective) mode of analysis, while the two "nonrational" categories represent an emphasis on a normative framework.

Among other things, Alexander has much of interest to say about the relation between nonrationality and voluntarism. The nonrationalist perspective on action, he says, emphasizes the internal voluntary aspect of human action. "Without presupposing the existence of nonrational action," writes Alexander, "it is impossible

---

[50] Ibid., p. 122.
[51] Jeffrey C. Alexander, *Theoretical Logic in Sociology*, vol. 1, *Positivism, Presuppositions, and Current Controversies* (London: Routledge & Kegan Paul, 1982).
[52] Ibid., p. 65.
[53] Ibid., p. 122.

to formulate the possibilities for voluntarism upon which all ideological arguments for increased freedom depend."[54] In other words, freedom is dependent upon the nonrational through the mediation of voluntarism. A theory can, then, be voluntarist while collectivist and nonrational. In fact, says Alexander, "To maintain the voluntary, intentional quality of action it is necessary to relate social order, in part or in whole, to the normative, nonrational elements of action. In doing so, we create a conception of collective *internal* order."[55]

Although social order can be accounted for by both rational and nonrational elements of action, Alexander claims that the nonrational account—with its collective internal order—has the consequence of maximizing the voluntary elements of action. From this perspective, social order is the result of collective ordering that arises through voluntary internal commitments to nonrational elements of action.

What, then, is "nonrationality," and how does it differ from "rationality"? For Alexander, to argue that action is rational is to assume that it is guided by ends of pure efficiency. One can, he notes, describe rationality as "being guided only by 'technical' concerns as compared with substantive moral ones."[56] Alexander contrasts this notion of rationality with nonrationality:

> In action conceived to be nonrational the actor's goals are not considered to have been chosen as the most efficient path for the realization of more general norms in the face of extant conditions. They are, rather, viewed as produced by the substantive ideal contents of the norms themselves. Norms, therefore, do not appear to be exhausted by the actor's reliance on instrumental calculation; nor do his goals appear effectively to be reduced to the status of means. Because the ideal reference is to be explicitly preserved, action does not take on a purely technical quality. Accordingly, the internal voluntary aspect of human action is maintained and a purely determinist perspective prevented.[57]

With nonrational action, according to Alexander, individuals voluntarily commit themselves and orient their conduct on the basis of norms, goals, values, ideals, and the like. But all such commit-

[54] Ibid., p. 89.
[55] Ibid., p. 103.
[56] Ibid., p. 73.
[57] Ibid., p. 76.

ments to substantive normative phenomena are viewed by Alexander as completely subjective and, of course, nonrational. People may voluntarily commit themselves to a belief in particular norms and values—thus, sometimes at least, assuring social order—but the norms and values themselves can in no way be rationally justified.

Alexander makes his position clear elsewhere when he emphasizes the inevitable conflict over the rationality of values and denies that any particular norms or values can ever be justified. In criticizing Habermas's ideas about the possibility of indeed justifying specific social norms, Alexander says the following: "Cognitively," those persons who accept the idea of normative truth, "may see more clearly, and we would all like the fruits of their vision. But morally they may be no better than the *lumpen* hipster, the petit bourgeois corner druggist, the falsely conscious worker, the opiated priest. The question of moral rationality must be argued on a deeper plane, and we must be prepared to accept certain inevitable differences of opinion."[58]

In common with Durkheim, Parsons, Collins, Gouldner, and, in fact, most other sociologists, Alexander holds that there can be no rational justification of the "normative" phenomena that are so important in helping to assure social order. Given Alexander's recognition of the dangers of relativism in regard to science, however, I find his standpoint rather surprising.

Alexander acknowledges the vast possibilities for relativism in his own nonpositivist position, but says that this need not mean that we must abandon the search for rational intellectual standards. Instead, one must give systematic attention to the development of postpositivist standards of rational knowledge. Interestingly, at this point Alexander appeals to Habermas. He says: "Instead of relying simply on deductive reasoning and empirical proof, one must establish objectivity, as Habermas argues, 'by means of the justification of a choice of standards.' "[59] He then quotes Habermas's assertion that "The approval of a procedure or the acceptance of a scientific norm can be supported or weakened by argument; it can at least be rationally assessed. And this is precisely the task of critical theoretical talk."[60]

But—as I will make clear in the following chapter—it is not only

[58] Jeffrey C. Alexander, "Looking for Theory: 'Facts' and 'Values' in the Intellectual Legacy of the 1970s," *Theory and Society* 10 (March 1981): 286.

[59] Alexander, *Positivism*, p. 114.

[60] Ibid.

"scientific" norms, as Alexander accepts, that are capable of a rational justification. Habermas also holds that the acceptance of more general norms and standards can be supported or weakened by argument. Unfortunately, however, Alexander fails to take seriously Habermas's arguments in this regard.

Just as do those positivist thinkers whose views he purports to reject, Alexander accepts that in the normative sphere all is subjective and nonrational. Consequently, his new theoretical logic leaves him completely silent about the rational justification of those norms and standards to which individuals voluntarily commit themselves. This means, of course, that he is unable to distinguish between a social order based on completely arbitrary normative elements and one resting on values and standards that are capable of being argued for and rationally defended.

Giddens's Position

Although he labels the centrality of the "problem of order" in the history of social thought to be a great "myth," Anthony Giddens has nevertheless devoted considerable attention to the issue of social order.[61] In recent work he has attempted to distinguish his own conception of the problem from that of Parsons and other sociologists in the consensus tradition. "The true locus of the 'problem of order,' " he states, "is the problem of how the duality of structure operates in social life; of how *continuity of form* is achieved in the day-to-day conduct of social activity."[62]

Much of Giddens's work is focused on the gap between action theory and institutional analysis.[63] Roughly, action theory refers to the writings of Goffman, ethnomethodologists, and sociologists in the tradition of symbolic-interactionism, while institutional analysis refers to the concern with structure, institutions, and such, found in the work of sociologists like Durkheim and Parsons. Action theory, Giddens says, suffers from a neglect of the temporal and spatial regularities of social action. Institutional analysis, on the other hand, neglects human agents as capable and knowl-

---

[61] Anthony Giddens, "Four Myths in the History of Social Thought." *Economy and Society* 1 (1972): 358–61, 365.

[62] Anthony Giddens, *Central Problems in Social Theory: Action, Structure and Contradiction in Social Analysis* (London: Macmillan, 1979), p. 216.

[63] Ibid., "Agency, institution and time-space analysis," in K. Knorr-Centina and A. V. Cicourel, eds., *Advances in Social Theory and Methodology: Toward an Integration of Micro- and Macro-Sociologies* (Boston: Routledge & Kegan Paul, 1981), pp. 161–74.

edgeable actors. Giddens attempts to bridge this gap through his "theory of structuration."

Especially important in this connection is Giddens's concept of the duality of structure. The traditional dualism of action theories and institutional theories can be avoided, Giddens argues, by "the emphasis that action and structure . . . form a duality. That is to say, action and structure stand in a relation of logical entailment: the concept of action presumes that of structure and vice versa."[64] Social structure, then, is both the medium and outcome, condition and product, of everyday life.

Structure itself, in Giddens's view, consists of rules and resources that are instantiated in social systems. "Rules," writes Giddens, "are social conventions, and knowledge of them includes knowledge of the contexts of their application."[65] "Resources," refer to what Giddens terms "capacities of making things happen," i.e., of bringing about certain states of affairs.[66] It is by drawing upon these rules and resources in everyday life that actors "structure" their actions. At the same time, these actions reproduce the structural qualities that generate social action. Structure, for Giddens, has no existence independent of the routines of day-to-day life.

Central to Giddens's theory is the claim that actors have both "capability" and "knowledgeability." The former term refers to the possibility that the agent "could have done otherwise," while the latter refers to "the fact that the members of a society know a great deal about the workings of that society."[67] More than any other sociologist, states Giddens, Goffman shows a recognition of the significance of capability and knowledgeability:

> Goffman's writings display a strong awareness of these features of human action . . . Goffman treats human beings as capable and knowledgeable agents, who employ such capability and knowledgeability routinely in the production and reproduction of social encounters. The subjects Goffman portrays for the most part know what they are doing and why they are doing it: but much of this knowledge does not operate at an immediately "conscious" level. . . . Goffman, in my view, is interested in laying bare the *tacit rules* and resources which competent actors employ in the course of day-to-day life. . . .

[64] Giddens, "Agency," p. 171.
[65] Ibid., p. 170.
[66] Ibid.
[67] Ibid.

33

Of course, this is not to say that Goffman is only concerned with tacit knowledge or practical consciousness; rather, he shows how the tacit and the explicit are interwoven in the texture of everyday social activity.[68]

According to Giddens, Goffman's account of human agency is similar to his own conception; they both employ a model of the human actor as a skilled and reflective being. Because of the similarity of their views, many of the criticisms that I levelled earlier at Goffman—as well as at the ethnomethodologists—apply to Giddens as well.

In Goffman's work, there is a virtual disappearance of the self. The self has been liquidated into role-playing and trying to keep up an "image" or "front." Insofar as someone has a sense of self, it is seen as being generated from social interaction in all those various situations that make up his or her life. From that perspective, an individual's self is fully constituted by various situational factors. There is, then, no room for a conception of self that is detached from the influence of one's surroundings.

In following Goffman, Giddens rejects the emphasis on values, norms, and constraints that is so central to the position of Parsons and consensus theorists. Value-consensus, normative agreement, the internalization of values, and the like, are generally ignored in Giddens's actor-centered theory. But he goes so far in rejecting a concern with factors that constrain social action and assure social integration that he is left with a view of action consisting largely of interactive strategies, on the one hand, and routinized activities, on the other.

It is undoubtedly true, as Giddens argues, that highly patterned and routinized behavior in daily life helps provide continuity and social order. And it is also true that many persons are often narrowly self-interested and "rationally" go after what is materially and politically useful to them within the context of one or another specific situation. But surely not all social action can be accurately characterized in such terms.

Giddens asserts boldly that *"orthodox sociology lacked a theory of action,"* and makes it clear that his theory is intended to fill this gap.[69] He notes quite correctly that Parsons's "action frame of reference" has been the most influential over-all scheme in sociology, and severely criticizes Parsons for his failure to depict human

[68] Ibid., pp. 163–64.
[69] Giddens, *Central Problems*, p. 253.

34

beings as acting for reasons, as reflexively monitoring their own conduct, and as being capable, knowledgeable agents.[70] In fact, says Giddens, "recognisably human agents seem to elude the grasp" of Parsons's scheme.[71]

But Giddens's own scheme seems to suffer much the same weakness. He leaves little, if any, conceptual room for human agents whose actions are shaped not only by interactive strategies and adherence to conventions but also by ideas of what is right, good, and just for oneself and others. There is no fixity of character, no sense of human agents who—being the kind of persons they are—affirm particular ends and choose to do this rather than that. Missing from Giddens's work is a conception of men and women as human agents who are capable of deciding how they should act, of determining what they ought to do, in terms of some values and standards more lasting than the demands of the immediate situation.

What is lacking is a conception of the human being with a history, with inner depths, and a sense of self and personal identity. Like Goffman and the ethnomethodologists, Giddens seems to view action as involving mainly short-term tactical "moves." But action also has a long-term perspective. Action is more than a matter of manipulating, winning, getting ahead, solving specific problems, and the like. It is also often guided by the ideal of achieving a completed and fulfilled life. In short, the actions of human agents involve not just the present, but also the past and the future. By ignoring such considerations, Giddens presents a theory that centers around an impoverished understanding of the human personality.

Up to this point, my comments about the different approaches to the problem of social order have been largely negative in character. But this is not to deny that there are some positive elements in these approaches as well. This is especially the case with the consensus theorists' view of social order. Despite my criticisms of their general standpoint, there is much in their approach that I find extremely useful and important.

Certainly, I share the view of Durkheim and Parsons, and indeed of most sociologists, that individuals must be motivated to act in conformity with normative standards, and that the internalization of these standards can help provide much of the restraining control

[70] Ibid., pp. 253–54.
[71] Ibid., p. 253.

necessary for social order. I also share their view as to the importance of "moral" values and standards in helping to provide for social integration and solidarity. I agree with Parsons that the maintenance of social order requires the mechanisms of socialization and social control. And I further agree with him in his emphasis on guilt and shame as the relevant sources of internal control necessary for social order.

To a considerable extent, then, I am in basic agreement with the general analytic framework utilized by many theorists in the consensus tradition: social order is (or may be) made possible by consensus within a social system as to normative standards, and motivation to observe these standards can be best assured through the mechanisms of socialization and social control. That is not to say, of course, that I share all of their views. Insofar as their *explanatory* views are concerned, as I noted earlier, they are unable to satisfactorily account for social conflict. And certainly they exaggerate the extent to which people actually *are* guided by internalized normative standards. Further, I believe that the consensus theorists do—as the private interests theorists and situational analysts point out—underestimate the extent to which people are frequently guided by self-interests and situational demands and expectations.

My principal source of disagreement with the consensus theorists, as should by now be apparent, is their treatment of normative and moral considerations. In their view, anything that threatens social order is seen as deviant or dysfunctional, as properly requiring improved modes of socialization and/or increased social control to restore the social system to the state of social order ("equilibrium") that it requires. They do, then, make a strong normative commitment: Whatever promotes social order is good. The appropriate moral standards or values are whatever will, in the given circumstances, achieve the greatest degree of social order.

However, the consensus theorists never consider the possibility of rationally justifying those dominant moral standards and values. But, of course, they should not be expected to. In common with other social scientists, they reject the possibility of ever providing such a rational justification. For that reason, the correctness of value-judgments cannot be demonstrated and evaluations must always be avoided. Since I am in complete disagreement with this point of view, I now must indicate why I think it is wrong. Let us, then, consider the issue of value-judgments in somewhat more detail.

36

II

Justifying Value-Judgments: The Status of Normative Theorizing

"Value judgments," Parsons asserts, "cannot claim the objective validity of science, and science must, as a methodological ideal, be kept free from them."[72] There is no way, he holds, that particular value-judgments (or moral principles) can be objectively demonstrated as true or correct. This is, of course, the dominant standpoint within the social sciences.

Most social scientists defend the methodological requirement that they be objective and "value-neutral" in their work. They try to adhere to this postulate of value-neutrality, which has its origin in the neo-Kantian premises that set up a dualism between "is" and "ought," between what is and what ought to be. Under the influence of Max Weber's methodological essays and the later writings of the logical positivists, this was transformed into a dualism between facts and values, between the descriptive and the prescriptive, between the empirical and the normative. The outcome was the view that only judgments relating to the regularities of empirical phenomena can be true or false, while those judgments concerning the normative sphere cannot be considered in this manner.

Since Weber is frequently taken as *the* authority for the claim that value-judgments must be avoided by the social scientist, I will begin by considering his views in this regard. As I will try to make clear, Weber was mistaken in thinking that explanatory theories occupy a privileged epistemological position vis-à-vis normative theories. Consequently, he was also mistaken about the standing of value-judgments.

Time and time again, Weber insists on the rigorous distinction between empirical knowledge and value-judgments. "When we distinguish in principle between 'value-judgments' and 'empirical knowledge,' " says Weber, "we presume the existence of an unconditionally valid type of knowledge in the social sciences, i.e., the analytical ordering of empirical social reality."[73] Social scientists

---

[72] Parsons, *Essays*, p. 593. That this is no longer readily accepted by all social scientists is shown by the excellent recent book by Norma Haan and her associates. Unfortunately, this book reached me too late for detailed consideration here. It is clearly, however, opposed to the dominant position in the social sciences today. See Norma Haan et al., *Social Science as Moral Inquiry* (New York: Columbia University Press, 1983).

[73] Max Weber, " 'Objectivity' in Social Science and Social Policy," in Maurice Nathanson, ed., *Philosophy of the Social Sciences* (New York: Random House, 1963), p. 369.

must, then, avoid making value-judgments, since "to *judge* the *validity* of such values is a matter of *faith*."[74]

As is known, Weber laid heavy emphasis on the "absolute heterogeneity" of facts and values, insisting that the social scientist should be concerned only with the factual side of the dichotomy. But the main criterion by which he attempts to exclude normative judgments is not just logical, but epistemological.[75] This can be seen from his discussion of value-judgments in the editorial statement that appeared in the *Archiv für Sozialwissenschaft und Sozialpolitik*:

> It has been and remains true that a systematically correct scientific proof in the social sciences, if it is to achieve its purpose, must be acknowledged as correct even by a Chinese—or more precisely stated—it must constantly *strive* to attain this goal, which perhaps may not be completely attainable due to faulty data. Furthermore, the successful *logical* analysis of the content of an ideal and its ultimate axioms and the discovery of the consequences which arise from pursuing it, logically and practically, must also be valid for the Chinese. At the same time, our Chinese can lack a "sense" for our ethical imperative and he can and certainly often will deny the ideal from it. . . . There is one tenet to which we adhere most firmly in our work, namely, that a social science journal, in our sense, to the extent that it is *scientific* should be a place where those truths are sought, which—to remain with our illustration—can claim, even for a Chinese, the validity appropriate to an analysis of empirical reality.[76]

What Weber is arguing is that the norms of correct science are so universal that "everyone" (even a Chinese) who is in possession of the relevant data and clearly understands the methods of science would reach the same conclusion as to the truth or falsity of a proposition. A proposition is "scientific," then, only if there are adequate data and a shared method, which allow all persons to agree whether it is true or false. A proposition that is a value-

---

[74] Ibid., p. 362.

[75] In the following discussion I draw on the example provided by Miller in an excellent article from which I have strongly benefited. Richard W. Miller, "Reason and Commitment in the Social Sciences," *Philosophy and Public Affairs* 8 (1979): 241–66.

[76] Max Weber, *The Methodology of the Social Sciences*, trans. Edward A. Shils and Henry A. Finch (Glencoe, Ill.: Free Press, 1949), pp. 58–59.

judgment, does not, Weber says, meet these requirements. In other words, scientific truths are, in principle, demonstrable, while value-judgments are not. Consequently, value-judgments must be excluded from the realm of science.

The universality of scientific practice, according to Weber, means that (again, in principle) even a Chinese can agree that one or another proposition is scientifically true. So long as the Chinese inquirer possesses the relevant data and employs the (universally shared) methods of science, he or she will reach the same conclusion as the Western investigator. Thus, scientific truths are everywhere demonstrable. But the truth of normative statements (value-judgments) does not meet this demand for universality. "Normative standards of value can and must be the object of *dispute* in a discussion of a problem of social policy," Weber says, "because the problem lies in the domain of general *cultural* values."[77]

In the case of someone who is Chinese, Weber points out that he "can lack a 'sense' for our ethical imperative and he can and certainly often will deny the ideal itself and the concrete value-judgment derived from it." If Weber's thesis is correct, we should expect to find widespread agreement about the truths of various propositions and theories in the social sciences and little or no agreement about the truth of normative statements or value-judgments.

In point of fact, however, there is only limited agreement among social scientists about the truths of propositions or theories. Despite the claims of Weber and others, there is very little in the social sciences that resembles or even approximates universal agreement in this area. Whether it be Weber's own theory concerning the Protestant ethic and the spirit of capitalism, Durkheim's theory of suicide, functionalist theory (of one or another stripe), systems theory, social exchange theory, or whatever, the agreement that Weber emphasized has never been realized.

What, then, about agreement concerning value-judgments? Since agreement about the truth of social "scientific" propositions is almost totally nonexistent, shouldn't we expect, following Weber, that this will also be the case with regard to normative judgments? After all, the methods of science are viewed as universal and at least provide the possibility for agreement. With value-judgments, the Chinese may lack a sense of "our" ethical imperatives, and, in

---

[77] Weber, "Objectivity," p. 362.

fact, there is such a plurality of value-systems and ethical imperatives that it seems highly unlikely that any agreement at all can be found regarding value-judgments. However, this does not appear to be the case. Consider, for example, value-judgments concerning incest, cannibalism, murder, and lying. These are almost everywhere considered morally wrong. Some incest prohibitions are universal, and nowhere are cannibalism, murder, and lying a regular practice.

Or consider the following value-judgment: "Hitler's 'Final Solution' to the so-called 'Jewish Question' was morally wrong." As Miller, who offers this example, suggests, the extent of agreement about the truth of this judgment far exceeds the extent of agreement about any single "scientific" proposition in the social sciences.[78]

But, of course, the fact (if it is a fact) that there is considerable agreement about the truth of this value-judgment is not, by itself, sufficient reason for us to accept it as correct. What is also required is that those making (or agreeing to) this value-judgment be in possession of the relevant data and that they clearly understand all relevant arguments. My assumption here is that when people know the relevant facts about Hitler's extermination of the Jews and when they understand the relevant moral arguments concerning the killing of innocent human beings, they will agree that it was morally wrong. This is not to claim that everyone will reach the same conclusion as to the moral wrongness of Hitler's policy, for this is demonstrably not the case. Nor is it to claim that the fact that a numerical majority may agree with a value-judgment necessarily says anything at all about the status of that value-judgment. If, for example, 75 per cent of the population agrees with the value-judgment that "Blacks are inherently inferior to whites," this says nothing about the correctness of that value-judgment.

In the last two sentences above I have spoken of the "status" and the "correctness" of a value-judgment. Let me now attempt to insert the term that Weber applied to social scientific propositions and withheld from normative judgments: "scientific." Weber's argument, to repeat, is that a proposition is scientific only if there are adequate data and shared methods that allow for the possibility of agreement about whether it is true or false. What I am saying is that some value-judgments and normative theories do meet these requirements and are, therefore, in Weber's sense, "scientific." My conclusion is that a value-judgment (and the normative thinking

---

[78] Miller, "Reason and Commitment."

supporting it) such as "Hitler's 'Final Solution' to the so-called 'Jewish Question' was morally wrong" is no less (and, in fact, I believe considerably more) scientific than most of the non-normative propositions and theories found in the social sciences.

The important point here is not the application or withholding of the honorific term "scientific" with regard to normative judgments and theories. I personally prefer to speak of the "rational justifiability" of a proposition or theory, rather than of its scientific status. What is important is that there be shared *standards* that all truth- and knowledge-claims must meet. Questioning a theoretical or empirical claim takes the form of asking, "How do you know?" or, "Why do you hold that that is so?" And assessing the claim is a matter of determining whether it meets the agreed-upon standards of the relevant scientific or intellectual community or audience. Exactly the same holds true for normative claims. A normative claim is in principle just as much susceptible to justification as a claim of the strictly empirical or theoretical kind. Why, then, can't most social scientists see this?

Two Views of Science

The principal reason why many social scientists seem to be unable to recognize this is that they are guided by a view of science that considers all statements other than those that are either empirical or logical and mathematical as meaningless, without any cognitive content. Science, from this perspective, is an enterprise, controlled by logic and empirical facts, whose purpose is to formulate truths about the laws of nature. For those holding this view, statements are cognitively meaningful only if they are verifiable. "Scientific" meaning is seen as a property only of propositions that can be tested, directly or indirectly, by means of observation. The truth of different propositions rests on their correspondence to what exists in the outside world. The actual practice of science involves the division of propositions into two disjunctive classes— accepted and nonaccepted propositions. Since there is a logical gulf between so-called factual or descriptive discourse and so-called normative or evaluative discourse, the scientist must never make an evaluative utterance.

For those in this tradition, the world we know is a collection of individual facts. Science has the goal of ordering these facts, and it is only because of this ordering activity that a practice becomes a "true" science. The facts themselves are what they are no matter what scientists call them. In this view, words are labels and lan-

41

guage is our means of referring to what exists "out there" in the world. Hence, language and the world are separate, though correlatable. Truth, then, is correspondence with the facts as disclosed by experience or observation; knowledge of extra-logical truths must be empirical.

Such a view of science also rests on the assumption that science must begin from a foundation where certain things are beyond doubt, whether this foundation be first principles, sense-datum statements, or something else. Because, it is argued, there are neutral and unquestionable basic propositions in science, different theories can be put in *direct* confrontation with one another. Scientific progress is guaranteed by working from this foundation and by introducing hypotheses or theories, which then must be closely examined both for their logical consistency and for their corroboration in reality.

This dominant view of science has long been firmly entrenched and taken for granted by philosophers and practicing scientists alike. Slowly, however, this image is being replaced by a new image, where science is viewed as a *social* activity. This new image is represented by the work of such persons as Kuhn, Sellars, Quine, and Rorty.[79] Although these scholars hold varying viewpoints, they are in agreement on certain essential points.

Among other things, they agree that "strict justification"—where there is a solid foundation that can carry the weight of absolutely certain knowledge or truth—simply does not exist.[80] The very idea of strict justification, they point out, has to be seen for what it is: a fetish of first philosophy, part of the legacy of Descartes's *Meditations*. Rather than viewing certain propositions, whether analytic or synthetic, as eternally unassailable, those advocating this new

[79] Thomas S. Kuhn, *The Structure of Scientific Revolutions* (Chicago: University of Chicago Press, 1962); Willifred Sellars, *Science, Perception and Reality* (London: Routledge & Kegan Paul, 1963); W. V. Quine, *From a Logical Point of View* (Cambridge, Mass.: Harvard University Press, 1953); Richard Rorty, *Philosophy and the Mirror of Nature* (Oxford: Basil Blackwell, 1980). My own efforts in this direction are presented in Derek L. Phillips, *Wittgenstein and Scientific Knowledge* (London: Macmillan, 1977).

[80] Those sharing this view, especially social scientists, also call into question the rigid distinction between descriptive and evaluative discourse. A given framework in sociology or political science, for example, will tend to support an associated value position since it secretes its own norms for the assessment of institutional arrangements. See in this regard, Charles Taylor, "Neutrality in Political Science," in Peter Laslett and W. G. Runciman, eds., *Philosophy, Politics and Society*, third series (Oxford: Basil Blackwell, 1969), pp. 25–57.

view argue that the real unit of meaning in a science is the language shared within that discipline.

They emphasize that the sensibility of the demand for ultimate justification itself turns on the belief in absolute distinctions between logic and language, language and reality, theory and practice. Such a belief, they show, is untenable. Thus, ultimate (strict) justification is impossible to realize. These various thinkers share the view that presuppositionless inquiry is impossible. They agree that the notion that scientific knowledge is an accurate representation of what is "out there" needs to be abandoned. Instead, they agree that the over-all "best" theories are those that are *agreed upon* as most adequately coordinating coherence and consistency requirements with the needs of successful scientific practice.

The advocates of this new image conceive of science as a social enterprise, with an organized consensus of scientists determining what is and is not to be warranted as truth or knowledge. The members of various scientific communities appeal to the agreed-upon criteria within their particular communities for warranting scientific truth and knowledge. To the extent that there is ever "rational certainty" about one or another fact or theory, then, it is the result of victory in *argument* rather than its relation to what is thought to be known. As Rorty puts it: "We understand knowledge when we understand the social justification of belief, and thus have no need to view it as accuracy of representation."[81]

This does not mean, however, that science is not "objective." It is indeed not objective in the sense long espoused by the dominant tradition in science, i.e., as "a representation of things as they really are." Since we cannot stand outside our current language and structure of thought, science can never be objective in that sense. But science is "objective" in the sense of being characterized by what would be agreed upon as a result of argument unreflected by irrelevant considerations. The only usable notion of objectivity, Rorty notes, is "agreement" rather than "mirroring."[82]

One important consequence of the new image of science is that none of the empirical sciences has a privileged status in the sense of being able to claim an essential grasp of reality. Of course, in some sciences there are truths (agreements) that are rather well established, i.e., that have been generally defended successfully against all comers. Certain statements and theories maintain the

[81] Rorty, *Mirror of Nature*, p. 170.
[82] Ibid., p. 335.

status of truth as long as nobody provides an interesting alternative that would lead other scientists to question them. But, ultimately, scientific truth and knowledge are always decided in the social context of justification.

A second consequence of the new image of science is that it is an illusion to think that sociology, political science, or even physics, is objective and rational in some way that moral philosophy, aesthetics, or poetry may not be. More importantly for my interests here, explanatory theories have no special objective or rational status vis-à-vis normative theories. All of these disciplines and theories are concerned with justifying their truth- and knowledge-claims, but none is more privileged in its foundation than any of the rest. *Conversation* is the ultimate context within which knowledge is to be understood.[83]

To the extent that normative theorizing operates with strict coherence and consistency requirements, its epistemology is identical to that found in explanatory theorizing. But it is often claimed that explanatory theories also have an empirical basis, while normative theories do not. According to the dominant view of science, scientific discourse occupies a privileged position because of its observational basis, while normative theories lack such "observationality." In principle, at least, scientists are in agreement about what is necessary for "scientific" statements to be true and how to go about checking or confirming whether they are indeed true. The truth of value-judgments, on the other hand, is not usually seen as resting in the same way on empirical facts and observation. This is, however, a mistaken view. Contrary to what is widely believed, normative and scientific theories are parallel in this regard.

The new view of science emphasizes, as already noted, that there is no place to stand outside our beliefs and our language. Nevertheless, our theories have an oddly reciprocal relationship between language and nature.[84] Explanatory theories do, now and again, break through the linguistic barrier. There is sometimes feedback from nature, and theoretical accounts are adjusted accordingly. Although never totally free of theoretical influences, it is this feedback that is viewed as constituting the "empirical foothold" or "empirical control" that constitutes the intersystematic checks in

[83] Ibid., p. 390.
[84] Phillips, *Wittgenstein and Scientific Knowledge.*

science. One or another sort of feedback provides, then, the empirical foothold of explanatory theories.

Exactly the same holds for normative theories. Here the corresponding role is played mainly by practice.[85] One way to find out whether a particular normative theory or principle is correct is to practice it, to try it out, to base individual conduct and institutional arrangements on such a theory or principle. The value of truth-telling, for example, is maintained not merely because of intersystematic consistency requirements but also because it usually works: telling the truth tends to help maximize our aims and interests. One empirical foothold for a normative theory or principle, therefore, is the *consequences* of observable actions or conduct. Actions or conduct based on a normative theory receive feedback that is relevant to evaluating the correctness of the theory.

Actual practice is not the only way, however, that normative theories are tested. Theories involving various conceptions of freedom, equality, or justice, for instance, allow us to engage in imaginary practices, to try out different *Gedanken* experiments, and to utilize feedback mechanisms that are cortical rather than the results of direct testing. Thus, we may imagine the various consequences arising from, say, application of a normative principle requiring an absolute equality of incomes, and compare these with the consequences arising from other distributive principles.

Just as with explanatory theories, the feedback about the quality of our predictions and practices is never perfect. This is due to the unavoidable mediation of theoretical and conceptual schemes. That is, explanatory and normative theories are faced with the identical problem that there are no completely independent checks (arising from presuppositionless inquiry) available by which theories can be tested. All explanatory theories—most especially in the social sciences—are radically underdetermined by observation. Exactly the same holds for normative theories; it is always difficult to get a clear-cut message from nature. But explanatory and normative theories alike require practice (both actual and hypothetical) as a form of self-criticism, as a means of self-correction, as a means of trying out (and adjusting) our ideas, and as a means of escaping vicious circularity.

For anyone who accepts the new image of science in preference to the dominant view, then, there will be no methodological pro-

---

[85] In the following discussion I draw on Owen J. Flanagan, Jr., "Quinean Ethics," *Ethics* 93 (October 1982): 56–74.

hibitions against making value-judgments and normative claims. But these judgments and claims must be rationally justified. Whatever the content of a scientific, moral, or political theory, to rationally justify it (or to choose one theory over another) is to give reasons and arguments for its acceptance that a reasonable person ought to find persuasive.[86] Justification involves the providing of a solid, well-grounded argument that other persons should respect as substantial—even though the argument is never totally compelling nor the conclusion necessarily the only one that could have been reached. With justification, the status of truth or knowledge is granted (always provisionally) to the propositions and theories that have survived the criticisms and objections of the particular audience to whom they have been directed. Justification, then, is a fully social phenomenon, not a transaction between the inquirer and "reality."

It is true, of course, that there will often be conflicts and differences of opinion regarding value-judgments and normative conclusions. But such conflicts and differences of opinion are in no way peculiar to normative theories. The literature of science (especially social science) exhibits an enormous diversity of explanatory theories, and conflicts and disagreements about the cognitive adequacy of these theories receive considerable attention from the various defenders and opponents of an explanatory theory. The absence of widespread consensus about the correctness of particular normative theories does not, then, serve to distinguish their status from that of explanatory theories. Both are equally rational.

What makes science "rational" is not the fact of consensus about particular propositions or theories, but the fact that there is a commitment to certain modes of argument (methods) whose very nature is to lead to (or allow for) agreement. Without the hope of agreement, of course, argumentation would be pointless. But the rationality of science lies in general agreement about certain "methods" (including what constitutes scientific procedures, evidence, reasons, a good argument, and the like) that allow for the possibility of consensus about specific propositions and theories, and for the resolution of disagreements about competing propositions and theories. In Sellar's words, "Science is rational not because it has a

---

[86] See, for example, John Rawls, *A Theory of Justice* (Cambridge, Mass.: Harvard University Press, 1971); Virginia Held, "Justification: Legal and Political," *Ethics* 86 (1975): 1–16; Alan Gewirth, *Reason and Morality* (Chicago: University of Chicago Press, 1978); Jürgen Habermas, *Communication and the Evolution of Society*, trans. Thomas McCarthy (Boston: Beacon Press, 1979).

foundation, but because it is a self-correcting enterprise which can put *any* claim in jeopardy, though not all at once."[87] Similarly, with value-judgments and normative theories. What makes them rational is that they rest on arguments, reasons, and justifications that allow for their appraisal and evaluation.

Both explanatory and normative theorizing require the existence of a communication community, or a practice—it is the presupposition for all truth and knowledge. That is, argumentation and justification must take place within a *real* community. It is impossible to even conceive, for example, of the logical validity of arguments or of the correctness of truth-claims without positing a community of human inquirers who are capable of intersubjective communication and the reaching of agreement. In other words, what counts as true is determined by standards that are impersonal and objective within the practice of physics, sociology, political philosophy, or whatever.

Claims about validity, truth, and knowledge, then, are all basically dependent upon the justification of verbal or written arguments in the actual community of inquirers. This means, at the very least, that one basic moral norm must be assumed in scholarly and scientific discourse: truth-telling. Were lies the rule rather than the exception, discourse and argumentation would be impossible. Further, such discourse demands the willingness of all participants to explicate, defend, and justify their truth- and knowledge-claims. Thus, there is always a commitment to the equality of all the participants in scholarly or scientific discussion, i.e., all have the equal right to demand, and expect, an extended justification of whatever is claimed.

But in addition to the real communication community, where truth- and knowledge-claims are decided upon through interpersonal dialogue, anyone who engages in argumentation and justification presupposes an *ideal* communication community that would be capable of adequately understanding the meaning of one's arguments and judging their ultimate validity.[88] Such a community would consist of persons who have freed their reasoning from the limitations and partialities of standpoints characteristic of the real community. This ideal community has been spoken of by Peirce as the "Indefinite Community of Investigators" (in 1868!)

[87] Sellars, *Science*, p. 170.
[88] Karl-Otto Apel, *Towards a Transformation of Philosophy* (London: Routledge & Kegan Paul, 1980).

and by George Herbert Mead as the "Community of Universal Discourse."[89] Although this ideal community is presupposed in all scholarly and scientific discourse, it is only imperfectly realized in the actual (real) community of practitioners. It is because we are able to recognize that our scholarly discourse is often influenced by internal and external constraints—thus affecting our capacity to understand the meaning of an argument and to judge its validity—that we must presume the possibility of an ideal community where we would be free of the constraints existent in the real one.[90]

With regard to explanatory and normative theorizing, there is frequently an admixture of the two in the theories of most social scientists. Yet, they can be analytically separated and can be viewed as having obviously different concerns. While explanatory theories focus on accounting for various social actions and institutional arrangements, normative theories are concerned with evaluating the self-same actions and institutions. The former might be interested in explaining the institution of slavery, the existence of apartheid, or the presence of social inequality (e.g., social stratification), while the latter may focus on the evaluation and criticism of these social practices on moral grounds. If, for example, the morality of apartheid is not to be accepted equally with the morality of racial non-discrimination, then normative theories obviously require a rational justification of their various principles or criteria.

Although they have different concerns, both explanatory and normative theories have the same empirical base: the actions of human beings. Human actions comprise the factual matter of explanatory and normative theorizing alike; they provide the objective basis against which, respectively, empirical propositions and value-judgments can be checked for their truth or correctness. The statement that "Sweden is a more just society than the Soviet Union" is no less objective than the statement that "There is greater economic equality in Sweden than in the Soviet Union." Both are concerned with showing that a certain statement is correct (warranted) in terms of a particular set of rules of inquiry. And both

---

[89] Charles S. Peirce, *Collected Papers*, vol. 5, ed. V. C. Hartshorne and P. Weiss (Cambridge, Mass.: Harvard University Press, 1934); George Herbert Mead, *Mind, Self and Society* (Chicago: University of Chicago Press, 1934).

[90] While the positing of such an ideal is important, I do not share the views of Habermas (*Communication*), and Apel (*Towards a Transformation of Philosophy*) about the need to develop a "universal pragmatics" or a "transcendental hermeneutics." Such notions are the equivalent of the Platonic search for the foundation of knowledge.

are, of necessity, involved with conceptual classifications of relevant properties and relations, e.g., what "counts" as just or as equality. Common to both explanatory and normative theories at their best, then, is a shared emphasis on reason and rational justification. Both must meet coherence and consistency requirements, and both have an empirical foothold in practice. Thus, the logical status and structure of explanatory and normative theories is identical. Contrary to the views of many who emphasize value-neutrality and objectivity, normative theories do not have an inferior logical status to that enjoyed by explanatory theories.

None of this is intended to deny the fact that an extremely important function of the value-neutrality doctrine has been to increase the autonomy and help assure the scientific status of the social sciences. Without this heavy emphasis on value-neutrality, it is doubtful that sociology, for example, would have achieved whatever (modest) scientific standing it now enjoys. And certainly there is much that is correct in the claim of the defenders of value-neutrality that their opponents frequently assert the normative superiority of certain institutional arrangements without adequately defending or justifying their conclusions. On the other hand, I also don't want to contest the point made by many critics of mainstream social science that those social scientists who claim to be engaged in explanatory theorizing often smuggle in their own value-preferences. Rather, in opposition to both groups, I have tried to show that there are no logical or methodological prohibitions against, first, explaining or describing what *is* and, thereafter, providing a normative theory that allows for *evaluation* of what is and offers a rational justification for what *ought* to be. In short, I have been emphasizing the legitimacy, desirability, and possibility of engaging in social scientific inquiry that is *both* explanatory and normative.

III

Both explanatory and normative considerations are, therefore, crucial to my concern with a just social order. On the one hand, I want to explain how normative consensus about moral principles and standards provides for social order. On the other, I must provide a rational justification for those particular moral principles that help assure justice. Rationally justifiable principles have not only a preferred ethical standing, they are also preferable in a more strictly

49

sociological sense. As I will show later, moral principles that can be rationally justified are far more likely to gain widespread support than those that people accept because of ignorance, coercion, tradition, and the like. And shared consensus about justifiable principles is far superior to other bases for consensus in sustaining the social solidarity required for achieving and maintaining social order.

Since socialization and social control are crucial for helping to assure social order, examination of these two mechanisms also raises important normative questions. What sorts of socialization processes, for example, are themselves morally acceptable and/or preferable? When, and why, should people feel guilty or ashamed if they violate internalized norms? If external sources are necessary for taking up the slack when socialization fails, what social control mechanisms are morally justifiable? All of these are normative questions that connect to the general problem of a just social order.

TWO

Justice and Social Order

ACCORDING to Émile Durkheim, "all the moral institutions one encounters in history are equally natural in so far as they are founded in the nature of the societies which uphold them."[1] And, speaking about social inequalities, he goes on to say that these inequalities "would not have been permitted if they had not been founded in the nature of things. . . . For the outcome to have been otherwise, one would have had to be able to establish that such inequality did not correspond to any need or social necessity."[2] All of this is, of course, consistent with Durkheim's general sociological postulate that a human institution cannot rest upon an error or a lie.

Obviously, I reject all such claims about the "naturalness" of any particular moral institution or about society's "need" for a specific form of social inequality. With such views as Durkheim's, the moral rightness or correctness of various social patterns and institutional arrangements is simply taken for granted. By ignoring all questions concerning the moral justification of these patterns and arrangements, Durkheim and most other social scientists must stand mute with regard to questions about a society's normative status. For them, all societies occupy exactly the same moral position; from their perspective, all are equally natural and one cannot, therefore, even speak of a just or unjust society.

In contrast, my explicit concern is with a just social order, i.e., a social order where people's actions and the institutional arrangements to which they give rise are warranted in terms of a specified set of rationally justified first principles. Because we can imagine so-called theories of justice that conceive, for instance, of blacks or women as subhuman—so that it would be "just" to treat them as animals—any morally acceptable theory of justice must begin either with the notion of rights or of common interests. In other words, there must be something so fundamentally the same in (or for) all

[1] Émile Durkheim, *Essays on Morals and Education*. Edited with an introduction by W. S. F. Pickering (London: Routledge & Kegan Paul, 1979), pp. 32–33.
[2] Ibid., pp. 71–72.

human beings that there is no room for a standard or theory of justice that is not universally applicable. The specification of a just social order requires, then, a theory that pays attention to what is potentially generalizable to all human beings and explicitly considers the things that people may or may not do to one another. Such a theory must contain the principles by which a just social order is to be guided, and must provide a standard against which the moral status of given societies and institutions can be judged.

In this chapter I will consider the viewpoints of four leading theorists whose work has received considerable attention in recent years: John Rawls, Robert Nozick, Alan Gewirth, and Jürgen Habermas.[3] Each of these theorists has engaged in normative theorizing directed at locating moral principles that can, by virtue of their philosophical cogency, provide the foundation for a just society. Each holds to the possibility of formulating a coherent set of fundamental principles bearing on our moral lives.

The theories of Rawls, Nozick, and Gewirth are concerned (in varying ways) with people's "rights," while Habermas focuses on people's "common interests." But all four theorists demonstrate the crucial importance of trying to locate moral principles that will allow for the evaluation of particular laws and institutions from a moral standpoint *independent* of those laws and institutions. That is, each attempts to provide the means for examining the basic structure of society from the perspective of specified moral values or principles. In one way or another, each of these men is concerned with the connection between morality and action, between what is and what ought to be, between the just society and the means to achieve it.

Given the general lack of attention paid to normative theorizing by social scientists, I am assuming that the majority of readers will be unfamiliar with the work of at least some of these theorists. Therefore, I will discuss these four theories at greater length and in greater detail than would be necessary if normative theorizing occupied a more central position in social scientific inquiry.

In discussing these theories, my intention is threefold: first, to examine them in regard to the issue of *how* moral principles and

[3] John Rawls, *A Theory of Justice* (Cambridge, Mass.: Harvard University Press, 1971); Robert Nozick, *Anarchy, State, and Utopia* (New York: Basic Books, 1974); Jürgen Habermas, *Theory and Practice*, trans. John Viertel (Boston: Beacon Press, 1973); Jürgen Habermas, *Legitimation Crisis*, trans. Thomas McCarthy (Boston: Beacon Press, 1975); Alan Gewirth, *Reason and Morality* (Chicago: University of Chicago Press, 1978).

judgments are to be justified; second, to consider the separate issue of *which* particular moral principles are justifiable; and, third, to present enough of the *content* of these theories to set the stage for my later consideration of various elements contained within each of them. Although, as will become clear, my overall assessment is that one of these theories is superior to the other three, I will draw on different aspects of all of them in later chapters.

I

Rawls's Theory of Justice

John Rawls's *A Theory of Justice* has been widely acclaimed as a work of great significance for moral and political theory. The importance of this book is clearly reflected in the huge literature to which it has given rise since its publication in 1971.[4] It has had an enormous impact on the discussion of central questions in moral and political philosophy over the past decade, and it constitutes the major point of reference for all subsequent discussions concerning justice. It is not my intention here, however, to deal with the general substance of Rawls's long and complex book. Instead, my concern is much more modest; I am going to focus exclusively on the main tenets in Rawls's theory. Since these are crucial to his whole enterprise, they deserve careful inspection.

"Justice," Rawls says, "is the first virtue of social institutions, as truth is of systems of thought."[5] Since there is a wide variety of competing principles of justice, and since no one has been able to bring order out of these competing principles, we require a philosophical foundation that provides a firm set of justifiable principles for choosing among various social arrangements and institutions. Rawls utilizes a version of inductive justification in arriving at his general principles of justice. He attempts to justify his general moral principles by showing that they conform with particular moral judgments that we actually do make and accept, and that the particular judgments themselves are, in turn, justified by being shown to be in accordance with the general principles of morality. This circularity, Rawls claims, allows the general principles and the particular judgments to be brought into agreement or "reflective equilibrium" with one another.

The technique of reflective equilibrium presupposes that each of

[4] Rawls, *A Theory of Justice*.
[5] Ibid., p. 2.

us entertains and accepts certain judgments about justice, equality, freedom, and other moral notions. Some of us may, for example, make the moral judgment that slavery is unjust or that men and women should be treated equally in the same circumstances. That is, we all make certain moral judgments simply because they seem "right" to us. These ordinary, unreflective moral beliefs or judgments are what Rawls terms "considered judgments." With the technique of reflective equilibrium, the task of moral theorizing is to provide a structure of general principles (a theory) that supports those immediate judgments about which we are more or less certain.

The equilibrium idea is a two-way process: we move back and forth between adjustments to our judgments and adjustments to our general theoretical principles until we find a satisfactory fit between them. The aim is not, says Rawls, to specify principles of justice suitable for all societies regardless of their particular social or historical circumstances. Instead, the concern is with the just form of basic institutions within a democratic society under modern conditions.

The goal of Rawls's work is to develeop a moral theory about justice. For him, moral thinking is a fully rational, highly systematic activity. "One may think of a public conception of justice," Rawls states, "as constituting the fundamental charter of a well-ordered association."[6] Thus, the primary subject of justice is the basic structure of society. Rawls assumes that conflicts are inevitable in any society, and that morality is a necessary regulative mechanism for settling such conflicts. He points out that

> although society is a cooperative venture for mutual advantage, it is typically marked by a conflict as well as by an identity of interests. . . . Thus principles are needed for choosing among the various social arrangements which determine [the] division of advantages and for underwriting an agreement on the proper distributive shares. These requirements define the role of justice.[7]

A conception of justice, then, provides a *standard* against which we can assess the distributive aspects of the basic structure of society.[8] It serves as a point of comparison to be used in appraising

[6] Ibid., p. 5.

[7] Ibid., p. 4.

[8] John Rawls, "Kantian Constructivism in Moral Theory," *The Journal of Philosophy* 79 (September 1980): 523.

the ways in which social institutions distribute to individuals the benefits and burdens of their shared social existence.

Central to Rawls's theory is the idea of the "original position," a hypothetical situation where men and women come together to form a social contract. The original position describes an initial situation of fairness where individuals—as equal, rational, and moral beings—must choose the principles of justice that will regulate the just society. Rawls's theory differs from other contractarian theories, however, in that the parties to the contract must choose their principles from behind a "veil of ignorance," that is, what the parties in the original position do *not* know.

The intention of the veil of ignorance is to assure that they do not know anything that would distinguish one individual from another. Thus, all parties lack any knowledge of their social position in society (for example, their sex, race, class, income, status, or power), of their own natural assets and abilities (e.g., strength, intelligence), and of their values, aims, preferences, purposes in life, and conceptions of the good. Nor do they know the particular circumstances of their own society (e.g., its economic or political situation), or even to which generation they belong.[9] These, then, are the things that the parties to the original position do not know. All such knowledge and information is excluded so that no one will have a disparate bargaining position. This is necessary to assure that the principles of justice will be chosen under conditions of equality and fairness.

Rawls also specifies that there are certain things that the parties in the original position *do* know. Although they don't know what these are, the parties do know that they all have various values, aims, and purposes, as well as conceptions of the good. Further, they know the "general facts" about human society, e.g., the principles of economic theory and the laws of psychology.[10] In addition, they know that each and every individual values certain "primary goods." Prime examples of such goods are rights and liberties, self-respect, opportunities, income, and wealth.[11] It is assumed that all persons would prefer to have more rather than less of these primary goods since they are useful in pursuing whatever ends an individual may have. Despite the lack of knowledge—behind the veil of ignorance—of their own particular ends or purposes, the parties

[9] Rawls, *A Theory of Justice*, pp. 136–37.
[10] Ibid., p. 138.
[11] Ibid., p. 162.

to the original position are all assumed to be motivated by the desire for certain primary goods.[12] It is this notion of primary goods that provides the motivation necessary to generate the problem of rational choice and to make possible a determinate choice for the principles of justice.

The original position, together with the veil of ignorance, incorporates what Rawls calls "pure procedural justice." This means that whatever principles the parties select from among alternative principles of justice *are* just. Apart from the procedure of choosing these principles, there are no reasons of justice. Pure procedural justice obtains where there is no independent criterion for the right result. The idea of pure procedural justice is meant to contrast with "perfect" procedural justice, where there is an independent and already given criterion of what is just and where a procedure exists to ensure a result that satisfies this standard. With pure, as opposed to perfect, procedural justice, there exists no independent criterion of justice; what is just is defined by the outcome of the procedure itself.[13]

In the original position, behind the veil of ignorance, individuals who are motivated by the desire for certain primary goods must choose the principles of justice applying to the basic structure of society. Because they are all similarly situated, no individual is able to design principles that favor his particular situation. Thus, the principles chosen are the result of a fair bargain.[14] In Rawls's words: "The idea of the original position is to set up a fair procedure so that any principle agreed to will be just. The aim is to use the notion of procedural justice as a basis of theory."[15] Under these conditions, the contract becomes an instrument of justification.

Rawls says that the parties in the original position will agree upon two principles of justice. His final statement of these two principles reads as follows:

First Principle
Each person is to have an equal right to the most extensive total system of equal basic liberties compatible with a similar system of liberty for all.

[12] Ibid., p. 144.
[13] Ibid., p. 86.
[14] Ibid.
[15] Ibid., p. 136.

Second Principle

Social and economic inequalities are to be arranged so that they are both:

(a) to the greatest benefit of the least advantaged, consistent with the just savings principle, and

(b) attached to offices and positions open to all under conditions of fair equality of opportunity.[16]

In speaking of "basic liberties" in the first principle, Rawls means, he says, freedom of speech and assembly, freedom to hold private property, and freedom from arbitrary arrest and seizure.[17] All citizens in a just society are *equally* entitled to all of these liberties. The second principle stresses that positions and offices in the hierarchy of organizations must be equally open to all, but it does *not* require that the distribution of wealth and income (or status and power) be equal. Whatever the distribution, however, it must be to everyone's advantage.

The two principles of justice formulated by Rawls are to be arranged in a serial order, with the principle of equal liberty (understood in terms of the enumerated basic liberties) having absolute priority over the second. Rawls writes: "This ordering means that a departure from the institutions of equal liberty required by the first principle cannot be justified by, or compensated for, by greater social and economic advantage."[18] If one social arrangement is better than another with regard to the first principle, by however narrow a margin, then it is to be preferred to that other arrangement even if the latter arrangement is superior on the basis of the second principle. Rawls states:

> Now it is possible, at least theoretically, that by giving up some of their fundamental liberties men are sufficiently compensated by the resulting social and economic gains. The general conception of justice implies no restriction on what sorts of inequalities are impermissible; it only requires that everyone's position be improved. . . . Imagine . . . that men forego certain political rights when the economic returns are significant and their capacity to influence these rights would be marginal in any case. It is this kind of exchange which the two principles as stated rule out; being arranged in a serial order they do not

16 Ibid., p. 302.
17 Ibid., p. 61.
18 Ibid.

permit exchanges between basic liberties and economic and social gains.[19]

This emphasis on the priority of liberty is of crucial importance to Rawls's theory, and has frequently been misunderstood by some of his critics.[20] The precedence of liberty over the second principle of justice means that liberty can be restricted only for the sake of liberty itself. Only when those with lesser liberty require compensation, can there be a restriction of other people's liberty. Rawls formulated his "priority rule" as follows:

> The principles of justice are to be ranked in lexical order and therefore liberty can be restricted only for the sake of liberty. There are two cases: (a) a less extensive liberty shared by all, and (b) a less than equal liberty must be acceptable to those citizens with the lesser liberty.[21]

Once a certain level of material well-being has been achieved, Rawls says, liberty is not to be traded off for other social goods. The basis for the priority of liberty in the original position is described by Rawls in this manner: "As the conditions of civilization improve, the marginal significance of further economic and social advantages diminish relative to the interests of liberty. . . . Beyond some point it becomes and then remains irrational from the standpoint of the original position to acknowledge a lesser liberty for the sake of greater material means and amenities of office."[22]

Highly important in Rawls's theory is the "difference principle," which is part of clause (a) of the second principle of justice: social and economic inequalities are to be arranged so that they are to the greatest benefit of the least advantaged. This means that an unequal distribution of income or wealth is justifiable if and only if it will maximize benefits to the least-advantaged group in society.

The difference principle requires that persons with unusual (i.e., highly valued) natural assets and abilities must accept restrictions on the degree to which they can benefit from their natural endowments. This is done with the goal of improving the position of the least advantaged.

Rawls distinguishes between "fundamental rights and liberties"

---

[19] Ibid., pp. 62–63.
[20] For example, Irving Kristol, "About Equality," *Commentary* 54 (1972): 41–47.
[21] Rawls, *A Theory of Justice*, p. 250.
[22] Ibid., p. 542.

and "economic and social benefits."[23] The former are to be equally available to everyone, but the latter are to be distributed in accordance with the difference principle. In its most general form, the difference principle states:

> In a basic structure with n relevant representatives, first maximize the welfare of the worst-off representative man; second, for equal welfare of the worst-off representative, maximize the welfare of the second worst-off representative man, and so on until the last case which is, for equal welfare of all the preceding n-1 representatives, maximize the welfare of the best-off representative man. We may think of this as the lexical difference principle.[24]

For the most part, however, Rawls uses the difference principle in its simpler form: social and economic inequalities are to be arranged so that they are to the greatest benefit of the least advantaged.

Utilization of the difference principle is basic to distinguishing between what Rawls terms liberal and democratic equality. The "liberal" conception is a sort of fair meritocracy in which social and economic inequalities are mitigated by equality of opportunity and the attempt to provide everyone with an equal start. But the liberal conception of equality is flawed, says Rawls, because it

> permits the distribution of wealth and income to be determined by the natural distribution of abilities and talents. Within the limits allowed by the background arrangements, distributive shares are decided by the outcome of the natural lottery; and the outcome is arbitrary from a moral perspective. There is no more reason to permit the distribution of income and wealth to be settled by the distribution of natural assets than by historical and social fortune.[25]

By contrast, the "democratic" conception, which is based on the difference principle, does not permit income and wealth to be determined by natural assets and abilities. The accidents of natural endowments and the contingencies of social circumstances must be *nullified*. This is because, Rawls states, we must leave aside "those aspects of the social world that seem arbitrary from a moral point of view."[26]

[23] Ibid., p. 63.
[24] Ibid., p. 83.
[25] Ibid., pp. 73–74.
[26] Ibid., p. 15.

Therefore, argues Rawls, the distribution of natural abilities must be seen as constituting a "common asset" within a society. He says that

> the difference principle represents, in effect, an agreement to regard the distribution of natural talents as a *common asset* and to share in the benefits of this distribution whatever it turns out to be. Those who have been favored by nature, whoever they are, may gain from their good fortune only on terms that improve the situation of those who have lost out. . . . No one deserves his greater natural capacity nor merits a more favorable starting place in society. But it does not follow that one should eliminate these distinctions. There is another way to deal with them. The basic structure can be arranged so that these contingencies work for the good of the least fortunate.[27]

Thus the operation of the difference principle (working for the least fortunate) requires that everyone has some claim on the totality of natural assets and abilities, i.e., on everyone else. Democratic equality follows, then, from the difference principle; social and economic inequalities, to repeat, are just only in as far as they improve the situation of the least-advantaged persons in society.

All of this represents, of course, only a very limited view of the central ideas in Rawls's *A Theory of Justice*. Among other things, he gives detailed consideration to the kinds of institutional arrangements following from his two principles of justice. Despite the enormous importance of Rawls's achievement—not least in stimulating a rebirth of normative philosophy and theorizing—there are serious weaknesses in his work, which demand attention. So far as my own interests are concerned, there are two shortcomings in his basic tenets that disqualify Rawls's theory as the source for the rationally justifiable first principles that ought to regulate a just social order.

First of all, there are problems in the justification that Rawls provides for his general principles of justice. With the inductive justification, which he utilizes, it is assumed that we can distinguish the morally right from the morally wrong in our particular moral judgments and can, hence, infer what are the morally right general moral principles by generalizing from the morally right particular judgments.

But what if there are serious disagreements about the particular

[27] Ibid., pp. 101–02.

judgments, i.e., what if different people do not have similar views about what is right and wrong? What if, for instance, the considered judgments about freedom and equality held by someone (or persons, more generally) in Cuba or Sweden were different than those held by ourselves and by John Rawls? After all, Rawls says that in addressing the public culture of a democratic society he "hopes to bring to awareness a conception of the person and of social cooperation conjectured to be implicit in that culture, or at least congenial to its deepest tendencies when properly expressed and presented."[28]

But how is any one of us to respond to the possible charge that our very judgments about persons, social cooperation, and the like, have been tainted by an unjust social structure? To appeal to general moral principles in such a dispute would beg the question, since the general principles rest exclusively on the particular judgments that opponents may be disputing. If we assume that every individual's judgments are to a large extent the historical product of living in a particular society and cultural situation, then we cannot allow Rawls to simply take *his* considered judgments (even if they are ours as well) as given in his exercise of reflective equilibrium. What is obviously required is an independent justification for moral judgments about competing judgments.

The second shortcoming of Rawls's basic tenets also concerns the issue of justification. There is, I believe, a fundamental problem with Rawls's notion of the hypothetical contract in the original position. As noted earlier, the parties must *choose* the principles of justice that will apply to the basic structure of society. The purpose of the double stipulation of the original position and the veil of ignorance is, of course, to assure that hypothetical social contractors will choose the principles of justice from a similar situation. Whatever principles the parties select from among alternative principles of justice *are* just. With pure procedural justice, that is, there exists no independent criterion of justice; what is just is defined by the outcome of the procedure itself. In other words, the correct principles are to be chosen and not discovered. In my view, however, the conditions for choice are absent behind the veil of ignorance.

With regard to selecting the principles of justice, Rawls's standpoint appears to be quite clear. He states repeatedly that the parties in the original position must "choose" or "agree" to specific prin-

[28] Rawls, "Kantian Constructivism in Moral Theory," p. 569.

ciples.[29] For instance, he says that free and rational persons must choose "the principles which are to assign basic rights and duties and to determine the division of social benefits. Men are to decide in advance how they are to regulate their claims against one another and what is to be the foundation charter of their society."[30] Thus, principles of justice are chosen for regulating conflicting claims (were they not "conflicting," neither contracts nor principles would be necessary). Rawls says the same thing, pointing out that

> principles of justice deal with conflicting claims upon the advantages won by social cooperation; they apply to the relations among several groups or persons. The word "contract" suggests this plurality as well as the condition that the appropriate division of advantages must be in accordance with principles acceptable to all parties.[31]

Agreement about the principles of justice involves, for rational persons in the initial situation, choice from among alternative conceptions of justice.[32] Rawls says that while ideally individuals are to choose from among all possible conceptions of justice, he will assume that all parties are presented with a short list of different conceptions of justice and are "required to agree unanimously that one conception is the best among those enumerated."[33] The parties in the original position are all able to advocate their own preferred conceptions, and all can "make proposals, submit reasons for their acceptance, and so on."[34] They must jointly evaluate various proposals and make a decision as to which are to constitute the principles of justice that will apply to the basic structure of society.[35]

In order for there to be an agreement about the principles of justice, then, there must be parties who evaluate alternative conceptions of justice. A "choice" of the preferred conception of justice is, therefore, possible only when two conditions are satisfied: (1) a plurality of agents must be present, and (2) alternative conceptions of justice must be available. That is, different agents must jointly make a choice from among different conceptions of justice. I am going to argue that the first condition is not satisfied in Rawls's

[29] Rawls, *A Theory of Justice*, pp. 13–14, 17, 136, 138–39.
[30] Ibid., p. 11.
[31] Ibid., p. 16.
[32] Ibid., p. 17, 122.
[33] Ibid., p. 122.
[34] Ibid., p. 19.
[35] Ibid., pp. 137–38.

portrayal of what occurs behind the veil of ignorance, i.e., that there is no plurality of agents. This means, of course, that there can be no possibility of agents choosing from among different conceptions of justice.

In developing his conception of justice as fairness, Rawls is highly critical of utilitarianism as a system of choice, whereby an impartial spectator selects the principles of justice by extending to everyone the principle of choice for one person. A principle of social choice cannot be arrived at this way, Rawls says, because it does not "take seriously the plurality and distinctiveness of individuals."[36] A plurality of distinct persons with separate systems of ends, he states, is an essential feature of human societies.[37]

Just as in actual societies, there must be a plurality of persons in the original position where contracting takes place. Such a plurality demands that persons be distinguished from their ends. That is, there must be autonomous selves who are *prior* to whatever they want to acquire or achieve. In this regard, Rawls says that the parties in the original situation "think of themselves as beings who can and do choose their final ends" and they "see themselves as primarily moral persons with an equal right to choose their mode of life."[38]

Let us now consider those doing the choosing in the original position. If all parties to the contracting situation are stripped of every trace of their own concrete individuality, can they even be expected to have a viewpoint about the choice of principles applying to the basic structure of society? Of course, they know that they "have" different preferences and interests, although these are unknown to them. The question is *who* has preferences and interests? One expects that the answer is "persons." But to be a person is to be a subject whose identity is given *independently* of what he has in the way of interests and the like. If, however, agents are deprived of all knowledge of their own specific identity, what is the nature of the "beings" who are supposed to think about social justice?

The notion of a person or a "self" signifies a distinction between one being and another, the acquisition of self-consciousness, and the capacity for self-reflection. The very idea of an individuated, distinct self involves a coherence and continuity in who one *is*.[39]

---

[36] Ibid., p. 29.
[37] Ibid.
[38] Ibid., p. 563.
[39] The notion of identity will be discussed in Chapter 5.

And, of course, the acquisition of a distinct self with a specific identity is largely the result of one's prior relationships with other human beings. Through contacts and comparisons with others, the individual acquires a consciousness of him- or herself as a unique and separate person. Each individual's history and experiences, attachments and commitments, contribute to his or her distinct identity.

As noted above, a choice among principles in the hypothetical original position requires a plurality of persons. But behind the veil of ignorance, people don't know anything that could provide the necessary basis for distinguishing themselves from others; everyone lacks knowledge of his or her age, sex, family relationships, values, interests, preferences, and aims. By stripping everyone of all characteristics that might distinguish one person from another, Rawls has made the individual completely invisible. Nothing remains that could possibly establish a plurality of persons.

It is, I realize, the intent of the veil of ignorance to deprive all parties to the original position of any and all distinguishing characteristics. In fact, Rawls emphasizes the point that they are all "similarly situated."[40] But surely this is a rather dramatic understatement. Since all individuating qualities and characteristics are excluded, the parties to the original position are, in fact, *identically* situated. Given that they are identically situated, there remains no basis to even distinguish one person from another. Thus, there is in Rawls's scheme no plurality of agents who are able to bargain with one another and agree to the principles of justice required for regulating society.

In the absence of a plurality of distinctive, individuated social agents, there is no room for such notions as bargaining or discussion (making proposals, submitting reasons, and the like). Unless there is some *difference* in the characteristics of the "bargainers," it is difficult (impossible?) to imagine who is involved in bargaining or what would constitute the basis of such bargaining. Nor, for the same reason, is it even imaginable that the various persons (*sic!*) could engage in anything that resembles a discussion. There simply is no plurality of parties to even attempt to reach an agreement about the principles of justice.

Although Rawls says that there must be a plurality of agents behind the veil of ignorance who come to a unanimous agreement about the principles of justice, this cannot be an agreement based

[40] Rawls, *A Theory of Justice*, p. 12.

on deliberations engaged in by a plurality of individuals with different characteristics. The veil of ignorance is employed to assure that there are no such differences. Consider the following statement in this regard:

> To begin with, it is clear that since the differences among the parties are unknown to them, and everyone is equally rational and similarly situated, each is convinced by the same arguments. Therefore, we can view the choice in the original position from the standpoint of one person selected at random.[41]

In other words, there is no question of a plurality of persons choosing together, no question of a group of persons deciding, no question of bargaining or engaging in discussion. In fact, writes Rawls, "If anyone after due reflection prefers a conception of justice to another, then they all do, and a unanimous agreement can be reached."[42]

Obviously, however, the phrase about reaching unanimous agreement is totally superfluous. After all, Rawls specifies that all parties to the original position will prefer the *same* conception of justice (if anyone does, "then they all do"). If they all have the same preference, then there is no need at all for any discussion, choice, or agreement. Instead of there being a plurality of persons behind the veil of ignorance, then, there is only a single subject.

In the absence of a plurality of distinct persons in the original position, it would appear that—just as in the utilitarian view that Rawls rejects—someone akin to the impartial spectator approves of or selects the principles of justice by extending the principle of prudence to everyone. But this single subject does not *choose* the principles for the just society. As I indicated earlier, Rawls himself specifies that choice is possible only when there is a plurality of persons who consider and evaluate alternative conceptions of justice. Since there is no such plurality behind the veil of ignorance, a choice about the principles of justice cannot occur in the original position.

Whatever his talk about discussions, bargaining, decisions, and choices in the original position, Rawls has developed an interesting and highly original way of showing which principles of justice ought to be preferred, i.e., those advanced and defended by Rawls himself. But this is something else than specifying a procedure

[41] Ibid., p. 139.
[42] Ibid.

under which the parties in the initial situation will choose the principles applying to the basic structure of society.

If I am correct, then Rawls's emphasis on pure procedural justice is clearly misleading. With pure procedural justice, it may be recalled, what is just is defined solely by the outcome of the procedure itself. But if, as I have been arguing, Rawls has (perhaps unknowingly) designed the procedure so that his own preferred principles must be selected by a single subject—and not a plurality of persons—then Rawls apparently holds that these principles are correct or *valid*. This being the case, we have an example of perfect procedural justice. In such an instance, it is assumed that there exists an independent criterion for the validity of the two principles of justice. What, then, is that criterion (external to the contract argument) which ultimately justifies Rawls's preferred principles of justice?

Given these problems with the justification of the principles, Rawls's theory will not be the source of those rationally justifiable first principles that ought to regulate the just social order. Nevertheless, there are several aspects of Rawls's work that are relevant and useful to the present project. I will have occasion to discuss and draw on them in later chapters.

II

Nozick's Theory of Justice

In contrast to Rawls's theory, which is concerned mainly with one or another pattern of distribution, Robert Nozick focuses on the *processes* through which distribution comes about. He argues that it is the history of a distribution, rather than its pattern, that determines whether or not it is just. His standpoint is similar to Locke's position on the justice of competition, namely, that it is the way in which competition is carried out, not its result, that counts.[43] That is, it is the acts themselves that are of paramount importance so far as justice is concerned.

Nozick's *Anarchy, State, and Utopia* consists of three parts. The first is an argument against the anarchists, where he shows how, in a Lockean state of nature, a minimal state—a "dominant protective association"—will arise by way of rational voluntary choice on the part of individual actors. In contrast to contractarians like Rawls,

---

[43] See F. A. Hayek, *Law, Legislation and Liberty*, vol. 2, *The Mirage of Social Justice* (London: Routledge & Kegan Paul, 1976).

Nozick argues that the origin of the state is not to be explained by the coordinated actions of rational, self-interested actors. Instead, Nozick utilizes the idea of an "invisible-hand" explanation to account for the origin of the state. This type of account "explains what looks to be the product of someone's intentional design, as not being brought about by anyone's intentions."[44] Without anyone having the idea of a state in mind, he says, the self-interested and rational acts of persons in a state of nature will lead to the formation of a minimal state.

Part II demonstrates how nothing more extensive than a minimal state can be morally justified, that is, can be achieved without violating individual rights. The last section ("Utopia") considers how particular communities, within the framework of utopias, might be combined with a minimal state to arrive at a variety of different types of societies. Since my main interest here is with justice and moral values, I will focus my discussion on Part II of Nozick's book, where he puts forth his own theory of justice: the "entitlement theory."

According to Nozick, Rawls's theory of justice violates people's rights and, therefore, cannot be morally justified. In common with most other theories of justice, Rawls's theory ignores the issue of people's *entitlements*. It forgets that whatever is to be distributed (equally or not) comes already tied to people. Most theories of distributive justice, Nozick points out, focus only on the *end* distribution of holdings. They pay no attention to the processes by which holdings were acquired. An additional characteristic of most theories of justice (including that of Rawls) is that they are *patterned*. They specify that "a distribution is to vary along some natural dimension, weighted sum of natural dimensions, or lexicographic ordering of natural dimensions."[45] Distribution according to need, merit, work, and so on, are all patterned.[46] Nozick asserts that "To

---

[44] Nozick, *Anarchy, State, and Utopia*, p. 19. The idea of an invisible hand has its origins in the writings of Smith and Mandeville. See Adam Smith, *Wealth of Nations* (New York: Modern Library, 1937); and B. Mandeville, *The Fable of the Bees* (1724). Edited with an introduction by Philip Harth (London: Penguin, 1970). In the following discussion of Nozick's theory, I draw on my own earlier presentation, pp. 91–96, in Derek L. Phillips, *Equality, Justice and Rectification* (London: Academic Press, 1979).

[45] Nozick, *Anarchy, State, and Utopia*, p. 156.

[46] Functional theories of stratification are similarly patterned: income and status are distributed according to (a) the social "importance" of various positions, and (b) the amount of training and education required to get people to fill them. I take a critical look at such theories in a later chapter.

think that the task of a theory of distributive justice is to fill in the blank in 'each according to his ———' is to be predisposed to search for a pattern; and the separate treatment of 'from each according to his ———' treats production and distribution as two separate and independent issues."[47]

The major weakness of end-state and patterned principles of distributive justice, Nozick contends, is that they can only be achieved and maintained by *continuous interference* with people's lives (i.e., by violating their rights). Consider how this would work in the case of Wilt Chamberlain (Nozick's example), although one could substitute Joan Sutherland or Mohammed Ali and the lesson would be the same. Let's say that incomes in the United States are distributed according to whatever distributive pattern you prefer, and call this particular distribution of incomes D_1. Suppose that your favorite distributive pattern is one of equal incomes for everyone. Imagine, further, that there are people all over America who want to see Chamberlain play basketball. In order to get him to perform in your home town, the local team offers him a contract where, in each home game, twenty-five cents from the price of each ticket sold goes directly to Chamberlain. Tens of thousands of people attend the games, with full knowledge that Chamberlain will get twenty-five cents from every ticket sold. Everyone enjoys seeing him perform, and they all consider it well worth the extra price of admission (without the added cost, he would play elsewhere). Because so many people attend the games, Chamberlain receives $250,000 at the end of the season—a figure that is far above the equal income that everyone else gets.

All who attended the games voluntarily chose (i.e., exercised his or her freedom) to give twenty-five cents extra of his or her money to Chamberlain in exchange for seeing him play basketball. Nozick asks: "If D_1 was a just distribution, and people voluntarily moved from it to D_2, transferring parts of their share they were given under D_1 (what was it for if not to do something with?), isn't D_2 also just?"[48] What we learn from this example, Nozick asserts, is that "to maintain a pattern one must either continuously interfere or take from some persons resources that others for some reason choose to transfer to them."[49] An egalitarian distributive pattern (or any other patterned system) can be maintained only if the state

[47] Nozick, *Anarchy, State, and Utopia*, pp. 159–60.
[48] Ibid., p. 161.
[49] Ibid., p. 163.

(or some other agency) prevents people from *voluntarily* transferring certain resources or holdings.

Because of such (potential) interferences with people's lives, Nozick rejects the patterned and end-state principles found in most theories of distributive justice. His own theory stresses the importance of *historical* principles; whether a distribution is just or not depends on how it came about.[50] "If the world were wholly just," according to Nozick, "the following inductive definition would exhaustively cover the subject of justice in holdings:

1. A person who acquires a holding in accordance with the principle of justice in acquisition is entitled to that holding.
2. A person who acquires a holding in accordance with the principle of justice in transfer, from someone else entitled to the holding, is entitled to the holding.
3. No one is entitled to a holding except by (repeated) applications of 1. and 2."[51]

Nozick's entitlement theory is concerned with the subject of justice in holdings, consisting of three parts. First, is the question of the *original acquisition of holdings*. How may previously unheld things come to be held? What are the processes involved in a just acquisition? The second topic focuses on the *transfer of holdings* from one individual to another. What mechanisms allow people to justly transfer their holdings, and by what processes may someone justly acquire holdings from another person? These two principles constitute the principle of justice in acquisition and transfer. The third topic in Nozick's entitlement theory concerns the existence of past injustices (i.e., violations of the first two principles), and focuses on the *rectification* of injustices in holdings. Here Nozick raises several interesting questions:

> If past injustice has shaped present holdings in various ways, some identifiable and some not, what now if anything, ought to be done to rectify these injustices? What obligations do the performers of injustice have toward those whose position is worse than it would have been had compensation been paid properly? How, if at all, do things change if the beneficiaries

---

[50] Although differing in almost every other respect, the Marxist theory of exploitation and Nozick's theory of justice share the feature of being *historical* as opposed to end-state theories.

[51] Nozick, *Anarchy, State, and Utopia*, p. 151.

and those made worse off are not the direct parties to the act of injustice, but, for example, their descendants?[52]

Nozick's theory contains a special proviso similar to Locke's proviso that there be "enough and as good left in common for others," the central idea being that the position of others at liberty to use a thing is not worsened by an individual's appropriation. Nozick's proviso would prohibit someone from appropriating the only water hole in the desert and charging what he will for its use. Except perhaps when everyone else's water holes go dry due to their own negligence, the situation would not change if one person's water hole remains while all the others dry up. It is not that the individual whose water hole remains full has no right to his water supply, but that right may sometimes be "overridden." The intent of Nozick's proviso is to assure that some people's appropriations of property (or other holdings) do not result in a net loss in what remains for other persons to use, i.e., that there be a "counterbalance" so that others are not worse off.[53] If people are on balance worse off because of an individual's appropriations, then his rights may be overridden to avoid some catastrophe.

Probably the most important aspect of Nozick's general argument is that it serves as a strong reminder that whatever is to be distributed (whether on the basis of need, merit, work, or whatever) comes already attached to other people. Not surprisingly, then, Nozick is highly critical of Rawls's assumption that everyone has some claim to the totality of natural talents within a society. This is not, of course, because people's endowments are not highly valued. "People's talents and abilities," Nozick writes, "are an asset to a free community; others in the community benefit from their presence and are better off because they are there rather than elsewhere or nowhere. (Otherwise they wouldn't choose to deal with them.) Life, over time, is not a constant-sum game, wherein if greater ability or effort leads to some getting more, that means that others must lose. In a free society, people's talents do benefit others, and not only themselves."[54] Similarly, he rejects Rawls's view that people's natural endowments and abilities, being undeserved, are "arbitrary from a moral point of view." Nozick questions whether it is correct to regard people's assets as morally

---

[52] Ibid., p. 152. I consider rectification at some length in *Equality, Justice, and Rectification*, Part III, "The Rectification of Injustices."

[53] Nozick, *Anarchy, State, and Utopia.*

[54] Ibid., p. 228.

arbitrary. But even if they are, he says, people are *entitled* to them and to what flows from them.[55] Much of Nozick's entitlement theory is aimed directly at Rawls's theory of justice. His intention is to use his theory of justice in holdings to "probe" Rawls's theory, to uncover its shortcomings and inadequacies.

Nozick's own theory constitutes a partially developed alternative view. His entitlement conception of justice in holdings is, as I have tried to indicate, a very special kind of theory of distributive justice. Nozick emphasizes this point, stating:

> The term "distributive justice" is not a neutral one. Hearing the term "distribution," most people presume that some thing or mechanism uses some principle or criterion to give out a supply of things. . . . However, we are not in the position of children who have been given portions of pie by someone who now makes last minute adjustments to rectify careless cutting. There is no *central* distribution, no person or group entitled to control all the resources, jointly deciding how they are to be doled out. What each person gets, he gets from others who give to him in exchange for something, or as a gift. In a free society, diverse persons control different resources, and new holdings arise out of the voluntary exchanges and actions of persons. There is no more a distributing or distribution of shares than there is a distribution of mates in a society in which persons choose whom they shall marry. The total result is the product of many individual decisions which the different individuals involved are entitled to make.[56]

Nozick's theory of justice, then, is quite different from other theories of distributive justice. It is a theory of justice in holdings, a theory that argues that just distributions come about necessarily, and only, from just original acquisitions plus just transfers in holdings. As with Rawls's theory, however, there are several serious weaknesses in Nozick's theory of justice.

First of all, Nozick fails to provide any justification for those individual rights that he stresses so strongly. In the opening paragraph of his book, he states: "Individuals have rights, and there are things no person or group may do to them (without violating their rights). So strong and far-reaching are these rights that they raise the question of what, if anything, the state and officials may

[55] Ibid., p. 226.
[56] Ibid., pp. 149–50.

do."[57] Although Nozick emphasizes the importance of these rights, he never deals satisfactorily with the question of where they come from or why they should be recognized and upheld by rational persons. Since his major argument is that people's exercise of their right to freedom or liberty will upset any (Rawlsian) patterned distribution of holdings, his case hinges on the justification he can provide for such a right to freedom. Even though he makes much of the crucial importance of rights, Nozick merely *assumes* a set of rights (and assumes that the link between personal freedom and private property rights is obvious). Having made this assumption, he then examines the political structure (institutions) that could arise—through the invisible-hand mechanism—within the constraints set by these rights. The total absence of a general argument for his framework of rights is apparent in his preface, where he says, "This book does not present a precise theory of the moral basis of individual rights."[58] Since Nozick's argument requires an acceptance of the existence of fundamental rights merely to get off the ground, this is a striking omission.

Second, there are problems with the principle of acquisition. Although a welcome alternative to various end-state theories of justice, Nozick's entitlement theory has the serious shortcoming of not adequately addressing the question of what constitutes an *originally just* holding. Since his first principle rests on the notion of a just acquisition of holdings, one needs to know what that is. This is crucial because the complex problem of rectification is dependent on judgments concerning the original acquisition of the things in question. The issue of how property rights arise and should be allocated is of critical import. Consistent with Locke, Nozick apparently wants the "natural" right of property that supposedly obtains in the state of nature to be maintained in civil society.[59] However, he is far from clear on this matter. Locke's theory of original acquisition is briefly mentioned, but never pursued. Nozick is forthright in acknowledging that to construct a more fully adequate theory, he would "have to specify the details of each of the three principles of justice in holdings."[60] And, he adds, "I shall not attempt that task here."[61] But it seems clear to

---

[57] Ibid., p. ix.

[58] Ibid., p. xiv.

[59] See my discussion in Phillips, *Equality, Justice and Rectification*, Chapter 4, "Property Rights."

[60] Nozick, *Anarchy, State, and Utopia*, p. 153.

[61] Ibid.

me that the accomplishment of that task is necessary if we are to take seriously (or accept) Nozick's theory of justice in holdings.

Third, Nozick's attempt to formulate a proviso similar to Locke's proviso that there be "enough and as good left in common for others" is unsuccessful. This is because Locke argued that property rights in unowned things must not involve the appropriation of more than the acquirer can "use and consume," and must be acquired "without waste and spoilage."[62] It is somewhat surprising that Nozick claims to have derived an entirely different (and much weaker) proviso from an examination of Locke's writings. The reason for this, I believe, is that Nozick confuses Locke's remarks on property acquisition in a "state of nature" with what is permissible in civil society.

Finally, the emphasis on individual freedom in Nozick's theory is not only ungrounded, but also appears to be far too exclusive. His entitlement theory of justice in holdings—based on principles of acquisition, transfer, and rectification—defends *any* distribution of wealth at all so long as it has resulted from voluntary or contractual agreements that ensue from an initial, presumably just acquisition. But this totally ignores the extent to which unfavorable familial and social backgrounds (for example, being female or black in a sexist or racist society) severely limit some people's abilities to exercise their right to freedom. Even if we grant that each person does have the right to freedom, there are certain necessary preconditions that are required in order for someone to exercise such a right. A minimum of "life's necessities"—such things as food, shelter, and protection—must be available to a person in order for him or her to even engage in social relations and economic transactions with other persons. At the very least, one would expect Nozick to give some attention to the situation of those whose initial position in life subjects them to serious disadvantages and handicaps. This he does not do.

III

Habermas's Theory of Justice

Social scientists in the tradition of critical theory reject the idea of value-neutral inquiry, endorsing, instead, a critical, dialectic-hermeneutic approach to social theorizing. They appraise existing states of affairs in terms of standards that derive from knowledge

[62] See *Equality, Justice and Rectification.*

of something better than what already exists. Their concern is the achievement of a theoretical understanding, which can be used to help transform society. Jürgen Habermas, the best known of contemporary critical theorists, formulates the primary problem of political and social theory as follows:

> How, within a political situation, can we obtain clarification of what is practically necessary and at the same time objectively possible? This question can be translated back into our historical context: how can the promise of practical politics—namely, of providing practical orientation about what is right or just in a given situation—be redeemed without relinquishing, on the one hand, the rigor of scientific knowledge, which modern social philosophy demands in contrast to the practical philosophy of classicism? And on the other, how can the promise of social philosophy to furnish an analysis of the interrelationships of social life be redeemed without relinquishing the practical orientation of classical politics?[63]

Habermas distinguishes between practical and technical (instrumental) knowledge. The practical is the sphere of fully human activity; it is knowledge that can be reached only by open human discourse. In contrast, the technical is the area of work, science, and those narrowly rational processes by which material means are fitted to material ends. Living in a time of extreme and highly developed technical consciousness, there is a strong tendency to suppress this distinction between the practical and the technical, and to treat all problems as merely technical. But technical rationality can be criticized, says Habermas, because it "severs the criteria for justifying the organization of social life from any normative regulation of interaction. . . ."[64] He goes on to add that "Technocratic consciousness reflects not the sundering of an ethical situation but the repression of 'ethics' as such as a category of life."[65]

As technical control expands, people are not only technologically manipulated, but that manipulation is normalized in order to maintain the system as it is. When, however, the "legitimacy" of technical control and state regulation is seriously called into question—when legitimacy fails—a social order maintained by normative motivations becomes highly problematic. In other words, people

---

[63] Habermas, *Theory and Practice*, p. 44.

[64] Jürgen Habermas, *Toward a Rational Society*. Translated by Jeremy J. Shapiro (Boston: Beacon Press, 1970), p. 64.

[65] Ibid., p. 112.

become increasingly less willing to act in accordance with the so-called requirements of the system. A "legitimation crisis," according to Habermas, "must be based on a motivation crisis—that is, a discrepancy between the need for motives declared by the state, the educational system and the occupational system on the one hand, and the motivation supplied by the socio-cultural system on the other."[66] Such a crisis of legitimacy is, Habermas points out, widespread in the contemporary world. Legitimation problems have arisen in developed capitalist countries, he argues, "because of a fundamental conflict that is built into their very structure: a conflict between the fundamental conditions of the capitalist society itself and the social welfare responsibilities of mass democracies."[67] The "steering capacity" of the system is overloaded by this basic conflict.[68]

Recent years have seen an outpouring of books and articles focusing on the general problem of legitimacy. Habermas, Bell, O'Connor, Wolfe, Schaar, Pitkin, and Stanley are only a few among the many scholars who, in one way or another, have dealt with various problems regarding legitimacy.[69] In this connection, Pitkin notes that "Men rarely question the legitimacy of established authority when all is going well; the problem of political obligation is urgent when the state is sick, when someone is seriously contemplating disobedience or revolt in principle."[70] But the fact that people seldom question the legitimacy of this or that authority or institutionalized arrangement when "all is going well" certainly should not be taken to imply that the problem of legitimacy is not significant in its own right. Whatever the extent of the legitimation crisis, and whatever the explanations offered to account for it, the problem of legitimacy has always been central to political and social

[66] Habermas, *Legitimation Crisis*, pp. 74–75. Although I disagree with many of his conclusions, I learned much from the article by Nil Disco, "Critical Theory as Ideology of the New Class," *Theory and Society* 8 (September 1979): 159–214.

[67] Habermas, *Legitimation Crisis*.

[68] Ibid.

[69] Ibid.; Daniel Bell, *The Cultural Contradictions of Capitalism* (New York: Basic Books, 1976); James O'Connor, *The Fiscal Crisis of the State* (New York: St. Martin's Press, 1973); Alan Wolfe, *The Limits of Legitimacy* (New York: Free Press, 1977); John Schaar, "Legitimacy in the Modern State," in Philip Green and Sanford Levinson, eds., *Power and Community* (New York: Vintage Books, 1970); Hannah Pitkin, "Obligation and Consent," in Peter Laslett, W. G. Runciman, and Quentin Skinner, eds., *Philosophy and Society*, fourth series (Oxford: Basil Blackwell, 1972); and Manfred Stanley, *The Technological Conscience* (New York: Free Press, 1978).

[70] Pitkin, "Obligation and Consent," p. 46.

theory. Nor is it correct to argue, as does Habermas, that legitimacy is a problem simply *because* of its being associated with one or another crisis in contemporary capitalist societies. Legitimacy is a problem whenever we evaluate alternative forms of government and ask what kinds of regimes are to be regarded as more legitimate than others.[71] It is, in fact, a problem that preoccupied Locke, Hobbes, and Rousseau, and has engaged the attention of social and political theorists to the present day.[72]

In his book, *Legitimation Crisis*, Habermas conceives of the life-world (*Lebenswelt*) as being organized around behavioral norms, which derive their ultimate authority from their rational justifiability.[73] Within the sphere of practial reason, communicative praxis, and interaction, the individual motivations necessary for the maintenance of the social systems are produced. This raises the issue of the grounding of norms, what Habermas terms "the discursive redemption of normative validity claims."

As I noted earlier, Weber saw norms as basically arbitrary. "The relations of law, conventions, and 'ethics' do not constitute a problem for sociology," says Weber.[74] He goes on to write: "From a sociological point of view an 'ethical' standard is one to which men attribute a certain type of value and which, by virtue of this belief, they treat as a valid norm governing their action."[75] Thus, there is ultimately no way of defending the "rightness" of one or another ethical standard; valid norms are those to which people lend their belief. For Habermas, on the other hand, every norm contains the supposition that it could be justified through reasonable argument. Contrary to the view of Weber and most social scientists, he holds that moral norms and values do admit of rational justification. Habermas asserts that "political and practical [i.e., moral] questions" can be true or false: "The truth of statements is linked in the last analysis to the intention of the good and true life."[76]

The appropriate model for explaining the validity claims of various norms is the communication community "of those affected,

[71] See, for example, James Fishkin, *Tyranny and Legitimacy* (Baltimore: The Johns Hopkins Press, 1979).

[72] Ibid.; A. John Simmons, *Moral Principles and Political Obligations* (Princeton: Princeton University Press, 1979).

[73] Habermas, *Legitimation Crisis*.

[74] Max Weber, "The Concept of Legitimate Order," reprinted in Talcott Parsons et al, *Theories of Society*, vol. I (New York: Free Press, 1961), p. 237.

[75] Ibid.

[76] Jürgen Habermas, *Knowledge and Human Interests*, trans. Jeremy J. Shapiro (Boston: Beacon Press, 1978), p. 317.

who as participants in a practical discourse test the validity claims of norms and, to the extent that they accept them with reasons, arrive at the conviction that in the given circumstances the proposed norms are 'right.' "[77] Insofar as norms express generalizable interests, Habermas writes, "they are based on a *rational consensus* (or they would find such a consensus if practical discourse could take place)."[78]

This notion of a rational consensus can be viewed as an alternative to the widely accepted distinction between a pragmatic and a normative consensus.[79] With a *pragmatic* consensus, people accept a political order, for example, as legitimate because they see no realistic alternative to it or because it would be dangerous not to lend it their support. With a *normative* consensus, people accept, give their allegiance to, and internalize, widely shared normative standards that pertain to the political order. Because both pragmatic and normative consensus may be what Habermas terms "forced," it is necessary to introduce a third type of consensus, one concerned with the relation of legitimation to truth: rational consensus. A *rational* consensus is a consensus arrived at by people who are free and equal.[80]

Thus Habermas argues against a view that authorizes decisions on the basis of people's "belief" in their legitimacy or on the fact that such decisions have legal standing. He recognizes that people's obedience may be the result of habit, coercion, insufficient knowledge, or lack of understanding. His attempt is to locate rational grounds for distinguishing between the "ought" of false beliefs, or the fear of the consequences of not obeying, and the "ought" of intersubjectively acceptable justifiability of the particular normative standards or expectations in question.

For Habermas, then, legitimate authority is, in principle, rationally justifiable authority.[81] This raises the obvious problem of the grounds on which a choice can be made for norms that are rationally justifiable. Building on the work of Wittgenstein, Austin, and Searle, Habermas argues that all linguistic communication assumes a background consensus, involving four different validity claims.

[77] Habermas, *Legitimation Crisis*, p. 105.

[78] Ibid., p. 11.

[79] Michael Mann, "The Social Cohesion of Liberal Democracy," *American Sociological Review* 35 (June 1970): 423–39.

[80] Habermas, *Legitimation Crisis*.

[81] Jürgen Habermas, *Communication and the Evoluation of Society*, trans. Thomas McCarthy (Boston: Beacon Press, 1979), p. 202.

These claims are constituted by the *truth* of the utterance or proposition, the *correctness* or rightness of an utterance in relation to a recognized normative context, the *veracity* of the speaker, and the *comprehensibility* of the semantic content of the utterance or proposition.[82] In normal contexts of communicative action, these four claims are not questioned; that is to say, there exists a background consensus. But in those cases where the background consensus breaks down or is nonexistent, there arises what Habermas refers to as "discourse." With discourse, the norms and opinions that are "taken for granted" in communicative action are problematized; the validity of these naively accepted norms and opinions can be consensually ascertained through discourse.

The output of discourse "consists in the recognition or rejection of problematic truth claims. Discourses produce nothing but arguments."[83] The aim of such discourse is to distinguish between a merely *accepted* consensus—the one that is now being challenged or called into question—and a *rational* consensus.[84] The presuppositions and procedures of discourse, Habermas holds, are the basis for establishing both the truth of statements and the correctness of norms.

But if decisions about the rationality of consensus themselves rest on argumentation, shouldn't we then ask about the criteria of argumentation itself? Since argumentation presupposes a consensus, how are we to distinguish between good and bad, sound and unsound arguments? Isn't there the danger here of an infinite regress? Habermas is aware of such a possibility and, in fact, directs explicit attention to it. The solution, he argues, is to be found in the idea of the "ideal speech situation":

[82] Jürgen Habermas, "Some Distinctions in Universal Pragmatics," *Theory and Society* 3 (Summer 1976): 161.

[83] Jürgen Habermas, "A Postscript to *Knowledge and Human Interests*," *Philosophy of the Social Sciences* 3 (1973): 168.

[84] Among others concerned with a theory of rationality in recent years are Rawls, *A Theory of Justice*; S. I. Benn and G. W. Mortimer, eds., *Rationality and the Social Sciences* (London: Routledge & Kegan Paul, 1976); Alvin W. Gouldner, *The Dialectics of Ideology and Technology* (New York: Seabury Press, 1976); Bryan A. Wilson, ed., *Rationality* (New York: Harper Torchbooks, 1970); Martin Hollis and Steven Lukes, eds., *Rationality and Relativism* (Oxford: Basil Blackwell, 1982); Thomas S. Kuhn, *The Structure of Scientific Revolutions* (Chicago: University of Chicago Press, 1962); Imre Lakatos and Alan Musgrave, eds., *Criticism and the Growth of Scientific Knowledge* (Cambridge: Cambridge University Press, 1970); and Stephen Toulmin, *Human Understanding*, vol. 1 (Oxford: Clarendon Press, 1970).

Discourse can be understood as that form of communication that is removed from contexts of experience and action and whose structure assures us: that the bracketed validity claims of assertions, recommendations, or warnings are the exclusive objects of discussion; that participants, themes and contributions are not restricted except with reference to the goal of testing the validity-claims in question; that no force except that of the better argument is exercised; and that, as a result, all motives except that of the cooperative search for truth are excluded.[85]

This, says Habermas, is an ideal underlying all subjectivity and intersubjectivity. In the ideal speech situation, *consensus* is achieved in unrestrained and universal discourse. A grounded, rational consensus is one that arises from a speech situation totally free from all internal and external constraints, i.e., one that is due entirely to the force of the better argument. The stipulation that the consensus arrived at must be constraint free guarantees that the consensus expresses the desire of all—the *common interest*. Thus, ideal speech requires the existence of an ideal community, for only in such circumstances is there the equality of communicative competence, and the exclusion of all motives "except that of the cooperative search for truth." The ideal speech situation itself represents an ideal, but its significance goes beyond that. As Habermas explains it:

the ideal speech situation is neither an empirical phenomenon nor simply a construct, but a reciprocal supposition unavoidable in discourse. This supposition can, but need not be, counterfactual; but even when counterfactual it is a fiction which is operatively effective in communication. I would therefore prefer to speak of an anticipation of an ideal speech situation. . . . This alone is the warrant which permits us to join to an actually attained consensus the claim of a rational consensus. At the same time, it is a critical standard against which every actually realized consensus can be called into question and tested.[86]

Since the rational consensus attained in the ideal speech situation is the ultimate criterion of the correctness of all norms, this means

[85] Habermas, *Legitimation Crisis*, pp. 107–08.
[86] Jürgen Habermas, "Wahrheitstheorien," in H. Fahrenback, ed., *Wirklichkeit und Reflexion* (Pfüllingen: Neske, 1973), p. 258.

that the norms for legitimate authority must be arrived at by rational consensus. Such a rational consensus, Habermas observes, is obviously lacking. It is not surprising, therefore, that part of Habermas's attack is directed at parliamentary politics for producing non-discursive laws in the form of "false consciousness." He bases his argument here on the thesis of what he calls the "suppression of potentially generalizable interests." Habermas uses the term "interests" to refer to "needs that are . . . rendered subjective and detached, as it were, from the crystallizations of commonly shared values supported by tradition (and made binding in norms of action)."[87] Some of these interests are "potentially generalizable," i.e., are interests that, under conditions of practical discourse, would turn out to be *common* interests. In Habermas's words: "The interest is common because the constraint-free consensus permits only what all can want; it is free of deception because even the interpretation of needs in which *each individual* must be able to recognize what he wants becomes the object of discursive will-formation."[88]

In order for people to determine the generalizability of interests, a practical discourse is necessary. Practical discourse itself, that is, people engaged in argumentation directed toward rational will-formation, can only occur when the material conditions required for such discourse are concretely realized. When these conditions are lacking, when compromises are achieved that foreclose on shared needs, we can speak of the suppression of potentially generalizable interests. In such cases, the critical theorist engages in "virtual" political discourse, which takes the form of comparing the extant normative structure and an imagined structure, which—so it is argued—would have been achieved had practical discourse *actually* taken place. What is then asked, Habermas says, is:

> [H]ow would the members of a social system, at a given stage in the development of productive forces, have collectively and bindingly interpreted their needs (and which norms would they have accepted as justified) if they could and would have decided on organization of social intercourse through discursive will-formation, with adequate knowledge of the limiting conditions and functional imperatives of their society?[89]

[87] Habermas, *Legitimation Crisis*, pp. 113–14.
[88] Ibid., p. 108.
[89] Ibid., p. 113.

When such a comparison reveals a significant suppression of generalizable interests, this serves as evidence for the fact that a rational consensus is lacking.

What Habermas is attempting to provide, in short, is a philosophical theory that rationally evaluates the quality of social and political life, i.e., a theory that is "normative," in the best sense of the word. Among other things, he recognizes the value of liberty, or the idea that will, not force, is the basis of government, and the value of justice, or the idea that right, not might, is the basis of all political society. The emphasis by Habermas on the normative character of practical discourse means, as Gouldner notes, that "Language behavior is seen as the intervening variable between social institutions, the class system, and the state, on the one side, and, on the other, persons' capacity to interpret the social world rationally and to do something with others to change it."[90] Habermas underscores the need for working toward the achievement of a society in which practical discourse (unlimited and nonrepressive communication) can be concretely realized. While he admittedly has little to say about how this ideal is to be achieved, the ideal itself is useful as a standard of comparison against which we can assess and evaluate the existing institutional structures of a society.

In a sense, Habermas can be viewed as offering a *methodology* for arriving at a "practical consensus" about the validity of norms. More generally, he notes that ultimate grounds for the justification of norms and actions can be made plausible and that, therefore, *"the formal conditions of justification themselves obtain legitimating force."*[91] That is, the procedures and presuppositions of rational agreement themselves become principles.

Clearly, there are similarities between Habermas's discussion of consensus arrived at in the "ideal speech situation" and Rawls's arguments concerning the conditions under which people choose the guiding principles to govern their conduct. Only in a speech situation totally free from all internal and external constraints is it possible for a grounded, rational, consensus to arise. This ideal speech situation, as noted earlier, requires the existence of an ideal community. Whereas Rawls's actors choose their principles of justice behind a veil of ignorance in the hypothetical original position, Habermas's actors would choose their principles of justice within the ideal speech situation. Rawls and Habermas share a concern

[90] Gouldner, *Dialectics*, p. 146.
[91] Habermas, *Communication*, p. 184.

with an *ideal* situation under which social agreements take place. Rawls considers this in terms of the principles of justice that would be arrived at under a *hypothetical* original position, while Habermas focuses on the formal conditions that would *have to be realized* in order for any set of moral principles to be justifiable. They both seem to utilize the notion of what Rawls terms "pure procedural justice"; they are in agreement that there exists no independent criterion of justice. What is just is defined by the outcome of a consensus under certain specified conditions.

Habermas himself has recently acknowledged the similarity of his linguistic theory of rationality and the theory of justice developed by Rawls. "In contract theories, from Hobbes to Locke to John Rawls," he writes, "the fiction of a state of nature or of an original position *also* has the meaning of specifying the conditions under which an agreement will express the common interest of all involved—and to this extent can count as rational."[92] In other words, moral values and principles are not to be dealt with either empirically (in terms of people's "beliefs") or normatively (in terms of ultimate grounds) but with regard to the *formal conditions* for a possible consensus. In Habermas's words:

> Only the rules and communication presuppositions that make it possible to distinguish an accord or agreement among free and equals from a contingent or forced consensus have legitimating force today. Whether such rules and communicative presuppositions can best be interpreted and explained with the help of natural law constructions and contract theories or in the concepts of transcendental philosophy or a pragmatics of language or even in the framework of a theory of the development of consciousness is secondary in the present context.[93]

Rawls and Habermas both claim that the justification for particular moral principles and values should proceed from some consensus. This is in the nature of justification. They both argue that the force of an argument justifying moral principles depends on the features of the consensus appealed to. Rawls stipulates the existence of an original position and the veil of ignorance, while Habermas emphasizes certain conditions under which rational consensus can (ideally) take place. Both seem to hold in common,

[92] Ibid.
[93] Ibid., p. 188.

however, the view that a moral (or other) principle is valid only to the extent that it would be mutually acknowledged under certain ideal conditions—freedom, rationality, equality, knowledge—by all agents to whom it applies. Those moral principles about which there is publicly acknowledged consensus under the specified conditions are, then, *valid* moral principles.

The theories of justice formulated by Rawls and Nozick represent a return to older traditions of "substantive" social and political philosophy. Their approaches constitute a sharp contrast to the work of positivist philosophers and to many of those philosophers working in the analytical tradition. Both seem to hold the view that social and political theory is to be construed as moral theory— "moral theory" in the seventeenth- and eighteenth-century meaning of the term, where the concerns were primarily normative and frequently critical of the societies in which they were conceived.

Although Habermas is a "critical theorist" and normative concerns are central to his work, it is never clear—to me, at least— how he regards the *moral* element in social theory and social life. Does he intend, for example, that "rational" consensus should be equated with "moral" consensus? Though some writers concerned with rationality do include moral elements as part of rational action, others do not. Rawls speaks of rationality in the sense that, when people choose from among principles, each individual tries as best he can to advance his own interests.[94] Since principles (those chosen behind the veil of ignorance) must have, in his words, "some rational connection with the advancement of human interests broadly defined," they are necessarily moral.[95] On the other hand, Goodin in his *The Politics of Rational Man* writes: "What an individual ought prudentially to do is not necessarily deserving of any moral accolades."[96] And later he adds that, with regard to political morality, "immorality can be a rational choice for men who are sufficiently confident of a sufficiently stronger position to have a reasonable expectation of being able to beat back challengers regularly."[97]

In much of his writings, Habermas discusses rationality and rational consensus without specifying whether these terms are to be taken to signify moral rationality or moral consensus. But since he

---

[94] Rawls, *A Theory of Justice*, p. 142.

[95] Ibid., p. 149.

[96] Robert E. Goodin, *The Politics of Rational Man* (London: Wiley, 1976), p. 10.

[97] Ibid., p. 86. This also appears to be the position of James M. Buchanan, *The Limits of Liberty* (Chicago: University of Chicago Press, 1975).

also speaks of the "rightness" of norms[98] and the "worthiness" of a political order to be recognized,[99] it seems clear that there is a (usually implicit) concern with the moral as well as (or as part of) the rational. Thus, I believe it correct to conclude that, like Rawls and Nozick, Habermas conceives of social and political theory as moral theory.

Rawls, as I showed earlier, assimilates justice to fairness (i.e., to what would be considered fair by persons lacking knowledge of what positions they would occupy in society); Nozick assimilates it to legitimacy (i.e., propriety in the way the system emerged); and Habermas assimilates it to consensus (i.e., to that which would command rational consensus under certain specified ideal conditions). As a consequence of these differing approaches, Rawls and Nozick are able to specify principles of justice that would characterize a just society, while Habermas must be almost completely silent in regard to such principles of justice. This strikes me as a serious weakness in Habermas's theory, although it is not the only one.

The first problem in Habermas's consensus theory concerns the "ideal speech situation." As noted earlier, the formal properties of discourse that guarantee the necessary interrogative space are those realized when the discourse is conducted in an ideal speech situation. A number of things must happen for such a situation to be brought about. Habermas sums them up in his general symmetry requirement: that participants all have a fair chance to speak out and that, more specifically, every participant is equally free to open or continue any line of discussion; that each can put forward any assertion or call any into question; that the participants are equally free in their relations with one another to express their most intimate feelings; and that they are equally free to make demands on each other and offer each other help.[100]

There are a number of objections that need to be raised here. How, to begin, can it be ascertained that this general symmetry requirement is satisfied? A rational consensus that it is indeed satisfied would only push the question back one step further, for we would need to determine that *that* consensus is itself rational. But even if it could be ascertained that the general symmetry requirement was met, i.e., that there existed an ideal speech situa-

[98] Habermas, *Communication*, p. 142.

[99] Ibid., p. 176.

[100] Habermas, *Theory and Practice*, pp. 255–56.

tion, it is difficult to believe that this would guarantee interrogative space in a dialogue. If some persons are lazy or just "don't care," it is unlikely that any set of conditions—however ideal—would ensure that they would engage in radical argumentation. And although in an ideal speech situation participants are bound only by the power of argument, the ability to argue is also a power. It is difficult to see how *this* power could ever be distributed equally. Furthermore, we are never told whether the symmetry requirement sets limits on the kinds of theoretical and practical positions that can be established. How are we to judge the force of the better argument? How is it to be decided what kinds of evidence can legitimately be utilized for or against competing moral or political standpoints? As currently elaborated, the notion of the ideal speech situation does not resolve these crucial questions.[101] In fact, it seems to me that Habermas's model of the ideal speech situation is not only unrealized in our society but is unrealizable as well.

A second serious problem has recently been pointed out by Philip Pettit.[102] Granted, says Pettit, that discursive argument requires that a proposition must be able to survive radical interrogation in order to be consensually agreed upon, why does such radical interrogation require a number of people in open discussion with one another rather than having each of them thinking the matter out on his own?[103] In answering this question, Pettit distinguishes between two different notions of consensus: a distributive sense and a collective sense. A proposition admits of "distributive" consensus, Pettit says, if and only if each person assents to it—whether or not in awareness of what others think.[104] A proposition admits of "collective" consensus, on the other hand, if and only if the people involved all discuss it together and come to a unanimous decision about it.[105] Because Habermas conceives of the consensus by reference to which justice is to be identified as a collective consensus, he gives himself the problem of stating the conditions that assure the required interrogative space for everyone and guard against a failure of collective reason.[106] This is accomplished, ac-

---

[101] For these and related criticisms, see David Hull, *Critical Theory* (Berkeley: University of California Press, 1980).

[102] Philip Pettit, "Habermas on Truth and Justice," Paper to be published in C.H.R. Parkinson, *Marx and Marxism* (Brighton: Harvester Press, forthcoming).

[103] Ibid., p. 9.

[104] Ibid.

[105] Ibid.

[106] Ibid., pp. 10, 16.

cording to Habermas, by the realization of those conditions that define the ideal speech situation.

One can accept Habermas's main point that justice is to be identified by the potential agreement of all others, Pettit argues, but there is no reason to accept the requirement of collective rather than distributive consensus. The demand for distributive consensus is sufficient, and the requirement for collective consensus is *not* necessary. In Pettit's words:

> It is quite gratuitous to add the requirement that the agreement must be achieved in collective discussion and it is therefore quite unnecessary for an upholder of the theory to investigate how best to guard against collective irrationality. . . .
> [T]o be rational a person's assent must indeed be able to stand the test of rational argument. There is no reason to say that the assent must be forthcoming as part of a collective consensus achieved in an ideal speech situation; it may coincide with the judgment that would appear on such an occasion, but that is neither here nor there. The discourse in which Habermas says that questions of truth are raised is normally an interpersonal affair and it may be this which leads him to put a collective construction on the consensus required by his theory. But, as Habermas himself admits, discourse may also be internalized; it may only involve a single thinking subject.[107]

Pettit goes on to examine the consequences of construing consensus in a collective rather than a distributive manner. In order to be sure of the justice of a principle or norm, someone must be convinced by way of reasons in its favor that the principle or norm would rationally command everyone's agreement (i.e., consensus). If the consensus by reference to which justice is identified is a distributive consensus, then justice would be more readily within someone's grasp than it would be if the consensus required were collective.

An individual who has become convinced by radical argument in his own case that a principle or norm is just may take it—by analogy—that anyone else would response to the considerations offered in a similar manner. If consensus is understood distributively, then, the individual may assume that the principle or norm is just. If, on the other hand, consensus is understood collectively, this introduces a dimension of inscrutability. This is because, Pettit

[107] Ibid., pp. 10–11. Habermas makes this distinction in *Theory and Practice*, p. 28.

points out, the outcome of a collective consensus is more difficult to foresee than that of a distributive one.[108] Who is to say what outcome people would come to collectively? The outcome of a collective consensus might be identical or very much different than the outcome of a distributive one. But if justice can only be determined through collective consensus, then this has the striking consequence that there is no sense of anyone's trying to formulate principles for the just society in advance of the realization of the conditions that define the ideal speech situation. Since the ideal conditions of communication required by construing consensus as collective are far from being realized (assuming, in principle, that they are realizable), the collective requirement may be, in Pettit's words, lacking "not just in argumentative support, but also in strategic purpose."[109]

A related criticism concerns the noncognitive status of justice in Habermas's theory. His consensus theory of justice provides a procedural criterion of justice, identifying the just social scheme as that which would attract rational consensus. But since we live in an imperfect world, where the conditions that define the ideal speech situation are not realized, this criterion of justice cannot be applied. Thus, according to Habermas's argument, we cannot now know what would command rational agreement. Habermas's consensus theory of justice, then, does not allow him to formulate any particular position with regard to the just society. The reason for this is made clear by the following remark: "It is obvious that practical questions, which are posed with a view to the choice of norms, can only be decided through a consensus between all of those concerned and all of those potentially affected."[110] What this suggests is that any selection of the principles of justice must wait on the consensus of all "those concerned" and "potentially affected" before the selection is made. This appears to place a severe restriction on attempts by individuals to work out on their own the principles that would govern the just society. Instead of formulating and defining such principles in advance, Habermas requires us to wait and see what happens under ideal conditions of communication. In his view, we cannot trust our own judgments about justice, although we do know the ideal conditions under which our (collective) judgments would be trustworthy.

[108] Pettit, "Habermas on Truth and Justice," pp. 11, 16.
[109] Ibid., p. 11.
[110] Habermas, *Theory and Practice,* p. 270.

Habermas's consensus theory, then, does not itself force him to adopt any particular position so far as the just society is concerned. Were the ideal conditions of communication to be realized, "collective" consensus might result in the choice of any one of a wide variety of principles concerning justice. But this has the consequence, as Pettit emphasizes, "that putting justice out of cognitive reach may ultimately mean inhibiting social criticism, and indulging the dangerous idea that someday everything will be changed, changed utterly."[111] With a "distributive" consensus, on the other hand, individuals may be convinced by way of reasons in their favor that a specified set of principles concerning justice would rationally command everyone's agreement. The choice of a distributive rather than a collective consensus, however, would appear to ignore and perhaps eliminate much that is unique in the work of Habermas.

It must be recognized that Habermas has indeed provided an interesting way of conceptualizing the relation between rationality and human emancipation. Certainly his notion of the ideal speech situation is an attractive one, in that it specifies the conditions under which the interrogative space necessary for rational discourse is ensured. As an *ideal*, against which to compare existing conditions for discourse, it is enormously useful in sensitizing us to the existence of a wide variety of internal and external influences that act to prevent and distort rational discourse. But if the notion of the ideal speech situation is taken as a *necessary* requirement for speculation and argumentation about questions of justice and morality, then it appears to be a hindrance to articulating the demands of justice and to developing the social criticism that Habermas himself advocates.

IV

Gewirth's Theory of Justice

I will now consider a justification of moral principles that I regard as superior to the arguments offered by Rawls, Nozick, and Habermas: the justification advanced by Alan Gewirth in his book, *Reason and Morality*.[112] Like these authors, he attempts to provide a rational justification for moral principles that will allow us to objectively distinguish morally right actions and institutions from

[111] Pettit, "Habermas on Truth and Justice," p. 26.
[112] Gewirth, *Reason and Morality*.

morally wrong ones, but Gewirth's theory avoids many of the weaknesses contained in their theories.

First of all, he does not resort to the device of having *hypothetical* persons confront some *hypothetical* situation where they are required to choose a set of moral principles that will regulate a just society. That is, he does not require the two artificial stipulations of an "original position" and the "veil of ignorance" utilized by Rawls. Nor does Gewirth begin, as does Nozick, with a *fictional* state of nature where asocial nomads encountering one another for the first time are simply *assumed* to have a set of rights. Further, it is not necessary for him to theorize about an "ideal speech situation" that would have to be realized in order for any set of moral principles to be justified. In short, Gewirth is able to ground and defend specific moral rights without recourse to the fiction of an original position or a state of nature, and without awaiting, as Habermas must, the realization of an ideal speech situation. He does this, as I will demonstrate, by showing how substantive normative moral principles can be logically derived from the nature of human *action*. The justification of these moral principles, Gewirth argues, is to be found in the web of social relations with which we are all familiar.

As Gewirth himself emphasizes, the chief novelty of his new version of rational justification is the logical derivation of substantive moral principles from the nature of human action.[113] The definitive justification of these moral principles is provided, he shows, by applying reason to the concept of action.[114] Gewirth uses reason in a strict sense; it comprises only the canons of deductive and inductive logic. "Deduction and induction," he writes, "are the only sure ways of avoiding arbitrariness and attaining objectivity and hence a correctness or truth that reflects not personal whims or prejudices but the requirements of the subject matter."[115] Someone who accepts the reasons of deductive and inductive logic, including the evidence of empirical facts, is a rational agent.[116] Not only is there the formal necessity of principles of morality being entailed or deductively implied by various premises, but the content of the justificatory argument must have a rational necessity established by reason.[117] The problem, then, is to locate a subject

113 Ibid., p. x.
114 Ibid., p. 22.
115 Ibid., p. 22.
116 Ibid., pp. 89–90.
117 Ibid., p. 24.

matter common to *all* moralities and moral judgments; this will constitute the necessary content of morality.

Action and its generic features, Gewirth demonstrates, provide this necessary content of morality. All moral precepts, whatever their further contents, are concerned with how people "ought" to act. And although there is considerable variability in the specific modes of action required by different moral precepts, there are also certain invariant features that pertain generically to all action.[118] Just as action provides the necessary content of all morality, these generic features provide the necessary content of all actions.

Gewirth employs the term *action* in a way very familiar to social scientists (and reminiscent of Weber): moral and other practical precepts are set forth with the intention that those to whom they are directed will "more or less reflectively fashion their behavior along the lines indicated in the precepts."[119] Hence, it is assumed that the hearers are able to exercise unforced choice so as to either try to achieve the prescribed ends or contents or to intentionally refrain from complying with the precepts. Action is involved whenever people control their behavior for ends they regard as worth pursuing. This means that action is inherently *social* and *intersubjective*.

Action, Gewirth argues, has two "categorical" features: voluntariness or freedom, and purposiveness or intentionality. In speaking of an action as being voluntary or free, he means that its performance is under the agent's control in that, knowing the relevant proximate circumstances of his action, the agent unforcedly chooses to act as he does.[120] And in referring to an action as being purposive or intentional, Gewirth means that the agent acts for some end or purpose that constitutes his reason for action.[121] These two features—*voluntariness* and *purposiveness*—are the most general features characteristic of all actions, and are what Gewirth terms the generic features of action. It is these two generic features, Gewirth goes on to show, that constitute the logical justificatory basis of what he refers to as the supreme principle of morality (which will be discussed shortly).

His concern with the analysis of action is to differentiate from the many features of human behaviors those that constitute human

[118] Ibid., p. 25.
[119] Ibid., p. 26.
[120] Ibid., p. 27.
[121] Ibid.

action in the relevant sense.[122] Thus, behaviors performed as a result of a forced choice (handing over money because of a threat at gunpoint), external compulsion (a push), or internal causes (reflexes) would not be instances of action in Gewirth's scheme. This is reminiscent of Weber's statement that "we associate the highest measure of an empirical 'feeling of freedom' with those actions which we are conscious of performing rationally—i.e., in the absence of physical and psychic 'coercion,' emotional 'affects' and 'accidental' disturbances of the clarity of judgment. . . ."[123]

Whatever people's differing views about what particular actions are morally right, all agents must agree that action is the necessary and universal matter of all moral and other practical precepts.[124] There is no way that human agents can refrain from intentionally committing themselves to the context of the generic features of action. Any attempt at such refraining would itself exhibit the features of voluntariness (or freedom) and purposiveness. Someone who did seek to renounce or surrender his freedom could only do so by, literally, doing so freely. Thus he must value that very freedom that allows him to (freely) renounce it. Similarly with purposiveness; whatever the divergence in the purposes or goals of different agents, no individual could act or be an agent without purposing and without valuing his ability to act purposively. It is not that an agent makes a choice or a decision to commit himself to accepting these generic features; it is, rather, that every agent must recognize what is necessarily entailed by a neutral analysis of action.

Voluntariness and purposiveness provide the normative structure from which Gewirth logically derives the supreme principle of morality. In order for human behaviors or movements to be actions in the strict sense, and hence voluntary or free, certain conditions must be fulfilled.[125] Negatively, the behaviors must not occur because of either direct or indirect compulsion, or because of causes internal to the individual (for example, disease). Positively, the individual's behavior must be controlled by his own unforced and informed choice.[126] Voluntariness or freedom con-

---

[122] Ibid., p. 29.

[123] Max Weber, "On the Methodology of the Social Sciences," *The Methodology of the Social Sciences*, trans. Edward A. Shils and Henry A. Finch (New York: Free Press, 1949), pp. 124–125.

[124] Gewirth, *Reason and Morality*, p. 357.

[125] Ibid., p. 31.

[126] Ibid.

cerns the way actions are initiated or controlled by the agent as ongoing events. Purposiveness or intentionality, on the other hand, refers to the end of action. When an individual acts in a purposive manner, he does so with the intention of realizing certain ends or goods that constitute his reasons for acting. Whether an agent acts to do something because he regards it as his duty to do so, because he desires the goal he pursues, or for some other reason, he necessarily has some sort of pro-attitude toward the purposes of his action.[127]

Having established the essential nature of action, Gewirth then goes on to show that there are rationally necessary propositions that follow from the concept of action and, consequently, provide the rational justification of the supreme principle of morality. The basis of his thesis is found in the doctrine that action has a normative structure, and he presents this doctrine in three main steps:

> First, every agent implicitly makes evaluative judgments about the goodness of his purposes and hence about the necessary goodness of the freedom and well-being that are necessary conditions of his acting to achieve his purposes. Second, because of this necessary goodness, every agent implicitly makes a deontic judgment in which he claims that he has rights to freedom and well-being. Third, every agent must claim these rights for the sufficient reason that he is a prospective agent who has purposes he wants to fulfill, so that he logically must accept the generalization that all prospective agents have rights to freedom and well-being.[128]

Although Gewirth discusses these three steps in great detail, I will examine only briefly the various elements in his argument.

To begin with, it seems clear that every agent acts for ends or purposes that seem good to him or her. In acting, the agent envisages more or less clearly some objective, good, or preferred outcome that he wants to achieve. The fact that the agent unforcedly chooses to move from inaction to action shows that he regards the objective, goal, or outcome as worth pursuing; otherwise, he would not do so. Whatever it is that the agent values in terms of his action, so long as his action is not a case of coercion or forced choice, he must be seen as regarding the purpose or object of his action as good. It is enough that the purpose or object

127 Ibid., p. 41.
128 Ibid., p. 48.

seems good to him, according to whatever criteria are involved in his action, and not that it actually *be* good.[129] Thus, every agent makes an implicit judgment that the purposes for which he acts are good.

It is not only the particular purpose for which an agent acts that he regards as good, but also the generic features that characterize all his actions. Since an agent's action is a means of attaining some object or purpose that he regards as good, he must regard the voluntariness or freedom that is an essential feature of his action as a necessary good.[130] After all, without this freedom he would be unable to act for any purpose or good at all. Thus an agent's freedom has not only an instrumental value for him, but he also regards his freedom as intrinsically good, "simply because it is an essential component of purposive action and indeed of the very possibility of action."[131] In addition to valuing his freedom or voluntariness as a necessary good, the agent also values the generic purposiveness of his actions as a necessary good. Not only is each of the particular purposes for which he acts regarded as good, but he also regards as good each increase in the level of purpose-fulfillment whereby he achieves the goal or purpose for which he acts.[132]

The generic purposiveness of a rational agent's actions are seen by Gewirth as encompassing three kinds of goods: basic goods, nonsubstantive goods, and additive goods. Basic goods are the general necessary preconditions of action, and are comprised of the physical and psychological dispositions and conditions that are the preconditions of an agent's performance of any and all of his actions.[133] Since the rational agent views his purposes as good, he must regard these basic goods—things like "life, physical integrity, health, and its various contributing factors, general freedom, mental equilibrium, and the like"—as at least instrumentally good in achieving the purposes for which he acts.[134]

The agent also, says Gewirth, must value nonsubstantive goods, which consist in his retaining whatever he already has that he regards as good. The third kind of good involved in the generic purposiveness of action—additive goods—"consist in the means

129 Ibid., p. 51.
130 Ibid., p. 52.
131 Ibid.
132 Ibid., p. 53.
133 Ibid., p. 54.
134 Ibid., p. 211.

or conditions that enable any person to increase his capacities of purpose-fulfilling action and hence to achieve more of his goals."[135]

What Gewirth tries to show here is that "all purposive action is valuational, and that agents regard as good not only their particular purposes but also the voluntariness or freedom and purposiveness that generically characterize all their actions. Their valuation of this generic purposiveness in turn, extends to the basic, nonsubstrative, and additive goods."[136] The important conclusion from this is that every agent, simply on the basis of his engaging in purposive action, is logically committed to accept this value-judgment about necessary goods. Gewirth builds on this conclusion to show how it logically requires every agent to accept certain judgments about *fundamental* or *generic rights*.

Although, as already noted, the particular purposes for which different persons act may vary considerably, the capabilities of action that are necessary in order to fulfill one or another purpose and for maintaining and increasing their abilities are the same for each and every agent. Thus every agent must regard these capacities of action as necessary goods. Further, they must be seen by him as constituting his own well-being as an actor. "For him to function as an agent," writes Gewirth, "is to have and exercise these capacities, including the second-order abilities to retain and expand his first-order abilities to act to fulfill his purposes."[137] The agent's well-being is to be identified primarily with the generic abilities and conditions that are necessary for all his pursuits of his purposes. What this amounts to, then, is the inescapable conclusion from the standpoint of every agent that "My freedom and well-being are necessary goods."[138] Because they are the necessary conditions of his acting for any purposes, he holds that he *must* have them.

Since the agent must regard as necessary goods the freedom and well-being that constitute the generic features of his successful action, he must also logically hold that he has *rights* to these generic features, and he implicitly makes a corresponding rights claim.[139] Given that these conditions are necessary for the very possibility of his agency and for his chances of succeeding in his actions, he must hold that all other persons ought to refrain from interfering

[135] Ibid., p. 240.
[136] Ibid., p. 57.
[137] Ibid., p. 60.
[138] Ibid., p. 61.
[139] Ibid., p. 63.

with the conditions.[140] Such an "ought" entails correlative rights insofar as it signifies what the agent regards as his due. When duties are owed to him, he has a right to their performance or to compliance with them. Thus, the agent holds that he has rights to the necessary conditions of freedom and well-being.

That is, other persons have correlative duties to the agent because he has these rights. If he were to deny that he has these rights to freedom and well-being, he would have to accept that other persons may remove or interfere with his freedom and well-being, so that he *may not* have them. But this would contradict his belief that he *must* have them. Hence, from the agent's concluding that "My freedom and well-being are necessary goods," there logically follows his further judgment, "I have rights to freedom and well-being."[141]

The rights to freedom and well-being are, says Gewirth, *generic rights*.[142] They are generic in several senses: in that they are rights to have the generic features of successful action characterize one's behavior;[143] in that either they subsume other rights, which are specifications of the rights to freedom and well-being, or that they take precedence over other rights, which must not violate these two rights. In these respects, notes Gewirth, they may be called "fundamental rights."[144] It is these fundamental rights to freedom and well-being, as we shall see, that eventually enter directly into the supreme principle of morality.

[140] Ibid., pp. 63–64.

[141] Alan Gewirth, *Human Rights: Essays on Justification and Applications* (Chicago: University of Chicago Press, 1982), pp. 50–51. Gewirth provides the following, detailed proof: the agent "must accept (1) 'My freedom and well-being are necessary good.' Hence, the agent must also accept (2) 'I, as an actual or prospective agent, must have freedom and well-being,' and hence also (3) 'All other persons must at least refrain from removing or interfering with my freedom and well-being.' For if other persons remove or interfere with these, then he will not have what he has said he must have. Now suppose the agent denies (4) 'I have rights to freedom and well-being.' Then he must also deny (5) 'All other persons ought at least to refrain from removing or interfering with my freedom and well-being.' By denying (5) he must accept (6) 'It is not the case that all other persons ought at least to refrain from removing or interfering with my freedom and well-being,' and hence he must also accept (7) 'Other persons may (or are permitted to) remove or interfere with my freedom and well-being.' But (7) contradicts (3). Since, as we have seen, every agent must accept (3), he cannot consistently accept (7). Since (7) is entailed by the denial of (4), 'I have rights to freedom and well-being,' it follows that any agent who denies that he has rights to freedom and well-being contradicts himself."

[142] Gewirth, *Reason and Morality*, p. 64.

[143] Ibid.

[144] Ibid.

It needs to be emphasized that the concepts of "rights" and "ought" as here invoked by the agents are not yet *moral*. For morality, Gewirth points out, "is primarily concerned with interpersonal actions, that is, with actions that affect persons other than their agents."[145] Thus, in order to be moral there must be reference to the important interests of at least one person other than the agent. In Gewirth's words:

> The criteria on which he grounds these "rights" and "oughts" are not moral but rather prudential; they refer to the agent's own freedom and well-being as required for his pursuits of his own purposes, whatever they may be. . . . In holding that all other persons ought at least to refrain from interfering with his having freedom and well-being, the agent likewise appeals not to moral criteria but to prudential ones. This "ought"-judgment is made from within the agent's own standpoint in purposive action: what grounds his judgment is his own agency-needs, not those of the persons about whom he makes the judgment.[146]

The concept of a right, then, is *necessarily* connected with action. Rights are necessarily, and not contingently, connected with being human. The primary criterion for having rights is that all persons have certain needs, namely the needs for freedom and well-being as the necessary conditions of action. The basis of rights, that is, is located in the conviction necessarily held by every human agent that he has rights to freedom and well-being by virtue of his having purposes and pursuing goods.[147] From this claim made, at least implicitly, by every agent that he has rights to freedom and well-being, it follows that *all* prospective purposive agents have these same rights.

This conclusion necessarily follows because of the principle of *universalizability*, which says that whatever is right for one person must be right for any similar person in similar circumstances.[148] The principle of universalizability is not itself, however, a moral principle; it is rather a logical one. It is given a moral application when it is the case that if someone has a certain right because he has a certain quality (where the "because" is that of justificatory condition), then all persons who have the same quality must have

[145] Ibid., p. 129.
[146] Ibid., p. 71.
[147] Ibid., p. 103.
[148] Ibid., p. 105.

such a right. Hence, moral properties are supervenient upon unmoral ones.

Although the moral principle of universalizability is apparently egalitarian, it says nothing specific with regard to content; it allows for a wide variety in the specific qualities or criteria or relevant similarity for having the right to perform certain actions. Thus the principle itself would allow someone—without inconsistency—to claim that only persons who possess the qualities that he himself has (being male, white, over 21 years of age, courageous, or whatever) has the right in question.

Gewirth avoids such a conclusion by returning to the point that every prospective agent who has a purpose he wants to fulfill, must hold that he has rights to freedom and well-being. It is this description of the agent that constitutes, from the agent's own point of view, the criterion of relevant similarity when it is combined with the principle of universalizability. Hence, in claiming the rights to freedom and well-being for himself, the agent logically must admit that these rights belong also to all other persons who are relevantly similar to himself, i.e., to all other prospective purposive agents.[149] Every agent must hold that he has the generic rights to freedom and well-being for the sufficient reason that he is a prospective agent, and he must admit that *all* prospective agents have these rights for exactly the same reason.

If an agent were to deny or refuse to accept the generalization in the case of any other prospective purposive agent, he would contradict himself. That is, he would be in the position of asserting that being a prospective purposive agent both *is and is not* a sufficient justifying condition for having the generic rights. To avoid self-contradiction, then, every agent must accept the generalization that all prospective purposive agents have the generic rights to freedom and well-being.[150]

[149] Ibid., p. 109.

[150] Gewirth, *Human Rights*, p. 26. Of course, it might be asked: What's wrong with self-contradiction? In answering this question, Gewirth points out that there are numerous claims and counterclaims concerning the "correct" principles of morality. These conflicting claims, he argues, can be "rationally adjudicated in a non-question-begging way if we can show that one principle is such that logical inconsistency results from rejecting it, while this is not so with other principles. For this provides a conclusive argument in favor of the first principle, since a proposition whose denial is self-contradictory is itself necessarily true. This, then, is the point of emphasizing the criterion of logical consistency: not that of *superceding* moral criteria that use specifically moral concepts of persons and their interests but, rather, that of providing a culminating structural argument where other arguments fail of

Combining this conclusion (i.e., that all prospective purposive agents have rights to freedom and well-being) with the earlier conclusion that someone's having a certain right entails a correlative " 'ought'-judgment" that all other persons ought at least to refrain from interfering with that to which he has the right, has the following result: the agent must, on pain of contradiction, accept the judgment "I ought at least to refrain from interfering with the freedom and well-being of any prospective purposive agent."[151] Thus, any agent who harms or coerces other prospective agents violates a requirement he is rationally obliged to accept.

It follows from these considerations, states Gewirth, that every agent logically must acknowledge certain generic *obligations*:

> Negatively, he ought to refrain from coercing and from harming his recipients; positively, he ought to assist them to have freedom and well-being whenever they cannot otherwise have these necessary goods and he can help them at no comparable loss to himself. The general principle of these obligations and rights may be expressed as the following precept addressed to every agent: *Act in accord with the generic rights of your recipients as well as of yourself.* I call this the *Principle of Generic Consistency* (PGC) since it combines the formal consideration of consistency with the material consideration of rights to the generic features or goods of action.[152]

The PGC is, for Gewirth, the "supreme moral principle." The moral community to which this principle applies comprises all prospective purposive agents, and its application requires an equal distribution of the most general rights of action to all human agents. The PGC requires not only that agents not interfere with the freedom and well-being of others; they also have a duty to contribute positively to the well-being of others, considered as recipients of their actions or their possible actions.

The Principle of Generic Consistency, as the supreme principle of morality, is itself, as has been shown, derived from claims or judgments that are not moral but prudential. The PGC is logically derived from the agent's claim that he has the rights to freedom and well-being. The criterion of this rights-claim is prudential since the agent claims these rights for his pursuits of his own purposes.

---

conclusiveness. The appeal to consistency, then, is a second-order logical argument about first-order moral arguments."

[151] Gewirth, *Reason and Morality*, p. 133.

[152] Ibid., p. 135.

A principle or judgment only becomes "moral," as I noted earlier, when the person making or upholding it takes favorable account of the interests or well-being of at least some persons or recipients other than himself.[153] The derivation of the moral from the prudential is accomplished with the PGC at the point where, through the principle of universalizability, the agent logically must acknowledge that the rights to freedom and well-being he claims for himself are also had by all prospective purposive agents.[154] It is at this point that the agent acknowledges that the sufficient reason he must adduce to justify that he himself has these generic rights also justifies that these rights are had by all other persons who fulfill that sufficient reason. "The agent is logically compelled to make this transition from a prudential to a moral judgment," Gewirth emphasizes, "because if he did not he would be in the position of denying what he had previously had to affirm, namely, that being a prospective purposive agent is a sufficient justifying condition for having rights to freedom and well-being."[155]

What Gewirth demonstrates, by way of brief summary, is that determinate criteria of moral rightness can be *logically* derived from the generic features of action (freedom and purposiveness). Since every agent wants to fulfill his purposes, he must regard his freedom and well-being—the necessary conditions of his successful purposes—as necessary goods. Hence, he holds that he has *rights* to freedom and well-being. The right to freedom consists in an individual's controlling his actions and relations with others by his own unforced choice or consent. This right includes having a sphere of personal autonomy and privacy. The right to well-being, as already mentioned, consists of three components: basic goods (the essential preconditions of action), nonsubstantive goods (those abilities and conditions required for "maintaining" one's level of purpose fulfillment and one's capacities for particular actions), and additive goods (the abilities and conditions required for "increasing" one's level of purpose fulfillment and one's capacities for particular actions). The rights to freedom and well-being, Gewirth emphasizes, "have as their aim that each person have rational autonomy in the sense of being a self-controlling, self-developing agent who can relate to other persons on a basis of mutual respect

---

[153] Ibid., p. 145.
[154] Ibid., p. 146.
[155] Ibid., p. 147.

and cooperation, in contrast to being a dependent, passive recipient of the agency of others."[156]

To avoid self-contradiction, every agent must hold that he has these generic rights insofar as he is a prospective purposive agent, and he must respect in all other prospective purposive agents the same generic rights that as rational he necessarily claims for himself. Gewirth shows, then, that all of us are required by *logic* to agree to a basic moral injunction, namely, that we ought not to interfere with others' freedom and well-being. By virtue of this logical necessity, the Principle of Generic Consistency ("Act in accord with the generic rights of your recipients as well as of yourself") is rationally justified as a categorically obligatory moral principle.[157]

The most important point here is that the nature of human *action* provides all that is necessary for rationally justifying the fundamental *rights* to freedom and well-being and the *obligation* that are correlative with such rights. As noted earlier, these obligations may be either positive or negative. An obligation would be positive in the case where A has the right to have food (as part of his right to well-being) and cannot obtain it by his own efforts. In such a situation, B has the obligation of giving food to A. An obligation would be negative if, in the case of A exercising his right to freedom of movement (as part of his generic right to freedom), B is merely obligated to refrain from interfering with A's movements. Positive obligations, Gewirth points out, clearly make more demands on other persons than do negative obligations, and often they require a context of institutional arrangements for providing assistance to people.[158] This, of course, raises a number of difficult issues surrounding the rightness or wrongness of a variety of social relationships and institutional arrangements.

In this regard, Gewirth indicates that the PGC has both a direct and an indirect application.[159] With the "direct" application, the requirement to act in accord with the rights to freedom and well-being of all other persons is imposed on individual agents. With the "indirect" application, this requirement is imposed on social rules and institutions. Institutional arrangements must express or serve to protect the freedom and well-being of all persons subject to them. The state, with its legal and political institutions, is to be

---

[156] Gewirth, *Human Rights*, p. 5.
[157] Gewirth, *Reason and Morality*, pp. 147, 171, 198.
[158] Ibid., p. 141.
[159] Gewirth, *Human Rights*, pp. 60–61.

viewed as a means of protecting the generic rights of individuals. For that reason, the implementation and enforcement of those laws protecting the rights to freedom and well-being of everyone may result in coercion or harm to some individuals. But such coercion or harm does not constitute a "violation" of their generic rights. This is because the legal system that imposes such coercion or harm is itself justified by the principle of generic consistency. A criminal who is sentenced to prison, for example, is subject to coercion and harm. Yet this is morally justified on the basis of his having violated one or another law that is intended to protect *everyone's* rights to freedom and well-being.

V

Gewirth's theory is attractive not only because it avoids many of the problems encountered in other theories of justice, but also because his focus on action is one that he shares with many social scientists. Since Gewirth himself refers to Max Weber's views on action, it is useful here to consider the relation between their standpoints.

Weber defines action as follows: "In action is included all human behavior when and in so far as the acting individual attaches a subjective meaning to it."[160] Whether the acting individual attaches a subjective meaning to his behavior explicitly or tacitly, it is specifically social insofar as he takes account of the behavior of others and is thereby oriented in its course.[161] Weber distinguishes four types of social action: affectual, traditional, value-rational, and means-end rational action. These are characterized, respectively, by action that is determined by the actor's specific feelings, by conformity to tradition, by dedication to an absolute value, and by means-end rationality.[162] According to Weber, these four types refer to universal capacities of *Homo sapiens*. They are not, then, dependent for their existence on particular social, cultural, or historical circumstances. Instead, these types of action must be seen as anthropological traits of all men and women, whenever and wher-

---

[160] In Talcott Parsons, ed., *The Theory of Social and Economic Organization* (New York: Oxford University Press, 1947), p. 88.

[161] Max Weber, *Economy and Society*, trans. Guenther Roth and Claus Wittich, vol. I. (New York: Bedminster Press, 1968), pp. 3–4, 7.

[162] Ibid., pp. 24–25.

101

ever they might be found.[163] Gewirth expresses the same view when he states that "the generic features of action pertain to historically diverse patterns of conduct, including not only moderns, ranging from capitalist entrepreneurs (or 'men of action') to unskilled laborers, but also medieval saints, warriors, and plebians, ancient sages, tyrants, and 'benausoi,' and exponents of many different ways of life in all eras in which persons control their behavior for ends they regard as worth pursuing."[164]

Like Weber, Gewirth takes as his point of departure actors' subjective orientations to their projected actions. There is also a similarity in their treatment of rational action. Gewirth quotes Weber as saying that the traditional and affectual types of action are "very close to the borderline of what can be called meaningfully oriented action," the former because it is sometimes "almost automatic," the latter because it may be an "uncontrolled reaction."[165] These qualifications regarding rational action are similar to the distinction that Gewirth makes between occurrent and dispositional purposes.[166] Gewirth specifies that for human behavior or movement to be action in the strict sense, certain conditions must be fulfilled: negatively, the behavior must not occur because of direct compulsion, causes internal to the person, or indirect compulsion; positively, the person must control his behavior by his own unforced and informed choice.[167]

With Weber's value-rational and means-end rational action, individuals deliberate between alternatives and make a reasoned decision based on that deliberation. With affectual and traditional action, on the other hand, there may be a decision among available alternatives but with little or no antecedent deliberation. But this does not necessarily mean, says Gewirth, that the behaviors are determined by forced choices and are "hence not action in the strict sense."[168] (Weber would probably say "hence not 'rational action' in the strict sense.") Forced choice, according to Gewirth, has three

---

[163] See Stephen Kohlberg, "Max Weber's Types of Rationality: Cornerstones for the Analysis of Rationalization Processes in History," *American Sociological Review* 85 (March 1980): 1148.

[164] Gewirth, *Reason and Morality*, p. 30. For other views on action, see Richard J. Bernstein, *Praxis and Action* (Philadelphia: University of Pennsylvania Press, 1971); and Norman S. Care and Charles Landesman, eds., *Readings in the Theory of Action* (Bloomington, Ind.: Indiana University Press, 1968).

[165] Gewirth, *Reason and Morality*, p. 369.

[166] Ibid.

[167] Ibid., p. 31.

[168] Ibid., p. 32.

interrelated aspects: compulsoriness, undesirableness, and threat. In some cases, someone may not be able to exercise control and choice *occurrently*, i.e., in relation to the action as it directly occurs, but may have been able to exercise *disposititonal* choice, i.e., could have controlled his getting into the situation. Similarly with purposiveness; the purposes for which people act, Gewirth notes, "may be habitual, results of long-standing goal-directed behavior where the goals have ceased to occupy the center of attention. Such habits, however, do not indicate the complete absence of purposiveness, but only that the purposes can be achieved without being explicitly considered or aimed at. That they are still latently present, however, would be shown if attempts were made to interfer with the agent's attaining them."[169]

In other words, Gewirth argues that even Weber's affectual and traditional types of action are generally characterized by voluntary and purposive elements. So long as individuals control their conduct by either their own unforced occurrent or dispositional choices, they remain rational actions.[170] Only if control is permanently given up or taken from individuals can it be said that they cease to be rational actors. This might occur as the result of highly adverse social conditions, where people's ability to obtain the minimal necessities required for controlling their unforced choices are absent. But in most instances people have either dispositional or occurrent freedom to control their behavior and do, therefore, engage in what Weber terms "meaningfully oriented action." Thus, Gewirth views all four of the types of action considered by Weber (affectual, traditional, value-rational, and means-end rational action) as involving the two generic features of voluntariness or freedom and purposiveness or intentionality. As human beings we cannot avoid esteeming our freedom and well-being; our esteeming them is, in fact, the very condition of our being agents in the first place. These, then, are the most general features distinctively characteristic of the whole genus of action. And these two features, as shown earlier, give rise to the generic rights to freedom and well-being.

It may also be instructive to briefly examine the theory of action advanced by Talcott Parsons, since it is perhaps the most influential of contemporary sociological theories of action. For him, the starting point for analysis is the concept of an *actor*, who is characterized

[169] Ibid., p. 38.
[170] Ibid., p. 53.

as a motivated, goal-seeking individual. Parsons defines action as including the following qualities: (1) It is "behavior [of an organism] . . . oriented toward the attainment of ends or goals or other anticipated states of affairs. (2) It takes place in situations. (3) It is normatively regulated; and (4) It involves the expenditure of energy or effort or 'motivation.' . . ."[171]

But, of course, the individual actor cannot be considered apart from his relations with other actors. Here the concept of "interaction" is introduced as the first-order step beyond the action concept itself. The crucial reference points for analyzing interaction, Parsons says, are two: "(1) that each actor is *both* acting agent and object of orientation *both* to himself and to others; and (2) that, as acting agent, he orients to himself and to others and, as object, has meaning to himself and to others, in *all* of the primary modes or aspects."[172] From these premises, Parsons derives what he calls the "double contingency" of social interaction. In the process of interaction, the outcome is not only contingent on each party's own actions but also contingent on the response of the other(s). As a consequence of this double contingency, Parsons says, the possibilities of instability far exceed the possibilities of stability in an interaction system. It is because of this that an interaction system must be integrated by a "shared basis of normative order."[173]

Thus, the normative character of social practices is a result of the need to establish some distinction between desirable and undesirable lines of action, which can serve to stabilize interaction (and help assure social order). Consistent with Durkheim's general position, Parsons argues that this necessitates the need for a shared normative culture, which has a double significance: on the one hand, it becomes (ideally at least) internalized in the personalities of individual actors as a moral authority and, hence, functions as an internal sanction; on the other hand, it guides the actions of all individuals, because of their recognition that there will be the external imposition of rewards for conformity and negative sanctions for nonconformity to the norms.[174] All stable systems of social interaction, require, then, a set of agreed-upon, institutionalized, normative standards.

Although he never puts it this way, Parsons could be viewed as

---

[171] Talcott Parsons and Edward Shils, eds., *Towards a General Theory of Action* (New York: Free Press, 1977), p. 167.

[172] Ibid.

[173] Ibid., p. 168.

[174] Ibid., p. 169.

referring to the rights and obligations that are constitutive of the normative culture governing social interactions. Emphasizing, as he does, that action is "oriented toward the attainment of ends or goals," he seems to share Gewirth's view that "the agent acts for some end or purpose that constitutes his reason for acting."[175] But Parsons is not really concerned with the claims of rights and correlative obligations that are logically involved in all purposive actions. Despite his emphasis on normative considerations and their importance in social interactions, he has never been concerned with the rational justification of a particular set of moral values or principles. Thus, normative rights-language has never played a part in his analyses. But, of course, it really could not be expected to. After all, Parsons holds that those standards, values, or principles that normatively regulate social interactions cannot themselves be rationally justified.

A different conclusion is reached by Habermas, who also places an emphasis on the concept of action. In opposition to the views of Weber and Parsons about the unjustifiability of normative standards, Habermas argues that the very act of self-reflection is normative, and must be seen as motivated by a reasoned interest in emancipation. Such self-reflection reveals the interested character of all theoretical knowledge (regarding what is good, right, true, and the like), and hence presupposes the primacy of action. The concept of action, therefore, embraces a social, an ethical, and an epistemological dimension. Implicit in all of Habermas's theoretical work is a recognition of the primacy of the practical: action is the presupposition of all knowledge; wanting to act is the presupposition of being-able-to-know.[176] Although his work takes a much different direction than Gewirth's, as we have already seen, they share the view that substantive moral norms or principles are logically entailed by the nature of human action.

It needs to be emphasized, however, that Habermas is no more concerned with rights as such than are Weber or Parsons. In common with most other social scientists, then, these theorists ignore the subject of rights altogether. Social actors are considered in terms of their needs, interests, desires, motivations, and goals, but not as possessors of rights.

Despite the absence of a concern with rights in the work of

[175] Gewirth, *Reason and Morality*, p. 27.

[176] See the excellent discussion in Garbis Kortian, *Metacritique: The Philosophical Argument of Jürgen Habermas* (Cambridge, Mass.: Cambridge University Press, 1980).

Parsons and Habermas, they both conceive of action in a manner quite consistent with Gewirth's views. In opposition to the standpoint of Homans, Blau, and other sociologists who see action as being guided solely by technical concerns, Parsons and Habermas share with Gewirth the view that normative concerns and constraints are inevitably involved in action. While the first-named group above conceives of action entirely in an instrumental, calculative sense, the second emphasizes that action is oriented both to the external environment and by reference to ideal ends. The first standpoint is, then, highly deterministic; the ends sought by agents, as well as their ability to achieve them, are determined entirely by external constraints. On this view, there is no room for any intentionality or freedom at all.

For Parsons, Habermas, and Gewirth, on the other hand, there is a recognition of both coercive and voluntary elements in social life. Action is motivated and regulated, at least in part, by internal volition as opposed to external, coercive control. All three of these theorists recognize that some norms are held to be morally superior to others and, for that reason, they reject the view that action is purely calculative and externally conditioned. But Parsons, of course, never attempts to establish which particular norms are superior, and Habermas goes no further than specifying the conditions under which certain norms would be justified. Only Gewirth is able to successfully establish which moral norms or principles—the generic rights to freedom and well-being—are morally superior. Nevertheless, Habermas and Parsons, as well as Weber and Durkheim, share with Gewirth the recognition that people do not orient their actions solely on the basis of instrumental considerations.

In one way or another, all of these theorists emphasize that action is guided in part by the distinction between what people *ought* to do and what they *want* to do. They all acknowledge that many persons are, and should be, concerned with what is morally permissible and impermissible, with what human beings may and may not do. Gewirth and Habermas, along with Rawls and Nozick, however, go a step further than the others: they attempt to locate a set of *rationally justifiable* principles or standards for structuring our social relationships and institutional arrangements.

VI

The theories set forth by Rawls, Nozick, and Gewirth are all deontological in form. Such theories usually take either duty or rights as the basis of morality. Duty-based theories hold that some acts are morally obligatory regardless of their consequences. Kant, for example, thought that everyone had a duty to tell the truth. This was not because truth-telling promoted some societal goal (such as a high level of trust within the society), but because it was wrong to tell a lie. Rights-based theories differ from duty-based ones in that they do not treat a particular code of conduct (say, the duty to obey the Ten Commandments) as fundamental, but instead emphasize some fundamental right like the right to freedom or equality. A rights-based theory assumes that individual rights must be honored even at some cost to the general welfare. Both duty-based and rights-based theories focus primarily on the individual; he or she is always at the center of such theories.

Deontological theories can be contrasted with teleological theories. These theories judge actions on the grounds of their consequences alone. That is, a particular act, social institution, or whatever, is judged in terms of some specific end-state that is to be realized. From this perspective, one can only know whether something is right, ought to be done, or is morally good if one knows first the fundamental aims or ends that our activities are to promote. To many sociologists, for example, the fundamental end is social order, and whatever promotes social order is itself morally right or desirable. Thus, Durkheim remarks that "it is impossible to consider moral those practices which are subversive of the society in which they are observed; because it is everywhere a fundamental duty to ensure the existence of the fatherland."[177]

There are several recent philosophical studies in the teleological tradition that challenge the deontological theories of Rawls, Nozick, and Gewirth. Of particular importance here are the books of MacIntyre, Sullivan, and Walzer—all of which attempt to provide an alternative to the individual-oriented theories that are concerned with rationally justifying specific moral principles and standards.[178] Since these books have received considerable attention, they are deserving of brief examination here.

In his book, *After Virtue*, MacIntyre is highly critical of the concern with universal principles in analytical moral philosophy. There

---

[177] Émile Durkheim, *De la Division de travail social* (Paris: Alcan, 1983), p. 21, quoted in Lewis A. Coser, "Durkheim's Conservatism and Its Implications for His Sociological Theory," p. 220, in Kurt H. Wolff, ed., *Essays on Sociology and Philosophy* (New York: Harper & Row, 1964).

[178] Alasdair MacIntyre, *After Virtue* (London: Duckworth, 1981); William Sullivan, *Restructuring Public Philosophy* (Berkeley: University of California Press, 1982); and Michael Walzer, *Spheres of Justice* (New York: Basic Books, 1983).

are two important arguments, he says, against the theories of writers like Rawls, Nozick, and Gewirth.[179] First of all, they do not agree among themselves about either the character of moral rationality or the substance of that morality which is to be founded on rationality. As I noted in the previous chapter, however, such a lack of agreement is not peculiar to normative theories. Most especially in the social sciences, but even sometimes in the natural sciences as well, there is no general agreement as to the correctness of one or another explanatory theory. Thus, MacIntyre's first argument is in no way specific to normative theories.

His second argument is more important; none of the various theories, he says, succeeds. He selects Gewirth as an exemplary case, stating that Gewirth "is self-consciously and scrupulously aware of the contributions of other analytical moral philosophers to the debate and his arguments therefore provide us with an ideal test case."[180] Let us see what MacIntyre says in this regard.

It is Gewirth's position, as we saw earlier, that anyone who holds that the prerequisites for his exercise of rational agency are necessary goods is himself logically committed to holding that he has a "right" to those goods. MacIntyre attacks that step in Gewirth's argument in which he introduces the notion of rights, arguing that there are no such rights as freedom and well-being. This is because all rights presuppose the existence of a socially established set of rules. "Such sets of rules," MacIntyre asserts, "only come into existence at particular historical periods under particular social circumstances. They are in no way universal features of the human condititon."[181] According to MacIntyre, there was no expression of our concept of "a right" until near the close of the middle ages.

It is interesting that MacIntyre explicitly accepts all of Gewirth's arguments except for the step concerning rights. He says, "There is clearly no reason to quarrel with Gewirth's argument so far. It turns out to be the next step [i.e., that in regard to rights] that is at once crucial and questionable."[182]

Gewirth could, I believe, avoid MacIntyre's criticism by totally ignoring the term *rights*. He could simply restate his questionable step in terms of such notions as duty or wrongness. And from what MacIntyre says, he would have to agree with the conclusion that "All agents are logically required to conclude that they ought

[179] MacIntyre, *After Virtue*, p. 20.
[180] Ibid.
[181] Ibid., p. 65.
[182] Ibid., p. 64.

not to interfere with other people's freedom and well-being." To so interfere, is, then, wrong. With such a reformulation, rights disappear. But the basic moral injunction remains the same: we ought not to interfere with other people's freedom and well-being.

Gewirth need not, however, concede MacIntyre's point concerning rights. In fact, Gewirth anticipates the historical objection that the concept of a right is of relatively recent origin. He offers several answers to such an objection, saying that people might have and use the concept of a right without explicitly having a single word for it, and that a right might be upheld on moral criteria (as the idea of entitlements, e.g.) although it has no legal recognition.[183] Moreover, Gewirth concludes from a brief survey "that the historical view that restricts the concept of rights to the modern ear is mistaken as a historical thesis."[184]

But whether or not the concept of rights is—as MacIntyre insists—a peculiarly modern Western phenomenon, it follows from Gewirth's own rational justification that human beings *had* rights long before they generally came to recognize that they did. That is, rights existed even before they became elements in people's moral discourse.

Since Gewirth specifies the features by which someone is a possessor of a right—i.e., applying reason to action—it is difficult to envision "human beings" without rights. Recall that for Gewirth reason is used as comprising the canons of deductive and inductive logic. Might not there have been a people with no commitment whatsoever to the use of reason and thus incapable of engaging in the sort of reflection that Gewirth describes? I think not, for as Quine has observed "creatures unskilled at induction have the sad, but praiseworthy tendency, to become extinct."[185] And, of course, exactly the same can be said with regard to deduction. It seems safe to conclude, therefore, that a commitment to reason is to be found in all known societies and cultures. If people do accept the canons of induction and deduction, then—given the opportunity to reflect on their beliefs and desires—they must acknowledge that they have rights. Creatures who reject the canons of induction and deduction would be unable to follow a rule or learn a language, let alone to reflect on their own beliefs and desires. They would not, I assert, be full-fledged human beings.

[183] Gewirth, *Reason and Morality*, pp. 98–99.
[184] Ibid., p. 100.
[185] Quoted in David Zimmerman, "The Force of Hypothetical Commitment," *Ethics* 93 (April 1983): 477.

So contrary to what MacIntyre claims, a belief in rights is *not* "at one with belief in witches and unicorns."[186] But what, it might be asked, does MacIntyre himself offer as a rational justification for morality? Although he is highly inconsistent in this regard, he appears to believe that morality must be based on some kind of teleological view of action as morally right or correct if and only if it leads to some specified end or good. For him, what is required is a morality in which the "virtues" are primary. "We may understand the virtues," he says, "as having their function in enabling an individual to make his or her life one kind of unity rather than another."[187]

But this requires a conception of a unity and of a good that specifies an individual's *telos*. In this regard, MacIntyre says that "the good life for man is the life spent in seeking for the good life of man, and the virtues necessary for the seeking are those which will enable us to understand what more and what else the good life for man is."[188] But that is both vague and circular, and tells us nothing about what represents the good or *telos* for MacIntyre.

What, then, is the good for the individual? What is the good for man? What remedies are available to us? What must we do? MacIntyre has little to say about such questions. He does specify that such virtues as justice, courage, honesty, and patriotism are necessary for the survival of one or another living tradition. But which living traditions are preferable to others, and why? What we must do, says MacIntyre, is construct "local forms of community within which civility and the intellectual and moral life can be sustained through the new dark ages which are already upon us."[189]

Even if we grant the need for such local forms of community, what if different communities hold opposing conceptions of the good life? What if, that is, *our* conception of the good life is one that is antithetical to *their* conception? Aren't questions of morality often connected with what one ought to do in just such situations?

However admirable the quest for community might be for other reasons, I do not believe that we decide what is morally required of us on the basis of first determining what is involved in a good life within *our* local community. Rather, we often try to understand what would be the morally correct act in a variety of different

[186] MacIntyre, *After Virtue*, p. 67.
[187] Ibid., p. 189.
[188] Ibid., p. 204.
[189] Ibid., p. 245.

situations or even different communities. To know what justice requires, for example, we must look beyond the conventions of one or another concrete community. This requires a morality based essentially on principles, the sort of morality advocated by Rawls, Nozick, and Gewirth. On my reading, then, MacIntyre's attempts to undercut such theories and to advance his own so-called theory of the virtues is totally unsuccessful.

The same conclusion holds for William Sullivan's *Reconstructing Public Philosophy*, a book which shares MacIntyre's opposition to the search for universal moral principles. There are, in fact, many similarities in these two books. Robert Bellah notes this in the Foreword, saying that Sullivan's book can be seen as complementary to *After Virtue*.[190]

Sullivan's criticisms of the analytical moral philosophers run pretty much parallel to MacIntyre's, as do his suggested solutions. In opposition to the liberal individualism found in deontological theories like those of Rawls and Nozick, Sullivan advocates the kind of teleological approach represented in Aristotle's statement (quoted with approval by Sullivan) that "The good life is the chief end, both for the community as a whole and each of us individually."[191]

In place of liberal individualism, Sullivan argues, we require civic republicanism and an emphasis on virtue. "For the republican tradition," he writes, "civic virtue is the excellence of character proper to the citizen. It *is* freedom in a substantive sense, freedom understood as the capacity to attain one's good, where *goodness* describes full enjoyment of those capacities which characterize a flourishing human life."[192] He goes on to specify that living well requires a shared life and that this is possible only when the members of a community "trust and respect one another."[193] People's commitments, then, must be to the community, to the shared life, to civic life.

Like others who write in this tradition, however, Sullivan never faces the difficult problem of specifying the standards or criteria that allow us to choose among and evaluate communities. It is not sufficient to insist that we must foster the value of "community," that we must respect the significance of community, that our identity and well-being find their source there. For we are left in the

---

[190] Robert Bellah, Foreword in Sullivan, *Restructuring Public Philosophy*, p. ix.
[191] Sullivan, *Restructuring Public Philosophy*, p. 169.
[192] Ibid., p. 163.
[193] Ibid.

dark as to a way of distinguishing a community that deserves our support and commitment (say, one based on something like universal brotherhood, love, and understanding) and one that does not (such as one based on racism, sexism, and hatred for all outsiders).

Furthermore, Sullivan fails to see that people are not card-carrying members of one or another community. Instead, we are all "members" at various levels. Most importantly, one can simultaneously belong to distinct communities with different values and moral standards. Since Sullivan repeatedly speaks of what America needs, requires, must achieve, and the like, let us consider the situation for someone who is an American citizen.

Sullivan speaks in this regard of "America's deepest founding values."[194] At one level of analysis, it seems probable that the overwhelming majority of Americans share some "founding values," which help define a shared life and a sense of belonging to a community of "we" Americans as opposed, for example, to the supporters of Hitler or Mussolini (or to Russians today). But at another level, those Americans who uphold the values of the "Moral Majority" are not part of the relevant community to which many of the rest of us belong. At that level, where there are political traditions in conflict with each other, one must often make judgments about what morality demands. As soon as disagreements arise, we require just the kind of analytic principles Sullivan rejects.

A third recent book standing in opposition to the search for moral absolutes is Michael Walzer's *Spheres of Justice*. Walzer advances a theory of what he terms "complex equality," a theory consisting of two ideals: (1) that resources must be distributed in accordance with the principles appropriate to their "spheres," and (2) that success in one sphere must not be allowed to have an influence in another sphere (e.g., success in making money must not result in buying votes). Somewhat like MacIntyre and Sullivan, Walzer emphasizes the importance of people's shared understandings within particular traditions. What justice may require in one sphere, Walzer believes, should depend on the conventions and understandings within that sphere and not on what occurs in another sphere.

To find the appropriate principles for the distribution of specific goods—education, housing, medical care, etc.—we must look to the existing social conventions in the various spheres. What this means, Walzer says, is that the various social goods and distributive

---

[194] Ibid., p. 156.

spheres have first to be located through a process of empirical investigation and then understood through a process of interpretation. This clearly places a considerable burden and a tremendous responsibility on those responsible for conducting such empirical inquiries.

Be that as it may, Walzer speaks of justice as follows: "A given society is just if its substantive life is lived in a certain way—that is, in a way faithful to the shared understandings of its members."[195] This is obviously a relativistic view of justice. A society where women are placed in (what some of us call) a subservient position is just when its traditions (i.e., shared understandings) accept it. In such a society, it would then be unjust to distribute goods and resources equally among men and women. For the sorts of reasons spelled our earlier, such a conclusion is morally unacceptable.

Strangely, however, Walzer follows the above quotation concerning justice with these words: "(When people disagree about the meaning of social goods, when understandings are controversial, then justice requires that the society be faithful to the disagreements, providing institutional channels for their expression, adjudicative mechanisms, and alternative distributions.)"[196] Interpretation of this statement is extremely difficult. If people disagree, Walzer says, then "justice requires" a number of things, which he specifies. But what conception of justice imposes such a requirement? If justice is, as Walzer stipulates, a matter of following shared understandings, then what if there is no shared understanding about the social meaning of justice? In the absence of consensus about what justice *is*, there is obviously no way of establishing what "justice requires." This follows directly from Walzer's relativistic position regarding justice.

Whether or not there are shared understandings within a society or community, however, a theory that ties justice to conventions is unacceptable. As it now stands, Walzer's theory invites the criticisms of either relativism or incoherence.

Contrary to the arguments of MacIntyre, Sullivan, and Walzer, then, normative theories cannot rest on the elaboration of social arrangments as found in the tradition, community, or society. Instead, we require the sorts of deontological theories that aim at

[195] Walzer, *Spheres of Justice*, p. 313.
[196] Ibid.

rationally justifying those principles appropriate to justice in *any* society.

VII

In this chapter, I have examined the theories of Rawls, Nozick, Habermas, and Gewirth in considerable detail. I have also given attention to three recent attempts to provide alternatives to the principles-based theories of these men. My conclusions are two-fold. First of all, deontological theories are to be preferred to te-leological ones; moral principles that can be universalized are superior to those that have only a limited, local, application. Second, Gewirth's theory—where substantive moral principles are derived from the nature of human action—is superior to the other three theories, which also attempt to formulate a coherent set of fundamental principles bearing on our moral lives. His theory is also attractive, as I have indicated, because the justification of these moral principles is to be found in the web of social relations familiar to social scientists. But even though Gewirth's theory avoids the shortcomings contained in the work of Rawls, Nozick, and Habermas, there is much of merit in these theories as well.

The major strength of Gewirth's work is that he has successfully accomplished two important tasks: one, the meta-ethical task of examining how moral principles and judgments can be justified; the other, the ethical task of actually showing which moral principles are justifiable. With regard to the first, Gewirth has demonstrated how moral rights can be established on the basis of considerations of consistency and logically necessary connections. With the second, he has shown that two specific moral rights—freedom and well-being—can be justified on the basis of systematic reasoning. Gewirth makes it clear, then, that both the form and the contents of moral principles can be established as logically necessary.

In my view, Gewirth has provided all that is required in the way of a rational justification for the rights to freedom and well-being.[197] These two generic rights constitute, therefore, the moral "first principles," which should—normatively speaking—regulate the just social order. For me, a *just social order* is one regulated by two

---

[197] A book containing various criticisms of Gewirth's theory as well as his response to them has just recently appeared. See Edward Regis, Jr., ed., *Gewirth's Ethical Rationalism: Critical Essays with a Reply by Alan Gewirth* (Chicago: University of Chicago Press, 1984).

fundamental moral principles—the rights to freedom and well-being—and by the institutional arrangements to which they give rise.

In the remainder of this volume I will take it as having been established that all persons do indeed have the rights to freedom and well-being. But whereas Gewirth specifies three different components of well-being (basic, nonsubstrative, and additive goods), I will generally intend by the "right to well-being" simply the basic right to subsistence and security. Unless people have adequate food, clothing, shelter, and health care, they cannot meaningfully exercise their right to freedom. Similarly with security; unless individuals are physically secure—and not subject to murder, torture, rape, assault, and invasions of their privacy—they will lack a necessary condition for the enjoyment of their right to freedom. Thus, the right to freedom can be exercised only when people's right to well-being, i.e., to physical security and subsistence, is recognized and respected.

But it is also the case that the enjoyment of the right to well-being itself depends upon exercise of the right to freedom. It is only possible for individuals to effectively exercise the right to well-being (security and subsistence) if they have the freedom to demand certain social guarantees as a right. People without the right to freedom (that is, the ability to exercise voluntary control over their actions) might have their security and subsistence needs met, but they would not be enjoying this security and subsistence as a right. Rather, their well-being would be in the nature of discretions, indulgences, or privileges, dependent on the arbitrary will of others. Consequently, the right to well-being can be enjoyed as a right only when the right to freedom is recognized and respected. A mutual dependence holds, then, between enjoyment of the basic rights to freedom and well-being.

Since the rights to freedom and well-being constitute the valid moral principles that should regulate the just social order, the question arises as to how individuals are to come to learn and accept these principles. This involves a concern with the mechanism of *socialization*. Part II is devoted to a consideration of the general issue of socialization and morality.

II

Socialization

THE limitations on what people can and should do to (and for) one another in a just social order are to be provided by normative consensus about the rights to freedom and well-being and the obligations that are correlative with such rights. But it needs to be emphasized that it is *individuals* who require stability in their social relationships and not society or the social system as a whole. This is not to deny, of course, that "society" does affect the actions of individuals or that a variety of structural arrangements and conditions influence and constrain people's actions. It is rather to make the point, in opposition to the standpoint of many sociologists, that societies as such do *not* have distinct aims or interests (and certainly not rights) of their own.

Further, normative consensus about the generic rights to freedom and well-being is not to be founded upon a mere "belief" in their correctness or legitimacy, nor upon convention, coercion, ignorance, or blind obedience. Instead, such consensus must arise from the recognition that these fundamental rights can be rationally justified, i.e., that they can be logically derived from the nature of human action.

It seems to me that Freud and Marx and Engels made implicit use of something like the idea of rational justifiability in their arguments against traditional morality. Certainly Freud directed considerable attention to unmasking the traditional moral ideas and standards that were accepted by people on the basis of ignorance or mere belief.[1] And his criticisms of particular cultural standards were based on an implied recognition of the difference between a morality that is in some way rationally defensible and a morality that is uncritically accepted. Similarly, Marx and Engels saw a difference between the "ideological" status of certain Judeo-Christian moral injunctions and the moral principles that would forbid exploitative relations among human beings. They distinguished between that (existing) morality which has always been a class morality—justifying the domination and interests of the ruling class—and a really human morality that transcends class antagonisms.[2] Although they themselves espoused the view that no set of moral principles could have an independent validity, they nevertheless were agreed that people's acceptance of moral principles ought to

[1] Sigmund Freud, *Civilization and Its Discontents* (Garden City: Doubleday, 1958), pp. 69–71, 91, 139.

[2] Karl Marx, *The German Ideology* (New York: International Publishers, 1939); Lewis Feur, ed., *Marx and Engels: Basic Writings on Politics and Philosophy* (Garden City: Doubleday, 1959).

be based on something other than ignorance, distortion, belief, or false consciousness. This "something other," I believe, is rational justification. Habermas, whose ideas were discussed earlier, as well as Marcuse, make this distinction between an existing and a correct (or true) morality much more explicitly than did the earlier critics.[3]

If it is indeed the case that the rights to freedom and well-being constitute the valid moral principles that ought to regulate the just society, then the problem arises as to how individuals are to come to learn and accept these principles. Here I return to the idea of *socialization*. According to Parsons and most other social scientists, this concerns the internalization of the dominant value-orientations in the society and the preparation of the child for the various roles that he or she may be called upon to play in society.[4] The internalization of the dominant value-patterns in a society is required, says Parsons, so that human beings will be motivated to meet "the exigencies imposed on them by the imperatives of their culture and society."[5] At the individual level, the internalization of normative values provides the motives that impel the actor; on the societal level, such internalization provides the normative consensus that serves to assure social order.

Where I most strongly disagree with Parsons and other social theorists in the consensus tradition is in their emphasis on the need for individuals to internalize the "dominant" values in a society. As I emphasized earlier, these theorists totally ignore the moral standing or justifiability of one or another set of moral values. We can imagine, for instance, that there is "normative consensus" in a society regarding the moral superiority of whites and the inferiority of blacks. It may even be that blacks and whites alike have internalized this normative value so that their social relations are conducted in accordance with its dictates—thus assuring social order. So far as the consensus theorists are concerned, the particular moral values about which there is normative consensus, and which are to be internalized through the socialization process, need no further justification than the fact that they provide for stability and social order. The validity of one or another moral value is apparently to be determined entirely by the extent to which it helps

[3] Herbert Marcuse, *Reason and Revolution* (New York: Oxford University Press, 1941).

[4] Talcott Parsons and Edward Shils, eds., *Toward a General Theory of Action* (Cambridge, Mass.: Harvard University Press, 1951), pp. 277–78.

[5] Talcott Parsons, *Social Systems and the Evolution of Action Theory* (New York: Free Press, 1977), p. 98.

achieve normative consensus. So long as the internalization of moral values provides for consensus, restraint, and stability, there is nothing to be said for one particular set of values in comparison with another.

But such a conclusion is mistaken, not only in the sense that no attention is given to the *moral* rightness or correctness of the values themselves but also in a more sociological sense. It seems clear to me that moral values that can be rationally justified are far more likely to gain widespread consensus than those that people accept and internalize because of ignorance, coercion, tradition, and the like. Contrary to what many social scientists seem to suggest, socialization is not simply the passive imprinting of society upon each individual. While infants and young children may sometimes almost unthinkingly accept the correctness of certain values that are emphasized in their upbringing, surely they are not creatures who are merely "molded" to fit society's so-called needs or their parents' desires.

Especially as they become older and are exposed in school and elsewhere to competing systems of beliefs, values, and social practices, individuals come to raise questions about the justification and legitimation of a whole host of social arrangements. Even if someone has internalized a particular set of moral values very strongly, so that his or her life is guided by adherence to these values as the appropriate norms, there is always the possibilty of being called upon to defend and justify them against persons who are committed to a different set of moral values. Consequently, moral values that have the potential of being rationally justified are superior in terms of commanding normative consensus to moral values that lack such rational justifiability. Thus, rationally justifiable moral values and principles have not only a privileged moral status to those unable to command such rational justification, but they are also superior in their ability to assure normative consensus and social order.

In considering the socialization of children in the following three chapters, I will be concerned ultimately with the processes through which children learn and place a moral premium on the recognition and respect for everyone's rights to freedom and well-being. However, it is also necessary to ask whether there are limitations on what is psychologically and sociologically feasible with regard to the moral development of children. This is considered in the following chapter, where I examine the two dominant theoretical approaches to children's development. Moreover, it also needs to be asked whether there are limitations on what is morally acceptable for parents to do in socializing their children. This raises the question of whether or not children have rights, and the further question of what this means in terms of the rights of their parents and other social members. An attempt to deal with such questions will constitute the bulk of Chapter 4. Then, in Chapter 5, I will deal with the socialization process itself as it involves learning to recognize and respect the rights of freedom and well-being, and with the difficult problem of what sorts of emotions ought to be experienced by people when they violate (or contemplate violating) the moral values connected with these generic rights. Part II, then, is devoted to the general issue of socialization and morality.

THREE

Socialization and Moral Learning

SOCIALIZATION has long been a topic of interest to social scientists. Although it is frequently discussed as if it were confined to childhood, or to childhood and adolescence, socialization can better be understood as applying to the entire life cycle of each individual. After all, people must be socialized with regard to the different norms and expectations connected with becoming a doctor or lawyer, a bricklayer or beautician, a parent or grandparent, and with a whole host of other positions in the life cycle. Nonetheless, my concern in this and the following two chapters will be exclusively on the socialization of children, and most especially on the processes by which they come to acquire and accept moral values and principles.

In the presnt chapter, I focus on two of the dominant theoretical approaches to children's moral development: the identification-internalization approach endorsed by Freud and Parsons, and adhered to by many sociologists; and Lawrence Kohlberg's cognitive developmental approach.[1] Examination of these approaches provides part of the background to my later discussion of the ways in which children *ought* to be socialized so that they will learn and be guided by the principles required for a just social order.

I

The Identification-Internalization Approach

Most social scientists emphasize that socialization is concerned with those social norms and values "appropriate to their society."[2]

---

[1] These are two of the three currently dominant theoretical approaches to children's development. The third, the social-learning approach, is concerned with how specific principles of learning—reinforcement, punishment, and modeling—determine children's learning and development. Because so much of the research connected with this approach has been conducted in laboratory settings, and its relevance to situations outside the laboratory is extremely unclear, I will not consider that approach here. For an excellent overview of the three approaches, see Ervin Staub, *Positive Social Behavior and Morality*, vol. 2 (New York: Academic Press, 1979), pp. 21–57.

[2] See, for example, Talcott Parsons and R. F. Bales, *Family: Socialization and Inter-*

The traditional argument concerning socialization proceeds as follows. When the child comes into existence, he or she immediately encounters, and eventually internalizes, the social values and normative standards dominant within the society. In virtually all societies, the family is the agency of socialization responsible for seeing that children come to be motivated to act in conformity with the dominant cultural values and standards, thereby themselves providing the restraining control necessary for organized social life. From the vantage point of the larger society, socialization helps assure that individuals incorporate the relevant social values and normative standards into their personalities. From the vantage point of the individual being socialized, socialization prepares him or her for taking on an autonomous role in society.[3] But from either perspective, successful socialization requires that children learn and internalize the normative requirements of the society. "Otherwise," writes Parsons, "the *moral authority* of 'society' as an agency of the individual's action—as an agency of constraint, in Durkheim's sense—could not be understood."[4]

Thus, Parsons holds that it is the "internalization" of the appropriate values that assures the normative consensus necessary for social order. The internalization of these values, as need-dispositions in the personality, hence ensures a fit between the individual and society. Parsons says that he learned from Freud the enormous importance of both internalization (Freud's own term was introjection) and of "identification" with those responsible for one's upbringing.[5] The development of identification with significant adults is viewed as an essential mechanism in the socialization process.[6] The most important characteristic of identification is the child's acceptance of the adult's value; that is, "what the adult wants for the child, the child comes to want for himself."[7] The mechanism of identification also provides for the acceptance of still further discipline by leading to the development of the needs for

---

action Process (London: Routledge & Kegan Paul, 1956); Talcott Parsons, *Social Systems and the Evaluation of Action Theory* (New York: Free Press, 1977); Ralph L. Beals, Harry Hoijer, and Alan R. Beals, *An Introduction to Anthropology*, 5th ed. (New York: Macmillan, 1977).

[3] Parsons and Bales, *Family*.

[4] Talcott Parsons, *Essays in Sociological Theory: Pure and Applied* (Glencoe, Ill.: Free Press, 1949), p. 203.

[5] Parsons, *Social Systems*, p. 37.

[6] Talcott Parsons and Edward Shils, eds., *Toward a General Theory of Action* (Cambridge, Mass.: Harvard University Press, 1951), p. 17.

[7] Ibid., p. 18.

approval and esteem, which serve as a fundamental motivational basis for the acceptance of "socially necessary disciplines."[8] It is through the phenomenon of identification that the personality acquires, in Parsons' terminology, "a motivationally and cognitively meaningful role set and the social system acquires a member who can make meaningful contribution."[9]

Together, then, the internalization of moral (and other) values and the motivations for approval and esteem (acquired through identification) provide for the development of what Parsons calls the "self-ideal."[10] This self-ideal is made up of Freud's superego, consisting of internalized negative values for the types of behaviors in which one *should not* engage, and Freud's ego-ideal, consisting of acquired positive values for those types of behavior in which one *should* engage.

Once societal expectations are internalized, their violation may give rise to "guilt and shame," which are negative sanctions applied by the individual to himself "as punishment for his failure to live up to his own and others' expectations respectively."[11] Guilt is directed at the individual's own internalized standards, in such a way that he himself is the judge. Shame is directed toward the anticipated reaction of other persons in accordance with what are interpreted to be their standards of approval or esteem.[12] The normal individual always has moral sentiments toward himself and his acts. "He either has a rather high degree of 'self-respect,' " writes Parsons, "or in some sense or other feels 'guilt' or 'shame.' "[13] These moral sentiments are, Parsons argues, inculcated in early childhood and are deeply built into the structure of personality itself. Such sentiments are beyond the range of conscious decision and control, "except perhaps in certain critical situations, and even when consciously repudiated, still continue to exert their influence through repressed guilt feelings and the like."[14]

In his classic article, "The Oversocialized Conception of Man in Modern Society," Dennis Wrong has been highly critical of what

[8] Ibid., p. 150.
[9] Parsons, *Social Systems*, pp. 196–97.
[10] Parsons and Shils, *Toward a General Theory*, p. 311.
[11] Ibid., p. 157.
[12] Ibid., p. 142.
[13] Ibid.
[14] Parsons, *Essays*, p. 207.

he considers to be the misuse of Freud's theory of the superego. He writes:

> What has happened is that internalization has imperceptively been equated with "learning," or even with "habit-formation" in the simplest sense. . . . The whole stress on inner conflict, on the tension between powerful impulses and superego controls the behavioral outcome of which cannot be prejudged, drops out of the picture. And it is this that is central to Freud's view, for in psycho-analytic terms to say that a norm has been internalized or introjected to become part of the superego, is to say no more than that a person will suffer guilt feelings if he fails to live up to it, not that he will in fact live up to it in his behavior.[15]

Wrong goes on to point out that Freud himself recognized that many people fail to acquire superegos, and he quotes Freud in this regard: "Such people habitually permit themselves to do any bad deed that procures them something they want, if only they are sure that no authority will discover it or make them suffer for it; their anxiety relates only to the possibility of detection. Present-day society has to take into account the prevalence of this state of mind."[16] Because of this misrepresentation of Freud's views, Wrong concludes, sociological theory ends up with the oversocialized conception of man emphasized by Parsons and others.

Given Wrong's remarks about the misuse of Freud's theory in contemporary sociology, most especially as it relates to internalization and guilt in Freud's work, it is well worth looking more closely at what Freud actually did say about internalization and about the origins and functions of guilt feelings.

Freud held that guilt has its origins in the Oedipus complex and arises as a sequel to it. The child who has incestuous desires toward the parent of the opposite sex comes to fear retaliation from the same-sex parent. Because of his fear of retaliation, he represses his incestuous desires. His fear is internalized as guilt, and the image of the punishing parent is also internalized, as the superego.[17] The superego, as the internal governing agency, observes and judges

[15] Dennis Wrong. "The Oversocialized Conception of Man in Modern Society," reprinted in Lewis A. Coser and Bernard Rosenberg, eds., Sociological Theory, 4th ed. (New York: Macmillan, 1976), p. 106.

[16] Ibid., p. 107.

[17] Sigmund Freud, The Basic Writings of Sigmund Freud (New York: Modern Library, 1938).

conduct in relation to standards of right and wrong, punishing deviation from them. Most especially in his earlier writings, Freud saw the superego as regulated by guilty fear, oriented toward the figure of authority.

The term "guilt," Freud argued in *Civilization and Its Discontents*, is only appropriate in regard to manifestations of conscience, which are the result of superego development.[18] Since the superego comes into being as a sequel to the Oedipus complex, roughly in the fifth year of childhood, the terms "guilt" and "conscience" do not apply to children under four or five years of age. In discussing the development of the sense of guilt, Freud says the following about the use of the term guilt in regard to early manifestations of "bad conscience":

> This state of mind is called a "bad conscience"; but actually it does not deserve this name, for at this stage the sense of guilt is clearly only a fear of loss of love, "social" anxiety. In small children it can never be anything else, but in many adults, too, it has only changed to the extent that the place of the father or the two parents is taken by the larger human community. . . . A great change takes place only when the authority is internalized through the establishment of a superego. The phenomena of conscience then reaches a higher stage. Actually, it is not until now that we should speak of conscience or a sense of guilt.[19]

Freud ascribed the superego to the introjection of the parents by the child and his identification with them.[20] Operating largely unconsciously, it criticizes and controls dangerous impulses and becomes part of the child's fundamental attitudes. As conscience, the superego forbids destructive tendencies and links with the child's need for restraint and guidance. Guilt is described by Freud as the tension between the strict superego and the subordinate ego; it manifests itself in the need for punishment.[21] All of this, of course, is the result of an inner conflict between powerful instinctual impulses and superego controls. The resolution of such conflict is, for Freud, almost entirely unconscious.

There may, however, also be *conscious* feelings of guilt. Freud

[18] Sigmund Freud, *Civilization and its Discontents* (Garden City: Doubleday, 1958).
[19] Ibid., pp. 78–79.
[20] Sigmund Freud, "Mourning and Melancholia," stand. ed., vol. 14 (London: Hogarth Press, 1917).
[21] Freud, *The Basic Writings*, p. 77. Also see, p. 82.

makes this clear in remarking that "Patients do not easily believe what we tell them about the unconscious sense of guilt. They know well enough by what torments (pangs of conscience) a conscious feeling of guilt, the consciousness of guilt, can express itself, and so they cannot admit that they could harbor entirely analogous feelings in themselves without observing a trace of them."[22] Because people are indeed aware of conscious feelings of guilt (pangs of conscience) and apparently find it difficult to admit to such feelings on the level of the unconscious, Freud suggests "abandoning the term" unconscious feelings of guilt,' " which, he says, is an incorrect one psychologically, and substituting "for it a 'need for punishment,' which describes the state of things observed just as aptly."[23] The important point here is not Freud's suggestion that the term *unconscious feelings of guilt* be abandoned (a suggestion ignored, in any case, by most psychoanalysts) but, rather, his acknowledgment of the existence of conscious feelings of guilt. When he noted (in the citation quoted earlier) that some persons do not acquire superegos, and habitually "permit" themselves to do any bad deed so long as they will not be found out, he is pointing to the absence of *either* conscious or unconscious feelings of guilt. Nevertheless, he gave primary emphasis to the unconscious and the superego, and viewed conscious feelings and processes as often being the product of unconscious forces, about which the individual has little or no awareness.

For Freud, then, a norm may or may not be internalized. If it is, and if the superego is dominant in the conflicts with other impulses, then the individual may live up to the norm. If, on the other hand, the norm is internalized but the individual fails to live up to it, he will experience conscious and/or unconscious guilt feelings. But if a norm has not been internalized, the individual will certainly not follow it or live up to it (at least, not because of guilt feelings). And without the violation of an internalized norm, there is no occasion for feelings of guilt at all. Just as Wrong argues, then, Parsons and other sociologists have misused and misrepresented Freud's views concerning the development of the superego, the internalization of norms, and feelings of guilt.

Despite his peculiar understanding of some of Freud's ideas, Parsons can be classified with Freud as being committed to an

[22] Sigmund Freud, *Collected Papers*, ed. Ernest Jones (New York: Basic Books, 1959), p. 263.
[23] Ibid.

identification-internalization approach to children's development. Freud proposes the notion (taken over by Parsons) that children learn through identification with their parents, and claims that the effects of the first identification in earliest childhood will be general and lasting. It is this first identification, he says, that lies behind the origin of the ego-ideal.[24] The ego-ideal, the ideal and omnipotent part of the self, was a concept that Freud formulated before he fully developed his ideas on the superego. As noted earlier, Parsons has incorporated the ego-ideal into his own scheme, seeing it as consisting of acquired positive values for those types of behavior in which one should engage. Both Freud and Parsons see identification as providing the positively reinforcing capacity of being like the parents.

Although they differ about both the actual extent to which people do internalize societal values and the influence of such internalization on people's actions, Freud and Parsons are agreed that internalization is the essential step in moral development. They assume that it is through internalization that the dominant moral values of the society will be accepted by the individual as his own and will guide his actions.[25] Deviation from the internalized values or standards, they agree, frequently results in internal punishment—particularly in the form of guilt feelings.

Obviously much more could be said about the identification-internalization approach followed by Freud and Parsons and by many other social scientists. But I think that I have said enough to lay the groundwork for a critical examination of this general approach, and to allow for comparison with Kohlberg's theory of cognitive development.

To begin with, neither Freud nor Parsons is particularly concerned with autonomous, rational thought processes in the acquisition of moral values. For Freud, moral thinking is usually the product of unconscious forces about which the individual ordinarily has no awareness. Once the authority of the parents is internalized through the establishment of the superego, dangerous impulses and destructive tendencies are (ideally) forbidden or punished. In Freud's own words: "The chronological sequence would thus be as follows: first, instinct-renunciation due to dread of

[24] Sigmund Freud, "The Ego and the Id," stand. ed., vol. 19 (London: Hogarth Press, 1923), p. 31.

[25] For an interesting elaboration of the idea of internalization, see M. L. Hoffman, "Moral Development," in P. H. Mussen, ed., *Carmichael's Manual of Child Development* (New York: Wiley, 1970).

aggression by external authority—this is, of course, tantamount to the dread loss of love, for love is a protection against these punitive aggressions. Then follows the erection of an internal authority, and instinctual renunciation due to dread of it. . . ."[26] Since the superego is seen as primarily noncognitive and nonrational, moral values are internalized without any rational examination or judgment on the part of the individual. That is, there is no cognitive component involved in the internalization of such values. Whatever the values are that the child internalizes, they will continue to direct his or her actions in adult life.

Like Freud, Parsons gives very little attention to the place of cognitive thinking and rational thought processes in moral development. He argues that the primary structure of human personality is organized about the particular role structure of the society and its various subsystems.[27] Through identification, the child accepts the adult's values, so that what the adult wants for the child, the child comes to want for himself. The child internalizes the dominant value-orientations of his society and these become part of the superego structure of his personality.[28] The internalization of a superego element means, says Parsons, "motivation to accept the priority of collective over personal interests. . . ."[29] The emphasis, then, is on the child's internalizing the moral values and standards necessary for filling his appropriate niche as a socialized role-performer and meeting the collective interests of society. These moral values will continue to provide guidance and direction in the later years.

Parsons and Freud share the view that an individual's moral values and beliefs are primarily the result of the experiences of early childhood. This means that the particular moral values or standards that someone endorses and upholds are, by and large, not the result of his or her own inquiries, choices, or rational decisions. They are, rather, the outcome of unconscious processes, identification with one's parents and acceptance of their moral values, and of having learned the values appropriate to satisfying the needs and interests of the social system as a whole.

So far as the phenomenon of identification is concerned, however, there has been little research into its influence. When the motivational disposition of identification has been studied, it has

<hr>

[26] Freud, *Civilization and Its Discontents*, p. 82.

[27] Parsons, *Social Systems*, p. 82.

[28] Ibid., p. 22.

[29] Ibid., p. 150.

not been measured directly. Instead, it has been inferred on the basis of the similarity of values between parent and child. Summarizing the relative paucity of significant relationships, Hoffman concludes that identification is not an all-pervasive process in moral development.[30] Similarly, there is little consistent empirical evidence in support of internalization as the most essential step in moral development. This is not to deny that children do adopt their parents' values to some extent in most societies; it is only to say that there is limited support for the claim that this occurs through identification and internalization in early childhood. So far as the importance of a child's early years are concerned, Escalona states that the net result of a great many studies is that "no significant relationships have been demonstrated between parental attitudes toward a child during the first three or four years of life and the child's later characteristics."[31]

Given the general lack of persuasive evidence pertaining to the alleged influence of identification and internalization in the child's early years on the acquisition of moral values, those following the identification-internalization approach can be criticized for neglecting the place of conscious, rational thinking in the child's acquisition and acceptance of moral values and beliefs. This, then, is my first criticism of this approach to children's moral development.

My second criticism is related; it concerns the highly relativistic implications of the theories of Freud and Parsons. The assumption that people accept and uphold particular moral values simply as the result of unconscious processes or of early childhood socialization leads to the conclusion that people's moral values are completely relative to their social upbringing. The moral relativity argument holds that it is meaningless to say that the moral values or standards of one group or society are better (or worse) than those of another group or society. It also, of course, excuses people from any individual responsibility for the values they hold and act upon.

---

[30] M. L. Hoffman, "Identification and Conscience Development," *Child Development* 42 (1971): 1071–82.

[31] Sibylle Escalona, *The Roots of Individuality: Normal Patterns of Development in Infancy* (Chicago: Aldine, 1968), p. 13. A similar conclusion is reached by Arlene Skolnick, *The Intimate Environment, Exploring Marriage and the Family* (Boston: Little Brown, 1973), pp. 378–79. And Anna Freud, "Child Observation and Prediction of Development—A Memorial Lecture in Honor of Ernst Kris," *The Psychoanalytic Study of the Child*, vol. 13 (New York: International Universities Press, 1958), p. 98, states that "the environmental happenings in a child's life will always remain unpredictable since they are not governed by any known law. . . ."

My third, and last, criticism of the identification-internalization approach concerns its general standpoint regarding emotion as it relates to the violation of moral standards. Both Freud and Parsons give considerable attention to the tyranny of moral values and the expression of "negative" sanctions, especially guilt feelings, when the values are violated or transgressed. These negative sanctions are, for the most part, seen as operating unconsciously. Freud and Parsons emphasize that the content of the superego is mostly unconscious, although they do also acknowledge the existence of negative sanctions at the conscious level; Freud speaks of feelings of guilt, and Parsons mentions guilt and shame. But neither really gives serious consideration to the moral "appropriateness" or "inappropriateness" of certain emotional feelings. Had they given more attention to a cognitive component in internalization, they might have considered the possibility that someone who is consciously aware that he has violated a moral norm, which he has rationally and knowingly come to accept as correct, *ought* to experience guilt feelings. Such feelings would be the appropriate reaction to such a violation. Under such conditions, it would be a mistake to think of such feelings as entirely negative or destructive. The point here is that Freud and Parsons deal with guilt entirely as a reaction to whatever social norms have been internalized. They, therefore, separate guilt completely, from *moral considerations*.

The same line of reasoning applies with regard to positive emotions; there may be positive emotions that accompany or result from adherence to those standards that someone has knowingly and rationally accepted. Again, such emotions may be entirely appropriate. My general point, is, I think, clear; Freud and Parsons, in common with most social scientists, ignore questions about what emotions people ought or ought not to feel in certain circumstances.[32]

There are, then, three important weaknesses in the identification-internalization approach adhered to by Freud and Parsons and taken over by many sociologists: (1) it neglects the place of conscious, rational reasoning (and cognition more generally) in the acquisition and acceptance of moral values; (2) it constitutes an entirely "relativistic" view of moral values and human actors; and

---

[32] The need for giving more attention to these kinds of questions is emphasized by Bernard Williams, *Problems of the Self* (Cambridge: Cambridge University Press, 1973), pp. 207–09. I consider such questions at length in Chapter 5.

(3) it ignores questions about the moral appropriateness or inappropriateness of certain emotions that may accompany or result from adherence to or violation of moral values and principles.

II

Kohlberg's Cognitive Developmental Approach

I turn now to a consideration of the theory of moral development set forward by Lawrence Kohlberg, a theory that builds on the work of Piaget in the field of cognitive development. Because Kohlberg's theory is rooted in Piaget's work, it is useful to briefly examine some of Piaget's ideas before turning to an exploration of Kohlberg's theory.

Piaget's research focused mainly on the development of human intelligence in children. He proposed a developmental conception of intelligence, with cognitive development proceeding through a series of chronological stages. Each stage represents a particular organization in the forms of reasoning that children use in solving problems. Thinking at each stage is characterized by certain specified principles. In order for a child to move from one stage to another, a reorganization of thinking has to take place so that new principles take the place of the old ones. The stages are seen as hierarchical, with each succeeding stage representing a more advanced organization of thinking. According to Piaget, the progression through stages is invariant in sequence; each person's thinking, that is, has to proceed through the various stages in exactly the same order.[33]

Although his research was devoted primarily to the study of how intelligence develops throughout childhood, Piaget also gave specific attention to moral development in children. Based on his research with young children, he suggested that children move from a *heteronomous* morality, characterized by evaluating right and wrong on the basis of the consequences of an action (e.g., physical punishment), to *autonomous* morality, in which the person's intentions determine the evaluation of the act. In the heteronomous stage, moral realism prevails; the child regards rules as fixed in nature, absolute, and immutable. In the autonomous stage, how-

---

[33] Jean Piaget, *The Origin of Intelligence in Children* (New York: International Universities Press, 1952; Jean Piaget, *The Moral Judgment of the Child* (New York: Free Press, 1965), originally published in 1932.

ever, rules come to be viewed as relative—as man-made agreements, which are arrived at to ensure that everyone will act in similar ways in similar situations.[34] The move from the first to the second stage is not, however, a purely cognitive process. It is rather the result of children working out new sets of social relationships with other persons. As they come to interact more with others, especially their peers, their understanding of rules changes. Rules come to be respected not because they are immutable but because there is a feeling of involvement with others, and it is recognized that it is only fair for everyone to respect (i.e., abide by) the rules. Piaget's research on the moral development of children extended beyond the rules of games to include their understanding of responsibility, law, and justice. But his work was never concerned with children beyond the age of twelve. Nor did he ever attempt to work out the stages of moral development in any detail.

Kohlberg has considerably expanded and modified the ideas of Piaget. For him, the morality of a particular action or point of view lies not so much in the action or point of view itself but, rather, in the reasoning involved. Moral reasoning, the way in which someone explains *why* he is acting as he is or the manner in which he thinks about right and wrong, defines the level of a person's moral development in Kohlberg's approach. He makes an important distinction between the content of a person's thinking and the form or structure of thought. The *content* refers to the rules, values, or standards that someone advocates; whether he thinks an action is right or wrong, honest or dishonest, is a matter of content. But, Kohlberg argues, the content of someone's responses is not a reliable means for concluding anything about his "real" thinking. It is only by focusing on the *form* or structure of a person's reasoning, by considering why he holds a particular value or standard or how he justifies his judgment that an act is right or wrong, that it is possible to get at the *cognitive structure* of his thinking.[35] What is crucial in Kohlberg's view, then, is the underlying structure that guides moral thinking.

Kohlberg assumes, in common with Piaget, that human thinking is in accord with certain rules of logical operation, and that some of these rules are epistemologically superior to others. Development consists of the replacement of one logical means of organizing information with a better one. Moral judgment is, of course, a

---

[34] Piaget, *Moral Judgment*.

[35] Lawrence Kohlberg, "Stage and Sequence: The Cognitive-Developmental Approach to Socialization," in David A. Goslin, ed., *Handbook of Socialization: Theory and Research* (Chicago: Rand McNally, 1969).

cognitive process; it allows us to reason about and reflect upon our moral values. But moral development is predicated on cognitive development. There must be sufficient development in cognitive structures—so that the child proceeds beyond egocentristic thinking, for example—to create the preconditions for development in moral structure. Cognitive development is a necessary, although not a sufficient, condition for moral change. This will be made clear in the following discussion.

According to Kohlberg, there are six stages involved in the development of moral reasoning from middle childhood to adulthood.[36] He derives these stages through the evaluation of moral judgments made by individuals to hypothetical situations of conflict. Following Piaget's example, he uses a modified clinical method of interviewing subjects. Various stories describing moral dilemmas are used, all involving a character who finds himself in difficult circumstances. Each story is read to the subject, and several standardized questions are posed. The subject is asked how the character *should* resolve the problem, and *why* that would be the right way to act under the circumstances.[37] As noted earlier, it is the *reasons* given to justify the decision, and not the decision itself, that determine the level or stage of moral reasoning. The most frequently cited of the moral dilemmas used by Kohlberg is the following:

> In Europe, a woman was near death from a very bad disease, a special kind of cancer. There was one drug that the doctors thought might save her. It was a form of radium for which a

[36] Ibid.; Lawrence Kohlberg, "Moral and Religious Education and the Public Schools: A Developmental View," in T. Sizer, ed., *Religion and Public Education* (Boston: Houghton Mifflin, 1967). Kohlberg's six stages have several important characteristics: (1) Stages imply qualitative differences in modes of thinking. Two individuals at different stages may share a similar value, but there will be qualitative differences in their thinking about that value. They may both agree that we should place a positive value on saving a friend from drowning, if we can. But one may hold that we should do so because he is our friend, while the other may justify it in terms of our obligation to help "anyone" in similar circumstances. (2) Each stage forms a structural whole; a change from one stage to another implies a restructuring in how someone thinks about a greater number of moral issues. (3) Stages are invariant in sequence; a child must master cognitive operations at earlier steps in order to be able to move on to more complex operations characterizing the later stages. (4) Stages are hierarchical integrations. As a person's thinking develops from one stage to the next, the structures found at lower stages are integrated into the next stage. With further development, that is, individuals continue to be able to utilize their earlier acquired learning.

[37] Kohlberg, "Stage and Sequence." The dilemmas are not usually used for children younger than nine years of age.

druggist was charging ten times what the drug cost him to make. The sick woman's husband, Heinz, went to everyone he knew to borrow the money, but he could only get together about half of what it cost. He told the druggist that his wife was dying, and asked him to sell it cheaper or let him pay later. But the druggist said, "No, I discovered the drug and I'm going to make money from it." So Heinz got desperate and broke into the man's store to steal the drug for his wife. Should the husband have done this? Why?[38]

On the basis of individuals' reasoning concerning this conflict situation and others, Kohlberg concludes that there are three distinct levels of development, each of which is divided into two stages. The meaning of the three levels is described by Kohlberg in this way:

> One way of understanding the three levels is to think of them as three different types of relationships between the *self* and *society's rules and expectations*. From this point of view, Level I is a *preconventional* person, for whom rules and social expectations are something external to the self; Level II is a *conventional* person, in whom the self is identified with or has internalized the rules and expectations of others, especially those of authorities; and Level III is a *postconventional* person, who has differentiated his self from the rules and expectations of others and defines his values in terms of self-chosen principles.[39]

Kohlberg suggests that a different socio-moral perspective underlies each level of moral reasoning: a "concrete individual" perspective at Level I, a "member-of-society" perspective at Level II, and a "prior-to-society" perspective at Level III.[40] At Level I, someone is concerned with the concrete consequences for individuals in deciding one way or another, and not with what "society" defines as the right way to behave in a given situation. With regard to the Heinz dilemma, for example, a person adopting this perspective would ask the following kinds of questions. Can Heinz

[38] Lawrence Kohlberg, "Justice as Reversibility." In Peter Laslett and James Fishkin, eds., *Philosophy, Politics and Society*, fifth series (London: Basil Blackwell, 1979), p. 259.

[39] Lawrence Kohlberg, "Moral Stages and Moralization: The Cognitive-Developmental Approach," in T. Lickona, ed., *Moral Development and Behavior* (New York: Holt, 1976), p. 33.

[40] Ibid., p. 36.

live without his wife? Will he be punished for stealing the drug? At Level II, there is a shared perspective that focuses on the individual's relationships to the society and its moral norms. Here, someone responding to the Heinz dilemma might consider whether society can survive if it allows its members to break the law in such situations. "The conventional individual," Kohlberg points out, "subordinates the need of the single individual to the viewpoint and needs of the group or the shared relationship."[41] At Level III, moral problems are approached in terms of a concern with principles. The individual is able to see beyond the given norms and laws of his own society, and considers the principles upon which a good or just society ought to be based. His commitment to moral principles will take precedence over his accepting society's perspective. With regard to the Heinz dilemma, someone at this level of moral development might consider whether this may be an instance where breaking the law is morally justified by the need to save the life of an innocent person.

These three broad levels define the scope of moral development as described by Kohlberg. Level I most often characterizes the moral reasoning of children, although many adolescents and some adults persist in this reasoning. Level II usually arises during preadolescence, develops further during the adolescent years, and remains dominant in the thinking of most adults. Level III is the rarest of the three levels of moral development. It arises, if at all, during late adolescence or early adulthood, and seems to characterize the moral reasoning of only a tiny minority of adults.

As I noted earlier, each of these three stages of moral development is divided into two stages. These are set out in Table 3.1. It is not my intention to discuss these six stages in detail, but I do want to make some brief remarks about each of them. Stage 1 thinking is dominant in children roughly between the ages of four and ten, and is characterized by an egocentric point of view. It resembles what Piaget called the heteronomous stage of morality. In stage 2, there is a development in the child's cognitive and role-thinking abilities, so that he begins to acquire the capacity to look at problems and social relationships from a more distanced, logical perspective. This stage begins to develop in the child when he or she is seven or eight years of age, and it remains the dominant stage througout the grade school years. In stage 3, which develops during preadolescence, the child acquires the ability to step outside

---

[41] Ibid.

Table 3.1
Kohlberg's Classification of Levels and Stages of Moral Development

I *Preconventional level*	
Obedience and punishment orientation	Egocentric deference to superior power or prestige, or a trouble-avoiding set, objective responsibility.
Instrumental hedonism	Right action is that instrumentally satisfying the self's needs and occasionally those of others. Naive egalitarianism and orientation to exchange and reciprocity.
II *Conventional level*	
Good-boy orientation	Orientation to approval and to pleasing and helping others. Conformity to stereotyped images of majority or natural role behavior, and judgments by intentions.
Law-and-order orientation	Orientation toward authority, fixed rules, and the maintenance of the social order. Right behavior consists of doing one's duty, showing respect for authority, and maintaining the given social order for its own sake.
III *Postconventional level*	
Contractual-legalistic orientation	Right action is defined in terms of individual rights and/or standards that have been initially examined and agreed upon by the whole society. Concern with establishing and maintaining individual rights, equality, and liberty. Distinctions are made between values having universal, prescriptive applicability and values specific to a given society.
Universal-ethical principle orientation	Right is defined by the decision of conscience in accord with self-chosen ethical principles appealing to logical comprehensiveness, universality, and consistency. These principles are abstract; they are not concrete moral rules. These are universal principles of justice, of the reciprocity and equality of human rights, and of respect for the dignity of human beings as individual persons.

SOURCE: Elliot Turiel, "Conflict and Transition in Adolescent Moral Development," *Child Development* 45 (1974): 14–29.

the two-person relationship and look at it from the perspective of "significant others" (parents, peers, the group). He becomes able to conceive how they will react to his actions or involvements with other individuals. This is the dominant stage during adolescence, and together with stage 4 remains the major stage for most adults in our society. In stage 4, individuals acquire the ability to take the shared point of view of the "generalized other." It is this ability to take the perspective of the whole social system, in contrast to the perspective of those who are closest or most significant to oneself, that characterizes moral development in this stage. The recognition that people are interdependent and that society is bound together by certain moral and social norms, provides a different basis for moral reasoning than was the case in earlier stages.

In stage 5 and 6, which make up the postconventional level, principled moral reasoning is dominant. These are not only the rarest stages for people to reach, but they are also the stages for which there is available the least empirical data. Stage 5 reasoning has as its mode, those agreements or social contracts to which people freely obligate themselves, while stage 6 reasoning involves a consideration of what any rational being acting in the role of moral agent should or should not do.[42]

Kohlberg's theory of stages implies that people's moral reasoning does not develop by internalization of the moral standards of the societies in which they live. Although individuals do learn different things in different societies, so that the *content* of someone's moral beliefs depends on the society in which he lives, Kohlberg reports that the *form* or structure of moral reasoning is culturally universal. Or, more precisely, he claims that there is a single sequence of stages of moral development that is the same for all societies.[43] This is not to say that every stage will be present in every society. But they will always develop in a given sequence (from stage 1 to 2, etc.), although the sequence may end at stage 3 or stage 4 in some societies. As far as internalization is concerned, Kohlberg believes that the existence of a universal unvariant sequence of stages of moral reasoning serves as evidence against the idea of the internalization of the particular moral values or standards of

---

[42] Kohlberg, "Justice as Reversibility." Also see Richard H. Hersh, Diana Pritchard Paolitto, and Joseph Reimer, *Promoting Moral Growth: From Piaget to Kohlberg* (New York: Longman, 1979).

[43] Lawrence Kohlberg, "Stages of Moral Development as a Basis for Moral Education." In C. M. Beck, B. S. Crittenden, and E. V. Sullivan, eds., *Moral Education* (New York: Newman Press, 1971).

one's own society. I will return to this point about internalization later.

Kohlberg's theory of the development of moral steps is, like Piaget's, an interactive theory of development. In the course of development, individuals come to interact with more and more other people at the various stages. It is the wide variety of such experiences and the nature of the interactions that influence the extent to which there are structural changes and movement toward higher stages of moral reasoning. The significance of parents or other child-rearers, peers, schooling, and other sources of human contact, then, is that they shape the child's opportunities for social interaction and various experiences. In common with Piaget, Kohlberg assumes that "equilibrium" is the specific mechanism by which changes in cognitive structure take place. Underlying the notion of equilibrium are Piaget's two complementary processes of assimilation and accommodation. "Assimilation" refers to the way an individual deals with an environmental stimulus (the way he or she perceives and interprets a new experience) in terms of existing cognitive organization; while "accommodation" refers to changes or modification in cognitive organization when it cannot— in its existing form—satisfactorily account for new experience. Turiel describes these changes in cognitive structure as follows:

> According to Piaget, movement from one cognitive structure to the next occurs when the system is in a state of disequilibrium. When a child who is in a state of disequilibrium is presented with operations that are developmentally close enough for him to consider, his assimilatory and accomodatory functions may act in complementary fashion to establish greater equilibrium. The child deals with the environmental event in accordance with the structure available to him. Change may occur when the inability to completely assimilate events to the existing structure leads to disequilibrium that motivates attempts to achieve new equilibrium. This more highly equilibrated stage allows better assimilation to the new experience.[44]

Thus, in Kohlberg's (and Piaget's) interactionist model of moral development, exposure to more adequate patterns of moral reasoning may result in cognitive disequilibrium for the individual.

[44] Elliot Turiel, "Developmental Processes in the Child's Moral Thinking," in P. Mussen, E. J. Langer, and M. Covington, eds., *Trends and Issues in Developmental Psychology* (New York: Holt, 1969), p. 126.

In trying to assimilate new information, he may have to alter his present structure of thinking to accommodate to greater complexity. Then the building of a new structure begins, resulting in development to the next higher stage of moral reasoning.

Moral development depends heavily, then, on opportunities for social interactions and on those experiences that will activate disequilibrium. Kohlberg specifies three aspects of "experience" that are influential for the development of moral reasoning.[45] The most important of these is apparently the opportunity for role-taking. Based in part on the ideas of George Herbert Mead and symbolic-interactionism, Kohlberg argues that higher stages of moral development are characterized by an increasing ability to engage in reciprocal role-taking. That is, there is a growth in the capacity to consider an action from an increasingly wide perspective. At the most advanced stage of development (stage 6), which involves a concern with justice and the sacredness of human life, moral reasoning is based on what Kohlberg terms "ideal role-taking."[46] This is the ability to reason from the perspective of all humanity in evaluating right and wrong.

A second sort of experience that is important in the development of moral reasoning is the moral atmosphere of the group or society in which the child lives. Kohlberg means by "moral atmosphere" the "justice structure" of the environment, which he quotes Rawls as defining as "the way in which social institutions distribute fundamental rights and duties and determine the division of advantages from social cooperation."[47] Thus, the more just the society, the more likely it is for individuals to reach a higher stage of moral development.

The third aspect of experiences mentioned by Kohlberg as contributing to moral reasoning is the existence of conditions that create cognitive-moral conflict. Exposure to different points of view and modes of reasoning may arouse internal contradictions, which are resolved by further moral development. This outcome is likely to occur, however, only if the conflict is moderate and is with significant others. Modes of reasoning completely at variance with

[45] Kohlberg, "Moral Stages and Moralization."

[46] Lawrence Kohlberg, "From Is to Ought: How to Commit the Naturalistic Fallacy and Get Away With It in the Study of Moral Development," in T. Mischel, ed., *Cognitive Development and Epistemology* (New York: Academic Press, 1971), pp. 151–235; Kohlberg, "Justice as Reversibility."

[47] John Rawls, *A Theory of Justice* (Cambridge, Mass.: Harvard University Press, 1971), p. 7.

one's own, which are followed by people whom one cares nothing about, are not apt to constitute the source of cognitive-moral conflict associated with moral development.

I turn now to a consideration of some of the more problematic aspects of Kohlberg's theory. To begin with, he seems to assume that individuals progressively evolve higher stages of moral reasoning simply through varied experiences; these higher stages apparently represent an unfolding of innate potential. In any case, Kohlberg believes that moral development takes place without an explicit inculcation of moral values and standards. That is, he argues that the universal moral values are not *directly taught* to children.[48] Rather, the basic values are embodied in common institutions found in every society: the family, the legal system, and the economy, among others. Although children are exposed to these institutions, the values associated with them are experienced in the home and peer group before the time that children actually participate in the institutions. Notions of fair exchange, for example, arise out of the child's experience of interacting with members of the family and with his peers. Because the function of these value concepts (like "fairness") is to regulate social behavior and because children develop moral concepts by having to get along with other people, the development of value concepts is a universally common experience. Thus, children develop moral values; these basic values do not have to be taught to them.

Kohlberg has two reasons for claiming that teaching morality does not work. One is that teaching involves a concern with "content," whereas it is changes in "structure" that constitute moral development. The second is that children can learn morality only from their own personal experience. Kohlberg argues that the child can develop understanding only by himself grasping the rule or principle that is to be understood—and this, it is claimed, cannot be taught to him. All of this seems to suggest a rather passive involvement by parents in the socialization process, at least with regard to the moral development of children. Kohlberg does acknowledge that parents can influence the extent to which there are opportunities for the child to have the "experiences" necessary for moral development, but he generally minimizes the extent to which parents more directly influence their children's morality. As noted earlier, he mentions three aspects of experience that are likely to affect development in moral reasoning: the opportunity for role-

<hr>

[48] Lawrence Kohlberg, "Stage and Sequence," pp. 397–401.

taking, the moral atmosphere of the group, and cognitive-moral conflict. I want now to examine these three aspects from the perspective of parents' influence on their children's moral development.

Role-taking is, of course, the opposite of egocentrism; it is the capacity to take the position of another person and to see and understand events or situations from his or her perspective. Kohlberg reports that the ability to engage in "ideal" role-taking is a characteristic of those at the highest stage of moral reasoning. It certainly makes sense to think that an ability to consider what is right and wrong from an increasingly wider perspective should be associated with moral maturity. Contrary to what Kohlberg seems to assume, however, the cognitive prerequisites of role-taking are probably already available in infants and young children. Even the reciprocal exchanges of smiles and gestures between infants and their parents may serve as preparation for eventual role-taking abilities on the part of the child.

In any case, it would appear likely that role-taking abilities might develop faster in circumstances where infants and children are encouraged to interact frequently with other persons in their social environment. If role-taking is a necessary skill for mature moral reasoning, then it would seem that parents and other child-rearers could do much to encourage this. Yet Kohlberg insists that children learn from their own experience and cannot be taught moral precepts. In response to studies finding that children who are encouraged to participate in discussions about moral issues are more likely to have reached a higher stage of development than those who are not encouraged in this manner, Kohlberg argues that this shows that providing role-taking opportunities leads to more advanced moral reasoning.[49] But one would expect that the very fact of parental encouragement of such participation would itself reinforce the tendency of the child to think about moral issues. And it seems highly unlikely that the parents' own views on these issues would have no influence on their children's moral thinking. It may be, as Kohlberg claims, that the actual changes in the child's moral reasoning do result from his own experience. Nevertheless, parents may be able to structure the environment so that children will not only have increased opportunities for role-taking and other interactive experiences but will also be able to optimally profit from them. The point here is that there may be more *direct* influence

[49] Ibid.

required (and, in fact, exerted) by adults than is acknowledged by Kohlberg.

With regard to the second condition for the development of moral reasoning, the moral atmosphere of the group,[50] it certainly seems reasonable that the moral atmosphere (i.e., the way rights and duties are distributed) of the group or society—including the family, school, and peer group—will influence the development of a child's moral reasoning. In the family situation, especially, it is likely that the way in which moral rights and duties are distributed among father, mother, and children may have a considerable influence on how someone thinks about moral issues. When the relationships among family members are just and fair, this itself may constitute an important ingredient in a child's moral development.

The third condition mentioned by Kohlberg as affecting moral reasoning, cognitive-moral conflict, has been dealt with by several investigators. Exposure to a higher level of reasoning may affect moral development, it is argued, because it stimulates disequilibrium. "Presumably, a sense of contradiction and discrepancy at one's own stage is necessary," Kohlberg writes, "for reorganization at the next stage."[51] Although the evidence for this is rather weak,[52] it seems safe to conclude that at least a moderate degree of conflict is necessary for moral development to occur. But I would think that the socialization of children inevitably involves exposure to moral reasoning more advanced than their own. And I suspect that these higher levels of reasoning would have most influence on the child's development when the parents' actions are consistent with the reasoning they employ. Unless the parents' behavior appears to follow from their own moral reasoning, it is unlikely that the child will experience a conflict that may lead to his or her further moral development.

[50] Kohlberg, "Moral Stages and Moralization."

[51] Kohlberg, "Stage and Sequence," p. 403.

[52] See, for example, J. Aronfreed, "Moral Development from the Standpoint of a General Psychological Theory," in Lickona, *Moral Development and Behavior*; P. Cowan, J. Langer, J. Heavenrich, and M. Nathanson, "Social Learning and Piaget's Cognitive Theory of Moral Development," *Journal of Personality and Social Psychology* 11 (1969): 261–74; J. Garbarino and U. Bronfenbrenner, "The Socialization of Moral Judgment and Behavior in Cross-Cultural Perspective," in Lickona, *Moral Development and Behavior*; G. R. Rotham, "The Influence of Moral Reasoning on Behavioral Choices," *Child Development* 47 (1976): 399–406; and Elliot Turiel, "An Experimental Test of the Sequentiality of Developmental Stages in the Child's Moral Judgments," *Journal of Personality and Social Psychology* 3 (1966): 611–18.

In my view, then, the influence of parents on their children's moral development may be more important than is acknowledged by Kohlberg. Be that as it may, it is obvious that most parents and other child-rearers *do* devote a good deal of attention to acquainting their children with the moral values that they themselves espouse. In fact, many parents consider this a crucial aspect in the socialization of their children. Because almost all children are initially socialized within the specific social system of the family, and because this will, at the very least, lay the groundwork for the child's eventual moral development, it is worth giving some further attention here to the socialization process itself.

Whatever the effects may be on their moral development in later years, it seems undeniable that young children do identify with their parents. And given their dependency upon them, children may be expected to try to gain their approval and avoid their disapproval. In the early years, the norms and values of the parents are those to which the children largely adhere. Some of these will contain a moral element, and the child may be rewarded for conforming and perhaps punished for deviating from them. He or she may be told, "Don't play with Jewish kids; they're no good," or, "Wash your hands; you're as black as a nigger," or, "Remember this; all people are equal," or he may overhear his parents talking about it being a world where everyone has to "look out for number one." The child may or may not internalize the moral values and norms associated with the above, but he or she is always brought up in the midst of moral norms and values. In short, there is an atmosphere of moral thinking in every family. It seems totally unlikely that such an atmosphere will not constitute an important influence on a child's moral development.

Whether or not the child comes to internalize these moral values and norms and make them his own (as Parsons claims is the case), he or she will certainly become aware of which particular values the parents espouse, and also which ones they comply with in their own behavior. And, as I noted earlier, the child will gain approval or disapproval from his parents for conformity or nonconformity to those values. This means that there are certain moral values that the child accepts (in varying degrees of intensity) that are carried with him or her into the world outside the family. The moral values encountered there—in the peer group, school, church, neighborhood, and elsewhere—may be the same or different from those dominant in the child's home. But, just as in the family situation, the child will learn (and not usually from being explicitly taught)

145

about right and wrong, good and bad, the superiority or inferiority of certain classes or groups, and the like. Again, as in the home, approval or disapproval will accompany the upholding or violation of these moral values and norms.

Throughout his or her later life, the individual will carry traces of these earlier experiences in which moral elements were involved. Many of us are able to recount such early influences, even though we may feel certain that our present thinking about moral issues is unaffected by them. Perhaps we learned (or were taught) that blacks are inferior and women inherently weak and emotional, or that our first loyalty is to our family, that only fools help strangers, and that we must always support our own country—right or wrong. Or maybe we learned that honesty is the best policy, that we should love our neighbor as ourself, or that all people are equal in the eye of God. As I said, we are all able to recall the existence of such moral "education" from our childhood. As I also indicated above, we may now claim that our present moral thinking and reasoning is generally unaffected by such moral precepts; we've managed to go beyond them, to overcome them, or to better understand them. In short, those earlier moral values may no longer play a part in our moral lives.

But, of course, it is very implausible to think that the atmosphere of moral thinking in our parents' home and in our childhood associations will have no influence at all on our present moral thinking and reasoning. Even if one accepts (as I, for the most part, do) the essential correctness of the scheme of moral development formulated by Kohlberg, there must be room in such a scheme for the lasting influence (both positive and negative) of early socialization experiences. By taking such influences into consideration, we may be better able to understand and make sense of the evidence regarding the relationship between people's level of moral development and their actions.

Kohlberg's theory is concerned specifically with moral reasoning, and not with moral actions as such. Still, it is important to determine the extent to which people do *act* on their moral judgments or principles. Kohlberg himself cites studies that show that people's moral actions are much more influenced by situational factors than by the values they espouse. Many persons who say that cheating is wrong, for example, will nevertheless cheat if they perceive a low risk of detection. Perceived risk of getting caught seems to influence their actions more than the values they hold about cheating.[53] But, needless to say, for someone to "say" that cheating is wrong (consistent with the general societal norms against cheating) says nothing about his or her stage of moral reasoning.

A study that does examine the relationship between the stage of moral development and resistance to cheating was conducted by Richard Krebs, a student of Kohlberg's.[54] He reports the following percentages of students who *resisted* cheating at each stage: stage 1: 19%; stage 2: 36%; stage 3: 22%; and stage 4: 45%. These findings do lend some support to what would be predicted from Kohlberg's theory; students at stage 4 were less likely to cheat than those at the lower stages. In line with his theory, it is to be expected that students whose moral reasoning is at a higher stage of development will be less likely to be influenced by situational factors (like risk of detection) and more likely to act consistently on their values. Nonetheless, it needs to be emphasized that the majority (55%) of those at stage 4 were unable to resist cheating (i.e., did indeed cheat).

In another study of cheating, Kohlberg reports that more than 40% of the college students at the conventional level (stages 3 and 4) cheated, compared to only 11% of those at the postconventional level (stages 5 and 6).[55] These findings represent somewhat more convincing evidence of the relationship between moral development and moral action. What is most striking, however, is the general paucity of studies directed at the presumed influence of moral reasoning on actual behavior. Although the development of moral thought is certainly of interest in its own right, up to now Kohlberg and his students have provided very little solid evidence concerning the extent to which people's actions correlate with their moral reasoning. This is a significant limitation on the usefulness or applicability of his theory as it concerns actual behavior.

Moreover, Kohlberg himself reports finding few individuals who have developed a stage 6 conception of morality. Similarly, Staub reports on two studies conducted with a total of more than 200 persons in which not a single person demonstrated stage 6 rea-

[53] Kohlberg, "Stage and Sequence." For evidence of the general absence of a relationship between what people say and what they do, see Derek L. Phillips, *Knowledge from What?* (Chicago: Rand McNally, 1971).

[54] Richard Krebs and Lawrence Kohlberg, "Moral Judgment and Ego Controls as Determinants of Resistance to Cheating." (Manuscript, Harvard University, 1973). Cited in Hersh et al., *Promoting Moral Growth*, p. 95.

[55] Cited in ibid., p. 96.

soning.[56] Thus, even if we assume that people at the highest stage of moral development will generally act in a manner quite consistent with their advanced moral reasoning, there are so few such persons as to lead to pessimism concerning the possibility of encouraging the development of moral thinking that will result in principled actions. So, it may be useful to look more closely at some of the above findings in order to better understand why moral actions are not more strongly correlated with the stages of moral reasoning.

I noted above that the majority of children at every stage in the Krebs study were unable to resist cheating. But now I want to focus on the 19% of stage 1 children who *did not* cheat and the 55% at stage 4 who *did* cheat. Since children at stage 1 are completely egocentric, and concerned only with themselves, why is it that almost one-fifth of them did not engage in cheating? Certainly one possible answer is that they had (as Freud and Parsons would suggest) "internalized" the norm that cheating was wrong (and leads to self-punishment). Because they are not yet capable of taking the perspective of the generalized other or of engaging in principled thinking, it may be that it is indeed superego control that is responsible for their honesty.

And how might we explain the 55% of stage 4 children who did cheat? At this stage, moral reasoning is characterized by the child's ability to take the perspective of the social system in which he participates—in this case, the whole group of students. Here, it seems to me, it may be the very orientation to the group itself that accounts for widespread cheating among these "conventional" students. The moral reasoning of children at this stage often involves asking, "What if everyone did it?" In fact, however, many did do it (cheat), so that cheating was the "norm" within the group. The 45% of stage 4 students who did not cheat may (like the 19% of non-cheaters at stage 1) be distinguished by having internalized the moral norm against cheating. Obviously, I have no way of knowing whether or not superego controls were influential in Krebs's cheating study. But whether students do or don't cheat is clearly not determined entirely, as Krebs's findings make abundantly clear, by their stage of moral development. Nor is it sufficient

[56] Ervin Staub, "Helping a Distressed Person: Social, Personality, and Stimulus Determinants," in L. Berkowitz, ed., *Advances in Experimental Social Psychology*, vol. 7 (New York: Academic Press, 1974).

to categorize all other possible influences into a residual category of "situational factors."

What seems likely to me is that cognitive moral development and moral *action* at every stage of moral reasoning is inescapably influenced by unconscious mechanisms, by earlier acquired moral precepts that are consciously available to individuals, and by the moral values and norms of the group and of the wider society. In fact, I believe that we can partially account for the relative scarcity of persons at the postconventional level of moral reasoning by recognizing that the moral values espoused by people at this level are *not* the moral values accepted by the vast majority of parents (at least so far as their actual behavior is concerned) or upheld in the institutional spheres of most societies (or advocated by Durkheim, Parsons, and most social scientists). Perhaps in a perfect world, the innate potentials apparently assumed by Kohlberg would be enabled to unfold so that higher stages of morality would progressively evolve. But in the world we live in, this is sadly not the case. Thus, there is good reason to give more attention than Kohlberg does to the ways in which parents and other child-rearers do influence the moral development of their children.

III

I want now to compare and contrast Kohlberg's psychological theory of cognitive development with the identification-internalization approach followed by Freud and Parsons. My concern will be with both the explanatory power of the two different theories and with their normative implications for moral thinking and action.

Beginning with the question of the ability of the two approaches to explain the change in moral reasoning from Kohlberg's stage 1 to the stage of "conventional" morality, it seems to me that the identification-internalization approach is equally able to account for such changes. In every society, Freud and Parsons would argue, children identify with their parents and accept their values. And because there are certain universal concerns (with regard to the regulation of sex, for instance) that are crucial for the functioning and survival of the social group and its members, it is to be expected that all children will be *taught* certain moral values in common. Given that children do identify with their parents and want to please them, it is not surprising that young children (stage 1) stick to the rules that are backed by the threat of punishment or disapproval.

The mechanism of identification is also seen by Parsons as leading to a more generalized need for approval and esteem, which provides the motivational basis for the acceptance of what he calls socially necessary discipline. Again, it would be expected from the identification-internalization perspective that individuals at the conventional level of moral reasoning will be oriented toward the approval of others, toward showing respect for authority, and maintaining the given social order for its own sake.[57] And, of course, the change in moral reasoning from stage 1 to conventional morality could also be accounted for by the idea of internalization. That very young children, who have not yet acquired a superego, move from a concern with immediate rewards and punishments for their actions to a higher stage, where their conformity is voluntary, can be seen as the result of the internalization of moral values and standards. So far as the similar age trends in moral reasoning across cultures goes, then, there may be little to choose between Kohlberg's theory and the identification-internalization approach; both theories are able to account for such trends.

This conclusion applies, however, only to the explanatory power of the two theories with regard to moral development from stage 1 to the stage of conventional morality. It does not hold, in my view, for questions relating to (a) the normative implications of the two theoretical approaches, or (b) the explanatory status of the two approaches with respect to the development of higher stages of moral reasoning.

Turning, first, to a consideration of the normative implications of the two approaches, it should by now be evident that "conventional" morality is very much the morality preferred and advocated by Parsons, Durkheim, and other social scientists in the consensus tradition. At stage 4, as noted earlier, the individual is oriented toward authority, fixed rules, and the maintenance of the social order. Individual relationships are considered in terms of their place in the system, and what is "right" is what contributes to the maintenance of the society, group, or institution.[58] Actions that threaten the solidarity and cohesion of the social system are morally wrong. At the level of conventional morality, to be "moral" is to adhere to the norms and laws of one's own society. Certainly Durkheim would see this level of reasoning as representing the ultimate in moral development, since he argued that the essence

[57] Kohlberg, "Moral and Religious Education," p. 71.
[58] Kohlberg, "Moral Stages and Moralization," p. 34–35.

of moral education is teaching children to limit themselves to the good of society.[59] Parsons seems to share this point of view.

Conventional morality, in short, is the morality required for social order. Were everyone to reach this stage of moral development, there would be normative consensus about moral values and standards within the society. The problem with conventional morality, of course, is its own moral standing. But since the conventional level of moral reasoning is that reached by most adults (at least in Western societies), theorists like Durkheim and Parsons would not even raise the question as to whether there may not be higher levels of moral reasoning. Given their acceptance of the adequacy of morality at the conventional level, they have no need to try to explain the development of more advanced levels of moral reasoning. In fact, advocates of the identification-internalization approach never attempt such an explanation. Thus, the explanatory status of Kohlberg's theory is vastly superior to the approach followed by Freud and Parsons in respect to the development of moral reasoning beyond the conventional level.

Theorists in the identification-internalization tradition (i.e., most social scientists) are apparently ready to accept the relativistic implications of conventional morality—so long as it assures normative consensus and social order. This is not, however, Kohlberg's position. Nor is it the position of those persons whose own moral reasoning is at the postconventional level. Kohlberg argues that "higher" stages of moral reasoning are not only higher in the sense that they come after or later than the other stages. They are also higher in that the moral reasoning is "better," that is, more adequate. In saying that some moral judgments are more "adequate" than others, Kohlberg means two things: that some moral values ought to take precedence over others, and that some ways of weighing values in a moral conflict situation are better than others.[60]

Regarding the first claim, Kohlberg argues that as a person's moral reasoning grows more adequate he will, for example, be able to differentiate the value of life from all other values and to see that it should take precedence over them. Thus in the Heinz dilemma, someone at the highest stage of morality would "choose the principle that there is a natural duty to life, or that a human's

---

[59] Émile Durkheim, *Moral Education* (New York: Free Press, 1961). Originally published in 1925.
[60] Kohlberg, "Stages of Moral Development," pp. 46–54.

right to life comes before another human being's right to property."[61]

The second claim concerning the adequacy of moral judgments is related to the first. Here the issue concerns judgments about legitimate moral claims in situations of conflict. Moral reasoning at the highest ("principled") stage involves ideal role-taking and is guided by a concern with moral principles. A moral principle, Kohlberg says, is to be understood as "a universal mode of choosing . . . which we want all people to accept in all [similar] situations."[62] Moral reasoning that involves moral principles is more adequate than lower levels of reasoning because it attempts to view conflicts from the perspective of any human being rather than from the perspective of being a member of a particular group or society. From the perspective of one's own society (and from the perspective of consensus theorists like Durkheim and Parsons), it might be argued, for example, that people ought to be loyal to their own country. But certainly many conventional Americans and Europeans also support dissidents in the Soviet Union whose "disloyalty" undercuts social order. Someone might maintain this position by formulating or accepting a principle that gives primary preference to the preservation of human rights over loyalty to his own country. And, of course, such a person could secondarily give preference to loyalty to his own country insofar as it preserves human rights. In saying that principled morality is more "adequate" than conventional morality, then, Kohlberg is himself making a moral judgment. In my view, his justification of this judgment is fully consistent with the ideas of Rawls and Gewirth that I discussed earlier.[63]

I noted above that those persons who are themselves at the highest level of moral reasoning also reject relativism. In fact, says Kohlberg, it may be a concern with relativism that motivates those individuals who do develop to stages 5 and 6. At the level of conventional morality (stage 4), the moral reasoning of an adolescent or a person in his twenties is consistent with the reasoning of most adults. What, it might be asked, could motivate such an individual to construct a new stage of moral reasoning? One possibility, Kohlberg suggests, is the "crisis of relativism."[64] This crisis

[61] Kohlberg, "Justice as Reversibility," p. 262.

[62] Kohlberg, "Stages of Moral Development," p. 58.

[63] It is also consistent with the emphasis on the need for a reasoned justification found in the work of Nozick and Habermas discussed in Chapter 2.

[64] Hersh et al., *Promoting Moral Growth*, pp. 77–78.

may arise when someone at this stage must confront and deal with moral values or ideas from outside his own system. It is, of course, characteristic of people at stage 4 to conceive of morality as a fixed system of laws and beliefs. This being the case, they cannot easily grant validity to other moral views without threatening their own. Nonetheless, someone who encounters moral values different from his own, especially if they are held by an individual whom he respects or cares deeply about (a teacher or a new love object, respectively) may be willing to at least consider the validity of the alternative conception of morality. In so doing, he may find that he has no good grounds for concluding that his own conception of morality is superior to the alternative. As a result, he may adopt a relativist perspective: what is moral depends upon what is right in your own group or society. This is, in my experience, a position frequently adopted by university students; morality, many of them argue, resides entirely at the level of "norms."

But Kohlberg's research suggests that relativism is not usually a stable moral position. Once people holding this position (which Kohlberg sees as a stage between stages 4 and 5)[65] enter positions of social responsibility within their society, they usually either return to their stage 4 reasoning or (less often) construct a "principled" rationale for moral reasoning. Those doing the latter, move directly to stage 5. Such a move can be viewed as a direct outgrowth of relativism, incorporating the relativist standpoint that moral values are relative to one's group or society but, at the same time, seeking a principle that will bridge these differences. As mentioned earlier, individuals at stage 5 frequently see morally right action as being defined in terms of individual rights and of standards that have been examined and agreed upon. Important here is the principle of social contracts; mutual agreements define the nature of people's obligations to one another. An example of stage 5 reasoning is provided by a philosopher who responded to the Heinz dilemma:

> It is a husband's duty to steal the drug. The principle that husbands should look after their wives to the best of their ability is one whose general observance does more good than harm. He should also steal it for a friend (close enough for it to be understood that they would do this sort of thing for each

---

[65] Lawrence Kohlberg, "Continuities in Childhood and Adult Moral Development Revisited." In P. B. Baltes and L. R. Goulet, eds., *Lifespan Development Psychology* (New York: Academic Press, 1973).

other). The reasons are similar to those in the case of the wives. If the person with cancer were a less close friend, or even a stranger, Heinz would be doing a good act if he stole the drug, but he has no duty to.[66]

In other words, the moral correctness of stealing the drug is viewed as contingent upon a prior contract or agreement (a formal contractual agreement in the case of marriage, and a less formal "understanding" in the case of friends). But this, too, can be viewed as relativistic; what is morally correct is seen as "relative" to whether or not there is some sort of prior agreement between the persons involved. It is only at stage 6, the highest stage, that moral reasoning totally escapes the effects of relativism. This is illustrated by the response of a different philosopher to the Heinz dilemma:

> If the husband does not feel very close to or affectionate with his wife, should he steal the drug?

> Yes. The value of her life is independent of any personal ties. The value of human life is based on the fact that it offers the only possible source of a categorical moral "ought" to a rational being acting in the role of a moral agent.[67]

Kohlberg's argument for stage 6 as the most adequate stage of moral reasoning is based on the concepts of reversibility and universalizability. The idea of "reversibility," Kohlberg writes, is "that we must be willing to live with our judgments or decisions when we trade places with others in the situation being judged."[68] A judgment is reversible in that we judge in such a way that we can live with the judgment afterward, whoever we are. Kohlberg also refers to reversibility as "ideal role-taking." The idea of "universalizability"is exemplified in Kant's maxim of the categorical imperative: act as you would want all human beings to act in a similar situation. In the Heinz dilemma, someone at the highest stage of moral reasoning sees the situation from the role of the person whose life is being saved as well as from the role of the person who can save the life (reversibility) and from the point of view of anyone filling these roles (universalizability).[69] Clearly, Kohlberg's arguments for the greater adequacy of moral reasoning at the higher

[66] Lawrence Kohlberg, "The Claim to Moral Adequacy of a Highest Stage of Moral Judgment," *Journal of Philosophy* 40 (1973): 639.

[67] Ibid.

[68] Kohlberg, "Justice as Reversibility," p. 258.

[69] Ibid., p. 261.

stages of moral development are grounded in a philosophical position opposed to relativism.

Up to this point in my comparison of Kohlberg's theory of moral development with the identification-internalization approach of Freud and Parsons, I have considered two of the three major weaknesses of the latter position: its neglect of conscious, rational reasoning in the acquisition and acceptance of moral values, and its relativist view of moral values. Let me, then, summarize the results of the comparison thus far.

Kohlberg's cognitive theory certainly gives far more attention to the manner in which children and adults think and reason than does the approach followed by Freud and Parsons. With the latter approach, what happens in infancy and early childhood is seen as all-important; through a process of emotional identification and learning, the child internalizes and makes his own the moral values of the significant others in his life. He or she is regarded as an almost totally passive creature, for whom internalization is viewed as a process like swallowing and digesting.

In sharp contrast to this view, Kohlberg emphasizes the capacity of human beings to think, to evaluate and give reasons, to attempt to resolve conflicts, and so on. Although Freud and (especially) Parsons do give attention to the importance of the child's relationships with other persons in his environment as a source of development, Kohlberg is far more explicitly concerned with showing how these relationships shape the child's opportunities for social interaction and various experiences upon which moral development depends. On the other hand, I do believe that Kohlberg underestimates the influence of more *direct* contributions by parents on their children's moral thinking and development. These more direct influences, as I suggested earlier, may help explain the apparently very limited impact of people's stage of moral reasoning on their actions. Certainly, the failure to present any persuasive evidence concerning the relationship between moral reasoning and people's actual behavior is a significant weakness in Kohlberg's work. Despite this weakness, Kohlberg's theory is better able to explain the acquisition and acceptance of moral values than is the identification-internalization approach followed by Freud, Parsons, and most sociologists.

Kohlberg's theory is also to be preferred with respect to the relativism issue. Freud and Parsons argue that the moral values or standards that people espouse depend on the internalization of the dominant norms in their society, and they hold that nothing can be said about the "rightness" of these norms. It is true that they might argue, as I indicated earlier, that because there are certain common concerns in every society (I mentioned the regulation of sex), all children will be taught some moral values in common. But, beyond that, Freud and Parsons see being moral as synonymous with adherence to the norms and laws of one's own group or society. Kohlberg, on the other hand, argues that some moral values ought to take precedence over others and that moral reasoning involving "principled" thinking represents the highest level of moral development. Moral reasoning characterized by reversibility and universalizability represents, as it were, the end point of the dimension of moral reasoning. Although some philosophers have suggested that his definition of the highest stages may be too narrow or restricted,[70] Kohlberg has provided a philosophical justification for his claims about the adequacy of the various stages of moral reasoning.

What, then, can be said about Kohlberg's theory with regard to the third criticism leveled earlier at the identification-internalization approach? This, it will be recalled, concerned the failure to give adequate attention to questions about the moral appropriateness or inappropriateness of certain emotions that may accompany or result from adherence to or violation of moral values and principles.

Here we encounter one of the most important limitations of Kohlberg's theory: the general neglect of the emotional and behavioral sides of moral development. Even though Piaget assumed that cognition and affect develop on parallel tracks,[71] Kohlberg has given far less attention to affect than to cognition. He does point to certain "sanctions" that are apparently seen as appropriate for moral development at the three levels—punishment at Level I, shame at Level II, and guilt at Level III—but these ideas are never developed at any length.[72] This is probably not unexpected, given his general criticism of theories that claim that children act morally to avoid guilt.[73] In any case, Kohlberg's theory shares with the identification-internalization approach a general failure to give serious attention to the appropriateness of certain emotional feelings. Whereas Freud and Parsons place too much emphasis on the neg-

---

[70] See, for example, Richard S. Peters, "A Reply to Kohlberg," *Phi Delta Kappa* 56 (1975): 78.

[71] Jean Piaget, *Six Psychological Studies* (New York: Random House, 1967).

[72] Kohlberg, "Stages of Moral Development."

[73] Lawrence Kohlberg, "Moral Development," in David L. Sills, ed., *International Encyclopedia of the Social Sciences*, vol. 10 (New York: Free Press, 1968), pp. 483–93.

ative aspects of the emotions, Kohlberg ignores these emotions almost altogether.

IV

In this chapter, I have examined two of the dominant theoretical approaches to children's moral development: the identification-internalization approach and Kohlberg's cognitive developmental approach. These have been compared and contrasted with regard to both their explanatory strength and their normative implications. My overall conclusion is that Kohlberg's theory is much to be preferred; it is better able to explain development, and it defends a conception of moral development that is grounded in an anti-relativist philosophical position.

Although Kohlberg's theory is the more adequate of the two approaches, it does have two serious weaknesses—both of which it shares to some extent with the alternative approach: (1) it is unable to demonstrate any strong relationship between the development of moral reasoning and moral actions; higher levels of moral reasoning do not necessarily mean that individuals are more moral persons; and (2) it fails to give serious attention to the relation of certain emotional feelings to moral action.

In my view, a more fully adequate theory of moral development would have to more satisfactorily locate the determinants of people's moral actions; and it would have to more explicitly deal with considerations about what emotions people ought or ought not to feel in connection with their moral actions. The fact that neither Kohlberg's approach nor the identification-internalization approach (nor any other, for that matter) is fully adequate is, of course, to be regretted. But the absence of a more adequate theory does seem to accurately reflect the present state of affairs with regard to sociological and psychological theories of moral development.

Furthermore, my review of these two developmental theories does provide some knowledge of what is sociologically and psychologically feasible with respect to my task in Chapter 5: a consideration of socialization as it pertains to the moral values and principles relevant to a just social order. That is, the findings of these other investigations must be viewed as imposing certain limitations on my own suggestions and speculations concerning socialization for a just social order. To ignore what appear to be some of the "realities" of socialization and child development would result in a line of argumentation far removed from the world of human beings like ourselves.

Just as there are limitations imposed by what is psychologically and sociologically feasible in socialization, there are also limitations on what is morally permissible in the socialization and upbringing of children. These are explored in the chapter that follows.

FOUR

Socialization and Children's Rights

SINCE the socialization of children involves their accepting the moral values of a society as their own, so that agreed-upon conceptions of desirable behavior are transmitted from one generation to the next, it might be expected that social scientists would devote attention to questions about what is morally acceptable and unacceptable in the socialization process itself. Certainly, there must be moral limitations as to what parents, and others, may or may not do in socializing children. For the most part, however, questions about what is morally permissible in the process of socialization have beeen totally ignored by social scientists.

In this chapter, I intend to focus explicit attention on the issue of "rights" as they pertain to the socialization of children. Rights, of course, set limits on what actions are morally permissible; they circumscribe what people may or may not do to one another.[1] A consideration of children's rights immediately raises a number of distinct normative questions. To begin with, there is the question: Do children have moral rights? And, if so, what rights do they have? If children do have rights, what consequences ought this to have for relationships between children and their parents, and between children and other persons in society? Do the rights of children impose obligations upon their parents and other persons? If so, what particular obligations are imposed? Those are only a few of the many questions that arise when we begin to think about children's rights. With few exceptions, neither sociologists, psychologists, anthropologists, nor others concerned with the socialization of the young, have seriously dealt with such questions.[2]

[1] For a general overview of rights, see Richard Flathman, *The Practice of Rights* (Cambridge: Cambridge University Press, 1976). See also my discussion in Derek L. Phillips, *Equality, Justice and Rectification* (London: Academic Press, 1979), chaps. 5–6.

[2] There is, however, a concern among philosophers. Examples are Onora O'Neill and William Ruddick, eds., *Having Children: Philosophical and Legal Reflections on Parenthood* (New York: Oxford University Press, 1979); Ferdinand Schoeman, "Rights of Children, Rights of Parents, and the Moral Basis of the Family," *Ethics* 91 (October 1980): 6–19; and Amy Gutmann, "Children, Paternalism, and Education," *Philosophy and Public Affairs* 9 (Summer 1980): 338–58.

These issues regarding moral considerations in the structure of relationships between parents and children must be examined before I can move, in the following chapter, to an exploration of the actual processes of socialization as they pertain to the moral values and principles relevant to a just social order.

I

The United Nations Declaration of the Rights of the Child, adopted unanimously by the U.N. Assembly, sets out a long list of children's rights. Among others, it speaks of children's rights to "adequate nutrition, housing, recreation, and medical services."[3] If, indeed, children do have these rights, then it must be asked: Where do these rights come from? Further, it needs to be asked: Who has the obligation to see that these rights are honored (or not violated)? According to the Preamble of the Declaration, "Mankind owes to the child the best it has to give."[4] However, saying that children's rights are owed to them "by mankind" is obviously very vague. Claims for adequate nutrition, housing, and the like, must be claims against specifiable others. "Mankind" cannot bathe an infant, change a diaper, or feed a child. Talk about children's rights can be taken seriously only if there is some specification of the persons (or class of persons) who should, morally speaking, be responsible for meeting the claims of one or another child. But the Preamble totally ignores the issue of who has the obligation to provide those benefits mentioned above. Since my concern here is with the socializing influence of child-rearers (usually parents) on children, I will consider the rights and obligations of both children and those responsible for their upbringing. My focus will be mainly on moral rather than legal questions about rights and obligations.

In most societies of the world, it is the child's biological parents who have responsibility for child-rearing and the duties involved therein.[5] But it is not the fact of procreation, that the biological parents have brought the child into existence, that is decisive so far as the child's rights and parental obligations are concerned. The moral issue is not who caused the child to exist but who has primary

---

[3] "United Nations Declaration of the Rights of the Child," Resolution 1386 (XIV), published in the *Official Records of the General Assembly, Fourteenth Sesssion, Supplement No. 16* (1960), p. 19.

[4] Ibid.

[5] A. L. Melden, *Rights and Persons* (Oxford: Basil Blackwell, 1977).

responsibility for the care and upbringing of the child.[6] It is those persons who have such responsibility who have special obligations to him or her. And it is not necessarily biological parenthood itself that imposes such obligations, but rather the social practices of one or another society. There have been societies in which the fact of causation was less relevant to parental duty than in most Western societies. In such societies, children are brought up by specially selected child-rearers or by the community at large. Their obligations toward upholding and honoring the rights of those children placed in their care are not, then, grounded in biological parenthood. Although bringing the child into existence is for most of *us* the special source of our obligations as child-rearers, it is not the case that biology is the special source of our obligations toward our children.

Be that as it may, child-rearing practices generally involve three separate and interrelated types of interests: those of the child, those of the parents or child-rearers, and those of "society."[7] The child has certain interests and needs, which can be met only by adult members of the community. Obviously, infants are incapable of taking care of themselves; they are inherently dependent upon others. Parents or other child-rearers have to take care of the infant's needs, and they must exercise enough control over the infant's environment to assure his or her survival. Young children, like infants, require nourishment, shelter, physical care, love and warmth, and continuity in their relationships with those persons who take care of them. They also need, especially as they become older, to be socialized for a life as independent adults. From infancy onward, children have certain interests that must be met by those responsible for rearing them.

As noted above, parents or child-rearers also have interests. Among them, is an interest in receiving love and affection from the child; in taking responsibility for helping give direction to another's life; in enjoying an intimate "family" relationship, where children are loved not only for themselves but as an outward sign of the parents' love for one another. They also have an interest in being free from interference by others in raising their children. And they have an interest in assuring that not all of their time and

---

[6] Jeffrey Blustein, "Child Rearing and Family Interests," in O'Neill and Ruddick, *Having Children*.

[7] Ibid.

161

attention is devoted to child-rearing, i.e., an interest in being free to pursue other desires and interests.

Since a society's children are its future citizens, societal members in general also have an interest in child-rearing practices. There is a concern with the maintenance of a certain level of procreation, and with the physical care and socialization of children. All children must also learn which kinds of interference in the lives of others are permitted and which are prohibited. Beyond this, the justification for one or another set of child-rearing practices is seen as depending largely on the general characteristics, dominant values, and wider social practices of a particular society. A highly industrialized society, for example, is widely viewed as requiring a higher level of literacy and specialized knowledge than does a society with a lesser degree of industrialization.

II

Children's Rights

Even though children have certain needs, this does not necessarily mean that they also have "rights." Does the child have any *moral* as distinct from *legal* rights? If so, what obligations do these impose on those persons responsible for his or her upbringing and on society as a whole?

Let us begin with the infant. Certainly, the young infant has needs and wants. Strictly speaking, however, it does not yet *have* interests, whether it be with regard to how it should be cared for or with regard to its own future development. Childhood is directed toward ends of which the infant can have no comprehension. But this is not to say that it is not *in* the infant's interests that its parents act one way rather than another toward him or her. In planning and preparing for its future development, they are acting in the infant's interests. It is, of course, true that these interests are presently unknown to the infant. This being the case, some persons would perhaps claim that the infant itself has no moral rights against its parents, that it has no right to have its interests satisfied. At a later stage of development, it might be acknowledged, the child does acquire moral rights, which place certain obligations on its parents.

But if that is so, if whatever rights an infant has are at best future rights, then parents cannot be said to be meeting their *moral obligations* as correlative to such rights when they act to promote its future development. Of course, it might be argued that parents, simply because they are parents, do have obligations toward an infant whom they have brought into the world. But this is really no answer. Granted that the young infant is completely dependent upon its parents or other child-rearers for survival and that parents do (usually) see that its elementary needs are met, the question remains as to the source of these moral obligations. The problem, then, is to provide a justification for the presumed rights of infants and children, and the obligations that such rights impose on their parents.

If it is assumed that certain rights accrue to all persons, then the problem may be seen as centering on the status of the infant as a "person." Our concept of a person, Melden states, "is the concept of a being who lives a life of which the present is only a segment."[8] The status of a being whom we call a person is determined not only by this condition now, during the present segment of his life, but also by the character of his life in the past and in the future. An elderly man lying in a hospital bed in a coma, in the very last stage of a terminal illness, we regard as a person. Even when he is incapable of any agency and unlikely to ever regain consciousness, we regard him as a person; we treat him as someone who has rights. This is not because we necessarily expect him to regain consciousness or to resume his daily life. Rather, it is because he is a person, a moral being, and not a cat or a dog, that we continue to ascribe rights to him.[9]

The newborn infant, like the elderly man lying in a coma, has no capacity for agency, no moral understanding, and no conscious interests. But if we continue to ascribe rights to persons who have in the present segment of their lives lost all capacity for entering into moral relationships with other persons, should we not perhaps do the same for infants whose moral capacities are yet to be developed? Like all other persons, the infant is a "developing" being. True, his or her moral agency will only gradually appear in the future. But this temporal development is a part of what it is to *be* (not become) a human being. To be a human being is to be a person for whom infancy is only one segment of life. It is, then, by virtue of the future, in the case of infants, that we count them as persons who possess rights. This means, concludes Melden, that infants do have moral rights and these rights impose corresponding obligations on those responsible for their upbringing. The infant's

[8] Melden, *Rights and Persons*, p. 222.
[9] Ibid., p. 219.

rights vis-à-vis its parents are moral rights grounded in the way their lives are joined then and there.

But it seems to me that there are serious problems with Melden's general line of argument and, in fact, with all similar arguments that attempt to ground rights in the notion of "personhood." According to that line of analysis, the main concern is with the proper conceptualization of what it is for an entity to be a person. Once that problem is resolved, i.e., once we know what a person is, then we know who has rights. This is because "persons" are viewed as rights-bearing entities; persons have rights, while other entities do not. Rights are seen as something that is held in full or not at all. Thus, the rights possessed by an infant or a young child are the very same rights that an adult human being has. The problems with this general position are, first, too much emphasis is placed on the issue of delineating the concept of a person and the rights that are seen as attaching to such a being, and insufficient attention is given to the *warrant* for such rights; and, second, this line of analysis has very little applicability to possible conflicts about rights between children and those responsible for their upbringing. This results from the conclusion that rights are held equally strongly by all persons. No attention is given to the possibility that rights might be something that differs in strength, something that people can have more or less of.

In my view, Gewirth's approach to rights—where they are viewed as necessarily rather than contingently connected with being human, and are logically derived from the nature of human action—avoids these difficulties and provides a far better basis for my own further consideration of the place of moral values in the socialization process. Let me, then, turn to his treatment of several issues pertaining to the question of children's rights.

Gewirth argues that not all entities that seem to pursue purposes are agents in the relevant sense. To be a prospective purposive agent, he writes, "requires having the practical abilities of the generic features of action: the ability to control one's behavior by one's unforced choice, to have knowledge of relevant circumstances, and to reflect on one's purposes."[10]

But these abilities are gradually developed in infants and young children, who will—normally, at least—eventually have them in full. Such abilities are largely lacking altogether in animals (espe-

---

[10] Alan Gewirth, *Reason and Morality* (Chicago: University of Chicago Press, 1978), p. 122.

164

cially the ability to reflect on one's purposes), and are had in varying ways by the insane and the mentally deficient. Whether one has the generic rights to freedom and well-being, Gewirth says, is determined by whether one meets the criteria for being a prospective purposive agent set out above.[11] Because entities fulfill these criteria to varying extents, animals, the insane, mentally deficient persons, infants, and children do not have generic rights in the full-fledged way that normal human adults have them. Nevertheless, members of these groups do approach having these generic rights in differing degrees. Consequently, the generic rights to freedom and well-being are held in *varying degrees* by different entities. This follows from the relation between the generic abilities involved for action and the having of purposes that one wants to fulfill. "For the lesser the abilities," states Gewirth, "the lesser one is able to fulfill one's purposes without endangering oneself and other persons."[12]

The Principle of Generic Consistency—act in accord with the generic rights of your recipients as well as your own—requires that every agent must respect the freedom and well-being of other persons and not treat them as objects to be used simply for the fulfillment of his or her own purposes. This principle applies to the moral population of all prospective purposive agents. Although entities differ in the extent to which they have the full-fledged rights to freedom and well-being, there are not differing degrees of actually being prospective purposive agents. In order to *be* an agent, as already noted, one must have the practical abilities of the generic features of action. But once one *is* an agent, the justifying ground for claiming to have the generic rights to freedom and well-being is to have purposes one wants to fulfill. "The point is," Gewirth writes, "that once a person is an actual or prospective agent, he has the generic rights in full; but if he does not fully attain to the generic features and abilities of action, then he has the generic rights in proportion to his degree of attainment of agency."[13]

Children, then, are not prospective agents, since they do not yet have the proximate abilities of the generic features of action. Rather, they have the status of *potential* agents. Unlike non-human animals, young children will normally attain the control, choice, knowledge,

[11] Ibid.
[12] Ibid.
[13] Ibid., p. 141.

165

and reflective abilities that enter into the generic features of action.[14] Because children are not yet prospective agents, they are not among the recipients whose rights to freedom must be *fully* respected in line with the Principle of Generic Consistency. But their status as potential agents means that "they have rights that are preparatory for their taking on the generic rights pertaining to full-fledged agency."[15] These preparatory rights include as much respect for freedom and well-being as is consistent with their goal of full-fledged agency.[16]

What Gewirth is arguing, then, is that children (and presumably fetuses and infants as well) have less than full rights. Although he does not use the term, it would seem correct to speak here of partial rights. As potential agents, fetuses, infants, and children all have "partial rights" to freedom and well-being. Further, the extent of these partial rights depends on the degree to which they have the practical abilities of the generic features of action. Because moral properties (generic rights) are supervenient upon nonmoral ones (the generic features of action), the degree to which individuals have rights to freedom and well-being depends on what might be termed "normal maturation." Adult human beings (prospective purposive agents in Gewirth's terminology) have full-fledged rights to freedom and to well-being. Adolescents are probably sufficiently like adults to be regarded as approaching the status of full-fledged rights-holders. Children's rights would be more "partial" in character, while infant's rights would be still more partial, with the rights of about-to-be-born babies and fetuses being the most partial of all.[17] In other words, the further from normal adulthood that someone is, the more partial or limited are his or her rights to freedom and well-being.

The notion of "partial rights" seems to me to be consistent with much of our moral thinking and discourse about rights and competing rights. Those of us who think one should save the life of the mother if it is necessary to choose between her life and that of the unborn, accept that the fetus does have such rights to well-being as is required for developing its potentialities for growth toward purpose fulfillment, but hold that this is less than the rights of its mother. In saying that a fetus is "less than a full person,"

---

[14] Ibid.

[15] Ibid.

[16] Ibid.

[17] Partial rights are also mentioned by Norman C. Gillespie, "Abortion and Human Rights," *Ethics* 87 (April 1977): 237–43.

the United States Supreme Court implies that its rights are indeed partial—not that it has no rights at all.[18] It is also the case that when parents raise their children there is ordinarily the assumption that the children will acquire more of the right to freedom (or self-determination) as they develop and approach adulthood. Thus, the notion of partial rights is one with which most of us have some familiarity.

By recognizing that children have less than full rights to freedom and well-being, Gewirth makes it possible to defend certain moral judgments in those frequent instances where the rights of parents and their children come into conflict. I am not denying that such conflicts may be genuine moral problems. Rather, I am emphasizing that the *comparative* strength of the rights at issue can sometimes be assessed and provide guidance for making judgments in cases of conflict. With the idea of partial rights, we are able to avoid some of the difficulties inevitably encountered by those who attempt to locate the properties that something or someone must have to be a "person." Once it can be determined what it is to be a person, according to that argument, it will be known who has rights, since to be a person is to possess rights. All of those beings who can be classified as persons have rights, and the rights of all persons are equal in strength. Many participants in moral discussions about abortion see the most serious problem as that of "drawing a line" between something that is and something that is not a person. If something is a person, it has rights, and the same moral status as an adult; otherwise, it has an entirely different moral status. Wertheimer, for example, claims that "our principles of justice apply solely to relations between persons," and not to a fetus, which has a separate status, just as animals do.[19] With Gewirth's idea of potential agents, on the other hand, principles of justice do indeed apply to a fetus. Although it has less than full rights, the fetus does have moral rights.

Thus, Gewirth's conception of rights and rights-holders has two distinct advantages over the standpoint of Melden, considered earlier. First of all, by arguing that rights are necessarily connected with being human, it avoids all of the many difficulties involved in trying to determine when it is that something becomes a "person." Assuming that an unfertilized ovum has no rights at all, a conceptus would have minimal rights, an almost full-term fetus

[18] Quoted in Ibid., p. 239.
[19] Quoted in Ibid., p. 241.

would have more, and so on up until adult status, with the full-fledged rights to freedom and well-being, is achieved. Secondly, by recognizing that there are differences in the comparative strength of rights, Gewirth provides a basis for making judgments in those instances where there are conflicts regarding the rights of children and their parents.

Children, to repeat, do have rights. Gewirth's principle, that we act in accord with the generic rights of our recipients as well as our own, requires that children be brought up in such a way that they will be enabled to become both agents who can make their behavior conform to this principle and prospective agents whose generic rights to freedom and well-being must be respected by other agents.[20] Although children have only partial rights, their upbringing should assure that they have lesser rights, especially to freedom, only to the extent that this is necessary for the protection of their well-being and their maturation into full-fledged agency.[21]

III

Rights, Obligations, and Parent-Child Conflicts

Children have (partial) rights to freedom and well-being. Before considering these rights further, as well as the obligations they impose on other persons, it is first necessary to give attention to the issue of parental rights to raise their children free from the interference of the state or other persons.

Given that parents have the same generic rights to freedom and well-being as all other normal adults in society, what *special* claim do they have to decide certain important matters involving their children? Why, that is, should parents have a privileged position in regard to their children's upbringing vis-à-vis all the rest of society?

The usual answer to this question is that the family is the natural or appropriate agency for child-rearing and socialization. Because of the crucial social function performed by the family as an institution, parents must be recognized as deserving the authority to exercise autonomy in bringing up their children.[22] This argument is sometimes advanced by sociologists who emphasize the func-

---

[20] Gewirth, *Reason and Morality*, p. 141.

[21] Ibid., p. 142.

[22] This is suggested by Elizabeth Anscombe, "On the Source of Authority in the State," *Ratio* 20 (1978): 1–28.

tional importance of the family in meeting certain social needs. But the same argument is also often set forth by persons whose focus is concentrated on the child's perspective and who conclude that the family is deserving of autonomy because it is the most efficient (or least detrimental) means of protecting the needs and rights of children. In either case, there is a recognition of certain exceptional circumstances under which such autonomy may be abridged by state interventions. Such intervention is viewed as appropriate only if there is a situation of clear and present danger. In such a situation, intervention is acceptable when two conditions are fulfilled: serious physical or emotional harm to the child is imminent, and intervention is likely to be less detrimental than the status quo.[23]

Whether the argument justifying parental autonomy is a functional one or one emphasizing efficiency with regard to the needs and rights of children, it has a serious weakness as a defense of parental autonomy. For should there emerge alternative means of raising children that were superior (relative to societal needs or the needs and rights of children, as the case may be), then this would have the consequence of depriving the family of its position of being necessary and hence immune in its claim to autonomy. If such superior means were to be found, says Schoeman, this would give rise to the following sorts of questions: "Would parents still have a claim on their children, as against society? And if so, what would its basis be?"[24] Thus, it seems clear that parental rights and prerogatives cannot be justified by arguments emphasizing the benefits that accrue to "others" (children, the larger society) through traditional family arrangements.

Arguments for the family as an institution necessary for meeting either the needs and rights of children or the so-called needs of society are characterized by a lack of concern for parents and their rights. Schoeman has recently attempted to provide a justification for parental autonomy as against the larger society, and for parental claims on their children, which is grounded in the recognition of the moral basis of family life. He argues that parents' moral claim to a private and autonomous relationship with their children can be understood only by acknowledging the significance of "intimacy" in people's lives.[25]

---

[23] Schoeman, "Rights of Children"; Michael Wald, "State Intervention on Behalf of 'Neglected' Children: A Search for Realistic Standards," *Stanford Law Review* 27 (1974–75): 985–1040.

[24] Schoeman, "Rights of Children," p. 12.

[25] Ibid., p. 6.

An intimate relationship, Schoeman points out, is one in which we "share our selves" with other persons who do the same with us.[26] Friendship, love, and family are relationships in which intimacy is central. Such unions are not only central to defining who one is, but human existence would lose much of its meaning if the possibility of such intimate relationships were cut off.[27] Because of the importance of intimate relationships to the self-image and meaningful existence of most people, they must have the privacy and autonomy necessary for such unions of intimacy. Only in settings characterized by privacy and autonomy are there opportunities for intimate relationships free from the intrusions of other persons. Thus, Schoeman emphasizes, the state should impose high standards on itself, like the clear-and-present-danger test mentioned above, before intruding upon such relationships.[28]

As with love and friendship relationships, the family must be understood to be entitled to certain rights of privacy and autonomy. In Schoeman's words:

> The right of privacy entitles the adults of the family to exclude others from scrutinizing obtrusions into family occurrences. The right to autonomy entitles the adults of the family to make important decisions about the kinds of influences they want the children to experience and entitles them to wide latitude in remedying what they regard as faults in the children's behaviors.[29]

So long as the minimum conditions for adequate upbringing are met, so that children's needs and rights are taken into account, the state has no right to violate the conditions of privacy and autonomy necessary for intimate family relationships.

Although Schoeman speaks of the rights of privacy and autonomy as if these were distinct and separate rights, provision for a sphere of personal autonomy and privacy can also be seen as being included in the generic right to freedom. It follows from the right to freedom that, within the limits imposed by nonviolation of other persons' rights, people have rights to a vast area of protected actions of their own. These include physical movement, speech and other forms of expression, assembly, sexual conduct, and religion.[30]

[26] Ibid., p. 8.
[27] Ibid., p. 14.
[28] Ibid., pp. 15–16.
[29] Ibid., p. 10.
[30] Gewirth, *Reason and Morality*, p. 256.

In those instances where someone is the potential recipient of other persons' actions, his right to freedom is, in the first instance, a right to be left alone unless he has unforcedly consented to participate in the transaction.[31] Schoeman's justification of family autonomy, then, is fully consistent with the recognition that all agents have the generic rights to freedom and well-being.

Because his argument on behalf of the family considers the rights and interests of *both* children and their parents, Schoeman's justification for family autonomy is to be preferred to those justifications that either concentrate solely on the child's perspective or on the needs and interests of society as a whole. If people choose to exercise their right to freedom by having intimate relationships in a family setting, they should be free from scrutiny and control in their relations with one another and with their children. Except in unusual circumstances, these familial relationships are not to be interfered with or violated by other societal members or even by the state itself.

I return now to the rights of parents. Because children have rights, the parents' autonomy to control and socialize them must be somewhat circumscribed by respect for these rights. The child's rights impose both prohibitions and obligations on the parents. For infants whose capacities for self-determination are totally undeveloped, it is their right to well-being that is of crucial importance. The infant's right to have basic goods, which are the necessary preconditions of action—among them, adequate nutrition, shelter, rest, health care, and affection—imposes corresponding obligations on those who are responsible for his or her upbringing. Unless this right to well-being is recognized and respected, the infant will never be in a position to become an agent with full-fledged rights to freedom and well-being. Thus, every infant has a moral claim on the child-rearers for whatever is physically and emotionally necessary in order to be able to eventually exercise its rights. But because the infant's rights are so partial that he or she is unable to exercise them him- or herself, it is usually not a recognition of the infant's rights but rather his or her needs that are paramount in the parent-infant relationship.

Once the young child is capable of some degree of rational deliberation and of doing more for him- or herself, the generic rights to freedom and well-being—which impose obligations on others—become increasingly central to the relationship between the child

---

[31] Ibid.

and those responsible for his or her upbringing. The fact that all children have these (partial) rights does not, of course, mean that they may not be limited by the full-fledged rights of others to raise and socialize them. In the early years, especially, it is inevitable that the child's rights to freedom will be enormously restricted. This follows from the fact that this right can be exercised only *after* the right to well-being has been met. Were there no restrictions on the exercise of the right to freedom, it is highly unlikely that the child would choose what is in its best interests so far as adequate nutrition, shelter, and other basic goods are concerned. By choosing for him, the parents do restrict his exercise of his rights. But these restrictions are necessary because of the child's inability to avoid harm or to promote his own welfare.

Even though the child's right to freedom may be restricted in order to assure his well-being and maturation into full-fledged agency, there is no hard and fast rule as to such restrictions. But, in general, they ought to be applied only to the aspects of a child's life that are relevant to protecting its physical, emotional, and psychological development.[32]

It is obvious, in any case, that restrictions of the right to freedom of young children are required to assure that their needs and interests are met, and to assure that they will not make decisions that will curtail their future freedom unnecessarily. With young children, it is morally justifiable to limit their exercise of the right to freedom in order to provide life's necessities and to avoid serious harm to the child. Thus, it is permissible to deny young children the freedom to, for example, choose their own diet, cross busy streets alone, or use matches—even though such freedom is accorded to adults. Not only are such restrictions on the rights of young children morally defensible, but the obligations imposed on parents by the children's right to well-being require such restrictions. Whether or not he or she is aware of it, every young child does have a right to adequate nutrition, health care, love and affection, and the general conditions necessary for achieving agency and the full-fledged rights to freedom and well-being. And the child's parents have the corresponding obligation to see that this right is honored.

Consider the relationship between the young child and its parents in terms of Gewirth's criteria for the attainment of full-fledged agency and the full-fledged rights that accompany it: the abilities

---

[32] Natalie Abrams, "Problems in Defining Child Abuse and Neglect," in O'Neill and Ruddick, *Having Children*.

to control one's behavior by one's own unforced choice, to have knowledge of relevant circumstances, and to reflect on one's purposes. The criterion of "unforced choice" is intended to emphasize that an individual's behavior should be under his or her control,[33] and not be the result of compulsion, threat, or undesirable alternatives.[34] Someone's choice is unforced only when he or she chooses on the basis of informed reasons that do not include any of these three negative features. Certainly the young child has only partially developed the ability to control his or her behavior through unforced choice, and the child's parents have the obligation to provide the physical, emotional, and psychological conditions necessary to the full development of such control.

The criterion of "knowledge of relevant circumstances" refers to knowledge beyond what is present to immediate awareness.[35] An individual must be able to bring such knowledge to bear in deciding on his or her actions. Among other things, this means knowing what action is being performed, the purposes of such action, who its recipients are, and its likely outcome.[36] Thus, an individual should have knowledge of the potential dangers or harmfulness of the proposed action. Again, the young child has only partially developed this ability, and parents have the obligation to raise the child under conditions conducive to the acquisition of such knowledge.

The third criterion, the ability to "reflect on one's purposes," points to the necessity of someone's being capable of reflecting on the purposes for which he or she acts—even if the person does not always do so.[37] An individual must have the capacity to reflectively appraise or evaluate his or her purposes before, after, or even during the time of acting. This idea of being able to reflect rationally refers to the ability to make problematic what would, without an awareness of alternatives, be experienced as intuitively given. Such an ability in the young child is probably the least developed of the three abilities required for full-fledged agency. It requires, among other things, a certain level of development in the child's powers of reasoning. As far as parents are concerned, they have an obligation to expose the child to, and make him or her aware of, alternative ways of life and lines of action.

[33] Gewirth, *Reason and Morality*, p. 32.
[34] Ibid.
[35] Ibid., p. 120.
[36] Ibid., p. 31.
[37] Ibid., p. 38.

In the relationship between a young child and its parents, then, the child's (partial) *rights* to freedom and well-being impose on his or her parents the *obligation* to provide the conditions necessary for the child to attain the abilities required for adult agency and full-fledged generic rights. Because the young child has developed these abilities to only a limited extent, many choices and decisions will be made on his or her behalf by the parents. But since the young child is not yet someone with full-fledged rights that he or she is able to exercise on his or her own, the rights of young children and their parents seldom come into serious moral conflict.

With older children, however, things become considerably more complex. As children grow older, they are able to do more for themselves, and they generally need less help from parents and other adults. They are increasingly able to control their actions by unforced choice, to acquire knowledge of relevant circumstances, and to develop the capacity to reflect rationally on their purposes. That is, they are approaching the status of being agents with full-fledged rights to freedom and well-being. Because of their greater physical maturity and psychological development, they more and more exercise their right to freedom. This is especially the case with adolescents. In fact, part of what it is to be an adolescent is to be someone who is learning to exercise freedom in a responsible way. It is during these years that serious conflicts may arise concerning the amount of freedom that older children should be allowed to exercise over their own lives. Aside from strictly legal prohibitions, children and parents may disagree about the justifiability of parental restrictions on the adolescent's freedom to purchase alcoholic beverages, drive an automobile, or choose his or her place of residence. In some instances, the older child's exercise of his right to freedom may come into direct conflict with the parents' exercise of the same right. While the child and his parents may both agree that he has the right to freely choose his own friends, they may not agree at all about how often his friends may be allowed to visit. Since the parents also have the freedom to choose and entertain their friends, they may feel that the constant presence of the child's friends in the house makes it difficult for them to successfully exercise their own freedom as they would like. Thus the right of the child and his parents come into conflict.

Let me now consider an example of a much more serious confict than that involving the entertaining of friends—one revolving around the religious socialization of a child. Say that the parents are practicing Catholics who, like all other normal adults, have a right to the free exercise of their religion. Assuming, as most people do, that this right extends to a right to educate their children into their own religion,[38] they raise their daughter in the Catholic religion. Parents in many countries do have a legal right to educate their children as they wish. In the United States, the Supreme Court has recognized a legally protected "liberty of parents and guardians to direct the upbringing and education of children under their control."[39] But, as noted, this is a *legal* right. Do parents also have a *moral* right to educate their children as they please?

It seems clear to me that their right to freedom does give parents a right to provide the kind of religious upbringing that they believe in and deem best for their child. Their general right to freedom allows them to engage in any actions that do not unjustly affect the freedom and well-being of others. In the case described above, the parents may believe that a Catholic upbringing is best for their child's moral character and development, and that only such an upbringing will assure her being an honest, humane, morally upright individual. In the early years of the child's socialization, the parents' exercise of their rights will constitute no problem for their daughter. She is, in a sense, surrounded by the religious life of her parents. Living in the midst of a particular religious way of life, she comes to share it. But as she grows older, as she comes into contact with different religious beliefs and ways of life, she may come to question or reject the teachings of the Catholic Church. Since she has the right to freedom, she may choose to exercise it by *not* continuing her life as a Catholic. In such a situation, there is clearly a conflict between the adolescent's right to choose *her* religious preferences and the right of her parents to live their religious life as they please—including *their* right to raise their child as they choose.

If the parents recognize and value both their own rights *and* those of their daughter, they will not force her to adopt their religious way of life. Although the parents may sincerely believe that their religious beliefs are preferable to others, they must (morally speaking) accept the value of their adolescent daughter's right to make her own religious choice. Once she has attained the control, choice, knowledge, and reflective abilities necessary for adult agency and full-fledged generic rights, she must be free to exercise her right

[38] Also see Gutmann, "Children, Paternalism, and Education."

[39] Kenneth Henley, "The Authority to Educate," in O'Neill and Ruddick, *Having Children*, p. 260.

175

to accept or reject the religious life of her parents and not to have it forced upon her.

Aside from not forcing their views upon her, it can be argued that the parents also have an obligation to provide the child with a number of choices as to various religious (occupational, or whatever) ways of life. If so, this immediately raises another problem. In preparing the child to exercise her right to freely choose her religious way of life, how many options must parents provide or allow her? How much should the parents do to assure that their child will learn about the variety of religious and nonreligious ways of life? How much control should they attempt to exercise over their child with regard to the various life-styles and ethical systems that are potentially available to her? The child's ability to exercise self-responsibility presupposes, of course, self-determination by means of exercising her right to freedom. But exercise of this right requires knowledge of alternative ways of life and possibilities of living. What, then, are parents' obligations in this regard?

Writing about just these kinds of questions, Ruddick points to two familiar extremes: the conservative and the libertarian.[40] The *conservative* view holds that parents need not prepare the child for anything different than the father's or mother's way of life. That is, the child should be prepared for the life of the parent of the same sex. The conservative feels no responsibility for providing options, for assuring that the child comes into contact with alternative ways of living. The parent counts on a world in which the child can and should reproduce the parent's own life, in other words, a world without cultural change. The *libertarian*, by contrast, believes that parents should provide as many different life possibilities as are permitted by their resources and the child's abilities. Thus, the libertarian allows for radical change, even in his or her own hopes and ideals. But by assuming a wide range of life possibilities, libertarians in principle discount their own parental preferences. This means, as Ruddick emphasizes,[41] that the parents ignore the ways in which the child's interests and life changes are themselves strongly dependent on the ideals and interests of the parents. "In avoiding the conservative's self-reproductive ambitions," Ruddick states, "the libertarian makes parenthood a selfless, temporary service, which, once rendered, allows parents and

---

[40] William Ruddick, "Parents and Life Prospects," in Ibid., pp. 123–37.
[41] Ibid., p. 130.

176

child to go their separate ways, psychologically as well as economically."[42]

What we require is a principle of parenthood that will provide for the individuation of a child's own life without necessitating that the parents be either completely self-serving, on the one hand, or entirely selfless, on the other. That is, both the child's needs and the parents' desires must be considered. And the rights of both must, so far as possible, be protected in preparing the child to eventually lead a life of his or her own. Ruddick suggests such a principle, which he terms the "Prospect Provision Principle." According to this principle, a "parent must foster life prospects which

1. jointly encompasses the future the parents and those they respect deem likely, and
2. individually, if realized, would be acceptable to both parents and child."[43]

With this principle, the number of different life prospects or possibilities that a parent must foster is left open. In a community or society that is both homogeneous and likely to remain more or less as it is, it would be morally permissible for the parents to socialize the child for independence in that way of life. In such a situation, the child would be prepared to assume the roles and responsibilities of the parent of the same sex: like father, like son; like mother, like daughter.[44] But such homogeneous and stable communities are exceedingly rare in today's world. Thus Ruddick's principle is mainly important insofar as it concerns people living in a heterogeneous, unstable culture like our own. Among the many futures that parents might today have to prepare a child for are futures with capitalist or with socialist institutions; with heterosexual marriages or without; with or without particular religious institutions; with a relatively open and equal opportunity structure (for education and occupations) or with closed and unequal opportunity structures; with a general moral consensus or with an almost complete absence of such consensus.

It is obvious that the more uncertain the future, the more parents are driven by Ruddick's principle in the libertarian direction. Does this mean, then, that parents should be expected to prepare the child for *any* conceivable life prospect or possibility? Have the par-

[42] Ibid.
[43] Ibid.
[44] Ibid., p. 131.

177

ents no rights of their own so far as their child's development is concerned? This problem is dealt with, says Ruddick,[45] by his second clause. This clause stipulates that a parent need not foster a life prospect that, if realized, would be predictably distressing. In Ruddick's words:

> A parent must ask, Will I approve in time of a life my child may in time come to choose? And if the answer is "yes," then the parent must make *some* provision for that life prospect, even if that provision is nothing more than allowing other adults to present that life prospect favorably.[46]

What Ruddick attempts with the Prospect Provision Principle is to provide some moral guidance for parents in making provisions about those life prospects that would *mutually* satisfy parents and children.

While Ruddick is to be praised for his effort, it seems to me that the second clause gives rise to the kinds of problems discussed above with the example of the Catholic parents and their daughter. If the parents are expected to make some provision for only a life prospect that, if realized, would not be distressing to them, then this may very well restrict enormously the life prospects open for exploration by their adolescent daughter. That is, it may interfere with the child's exercise of her rights. In fact, the right to freedom is emptied of almost all meaning if the child's choice is so restricted. A child who knows only about the Catholic way of life may choose to remain a Catholic. Such an action would certainly be voluntary. But it cannot be viewed as "free" if she could not have undertaken a different action.

Catholic parents who are not at all distressed by the possibility that their adolescent daughter might eventually choose a life as, for example, an atheist would have no objections to her reading books about atheism, having atheist friends, or the like. On the other hand, consistent with Ruddick's principle, parents who would be very much distressed by the prospect of their daughter living her life as an atheist need make *no* provision at all for her to learn anything about such a life. Such parents could be expected to do whatever they could do to avoid fostering such a life prospect. Thus, there would be many instances—as indeed there are in the world around us—in which the child who wants to learn more

---

[45] Ibid.
[46] Ibid.

about atheism (communism, homosexuality, Buddhism, or whatever) and the kind of life connected with such views would find her parents totally opposed to her exercising her right to freedom. Obviously, there are an enormous variety of life prospects and possibilities about which parents and child may strongly disagree.

Ruddick himself notes that the principle does not require present agreement about what will be mutually satisfactory in the future.[47] It allows children, and this would occur most frequently with adolescents, to criticize their parents' views on the matter. And parents, of course, may not agree with their children's views about one or another life prospect. But the principle does at least allow for the possibility, argues Ruddick, "of mutually adjusted and mutually endorsed prospects."[48] The major thrust of Ruddick's principle, then, is to resist ideas that parents are their children's masters or their servants, their guardians or their trustees, and to replace these ideas with the view that the most distinctive work of parenthood is life-giving. This includes providing the child with the possibility of leading a life of his or her own, a life that, ideally at least, is mutually acceptable to the child and parents alike.

But it seems to me that it may be possible to say more about such conflicts between adolescents and their parents. If, as Ruddick argues, parents have an obligation to provide the child with a number of choices as to various ways of life, including that upheld by the family itself, such an obligation must be correlative to the rights held by the child (adolescent) him- or herself. I noted earlier that limitations on children's partial rights to freedom should not extend beyond what is necessary for the protection of their wellbeing and their maturation into full-fledged agency. Since such preparation for adult agency requires the provision of those conditions necessary for the development of control, choice, knowledge, and reflective abilities on the part of the children, parents have an obligation to try to assure that such conditions are indeed provided.

Perhaps most important with regard to the issue of parents providing a number of life prospects and possibilities for their daughter (in the example considered earlier) is the development of her ability to rationally "reflect" on her own purposes. Only if she is made aware of alternatives to the religious life of her parents is there the opportunity for her to develop her reflective abilities, at least with

[47] Ibid.
[48] Ibid.

179

respect to religion. Where there is no awareness of alternatives, she is not being prepared to appraise, evaluate, and reflect upon her actions. Without such an awareness of alternative possibilities, whatever "is" will simply be accepted as natural or inevitable.

Of course, it is true that the child is likely to learn about and encounter other ways of life (including religious ways of life) in settings outside the family: in school, through friends, and by way of reading, movies, and the like. But this does not negate the parents' obligation to provide their daughter with alternative life prospects. Thus, I believe that the adolescent's right to have the conditions necessary for developing the ability of rational reflection imposes an obligation on her parents to make some provision for life prospects other than those they themselves prefer. The child's right to develop her reflective abilities is a necessary condition for the development of those capacities required for full adult agency. When there is conflict between the parents' right to make provision only for life prospects that, if realized, would not be distressing to them and the right of an adolescent child to have the life prospects necessary for the development of agency, the child's right must be given priority over the right of his or her parents.

IV

The Interests of Other Societal Members

Thus far, I have focused on the rights of children and of those responsible for their upbringing. As mentioned earlier, child-rearing practices must also take account of the interests of other persons in society. As already noted, these interests include a concern with the maintenance of a certain level of procreation, with the provision by parents of an adequate level of physical care for their children, and with the preparation of children for their place as citizens in the society. It would be a mistake, however, to speak about society having "rights" in this regard. Certainly, individual persons do have rights. But society is not an entity that can, properly speaking, be said to possess rights.

In a just social order—one in which people's actions are guided by recognition and respect for the generic rights to freedom and well-being of others—children must learn to be able to act in accord with others' rights as well as their own. Responsibility for the acquisition of this ability will be shared jointly by the parents and the state. Especially in the period before the young child enters school, it is his parents who have major responsibility for his so-

180

cialization. Thereafter, the preparation of the child for adulthood is shared by the parents or child-rearers and the formal education system. The state is, in a sense, charged with the protection of the public interest and, therefore, has some authority to educate children to meet the socially required standards of behavior. And the state, as Henley points out, has the *legal* authority "to remove the child from the parents if they do not, or cannot, provide a socialization which is minimally acceptable to society."[49]

But, of course, the state's legal authority as regards the child-rearing practices in one or another society in itself says nothing about the *moral* standing of such authority. In Nazi Germany, as we know, Aryan parents were thought to have a primary duty not to themselves or their children but to the Third Reich.[50] The state required some Aryan mothers to place their children in specially selected clinics, so that they were left to the care and socialization of state-appointed child-rearers. In some instances, the biological parents and their children were never permitted to see one another again. For anyone who takes the rights of children and their parents seriously, such practices are morally indefensible. They violate the rights of both children and their parents. The same conclusion would be reached in the case of a society that needed a certain number of slaves to assure its smooth functioning and required that either parents or the state see to it that some children be socialized into the role of slave. Child-rearing practices that are directed entirely toward satisfying the interests of society, whatever these might be, are obviously not grounded in a moral commitment to the rights of children and their parents.

The state does, however, have a legitimate interest—and say— in the child-rearing practices found within a particular society. The state has the legal and moral right to intercede in those situations where the parents of a child show a total disregard for his or her rights.[51] But even here, as Henley observes, "the courts have not consistently protected the rights of children; . . ."[52] The reason for this, Henley says, is that the courts often "insist on recognizing a liberty of parents so extreme that it is incompatible with the rights of the children."[53]

While the state or society is not an entity with rights of its own,

[49] Henley, "The Authority to Educate," pp. 257–58.
[50] See, for example, Blustein, "Child Rearing and Family Interests," p. 117.
[51] Abrams, "Child Abuse."
[52] Henley, "The Authority to Educate," p. 262.
[53] Ibid.

the state does have responsibility for protecting the interests and rights of all the individual members of society. Whatever the rights and obligations that children and their parents have vis-à-vis one another in their family relationships, neither is free to invade or violate the rights of other persons in the society. Just as the parents' rights are to some extent circumscribed by respect for the rights of their children, and the children's rights by respect for those of their parents, the rights of each individual in society are circumscribed by respect for the generic rights of all other members of society. Given those many instances where people's exercise of their rights—both within and external to the family—brings them into conflict with other persons, it is the state that is the final protector and arbiter as regards the legal rights of individuals. Whether or not the state's exercise of its legal authority is always morally justified (or justifiable) is, of course, another question. It is a question to which I will devote considerable attention in Part III.

V

Thus we see that any consideration of the place of moral values in the structure of the socialization process must take account of the interests of children, of their parents or other child-rearers, and of other societal members. Perhaps most importantly, the rights of children, parents, and all other individual members of society must always occupy a central position in such a consideration. It is because each and every human agent has the generic rights to freedom and well-being, which he or she is entitled to exercise, that conflicts in the exercise of such rights are frequently unavoidable. But there is no principle or set of principles that will allow us to "resolve" all such conflicts in advance. The resolution of conflicts between parents and children, for example, depends on the age and level of development of the children, the short- and long-run consequences of their being free to exercise their rights as they choose, and a host of other considerations. But it can certainly be said that, except in unusual circumstances, familial relationships are not to be violated by other members of society or by the state.

My concern with children's rights in this chapter has been focused mainly on the question of what parents, and other persons, may or may not do in socializing children. This, as noted earlier, is a topic that has been generally ignored by social scientists. I have tried to show that the socialization of children imposes both moral requirements and limitations on those responsible for the upbringing and welfare. These must be borne in mind in examining the actual processes of socialization through which children learn and accept the substantive moral values and principles relevant to a just social order. In the following chapter, these processes will be examined at length. My discussion here of the interests and rights of children and their parents has been intended to direct attention to the moral standing and humanity of both.

FIVE

Socialization for the Just Social Order

I

I HAVE argued earlier that all persons have rights to freedom and well-being, and that a just social order is one regulated by recognition and respect for these rights and for the institutional arrangements to which they give rise.[1] A society in which every person's actions are guided by the correct sense of justice is, then, inherently a *just social order*. It is a society characterized by both stability and justice. This means that a social order will be just if and only if (1) people recognize and respect everyone's generic rights to freedom and well-being, and (2) their actions are guided by this conception of justice. The presence or absence of these two conditions yields several different types of societies.

In one type of society, there is widespread endorsement of an alternative (and unjustifiable) conception of justice that also fails to provide adequate guidance for people's actions. Everyone might agree, for example, that justice requires people being rewarded in proportion to their contribution to the greater society. But this is clearly too vague or imprecise to put into actual practice. In a second type, everyone's actions are indeed guided by a particular conception of justice, although it is an incorrect one. People's actions might possibly be guided by a conception of justice (such as that advocated by Plato and Aristotle) that stipulates "equals should receive equal shares and unequals should receive unequal shares." In such a society, every person may know his or her "place," but stability or order would be achieved at the cost of endorsing an unjustifiable conception of justice. In a third type of society, people hold and endorse the correct conception of justice but it nevertheless fails to guide their conduct. This would be similar to the situation found among the many persons at Kohlberg's highest stage of moral development who fail to act in a way consistent with the moral principles that they endorse. In this type of society, individuals

---

[1] Alan Gewirth, *Reason and Morality* (Chicago: University of Chicago Press, 1978).

make the correct moral judgments but fail to "follow through" in terms of their concrete actions. Only a society in which *both* of the above conditions are fulfilled—where people hold the correct conception of justice and act in accordance with it—has a morally acceptable status. This fourth type of society is, of course, what I have termed the just social order. Here, every individual recognizes and respects the generic rights to freedom and well-being for himself and all others, and acts accordingly.

It should be clear that only the last named of these four types of societies (the just social order) can be characterized as having a "normative consensus" that is morally acceptable. Consistent with the views of Durkheim and Parsons, a society regulated by normative consensus about moral values will be one in which there is a high degree of predictability and stability in social relationships. But contrary to what they argue, the moral standing of such a society depends on the justifiability of those moral values about which there is consensus. And, of course, it is individuals who require predictability and stability in their social relationships and not the "social system" as a whole. What is necessary for a just social order, then, is that everyone live by the correct principles of justice.

In the real world, of course, it is totally unlikely that everyone would live in accordance with these principles. But still, the idea of all persons doing so does provide a standard against which we can compare existing states of affairs. Assuming, then, that it would be both morally and socially desirable for every person to recognize and respect the rights to freedom and well-being of everyone else, we need to consider how individuals might come to acquire such a sense of justice.[2] How is this to be accomplished through the process of socialization? To try to answer this question, it is first necessary to specify the various tasks that socialization must see to in regard to morality.

One of the primary tasks of socialization should be the devel-

[2] In focusing on the development of the correct sense of justice among children I am ignoring the question of whether those persons responsible for their socialization have themselves acquired this correct sense. I acknowledge that probably only a tiny percentage of child-rearers in the real world actually do have the requisite sense of justice. But there are undoubtedly some who do, that is, some who ascribe to something very much like the principles of justice formulated here. If the reader chooses, however, he or she may prefer to think of the problem of developing a sense of justice among children as one *concretely* faced by those few child-rearers who do themselves actually ascribe to the principles of justice.

opment in every person of a respect for the rights to freedom and well-being of all others. The recognition of these generic rights and the disposition to act in accordance with them is what Gewirth calls "the moral virtue of justice."[3] Thus, this is an important personal quality which needs to be developed in each child. A second kind of personal quality mentioned by Gewirth is self-esteem and the various virtues of character related to it. Every agent, Gewirth writes, "has an abiding self-esteem in that he views the worth of his goals as reflecting his own worth as a rational person whose life, freedom, and well-being are worthy of protection and development."[4] Without such self-esteem, the individual's ability to achieve many of his purposes becomes problematic. Certain virtues of character—such as courage, temperance, and prudence—are related to the agent's sense of his own worth; they serve to ground and reinforce his self-esteem, and contribute to his effectiveness in acting to fulfill his purposes.[5] Gewirth's principle of generic consistency requires that each person's "self-esteem must be reflected in a corresponding esteem for other persons."[6] This means that people ought to have an attitude of mutual acceptance and toleration toward one another, and that all moral agents have a duty to refrain from actions that hinder the development of the virtues of character in other persons. Because of the importance of self-esteem and those virtues of character to which it is related, its development constitutes a second task of socialization.

Although Gewirth speaks of "modes of education" with regard to the development of these two personal qualities—the moral virtue of justice, and self-esteem and the virtues associated with it—and notes that they can be fostered by the educational, political, and social institutions of the whole society,[7] I shall consider the problem of moral development almost entirely in terms of socialization within the setting of the family. Because most persons' capacities for self-development are initially acquired in a familial setting, socialization processes there will have a crucial determining influence on their moral development.

In addition to the two personal qualities emphasized by Gewirth, I will include a third as a major task of socialization: the development of the emotions that ought to accompany respect for peo-

---

[3] Gewirth, *Reason and Morality*, p. 319.

[4] Ibid., p. 241.

[5] Ibid., pp. 242–43.

[6] Ibid., p. 242.

[7] Ibid., p. 319.

ple's generic rights or their self-esteem and, perhaps more importantly, the emotions that ought to be felt when people's generic rights or their self-esteem are violated. It is not only that all persons must learn to respect the rights of others and esteem them, but they must also learn what emotions should—normatively speaking—accompany such respect and esteem. This aspect of morality is almost totally ignored by Gewirth.

Thus, I am concerned with three tasks in the socialization process: the development of children's ability to recognize and act in accordance with everyone's rights to freedom and well-being, the development of self-esteem within all children and a corresponding recognition of the need for self-esteem in all other persons, and the development of the capacity to experience the appropriate emotions as they relate to moral actions.

II

Gewirth makes it clear that rationality, the extent to which someone is rational and so behaves, is an important component of an agent's moral status. To act voluntarily and purposively, is to be disposed to "accept and act upon that to which the weight of deductive and inductive reason leads."[8] Someone who is able to exercise this commitment is a rational agent. This sense of "rational," Gewirth says, is the most minimal one, "involving consistency or the avoidance of self-contradiction in ascertaining or accepting what is logically involved in one's acting for purposes and in the associated concepts."[9] All normal human beings, he claims, are rational in this strict sense.[10] Consequently, as I have shown in Chapter 2, what a rational agent "ought" to do is to act in accord with the generic rights of his recipients as well as with his own rights.

Children are not yet rational agents in the above sense. Rather, they are potential agents and, as such, have rights that are preparatory for their taking on the full-fledged generic rights pertaining to full-fledged agency. Thus children must be given the kind of upbringing that will enable them to exercise their rights to freedom and well-being and to recognize and respect the same rights for all other persons. What, then, can parents or other child-rearers do to help assure that their children will acquire the status of full-fledged rational agents?

[8] Ibid., p. 46.
[9] Ibid.
[10] Ibid., p. 138.

I have shown in the previous chapter that infants and young children have ("partial") rights.[11] For them, it is the right to well-being that is of crucial importance. Their right to the basic goods that are the necessary preconditions for development—most importantly, adequate nutrition, shelter, rest, health care, love, and affection—imposes corresponding obligations on those who are responsible for their upbringing. Every child has a moral claim on the child-rearers for whatever is required for him or her to achieve adult agency and the full-fledged rights to freedom and well-being.

The child's needs for adequate nutrition, shelter, health care, and conditions of a more material character are quite obvious, but it is worth saying something about the significance of affection. This is because warmth and affection are crucial not only for the child's psychological development but for his or her moral development as well. There is considerable evidence showing that parental affection is important if children are to learn moral values and behavior.[12] Staub suggests several ways in which affection may influence the development of moral values and the tendency to behave "prosocially" (i.e., in a way that benefits other people):

> First, nurturance and warmth as the dominant mode of the parents relating to their children would make the children feel secure and would minimize self-concern in interaction with other people. . . . Second, an affectionate relationship with parents is likely to create a positive orientation toward other people, while a cold, hostile relationship is likely to create a negative one. Concern about other's well-being and the desire to help others may be greatly promoted by such a positive orientation. . . . A third consequence of parental nurturance may be that, by creating a positive emotional environment, it facilitates learning by the child. Tension, fear, and anxiety, which may result from lack of parental warmth, are known to interfere with learning. . . . Finally, parental nurturance may be an important source of identification with parents: if parents hold prosocial values and tend to behave prosocially, the affectionate relationships with the parent would contribute to

[11] I have used this term in Chapter 4 to refer to those rights which are not yet full-fledged rights.

[12] See, for example, M. L. Hoffman, "Moral Development," in P. H. Mussen, ed., *Carmichael's Manual of Child Development* (New York: Wiley, 1970); R. R. Sears, E. E. Maccoby, and H. Levin, *Patterns of Child Rearing* (New York: Harper Brothers, 1957).

the acquisition of a prosocial orientation through identification.[13]

Staub reports on a number of studies showing that, in fact, parental affection does contribute to all of the above.[14]

As I discussed in the previous chapter, there are three criteria for the attainment of full-fledged agency and the full-fledged rights that accompany it: the abilities to control one's behavior by one's unforced choice, to have knowledge of relevant circumstances, and to reflect on one's purposes.[15] With respect to "unforced choice," the child-rearers have an obligation to provide the physical, emotional, and psychological conditions necessary for the full development of such control in the child. If the child is to acquire the ability for self-control, so that he is able to exercise unforced choice, he must learn to delay immediate gratification, to see the immediate and future consequences of his actions, and to take on certain responsibilities. Certainly as the child grows older, there must be an emphasis on reciprocity so that the reciprocal rights and obligations of parents and child alike are recognized. Furthermore, as Gewirth points out, "children must increasingly participate actively in decisions affecting themselves as they increase in maturity."[16] To the extent that children are assigned responsibilities that make some actual contribution to the maintenance and functioning of the family, they are enabled to see how their own actions affect the welfare of other persons. A family environment in which there is sufficient parental control to limit harmful activities on the part of their children, an emphasis on the interdependence of family members, and enough autonomy for children so that they can learn from their mistakes in a supportive and just atmosphere, will allow children to gradually develop the ability to exercise their own unforced choices.

With regard to "knowledge of relevant circumstances," the parents or other child-rearers are obligated to raise the child under conditions conducive to the acquisition of such knowledge. The child requires parental guidance and preparation in being able to develop an awareness of the world beyond himself and outside

---

[13] Ervin Staub, *Positive Social Behavior and Morality*, vol. 2 (New York: Academic Press, 1979), pp. 111–12. This is a very useful summary and review of many studies related to moral development, and I will refer to it with some frequency in the following pages.

[14] Ibid.

[15] These come from Gewirth, *Reason and Morality*.

[16] Ibid., p. 141.

the home. He can only learn to function in a (relatively) autonomous fashion if he is enabled to acquire the necessary factual information and knowledge about the world he lives in. This, of course, involves the parents seeing that he obtains an adequate formal education, but it also involves an emphasis by the parents on the interdependence of human actions and activities, and a stress on the possibility of both intended and unintended consequences following from certain actions because of the complexity of the physical and social world. In addition to providing certain material resources for the child so that he can acquire formal training or instruction (schools, books, lessons), parents always have the difficult task of preparing the child to discriminate effectively among the many varieties of so-called knowledge that he will encounter, both formally and informally, outside the home. If the child is to eventually reach the status of a full-fledged agent, he must also learn various behavioral skills and strategies for interaction. Obviously, this requires more than the mere acquisition of knowledge, and a good deal of parental guidance is called for.

The third criteria for full-fledged agency, the individual's ability to rationally "reflect" on his own purposes, requires that parents expose the child to, and make him aware of, alternative ways of life and lines of action. As I noted in the previous chapter, without an awareness of alternatives, the child is not being adequately prepared to appraise, evaluate, and reflect upon his actions. This means that parents and other child-rearers have an obligation to assure that the child comes into contact with ways of life other than their own. Since I have already discussed this in Chapter 4, I will say no more about it here. With regard to the three criteria for the attainment of full-fledged agency and the full-fledged rights that accompany it, then, parents can obviously do much to provide the kind of upbringing that will assist their children in fulfilling these criteria.

But it needs to be emphasized that even if the child is provided with the necessary preconditions for development and is eventually able to meet the criteria for full-fledged agency, this does not necessarily mean that he or she will *observe* the demand of the principle of generic consistency to *act* in accord with the generic rights of all other persons. That is, someone may accept the analytic truth of this principle and, at the same time, fail to respect other people's rights to freedom and well-being. An individual who accepts the principle of generic consistency, who recognizes that all persons have rights, and yet commits murder is not acting in a self-con-

190

tradictory manner. That is, his violation of the person's rights does not mean that he is not a rational agent. What would be self-contradictory would be for him to accept that everyone has rights and still to assert that the person whom he murdered had no such rights. Thus, a rational individual can violate other people's moral rights without doing what is self-contradictory or logically impossible.[17]

Rationality, then, is a necessary but not sufficient condition for individuals to be able to act in accord with the moral rights of all other human beings. Only someone who is rational, in the sense specified earlier, is able to apply an "ought" to his own actions with regard to the generic rights of other persons. But, nonetheless, a person can be rational and recognize his obligation not to violate other people's rights and yet act in ways that are not consistent with this recognition.

III

Because rationality by itself is not a sufficient condition for acting morally, we need to consider what else the child-rearers can do to help assure that the child will learn to *act* in accord with the recognition of everyone's rights to freedom and well-being and their self-esteem. As will become clear in the following pages, it is difficult to provide answers that can command definitive empirical support from the literature of the social sciences. But there are some hints, especially in the more strictly psychological investigations, that, together with some of my own speculations, make it worthwhile to consider the question further. I will begin with a very brief and general discussion of the importance of "authoritative" child-rearers, will then consider the influence of "reflective understanding," and will conclude with a rather lengthy examination of the most neglected element in current discussions of socialization: the moral emotions.

To set the stage for my examination of these three aspects of socialization as they relate to the rights to freedom and well-being, it is first necessary to offer some comments about the need of all persons to acquire a sense of personal identity.[18] Later on in this chapter, I will return to the issue of identity and will contrast the

[17] Ibid., p. 181.
[18] Erik H. Erikson, *Childhood and Society*, 2nd ed. (New York: W. W. Norton, 1963).

model of identity formation sketched out here with the model dominant in the contemporary Western world.

Identity

Starting in early childhood, human beings begin to develop an identity, which—ideally, at least—becomes relatively crystallized and permanent during adolescence. Once this unitary, coherent, personal identity is established, it then remains more or less the same over the entire life cycle. Whatever else the tasks of socialization may be, the formation of personal identity is obviously one that stands central in the socialization process. The notion of identity implies the existence of an over-all *coherence* within the experiences and expressions of the individual, a *continuity* in the individual's memory as to who he or she is, and a *commitment* to a particular manner of both comprehending and managing one's own self.[19] In short, a sense of personal identity involves a continuity, a structure, and a policy.

The acquisition of a personal identity requires those kinds of secure, intimate, socially coherent, and articulated relations that are characteristic of the family at its best. The necessity for the presence of these conditions constitutes what Kovel refers to as a "transhistorical human need."[20] In order for the developing child to acquire a stable personal identity, an adequate level of security and intimacy are obviously important; they are the necessary conditions for the gradual acquisitions of his or her personal identity. But without the presence of a coherent set of behaviors on the part of parental figures and a consistent and articulated set of values, standards, and ideals on their part, the child is unlikely to acquire the self-identity required for morally right conduct.

As regards coherent actions and relations on the part of the parents or child-rearers, the adult must be perceived as being the same person throughout the range of his or her interactions with the child. Whatever the child may feel about the parents in terms of love, hate, or ambivalence, the parental figure must be someone who is him- or herself recognizable to the child as a distinct and unique human being. Similarly with the need for a consistent and articulated code of conduct; the child can acquire a stable sense of identity only if the child-rearers are experienced as persons who

[19] Vytautas Kavolis, "Logics of Selfhood and Modes of Order: Civilizational Structures for Individual Identities," in Roland Robertson and Burkhart Holzner, eds., *Identity and Authority* (Oxford: Basil Blackwell, 1980), p. 41.

[20] Joel Kovel, "Narcissism and the Family," *Telos* 44 (Summer 1980): 96.

are clear and consistent about what is permissible and impermissible, good and bad, right and wrong. Since the child's personal identity is acquired through a struggle over what one *ought* and *ought not* to do—as contrasted to what he or she simply *wants* to do—the demands and expectations of the child-rearers must be seen as having a certain coherence and logic.

The acquisition of a single, continuous sense of self, of sameness over time, requires also that the child experience and recognize the authoritative presence of the child-rearers. In order for him or her to acquire a specific identity *vis-à-vis others*, the child must come to terms with those authority figures first encountered in the early stages of socialization, i.e., the parental figures. Without the availability of authority and authority figures, there can be no meaningful and structured order within which the child's purposes can be pursued, a coherent life plan formulated, and moral development assured. Direct and intimate contact with living authority, from whom ensue right and proper demands that go beyond various situational immediacies, helps assure that there are recognizable models against whom the child can compare and contrast his or her own fantasies and conduct. In one sense, authority is superior to what it authorizes. That is, it is the form—and not just the content of authority—that makes it crucial to a child's moral development. Only the presence of real, living authority allows for the possibility of both identification with and eventual revolt against parents and other authority figures. In order for the "identity crisis," common to adolescents, to be successfully resolved, recognizable authority figures must be available to the developing child. Obviously, the family setting is where such figures are most likely to be encountered.

Part of what I am suggesting, of course, is that the child's eventual acquisition of a sense of identity is very much dependent upon he or she being raised and socialized by parental figures who themselves have coherent and well-integrated personal identities. The parental "self" that the child witnesses in the mother or father's contact and relations with friends, neighbors, and other acquaintances, must be seen by the child as consistent across a whole variety of different situations and relationships.

For the parent, as will eventually become the case for the child, a stable and coherent identity is ideally one built around commitments to work and love. Love is, of course, crucial as a cohesive force in the family and as a substantive model of self-other respect, restraint, and duty. Further, the child's very first experience and acquaintanceship with love occurs in the parent-child relationship. In fact, it would appear that the only way in which human beings could possibly have developed a familiarity with love, and certain expectations regarding it, is by having been the recipients of prolonged, reliable affection as infants and children. But love is also an important and necessary aspect of the personal identity of those adult figures who are involved in the socialization of the young. And certainly work is not only an instrumental activity that is necessary for the family's economic well-being and functioning; it is also potentially both a source of satisfaction and personal identity to the adult and an important component of the child's perception of who (and what) his mother and father are.

Freud is alleged to have said that the definition of maturity was to be found in the capacity to love and work.[21] He realized, of course, that most persons never realize this capacity in the full. But love and work, he claimed, combine to make civilization possible. Certainly, there are many elements common to these two phenomena. Among other similarities, both love and work are dependent on interpersonal relationships; both involve strong commitments to objects, both personal and impersonal; and both are governed by the search for lasting and socially responsible pleasure.[22] Love and work, then, are ancient prescriptions, necessary both for the survival of society and for the identity of all individuals.

With the ideal of love in the West, as Swidler observes, "Identity is symbolized through choosing whom to love and remaining true to one's choice against all opposition."[23] Successful identity formation, on this view, is measured by the capacity to make a commitment as to one's choice of partner and stick to it; to form a close attachment with him or her; to engage in self-sacrifice as the ultimate proof of love for one's spouse and children; and to sustain close and intimate relations with those whom one loves.[24] The realization of these ideals of commitment, attachment, self-sacrifice, and intimacy can provide a crucible for identity formation. When fully realized, love allows for a transformation, an expression

[21] Cited by Neil J. Smelser, "Issues in the Study of Work and Love." In Neil J. Smelser and Erik Erikson, eds., *Themes of Work and Love in Adulthood* (London: Grant McIntyre, 1980), p. 4.

[22] Smelser, "Issues in Work and Love"; Nathan Hale, "Freud's Reflections on Work and Love," in Smelser and Erikson, *Work and Love*, pp. 29–42.

[23] Ann Swidler, "Love and Adulthood in American Culture," *Work and Love*, p. 124.

[24] These ideals are discussed at length in ibid., pp. 120–47.

of self-definition, which helps create a more coherent and stable personal identity.

Work, too, can be a source of transformation. "History compels the judgment," says Ellul, "that it is in work that human beings develop and affirm their personalities."[25] But work must be distinguished from labor. To labor is to be imprisoned in an activity whose outcome or product has no personal meaning for the person's capacities and individuality. Labor is usually accompanied by boredom, a lack of commitment, and an absence of satisfaction with the activity in which one is engaged. To work, by contrast, is to have the outcome and product bear the stamp of one's own capacities and individuality. Work involves interest, commitment, and satisfaction; it contributes to an expanding and enriched life. As noted by John Dewey, work can be an experience in the fullest sense.

> A piece of work is finished in a way that is satisfactory; a problem receives its solution; . . . a situation, whether that of eating a meal, playing a game of chess, carrying on a conversation, writing a book, or taking part in a political campaign, is so rounded out that its close is a consummation and not a cessation. Such an experience is a whole and carries with it its own individualizing quality and self-sufficiency. It is *an* experience.[26]

Work, like the other activities listed above, contains the promise of what Dewey terms experience. It has the possibility of providing challenge, novelty, and satisfaction. Labor, on the other hand, is devoid of such a possibility.

The capacity to love and be loved and the capacity to enjoy meaningful work are, then, important components of our identity. Love and work are the two major ways in which we adults define our personal identity. They are also the bases on which others—including our children—presume to know who we are.

Having briefly discussed the need of each individual to acquire a coherent sense of personal identity, I turn now to an exploration of what parents and other child-rearers can do to help assure that the child will act in accord with the recognition of everyone's rights to freedom and well-being. Since this is my explicit concern in the section that follows, I will touch on identity formation only in

---

[25] Jacques Ellul, *The Technological Society* (New York: Vintage Books, 1964), p. 399.
[26] John Dewey, *Art as Experience* (New York: Balch & Co., 1934), p. 35.

passing. Nevertheless, the extent to which it is related to the topics under consideration should be obvious.

Authoritativeness

Many writers in recent years have pointed to the collapse of authority within the family, the traditional source of much moral teaching and guidance.[27] Arnold Rogow, for example, argues that American parents, alternatively "permissive and evasive" in dealing with their children, "find it easier to achieve conformity by the use of bribery than by facing the emotional turmoil of suppressing the child's demands."[28] Gilbert Rose writes that "Some parents . . . are incapable of such things as putting their child to bed in the face of protests or of curbing the child's aggression."[29] Christopher Lasch states: "Instead of guiding the child, the older generation now struggles to 'keep up with the kids,' to master their incomprehensible jargon, and even to imitate their dress and manners in the hope of preserving a youthful appearance and outlook."[30] And Philip Rieff echoes this when he writes, "How sad for our young that their elders imitate them."[31]

It is not my intention to speculate here about the various factors responsible for the lessening of parental authority. Instead, I want to consider why authoritativeness is important in the child's acquisition of moral principles and in his ability to act on such principles.

To begin with, many parents are not themselves clear as to what qualities they want their children to have. Obviously, such parental uncertainty gets communicated to the child and makes the acquisition of a consistent set of moral principles very difficult. Thus, parents who adhere to some basic philosophy of child-rearing are more likely to successfully socialize their child than those who lack such a guiding philosophy. Staub notes that parents must exercise control if they are to bring about acceptable conduct, and observes that "Love and affection without control may lead to licence, lack

[27] See, for example, Jules Henry, *Culture Against Man* (New York: Knopf, 1963); Arnold A. Rogow, *The Dying of the Light* (New York: Putnam's, 1975); Robert Nisbet, *Twilight of Authority* (New York: Oxford University Press, 1975); Christopher Lasch, *The Culture of Narcissism* (New York: W. W. Norton, 1978); Gilbert J. Rose, "Some Misuses of Analysis as a Way of Life," *International Review of Psychoanalysis* 1 (1974): 509–15.

[28] Rogow, *The Dying of the Light*, p. 67.

[29] Rose, "Misuses of Analysis," pp. 513–14.

[30] Lasch, *The Culture of Narcissism*, p. 169.

[31] Philip Rieff, *Fellow Teachers* (New York: Harper & Row, 1973), p. 156.

of self-discipline, and the inability to inhibit desired behavior that is harmful to others."[32] Several investigations show the influence of parents' firm enforcement on the behavior they expected of their children. Firm and consistent control, as opposed to lax or extremely restrictive control, seems to be highly important for children's moral development.[33]

According to Baumrind, "authoritative parents," whose child-rearing policies are characterized by firm enforcement, reasoning with the child and nurturance, and whose children tend to be socially responsible, are found to use "corporal punishment rather than ridicule, frightening the child, or withdrawal of love." They also generally use positive rather than negative reinforcement to obtain compliance.[34] In comparison with inconsistent parents, authoritative parents are better able to assure that their child will learn moral principles and values because their own actions, verbal communications to the child, and general style of interaction with him or her are all reasonably consistent with each other and with the principles and values to which the parents require adherence.[35] Summarizing several studies in which the effects of authoritative, permissive, and authoritarian child-rearing practices have been compared, Staub concludes that authoritative practices by parents contribute "not only to positive behavior with peers, rule following, and obedience to adult's authority but also to a reasonable degree of independence."[36]

"Reasoning" by parents, Baumrind shows, is an important component of the authoritative practices that contribute to socially responsible behavior in children.[37] Other investigations bear this out.[38] Hoffman, for example, reports that the most important antecedent of a child's learning and acting on moral values advocated by the parents is the parents' pointing out the harmful conse-

[32] Staub, *Positive Social Behavior and Morality*, p. 91.

[33] D. Baumrind, "Child Care Practices Antecedenting Three Patterns of Preschool Behavior," *Genetic Psychological Monographs* 75 (1967): 43–88; D. Baumrind, "Current Patterns of Parental Authority," *Developmental Psychology* 4 (1971): 1–101.

[34] D. Baumrind, *Early Socialization and the Discipline Controversy* (Morristown, N.J.: General Learning Press, 1975), p. 111.

[35] Staub, *Positive Social Behavior and Morality*, p. 93.

[36] Ibid., p. 110.

[37] Baumrind, "Child Care Practices," and "Current Patterns of Parental Authority."

[38] Sears et al., *Patterns of Child-Rearing*; Hoffman, "Moral Development"; J. Aronfreed, *Conduct and Conscience* (New York: Academic Press, 1968).

quences of the child's undesirable behavior for others.[39] With respect to the general influence of parental reasoning—i.e., using arguments and reasons rather than simple appeals to authority—on children's moral development, Staub writes:

> Verbal communication, together with the parents' behavior, may also shape children's conception of their own similarity to or difference from others. If children come to conceive of others as similar to themselves on important dimensions defining "human-ness"—basic needs, feelings, and the like—a close self-other connection may result, the capacity for empathy and identification may be enhanced, and a wide scope of prosocial values may develop.[40]

Authoritative parents who have clear ideas about how they want their children to act, who emphasize the moral desirability of certain kinds of actions, utilize reasoning in regard to their advocacy of specific sorts of conduct, stress the harmful consequences of some behaviors and demand some sort of redress for those whom their children might have harmed, and themselves engage in actions consistent with their reasoning, are more likely than either highly permissive or authoritarian parents to successfully engender the moral principles and standards required for a just social order. Since children first learn that certain actions are right or wrong from the standpoint of those responsible for the upbringing, authoritative child-rearers can certainly shape the child's ability to recognize and act in accord with other people's rights to freedom and well-being, and also help them develop feelings of self-esteem and the corresponding recognition of the need for self-esteem of all other persons.

Reflective Understanding

As noted earlier, Gewirth stipulates that the capacity for reflection is one of the criteria for full-fledged agency. This ability to reflect on one's own purposes must, of course, be acquired by individuals in their childhood years. But Gewirth also mentions a second kind of reflective ability that the child may need to acquire, although he refers to it only in passing. This is the reflective ability required of those to whom precepts are addressed, i.e., the recipients. Gewirth writes:

[39] Hoffman, "Moral Development."
[40] Staub, *Positive Social Behavior and Morality*, pp. 115–16.

The precepts must be presented not as mere incitements or goads to action, as threats or attempts at brain-washing, but rather as reasoned commands, as offering directives or guidance for action with the implicit assumption that these are the right ways to act because there are sound reasons for doing so (these need not be moral reasons). A related assumption is that these reasons can be *reflectively understood* by the persons to whom they are addressed.[41]

It is not, of course, necessary for those to whom precepts are addressed to agree with the prescribed objectives or the reasons offered for them, but they must be able to reflectively understand them.

Thus, Gewirth speaks of reflectivity in two different contexts: one, in regard to the agent's ability to reflect on his own purposes; the other, in regard to his ability to reflectively understand the reasons that are addressed to him in support of various precepts. It is the first of these that Gewirth includes as one of the criteria for full-fledged agency, and I shall say nothing more about that here. But the second, the ability to reflectively understand, is worth considering further. Although it is not directly relevant to the conditions for full-fledged agency, I believe that the differentially developed ability to reflectively understand reasons, precepts, other points of view, and the like, is highly relevant to the development of moral reasoning and action in children.

Since I do not know exactly what Gewirth intends when he makes brief mention of the ability to reflectively understand, I will not consider it in terms of his aims. Instead, I want to suggest some reasons why reflective understanding is important for moral development. I will consider the notion of reflective understanding explicitly in regard to Kohlberg's scheme of moral development discussed in Chapter 3.

According to Kohlberg, there are three levels of moral development, each of which involves a different type of relationship between the individual and society's rules and expectations. In his words:

> *Level* I is a *preconventional* person, for whom rules and social expectations are something external to the self; *Level* II is a *conventional* person, in whom the self is identified with or has internalized the rules and expectations of others, especially

---

[41] Gewirth, *Reason and Morality*, pp. 165–66.

those of authorities; and *Level* III is a *postconventional* person, who has differentiated his self from the rules and expectations of others and defines his values in terms of self-chosen principles.[42]

It seems obvious that a different level of reflective understanding is required for each of the three levels of moral development. The preconventional person needs to be able to reflectively understand and follow what other persons expect of him. He needs to be aware that people have different interests, and has to be able to himself engage in reciprocal actions and exchanges. The conventional person must be able to reflectively understand and follow (or deviate from) expectations that are connected with norms and values. This involves the capacity to shift from a reflective understanding of the concrete interests of specific individuals to the norms, standards, and laws of the group or society in which he participates. The postconventional person has to be capable of reflectively understanding the norms and values themselves. That is, he must be able to reflect on, and call into question, the validity of norms, standards, values, and the like, that are nonproblematic for conventional persons. Thus, the more advanced the level of moral development, the more advanced the degree of reflective understanding demanded from the individual.

What is most significant about different degrees of reflective understanding is the increased capacity to consider things from a wider perspective. Infants and young children view the world entirely from their own, individual, perspective. Eventually, they acquire the capacity to take the perspective of one other person at a time. Conventional persons (in Kohlberg's sense) have the ability to step outside the two-person relationship and look at it from a third-person perspective: initially from the perspective of "significant others," then from the perspective of the "generalized other." This ability to take the perspective of the generalized other involves the capacity to take the perspective of the whole social system in which the individual participates. Those persons with the most highly developed capacity for reflective understanding are able to view their own and other people's actions from the perspective of any human being, rather than as a member of a particular society. They are, of course, postconventional persons. Assuming, then,

[42] Lawrence Kohlberg, "Moral Stages and Moralization: The Cognitive-Developmental Approach," in T. Lickona, ed., *Moral Development and Behavior* (New York: Holt, 1976), p. 33.

that a highly developed reflective understanding involves the capacity for taking the perspective of "anyone" (or everyone), it is important to consider what aspects of socialization might be connected with higher degrees of reflective understanding.

Kohlberg himself emphasizes the importance of opportunities for "role-taking" as contributing to moral development. He speaks of role-taking ability as the capacity "to react to the other as someone like the self and to react to the self's behavior in the role of the other."[43] At the one extreme (stage 1 in Kohlberg's six-stage scheme), the egocentric child is unable to take the role of any other person; at the other extreme (stage 6), the individual is able to engage in "ideal role-taking" (involving, as I noted in Chapter 3, reversibility and universalizability).

There is extensive evidence that role-taking abilities increase with age, and this appears to be true for perceptual, affective, and cognitive role-taking alike.[44] As children become older, they are increasingly able to see and understand events from the perspective of other persons. With regard to affective role-taking, for example, the ability to accurately perceive, identify, or infer others' feelings is an important element in being able to take the perspective of other persons. Such accuracy requires, as Staub points out, "knowledge about how people react emotionally to different kinds of events" and "an understanding of the psychological meaning of events and knowledge about the antecedents of different classes of human emotions."[45] It is not to be expected that such understanding and knowledge will be found in very young children; it will be acquired (if at all) only with maturation.[46]

So far as the evidence concerning the relationship between increased abilities for role-taking and moral development is concerned, it seems correct to conclude that role-taking ability is a necessary but not sufficient condition for advanced moral reason-

[43] Lawrence Kohlberg, "Stage and Sequence: The Cognitive-Developmental Approach to Socialization," in David Goslin, ed., *Handbook of Socialization Theory and Research* (Chicago: Rand McNally, 1969), p. 398.

[44] Staub, *Positive Social Behavior and Morality*, p. 75.

[45] Ibid., pp. 74–75.

[46] With regard to cognitive role-taking, both Kohlberg and Piaget assume that role-taking is a prerequisite for moral development. In fact, the capacity to consider events from an increasingly broad perspective is an inherent aspect of moral development in Kohlberg's theory. What is required, and generally lacking, is research where cognitive role-taking abilities are investigated *apart* from their contribution to moral reasoning. It is also unfortunate that there are almost no studies of role-taking in the adult years.

ing.[47] Nevertheless, greater opportunities for role-taking do appear to contribute to the increased capacity for reflective understanding, which is a major component of advanced moral reasoning. But, to repeat a point made in an earlier chapter, the capacity to see events from another's perspective does not necessarily mean that the individual will always do so or that such a capacity will directly influence his or her actions.

Implicit in the above discussion is my assumption that individuals with an advanced capacity for reflective understanding will be more likely to act in accord with their recognition of everyone's rights to freedom and well-being, as well as their self-esteem, than will those persons with a less advanced capacity for such reflective understanding. If this is correct, and if opportunities for role-taking contribute to the capacity for reflective understanding, then—as I suggested in Chapter 3—parents and other child-rearers should do as much as possible to encourage and create such opportunities.

Reflective understanding is obviously an important component in the moral reasoning of persons at the highest stage of moral development in Kohlberg's scheme. Such persons have a capacity for ideal role-taking and a concern with moral principles; their reasoning is guided by universal principles of justice, by a recognition of the reciprocity and equality of rights, and by respect for the dignity of all individual persons.

In this connection, it is important to make brief mention of Carol Gilligan's recent work on moral development. In her book, *In a Different Voice*, she criticizes Kohlberg for his general lack of attention to differences in male and female moral development.[48] Her own research shows that while the moral imperative for males at a high stage of development is an injunction to respect the rights of other persons, the moral imperative for females is an injunction to care. Essentially, the difference is that men see morality mainly as a matter of justice as fairness, and women see morality more as a matter of caring and personal responsibility for those to whom they are connected. Kohlberg's individualistic theory needs to be supplemented, Gilligan argues, by attending to the ethic of responsibility and caring that grows out of people's relationships with one another.

[47] This is made clear in R. L. Selman, "The Relation of Role-Taking to the Development of Moral Judgment in Children," *Child Development* 42 (1971): 79–92.

[48] Carol Gilligan, *In a Different Voice* (Cambridge, Mass.: Harvard University Press, 1982).

Thus, in the move from rights to responsibilities, the fundamental premise of moral judgments shifts from balancing separate individuals in a social system equilibrated by the logic of equality and reciprocity to seeing individuals as interdependent in a network of social relationships. . . . Whereas justice emphasizes the autonomy of the person, care underlies the primacy of relationship. Thus, justice gives rise to an ethic of rights, and care engenders an ethic of responsibility.[49]

This ethic of responsibility, Gilligan argues, depends on a contextual mode of judgment, which she speaks of as "contextual relativism."[50] Based on the empirical results of her research of pregnant women who were considering abortion decisions, she concludes that the context and circumstances involved are far more important for women than for men. With regard specifically to abortion, women do not usually construe this as a dilemma involving the rights of the mother and the fetus. Instead, they place the dilemma of abortion in the context of the relationship in which it arises. They see the decision as placed at the juncture between two relationships: of man and woman, and of parent and child. Viewed in this context, a decision about abortion poses a problem of responsibility.

Gilligan claims that sensitivity to contextual relativism constitutes a "developmental advance" over the "principles morality" found among men in Kohlberg's highest stages of moral development.[51] It is clear from Gilligan's research that women are indeed more cognitively aware and sophisticated about situational factors than are men. At the same time, however, she points out that "In women's development, the absolute of care, defined initially as not hurting others, becomes complicated through a recognition of the need for personal integrity."[52] Gilligan mentions in this connection a lawyer whose earlier absolute injunction against hurting people has now been extended to include herself among those who ought not to be hurt. "Her moral inclusive morality," Gilligan observes, "now contains the injunction to be true to herself, leaving her with

[49] Carol Gilligan, "Do the Social Sciences Have an Adequate Theory of Moral Development?" In Norma Haan, et al., Social Science and Moral Inquiry (New York: Columbia University Press, 1983), p. 40.

[50] Gilligan, In a Different Voice, p. 22.

[51] J. M. Murphy and Carol Gilligan, "Moral Development in Late Adolescence and Adulthood: A Critique and Reconstruction of Kohlberg's Theory," Human Development 23 (1980): 166.

[52] Gilligan, In a Different Voice, p. 166.

two principles of judgment whose integration she cannot clearly envision."[53]

As it now stands, I fail to see why this view of morality constitutes a developmental advance. What Gilligan shows is that there are people (more often women than men) for whom moral judgments always involve the competing claims of two sorts of principles, what Gilligan refers to as "integrity" and "care."[54] Because of their contextual understanding of morality, such persons see a concern for self (integrity) and a concern for others (care) as in conflict.

In my view, however, contextual relativism is not a moral position at all. Unless we are told how context-sensitive individuals weigh and choose between things that they see as conflicting, we are not really dealing with how people decide to *act* when confronting various dilemmas of the sort discussed by Gilligan. If—as Gilligan herself indicates—people must sometimes act to resolve dilemmas, how do they do so? It seems to me that a conflict between, say, a principle of integrity and a principle of care must be resolved by reference to some other principle (unless, of course, both fall under a more general principle as with Gewirth's Principle of Generic Consistency). But neither Gilligan nor her subjects mention any such principle, emphasizing instead the existence of incompatible alternatives. For this reason, I have strong doubts about the so-called "advance" involved with contextual relativism.

Returning to Kohlberg's theory, his abstract and ethical principles appear very similar to the admonition of the Principle of Generic Consistency to act in accord with the generic rights of your recipients as well as with your own rights. But, of course, there is one very significant difference between this principle and the principles adhered to by people at the highest stage in Kohlberg's scheme. The Principle of Generic Consistency is concerned specifically with people's moral *actions*, while the principles followed at stage 6 are principles of moral *reasoning*. As I indicated in Chapter 3, there is surprisingly little evidence of any strong relationship between the development of moral reasoning and moral actions; higher levels of moral reasoning do not necessarily mean that individuals are more moral persons. In fact, the nature of the relationship between cognition and behavior more generally remains unexplicated.[55] Therefore, it seems very unlikely that an advanced

---

[53] Ibid., p. 165.
[54] Ibid., p. 164.
[55] Staub, *Positive Social Behavior and Morality*, p. 167.

capacity for reflective understanding by itself, or even in conjunction with authoritative child-rearing practices, will result in people being more moral persons.

What is further required, in my view, is an educating of the emotions so that the cognitive influences on moral reasoning will also affect people's emotional reactions and thus their actions.

The Emotions

I argued in Chapter 3 that neither Kohlberg's cognitive developmental theory nor the identification-internalization approach gives adequate attention to the appropriateness or inappropriateness of certain emotional feelings. While the advocates of the latter approach place too much emphasis on the entirely negative aspects of some emotions, Kohlberg neglects them almost altogether. Further, I noted that the emotions are generally ignored by Gewirth. Because I believe that people's emotional reactions can have a strong influence on their actions and may, therefore, contribute to their being more moral persons, I will consider the emotions at some length and in considerable detail.[56]

There is a long tradition that views the emotions as irrational, in fact, as threats to rationality. Many philosophers have espoused this view, demanding that Reason *conquer* Emotion. Kant held that no emotionally governed activity by an individual can contribute to our assessment of him as a moral agent. This is because, he claimed, the emotions are too capricious, are too passively experienced, and whether one experiences them or not is entirely the result of natural causation.[57] Aristotle, on the other hand, argued that a central part of moral education has to do with learning to

[56] I have found the following especially useful with regard to the emotions: William Alston, "Emotion and Feeling," in Paul Edwards, ed., *Encyclopedia of Philosophy*, vol. 2 (New York: Collier-Macmillan, 1979); M. B. Arnold, ed., *Feelings and Emotions: The Loyola Symposium* (New York: Academic Press, 1970); J. R. Davitz, *The Language of Emotion* (New York: Academic Press, 1969); Willard Gaylin, *Feelings: Our Vital Signs* (New York: Harper & Row, 1979); Anthony Kenny, *Action, Emotion and Will* (London: Routledge and Kegan Paul, 1963); R. S. Peters, in Arnold, *Feelings and Emotions*, pp. 187–204; Gerhart Piers and Milton S. Singer, *Shame and Guilt: A Psychoanalytic and a Cultural Study* (Springfield, Ill.: Charles C. Thomas, 1953); Robert C. Solomon, *The Passions* (Garden City, N.Y.: Anchor Press, 1977); Bernard Williams, *Problems of the Self* (Cambridge: Cambridge University Press, 1973); and, most especially, Amélie Oksenberg Rorty, ed., *Explaining Emotions* (Berkeley: University of California Press, 1980).

[57] Cited in Williams, *Problems of the Self*.

feel the right emotions.[58] And a contemporary philosopher, Bernard Williams, states: "If such [moral] education does not revolve around such issues as what to fear, what to be angry about, what—if anything—to despise, where to draw the line between kindness and a stupid sentimentality—I do not know what it is."[59]

Are emotions indeed irrational and a threat to rationality, as some persons claim, or are they a necessary and important part of human life? Perhaps we can attempt to answer such a question by first trying to conceive of a world without emotions, a world where no one expressed feelings of fear, anger, guilt, shame, pride, or jealousy. Such a world would be one where all social relationships involved creatures whose actions would be governed entirely by the exercise of a pure rational will. As Wittgenstein frequently emphasized, some of our concepts have roots that reach so deep into our lives that imagining them to be different involves virtually imagining different kinds of creatures. We can certainly imagine a form of being who never expresses feelings. For such beings, there would be no concept of shamming and there would be no point in having one. Without the concept of love, hate, anger, and the like, there would be no place for feigning emotions—pretending to love someone, simulating anger, or whatever. The life of such beings would run quite differently than ours. But it is certainly questionable whether we would consider them "human" beings. Yet, as Wittgenstein insisted, such forms of behavior are imaginable.[60] We can try to follow his advice to "imagine the facts otherwise than they are," but think *how much* we would have to imagine otherwise for the idea of a world without emotions to gain any foothold in our thinking.

I want to suggest that emotions are purposive actions and not disruptive occurrences. That is, emotions are not occurrences that happen to (or in) us, but are a species of activity that falls into the realm of responsibility. Though it cannot be said that we "choose" them (we cannot, for example, simply choose to love someone), they are under our control and there are reasons for them. They involve evaluation and appraisal and are subject to justification. As Louch observes, an emotion "is not, as held by many philosophers and psychologists, an irrational eruption for which, like

---

[58] Aristotle, *Nicomachean Ethics*. Translated, with introduction and notes, by Martin Ostwald, 2 vols. (Indianapolis, Ind.: Bobbs-Merrill, 1962), 2: 6.

[59] Williams, *Problems of the Self*, p. 225.

[60] Ludwig Wittgenstein, *Zettel* (Oxford: Basil Blackwell, 1967), pp. 383–90.

pimples and rashes, we seek the physical causes, but a form of rational response to standard situations of provocation."[61]

Consider anger, for example. Like many other emotions, anger can be either rational or irrational. It is rational insofar as there are adequate reasons for it. In many instances, anger is not simply an emotion that "overcomes" one; rather, it is open to rational control to some extent. Anger is irrational, on the other hand, when it fails to disappear despite evidence that shows it to be unfounded. Anger, like other emotions, can also be appropriate or inappropriate. Appropriateness is, in fact, the basic rational value of the emotions.[62] Anger is appropriate if, and only if, the evoking situation warrants that emotion.[63] It is inappropriate, in contrast, when the evoking situation warrants a different emotion.

Just as with anger, many other emotions may sometimes be both rational and appropriate. In fact, the possibility of asking about any emotion, "What makes you feel that way?" should by itself be enough to belie the conception that emotions are not cognitive mental phenomena. Not only are people frequently able to try to answer such a question, but the set of plausible answers is quite limited. If a woman were asked, "Why are you angry?" we would be astonished if she responded, "Well, I'm angry because snow is white," or, "I'm angry because today is Tuesday." Such responses might, of course, make sense under some circumstances. If it were the case, for example, that Tuesday was the day her husband always saw the woman with whom he was having an affair, then the second response would constitute a plausible answer to the anger question. For the most part, however, we are all able to assess the plausibility of responses to the question, "What makes you feel that way?"

When we ask people why they are angry, ashamed, jealous, or whatever, we judge not only the plausibility of their responses but also their appropriateness and rationality. If we ask someone who appears to be extremely angry why he is so angry, he could reply, "Because two plus two equals four." This would be an implausible answer, and we might decide that he misunderstood the question, was joking, drunk, or out of his mind. If, on the other hand, he

[61] A. R. Louch, *Explanations and Human Action* (Berkeley: University of California Press, 1969), p. 85.

[62] Patricia S. Greenspan, "A Case of Mixed Feelings: Ambivalence and the Logic of Emotions," in Rorty, *Explaining Emotions*, p. 245. See also Robert C. Solomon, "Emotions and Choice," ibid., pp. 251–81.

[63] Ronald de Sousa, "The Rationality of Emotions," ibid., p. 131.

replied, "I'm angry because someone just stole all my money," this would be a plausible answer. It would also be rational for him to be angry; there is good reason for him to feel that way. And, of course, anger is the appropriate emotion under the circumstances; given what occurred, he should feel angry, and not jealous, proud, or loving.

The Moral Emotions

There are also certain emotions that ought to accompany or result from the violation of moral standards and principles. If someone does something that he believes he ought not to have done, the most rational and appropriate emotion is often guilt.[64] An individual who accepts the moral prohibition against killing and yet violates this by killing someone ought to, under ordinary circumstances, feel guilty. Guilt is, in such a case, both rational and appropriate. But note that I say "under ordinary circumstances"; in a situation of war, it might be that pride—perhaps mixed with regret—is the rational and appropriate emotion to be experienced after killing another human being. I am not saying, of course, that all feelings of guilt (or pride, or whatever) are rational and appropriate. There is, after all, neurotic guilt, excessive pride, and the like. But these are aberrations, and they are not my concern here. My main point, to which I shall return later, is that guilt is the rational and appropriate (in short, the "correct") emotion for people to experience when they violate the generic rights of other persons or fail to give them the esteem to which they are entitled.

Just as guilt may be the rational and appropriate emotion in the

[64] Especially useful for guilt and shame are the following: David P. Ausubel, "Relationships Between Shame and Guilt in the Socializing Process," *Psychological Review* 62 (September 1955): 378–90; Charles Brenner, *An Elementary Text of Psychoanalysis* (Garden City, N.Y.: Doubleday Anchor, 1955); Joel Feinberg, *Doing and Deserving: Essays in the Theory of Responsibility* (Princeton: Princeton University Press, 1970); Freud, *Civilization and Its Discontents*; Sigmund Freud, *Collected Papers*, ed. Ernest Jones (New York: Basic Books, 1959); Clifford Geertz, *The Interpretation of Cultures* (London: Hutchinson, 1975); Bernard Gert, *The Moral Rules* (New York: Harper Torchbooks, 1973); Helen Merrel Lynd, *On Shame and the Search for Identity* (New York: Harcourt, Brace and Company, 1958); A. I. Meldon, *Rights and Persons* (Oxford: Basil Blackwell, 1977); Herbert Morris, ed., *Guilt and Shame* (Belmont, Calif.: Wadsworth Publishing Company, 1971); Piers and Singer, *Shame and Guilt*; John Rawls, *A Theory of Justice* (Cambridge, Mass.: Harvard University Press, 1971); Philip Rieff, *Fellow Teachers*; David Riesman, Nathan Glazer, and Reuel Denney, *The Lonely Crowd* (Garden City, N.Y.: Doubleday Anchor, 1956); Allen Wheelis, *The Moralist* (New York: Basic Books, 1973); Allen Wheelis, *The Quest for Identity* (New York: W. W. Norton, 1958).

above circumstances, there may be a more strictly positive emotion that should accompany or result from doing what one ought to do morally. I am not certain, however, what that emotion would be. Pride might be such an emotion, but pride seems to be associated more with doing well (i.e., with achievement) than with doing good, or what is right. To feel proud is to have certain qualities that are considered "desirable" and that, frequently at least, earn us the approval of others. Oftentimes, pride has the connotation of being an emotion that depends on the acknowledgment of others, although this need not be the case. It could be argued, I suppose, that if we ought to do what is right and feel guilty when we don't, then we should simply feel normal in the performance of right actions.

But it seems to me that Isenberg makes an important observation when he points out that "pride should be proportioned to the real value of the things of which we are proud. The pride taken in qualities of our own must run parallel to the respect which we should feel for the same qualities in another person, and this respect must in turn correspond to the actual worth of those qualities."[65] Thus, if I feel respect for people who uphold the correct moral standards, then having the same qualities in myself would constitute respect for myself. While we could call this pride, as Isenberg does, I prefer to use the term "self-respect." We might also think of such emotions as self-contentment or self-esteem here, but I believe that self-respect is superior to these terms in capturing the essence of an emotion that is rational and appropriate when we do what we should do morally. In this sense, Parsons is correct in saying that self-respect may be one of the moral sentiments that an individual has toward himself.[66]

Up to this point, I have argued that *guilt* is the rational and appropriate emotion when we do something that we ought not to do, and that *self-respect* is the rational and appropriate emotion when we do what we ought to do. I also mentioned in passing that we feel *respect* for other persons who do what they ought to do. With regard to those persons who violate the correct moral standards, *moral indignation* is perhaps the most rational and appropriate emotional feeling on our part. Moral disapproval strikes me as too weak, while moral outrage seems too strong an emotional

---

[65] Arnold Isenberg, "Natural Pride and Natural Shame," in Rorty, *Explaining Emotions*, p. 360.

[66] Talcott Parsons, *Essays in Sociological Theory: Pure and Applied* (Glencoe, Ill.: Free Press, 1949), p. 168.

response. Just as our self-respect runs parallel to the respect we should feel for the same qualities in other persons, our moral indignation runs parallel to the guilt we would feel if we were to violate the correct moral standards or principles that we accept. With moral actions, then, self-respect and guilt are the emotions we apply to ourselves, and respect and indignation are those we apply to others. Although respect and indignation are important in terms of our emotional reactions to other persons, my focus will be mainly on our emotional feelings in regard to our *own* moral actions. And even here, I will have far more to say about guilt than self-respect. But given the interdependence of guilt and self-respect, much of my discussion about guilt has obvious implications for self-respect.

The Need for True Guilt

As we know, there are many persons today who denounce guilt as being unnecessary, unhealthy, destructive, and neurotic. In fact, recent years have seen a proliferation of books and magazine articles with titles like "Stop Feeling So Guilty" and "Guilt: the Useless Emotion." A psychoanalyst, Dr. Theodore Rubin, calls guilt "a destructive form of self-hate."[67] And a philosopher, Walter Kaufman, writes: "Guilt feelings are a contagious disease that harms those who harbour them and endangers those who live close to them. The liberation from guilt spells the dawn of autonomy."[68] Rubin and Kaufman, like countless others, view guilt as an entirely negative emotion, as an emotion that people can (and should) do without. Laying heavy emphasis on its destructive quality, they advocate its total disappearance.

In opposition to those who stress the entirely negative aspects of guilt, I intend to argue two points in the following pages: first, that guilt is the moral emotion *par excellence*; and, second, that a just social order requires an increase—not a decrease or, as Kaufman argues, a total elimination—of guilt.

For Freud, as we know, guilt is derived from the transgression against ancient taboos, against parental and social tribunals. In terms of the (conjectural) history of the original momentous move from the family to the wider communal life, the "first" sons killed the "first" fathers, whom they simultaneously loved and hated.

[67] Quoted in Virginia Adams, "Behavioral Scientists Argue Guilt's Role," *New York Times*, 24 July 1979, p. C1.

[68] Walter Kaufman, *Without Guilt and Justice* (New York: Delta, 1975), p. 114.

210

Their guilt from this terrible act and their subsequent identification with their dead fathers led to the emergence of the superego.[69] In our own time, it is passage through the Oedipus complex that is seen as giving rise to guilt and the creation of the superego. The feeling of guilt expressed by the child is viewed as essentially the consequence of dread of punishment, as the result of the child's "loss of love," and perhaps even as "moral masochism."[70] Thus, Freud's emphasis is on the influence of unconscious feelings of guilt that function to keep people from selfishly pursuing their individual aims. Guilt, he believed, was the necessary price of civilization.[71]

Those aggressive impulses that cannot be expressed if civilization is to survive are inevitably turned inward against the self. The individual's aggressiveness, Freud writes, "is introjected, internalized . . . directed back towards his own ego. There it is taken over by a portion of the ego which sets itself over against the rest of the ego as the super-ego, and which now, in the form of 'conscience', is ready to put into action the same harsh aggressiveness that the ego would have liked to satisfy upon other extraneous individuals."[72] The resulting sense of guilt is then repressed, emerging in consciousness as anxiety, a sense of worthlessness, feelings of general discontent, and the like. This kind of guilt can be termed *neurotic* guilt. Neurotic guilt is generated by the superego and ordinarily remains unconscious, although the anxiety that accompanies it does become conscious.[73] Since everyone is supposed to have repressed hostile impulses toward his or her parents, everyone will be affected by such guilt.[74]

But Freud also recognized another kind of guilt. With the idea of the ego-ideal, he postulated that there is an internalized ideal of behavior by which we judge our own actions—and in our failures experience guilt. This guilt, as contrasted with neurotic guilt, is a form of self-disappointment, arising from the fact that we have

[69] Freud, *Civilization and Its Discontents*, pp. 101, 131–32.

[70] Freud, *Collected Papers*, 2: 255–68.

[71] Freud, *Civilization and Its Discontents*, p. 43.

[72] Ibid.

[73] See, for example, Ausubel, "Relationships Between Shame and Guilt"; Piers and Singer, *Shame and Guilt*.

[74] It is, of course, neurotic guilt associated with certain sexual feelings and behaviors, and manifesting itself in feelings that they are wrong or dirty, that psychoanalysis attempts to expunge.

fallen short of the standards incorporated in the ego-ideal. It is this kind of guilt that, in my view, is required for a just social order.

Hence, I am advocating an increased recognition of the importance of a kind of guilt that is conscious and reality-oriented, a guilt that I will refer to as *true* guilt. Feelings of true guilt are those that are (or ought to be) experienced by people who sometimes act wrongly, who suffer because of it, and see themselves as owing something to others because of their wrongdoing. This kind of guilt is not to be comprehended through such categories as "repression" or "becoming conscious." The bearer of true guilt is consciously aware of his guilt, knows why he feels guilty, and is able to reflect on it. This guilt, in the words of Martin Buber, "is not one that allows itself to be repressed into the unconscious. It remains in the chamber of memory . . ."[75] True guilt, as I am terming it, is associated with reflexivity; it is the result of our recognition that not everything is permitted, that certain actions are wrong or bad, and that we are responsible for our actions. In a certain sense, it might be said that our freedom is the necessary condition for our being able to experience true guilt. Only when there exists the possibility of acting other than we did can true guilt arise. Without this freedom, there would be no responsibility, and without responsibility no guilt (in fact, no morality).[76]

No guilt is true guilt except as it subserves moral precepts. Guilt is false, neurotic guilt, when it subverts moral precepts.[77] True guilt is associated with a concern with what is right or good, and not with what is customary or usual in terms of the social norms. Moral precepts—concerning freedom, equality, justice, and the like—are necessary for structuring and guiding our social relationships. As noted earlier, they function to assure the greatest possible freedom for everyone compatible with the restraints necessary for organized social life. We may, of course, sometimes not obey these moral precepts; that is, we may ignore or violate them. Even though I accept the moral wrongness of taking a human life, for example, it is conceivable that I might murder someone. If I did, I ought to feel guilty. Such guilt would obviously not be due to repression, to unconscious forces, or to other elements about which I have no awareness or recognition. My guilt would, in short, be true guilt and not neurotic guilt. It would arise as a result of my having

[75] Martin Buber, "Guilt and Guilt Feelings," in *The Knowledge of Man*, trans. and ed. Maurice Friedman (New York: Harper & Row, 1965), p. 80.

[76] Wheelis, *The Moralist*, p. 36.

[77] Rieff, *Fellow Teachers*.

unjustifiably violated a moral precept that I accept: thou shalt not kill. In such circumstances, my guilt would be rational and appropriate, and I should (morally speaking) welcome and embrace it.

True guilt is reparative and not persecutory.[78] It requires not only expiation but, if possible, reparation and redress in order to attempt to remedy the wrongs that one has committed. Someone who has intentionally violated a moral prohibition may not just torment himself but may seek to provide reparation for what he has done. True guilt is characterized, then, not only by feelings of remorse, self-regret, loss of self-respect, and the like, but also by a readiness to make atonement for having done wrong. It is usually a condition of true guilt that one would undo the action if one could.

This close tie of remedial action to true guilt is one of the elements that distinguishes it from a closely related emotion: *shame*. These two emotions serve a similar purpose, the facilitation of socially acceptable behavior required for social life. But whereas guilt relies entirely on sanctions that are *internal* to the individual, shame incorporates other persons directly into the feelings and involves, therefore, *external* sanctions. Shame requires an audience, if not realistically, then symbolically.[79] It is bound up with the idea of publicity, the idea of other people knowing what one has done. As Rorty observes: "the pain the person feels at the action is that of having been seen to perform it. (That is why the physical expression of shame involves motions of hiding oneself.)"[80] While guilt often drives us to seek exposure, shame, in contrast, retreats into privacy for repair.

True guilt, as I noted above, is a feeling that arises from the intentional transgression or violation of a specific moral standard or prohibition. (Of course, guilt can also result from violation of a taboo or a legal code, but I am focusing here on guilt in relation to morality.) It is only when the individual himself judges that he has unjustifiably violated an accepted moral standard or precept that he experiences guilt. He experiences this because of *his* awareness that he has violated a standard that is important to him. It makes no difference whether or not other persons are aware of his transgression; the individual feels guilt because he views himself as having unjustifiably broken some moral rule. Guilt reflects a

---

[78] Melanie Klein, *Envy and Gratitude* (New York: Delta Books, 1977).

[79] Gaylin, *Feelings*, p. 57.

[80] Amélie Oksenberg Rorty, "Agent Regret," in Rorty, *Explaining Emotions*, p. 498.

concern with one's person; it is, in fact, the most personal of emotions. Crucial to true guilt is the individual's *own* regard for his misconduct. And, as distinctive from shame, it wants exposure. In Gaylin's words: "True guilt seeks, indeed embraces, punishment. Guilt represents the noblest and most painful of struggles. It is between us and ourselves. It is alleviated or mitigated by acts of expiation."[81]

While guilt is a self-punitive, self-critical reaction of self-disappointment that accompanies or follows transgression or violation of a moral standard, shame is the feeling that comes with consciousness that other persons know or may find out that (in the case of moral considerations) we have violated a moral standard. More generally, shame arises when we fear other people's awareness of our faults, weaknesses, or other qualities deemed socially undesirable. It is experienced when others reproach or reprove us for violating a norm or standard. We feel shame when we act in ways that other persons judge (or could be expected to judge) as unpraiseworthy conduct. "Shame," Rorty points out, "tends to involve obsessive imagistic replays of the moment of exposure, to be expressed in the focused remembering of the event, as if time were arrested."[82] With shame, it is not so much the results of exposure that are dreaded, but the exposure itself. Shame reflects a concern with the others upon whom we depend to confirm the sense of our own worth. The more central and the more significant these others are for us, the more likely will we experience shame when we violate a norm or standard shared with them. But shame, in contrast to guilt, is not strongly tied to reparation and redress.

This distinction between true guilt and shame does not constitute a claim that guilt is a completely self-induced emotion characteristic of individuals who stand apart from or are completely independent of other human beings. Such a claim would be totally ill-founded. After all, in the absence of feelings of common humanity and respect for others, there can be no feelings of guilt when we misuse our fellows or commit wrongs against them. While shame requires actual (or anticipated) public exposure of one's wrongdoing and the reproval or reproach of other persons, true guilt is also an emotion that binds us to those others without whom none of us can survive. Together, shame and guilt constitute the two most important guardians of our morality. Both involve a degree of moral

[81] Gaylin, *Feelings*, p. 46.
[82] Rorty, *Explaining Emotions*, p. 498.

reflection that is apparently not developed in all human beings. An ability to reflect on our misdeeds and wrongdoings, to consciously think about and evaluate them, is necessary for feeling shame and guilt.

Oftentimes we think of shame and guilt in terms of "conscience," a term which appears to have been pretty much purged from the literature (and vocabularies) of sociology and psychology. Although psychoanalysts do emphasize the conscience as part of the superego, it is usually dealt with as an unconscious mechanism, characterized by its inaccessibility to rational thought processes. But whereas the superego is indeed largely unconscious, conscience may enter awareness as a mode of consciousness and thought about one's actions. Buber describes the conscience this way:

> Conscience means to us the capacity and tendency of man radically to distinguish between those of his past and future actions which should be approved and those which should be disapproved. . . . Conscience can, naturally, distinguish and if necessary condemn . . . not merely deeds but also omissions, not merely decisions but also failures to decide, indeed even images and wishes that have just arisen or are remembered. . . . One must bear in mind that among all living beings known to us, man alone is able to set at a distance not only his environment but also himself. As a result, he becomes for himself a detached object about which he can not only "reflect," but which he can from time to time confirm as well as condemn.[83]

Most frequently, the conscience is retrospective; it comes into play when we become conscious of, think about, and evaluate our past acts. We are most aware of our conscience, I believe, as a "bad conscience": as the feelings of guilt and shame that accompany or result from consciousness of our own actions as wrong or bad. Buber points out that man alone has the ability to engage in reflection and, therefore, man alone has a conscience. But, of course, not all men have a conscience. Hannah Arendt insists that "only good people are ever bothered by a bad conscience whereas it is a very rare phenomenon among real criminals. A good conscience does not exist except in the absence of a bad one."[84] Although I

[83] Buber, "Guilt and Guilt Feelings," p. 133.

[84] Hannah Arendt, "Thinking and Moral Considerations: A Lecture," *Social Research* 38 (Autumn 1971): 418. Quoted in James F. Childress, "Appeals to Conscience," *Ethics* 89 (July 1979): 315–35.

know of no evidence showing that a bad conscience is, as Arendt states, a rare phenomenon among real criminals, it is certainly the case that there are persons ("psychopaths" and "sociopaths") who lack a conscience altogether.[85] Such persons give no attention to moral considerations in their actions, and when asked to explain their behavior do not refer to moral elements as relevant to them. Those lacking a conscience are also, it is interesting to note, apparently totally immune to psychotherapy.[86] Thus there are persons for whom talk about a good, bad, dirty, or clear conscience is literally meaningless. They are capable of crimes and other misdeeds without remorse or contrition.

Most of us, I assume, are sometimes aware of the working of our conscience—most often, as I noted above, in terms of feelings of guilt and shame. Although both of these elements that constitute a "bad" conscience are important as guardians of our morality, guilt is the more important of the two. In my view, a concern with moral standards and prohibitions must allow for guilt as the most appropriate emotion to be experienced by those who violate or consider violating the correct moral principles. While shame may also function to reinforce certain prohibitions, there are two reasons for arguing that it is to be regarded as inferior to guilt: first, it is not a moral emotion in the same sense that guilt is; true guilt is a distinctly moral sentiment in that it rests on the individual's own recognition of his wrongdoing and his readiness to make atonement for having done wrong; and, second, shame is only effective in groups, or in a society small enough to assure that people (especially those in positions of authority) are able to exercise surveillance over one another. The first reason is a moral one, the second is sociological.[87] Since I have already considered guilt and shame from a moral perspective, I don't think they require any further discussion. But it is necessary to consider a bit further the *sociological* superiority of guilt over shame.[88]

[85] S. Arietti, *The Intrapsychic Self* (New York: Basic Books, 1967); R. D. Hare, *Psychopathology: Theory and Research* (New York: Wiley, 1970).

[86] W. McCord and J. McCord, *The Psychopath: An Essay on the Criminal Mind* (New York: Van Nostrand, 1964).

[87] In my view, the moral is the more important of the two. Guilt is to be preferred to shame as a moral emotion even if its social function were to be less. The point here is that guilt is both the superior moral emotion *and* can do more today to enhance social life.

[88] Some anthropologists have distinguished between "guilt cultures" and "shame cultures." See, for example, Clyde Kluckholn, "The Moral Order in the Expanding

Someone growing up in a small American or Western European town in the last century experienced a relatively homogeneous society. The prevailing norms, customs, and moral standards were of stable value, widely shared, and usually accepted without question. Far more likely than today, people grew up and spent their life in one place, and were under scrutiny by other persons who subscribed to the same moral standards. Under conditions of generally shared standards and ideals, where there is a permanency in people's lives, with the result that their actions are known about by other persons with whom they have relatively enduring relationships, shame can be a highly potent force for assuring people's conformity to shared moral standards. As Gaylin notes, shame "allows the community to join in the enforcement of moral behavior rather than leaving it exclusively in the hands of individual responsibility."[89]

But in heterogeneous societies, like those lived in by most of us today, the influence of shame is much less powerful. Customs, norms, and moral standards are far less widely shared than in the past, and are less often accepted without question. Enormous increases in geographical mobility, as well as changes in social mobility that minimize patterned sequences of work and career, result in large numbers of people living much of their lives among persons with whom they have only minimal and superficial social relationships. Under such conditions, where a sense of community and belonging is frequently absent, shame—which is the primary mediator of community-oriented conscience—will not prove effective. Thus it is guilt, the mediator of individually oriented conscience, which must take on the burden of helping to assure our morality. What this indicates, then, is that a primary task of socialization must be the cultivation of children's ability to experience true guilt.

There are, of course, important structural constraints on the acquisition of guilt in the contemporary world. To acquire a conscience and the capacity to experience true guilt requires highly intense, direct, personal relations, usually within a family setting. Yet, as Lasch, various writers of the Frankfurt School, and many

---

Society." In C. H. Kraeling and R. M. Adams, *City Invincible* (Chicago: University of Chicago Press, 1960); Melford Spiro, "Social Systems, Personality, and Functional Analysis," in Bert Adams, ed., *Studying Personality Cross-Culturally* (Evanston, Ill.: Row, Petersen, 1961). For a criticism of these views, see Christoph von Fürer-Haimendorf, "The Sense of Sin in Cross-Cultural Perspective," *Man* 9 (1974): 539–56.

[89] Gaylin, *Feelings*, p. 58.

others have emphasized, the family as the primary agency of so-cialization has lost many of its tranditional functions as these have been taken over by other institutions.[90] Despite this surrendering of many of its traditional responsibilities and the loosening of ties between parents and children, the family is almost certainly the only existing kind of institutional arrangement that has the pos-sibility of providing the human surroundings necessary for the moral development of the young.

One need not romanticize about the virtues of the classic bour-geois family to recognize that—at its best—it provides for secure and coherent human relations. And while there has undoubtedly been a weakening of ties within the family, nevertheless, the ex-isting ties are still considerably stronger than those that connect the individual to the wider community. However far it may have disintegrated, only the family is able to provide the stability, con-tinuity, and authority necessary for the moral development of a society's citizens. While the conditions for the effectiveness of shame are almost totally absent in contemporary industrialized societies, the family still has the potentiality for instilling a knowl-edge of true guilt in its young. Of course, whether the family (or any other mode of association, for that matter) has either the desire or the ability to successfully acquaint its members with feelings of true guilt under present historical circumstances remains to be seen.[91]

I want now to briefly consider what parents or other child-rearers can do to help assure that their children will acquire the capacity for experiencing true guilt. To begin with, it seems to me that they can do very much the same thing they do in "educating" other emotions. Just as adults have to teach children that some things are dangerous and that the child should learn to fear them, they should also teach their children that some things are morally wrong

[90] Lasch, *The Culture of Narcissism*; Jürgen Habermas, *Legitimation Crisis*, trans. Thomas McCarthy (Boston: Beacon Press, 1975); Jacques Donzelot, *The Policing of Families* (New York: Pantheon, 1979).

[91] I might note here that Rawls is the only one of the four theorists considered in Chapter 2 to devote systematic attention to guilt and shame. Although it seems to me that he sometimes confuses the two emotions, he has many interesting things to say about the education of the moral sentiments. This part of his well-known book has received surprisingly little attention. Becker also argues for the importance of "just conduct" and its general neglect in many theories of justice. "What existing theories of justice neglect is the fact . . . that justice is a way of life, not merely a set of conditions for a minimally acceptable life." Lawrence C. Becker, "Economic Justice: Three Positions," *Ethics* 89 (July 1979): 389.

218

and ought to be accompanied by feelings of guilt when they are done. Obviously, children have to be taught that this or that is dangerous or threatening, and that it is rational to react to what one takes to be a threatening object with some degree of fear. Similarly, with the child's ability to recognize and understand such things as compliments and insults; these are not instantly recognizable to the young child. He or she must learn to recognize what constitutes a compliment or an insult, and must also acquire the appropriate emotional reactions: pride, anger, or whatever. For children to learn what another person's action "means" and what is the appropriate emotional reaction is clearly an enormously complicated accomplishment. Yet most of us have learned to distinguish between objects that are threatening and those that are not, to recognize what constitutes an insult or a compliment, and the like, and we have also learned what emotional reactions are appropriate to the situation. I doubt seriously, however, that many of us are able to recall who taught us such things or how we managed to learn them.

Most of us are made familiar with the vocabulary of emotions by association with what de Sousa calls *paradigm scenarios*, "drawn first from our daily life as small children, later reinforced by the stories and fairy tales to which we are exposed, and, later still, supplemented and refined by literature and art."[92] These paradigm scenarios involve two aspects: first, a paradigm situation providing the characteristic objects of the emotion; and, second, a set of characteristic or "normal" responses to the situation.[93] If a child reacts with (what we call) fear when he is suddenly confronted by a large, snarling dog, for example, he may be told that such animals can indeed be dangerous and that there is good reason for him to be "afraid." Thus, his emotion is identified and he is given a name for it in the context of the scenario. Perhaps he will react the same way when he hears a particular loud noise, but this time will be told that it is only a vacuum cleaner and that his "fear" is not appropriate. In these cases, as in many others, the child is taught that he is experiencing a certain emotion and, further, that it is either appropriate or inappropriate under the circumstances.

Guilt—that is, true guilt—is a bit different. With guilt, it is not usually a question of the child being taught to "identify" an emotion that he is experiencing so much as it is his being taught to

[92] De Sousa, "The Rationality of Emotions," p. 142.
[93] Ibid.

experience the emotion in the first place. Whereas fear, rage, and perhaps lust are such primitive emotions that they need not be taught (although the child does have to learn to correctly identify them), the ability to experience true guilt can only be acquired through the process of socialization. I suspect that this emotion is acquired in something like the following way.

The child is taught that certain actions are right and others wrong. He is also taught that when he does things that are considered wrong certain things are expected of him. Imagine that little Tommy has taken some money from his brother, Bob, and spent it all on ice cream. Bob, who has been saving for some weeks in order to be able to go to the movies, discovers what happened and goes to his parents in tears. Presumably, the parents will explain to Tommy why his action was morally wrong, and they may try to get him to consider how he would feel if Bob were to take all the money he had saved for something he wanted. Tommy may be asked to apologize to Bob, or to ask his forgiveness, or to repay Bob from next week's allowance. And Tommy may, in fact, do these things.

But certainly Tommy does not yet experience guilt feelings. If he did, he would have gone to Bob and confessed and offered to make redress without his parents' urgings. Yet, Tommy can only acquire the capacity to feel guilty by first learning what stealing means (both socially and morally) and what the appropriate emotion is in such circumstances. Like every other person, Tommy has to be helped to acquire the capacity for experiencing true guilt. Only when the child who has committed a wrongdoing takes the initiative to apologize and ask forgiveness can he be said to be motivated by feelings of guilt. Certainly, there have to be many situations like the one described before the child is enabled to experience guilt. No doubt shame and guilty fear (the fear of getting caught) are emotional reactions that are acquired much more easily, and prior to, true guilt. But the child who is taught about stealing, lying, cruelty, and the like, and why they are morally wrong, and also what he ought to feel when he engages in such actions, is being prepared to experience feelings of true guilt. Further, as I noted earlier, these paradigm scenarios are reinforced by fairy tales and other children's stories and perhaps by such things as television and movies as well. When the day comes that Tommy, for example, wants (needs) to blurt out his confession of his wrongdoing and to atone for it, he can be said to have acquired the capacity for true guilt.

The above account is, however, almost certainly too simple. It is probably the case that children often learn certain moral principles and the moral emotions that ought to accompany their transgressions at the same time. That is, they may learn what lying is, why it is wrong, and how someone who tells a lie ought to feel, all more or less together. I doubt that the child first learns what it means to tell a lie, then learns why it is morally wrong, and, finally, why the liar should feel guilty. Sometimes, at least, all of these are acquired together.

Be that as it may, the child is obviously more likely to become acquainted with true guilt when he sees it manifested in the actions of those persons who are most significant for him. All of us, I assume, sometimes engage in actions for which we should feel guilty. And Tommy's parents, being like the rest of us, are no different. Imagine that Tommy's father has helped himself to some of the luscious red tomatoes from the garden of the people next door, who are away for the weekend. After dinner, Tommy hears his parents talking in the other room. His father says to his mother: "I feel terrible; I really shouldn't have taken those tomatoes. It wasn't right, and tomorrow I'm going over and tell them what I did. I hope they'll forgive me." Hearing his father saying all this in an uncharacteristically sad tone of voice, Tommy comes into the room and sees that his father has a rather strange look on his face. "Tommy," his father says, "I took those tomatoes from our neighbor's garden without asking. What I did was wrong, and tomorrow I'm going to talk to them about it." Tommy's response is immediate: "But, Dad, they have so many tomatoes that they'll never even know the difference. And they're not very nice people anyway. So I don't see what's so bad about it." "Yes, Tommy," replies his father, "but I know I took them, and I know that it was wrong to do so. Whether they're nice people or not has nothing to do with it." Tommy thinks about this for a minute, and then says: "But, Dad, if you know it was wrong to take the tomatoes and now you feel bad about it, shouldn't that be enough? Why do you also have to go and apologize to them?" "Because, Tommy," the father responds, "until I acknowledge to them what I've done, until I 'own up' to it, there is no way that I can hold my head up the next time that I see them. Maybe there is even some way that I can make it up to them."

Despite the somewhat "preachy" quality of this dialogue, it is the kind of paradigm scenario from which children do learn about true guilt. Tommy's father has done something that is morally wrong. He recognizes that he has done so, and experiences guilt feelings as a rational and appropriate reaction to his transgression. He also needs to acknowledge his wrongdoing to the neighbors, to ask their forgiveness, and to try to atone for what he has done. His actions are those of a moral agent, responsible for what he does. As such, he needs to seek exposure for his guilt. Tommy is, of course, fortunate that he has a father who is capable of experiencing true guilt; it will make it easier for him to acquire the same capacity. But his father is also fortunate, and the words of Philip Rieff seem appropriate here: "Be grateful for your sense of true guilt and doubly grateful if it has not been badly damaged. Without that guilt, an elaborately cultivated strength of inhibition preventing or punishing transgressive activity, there can be neither aristocracies of the feeling intellect nor democracies of obedience."[94]

The general point of the example of Tommy's father is that a child will be best able to acquire the capacity for experiencing true guilt when it is socialized under conditions where those responsible for its upbringing are themselves responsible moral agents. With regard to the generic rights to freedom and well-being and to self-esteem, children who have learned to recognize and respect everyone's generic rights, and not to interfere with the development of the virtues of character that are related to each person's self-esteem, *ought* to experience true guilt when they violate other people's rights or interfere with their self-esteem. Thus, when they engage in such wrongdoings they should seek to atone for what they have done. More importantly perhaps, persons with the capacity to experience true guilt will be far *less* likely than those lacking such a capacity to violate people's rights or to interfere with their self-esteem. That is, the capacity to react with anticipatory guilt may motivate resistance to morally wrong actions. Because guilt is a painful feeling that individuals are motivated to avoid, true guilt can be conducive to moral actions in line with the Principle of Generic Consistency. True guilt, then, has both preventive and remedial consequences.

If parents themselves accept that true guilt is the guardian of our morality and that it is an emotion that people should sometimes experience, they can do much to assure that their children will acquire the capacity for experiencing that emotion. But such acceptance is admittedly difficult today; it flies in the face of much

[94] Rieff, *Fellow Teachers*, p. 156.

of conventional morality and the teachings of some of the high priests of philosophy, psychoanalysis, and the social sciences.

For a child to acquire the capacity for true guilt requires a certain submission to authority; initially to the authority of the parents, and thereafter to the authority of moral principles. Only those parents who raise their children in an authoritative manner, who recognize their obligation to assure the moral character of their children, and who themselves have knowledge of true guilt, are likely to successfully assure the development of their children's capacity to experience true guilt when it is appropriate. Moral principles and moral emotions have to be taught; we human beings are not born with them. This means that responsible parents must act as moral draftsmen in the socialization of their children.

IV

Having considered what parents or other child-rearers can do to encourage moral development and to help assure that the child's actions will be in accord with the recognition of everyone's generic rights to freedom and well-being, I want now to briefly examine changing ideals of love and work and their implications for identity formation and moral development in the modern age. As I will try to show, a new, and very different, conception of identity formation has come to the fore in contemporary society.

A number of social theorists have argued that Western societies have entered a new type of societal order and historical era. This has been variously referred to as "cybernetic,"[95] "programmed,"[96] "post-industrial,"[97] and "post-modern."[98] Whatever label one prefers, there is widespread consensus that it is characterized by an expansion of markets and trade, a general and persisting prosperity, a shift from a manufacturing to a service economy, and an enormous increase in the importance of technological applications of theoretical knowledge to the productive sector. Taken together, these developments require that people be "rational and efficient"

[95] Daniel Bell, "Notes on the Post-Industrial Society," *The Public Interest* (Winter 1967).

[96] Alain Touraine, *The Post-Industrial Society, Tomorrow's Social History: Classes, Conflicts, and Culture in the Programmed Society*, trans. Leonard F. X. Mayhew (New York: Random House, 1972).

[97] Daniel Bell, *The Coming of Post-Industrial Society* (New York: Basic Books, 1973); Touraine, *The Post-Industrial Society*.

[98] Daniel Bell, *The Cultural Contradictions of Capitalism* (New York: Basic Books, 1976).

and that they be able to exercise a technical mastery in order to meet the needs of the post-modern society. This new type of society is accompanied by various structural and institutional arrangements and rearrangements that have brought about significant changes in the cultural-meaning systems of modern societies. These changing institutional arrangements and cultural-meaning systems have important consequences for identity formation in the modern age.

The growth of post-modern societies has contributed to the general undermining of many traditional social arrangements that helped provide and assure stable social relations: the family, neighborhoods, more or less personalized work settings, conventional religious practices. Further, the development of a managed and planned economy and an increasingly bureaucratized society have made the ideal of personal autonomy and responsibility far less plausible than it once was.[99] And the mass-consumption capitalist societies found in the West have undoubtedly encouraged a leisure-time "permissive" culture that challenges long-standing notions of identity and morality in the private expressive realm.[100]

It is most especially the "soft structures," which have traditionally been concerned with morality—the family, the schools, the churches—that have undergone enormous changes in recent decades. This is clearly so, as Bellah notes, with respect to "their capacity to transmit patterns of conscience and ethical values."[101] Without going into a detailed examination of these various changes as they pertain to the family and identity formation, I want to briefly consider certain changes in regard to the ideals of love and work that have obvious implications for the socialization and moral development of the young.

To begin with, the stable nuclear family with the husband at work and his wife at home with the children has ceased to be the modal household unit.[102] Various (welcome) changes—associated with the pill, the feminist movement, the availability of labor-saving devices, and changing requirements of the labor market—have helped to free women to lead lives of their own and to lessen their

[99] Dick Anthony and Thomas Robbins, "Spiritual Innovation and the Crisis of American Civil Religion," *Daedalus* 3 (Winter 1982): 218.

[100] Ibid.

[101] Robert Bellah, "Religion and Legitimation of the American Republic," in Thomas Robbins and Dick Anthony, eds., *In God We Trust: New Patterns of Religious Pluralism in America* (New Brunswick, N.J.: Transaction Books, 1981), p. 48.

[102] Andrew Hacker, "Farewell to the Family?" *New York Review*, 18 March 1982.

economic and psychological dependence on their husbands. But these changes have also tended to weaken marital and familial stability. In any case, the course of marriage and family life is becoming less continuous for adults and children alike. Work, too, is becoming less continuous as the demands of employment change in the direction of jobs that require greater mobility, flexibility, and a constant requirement for learning new skills and abilities.

With regard to the importance of love, I noted earlier in this chapter that identity formation depends partly on the individual's capacity to realize the ideals of commitment, attachment, self-sacrifice, and intimacy in the sphere of love, marital, and familial relationships. It seems clear that the status of these ideals is undergoing rapid modification in contemporary Western societies. Commitment is no longer highly valued as an aspect of one's personal identity; fewer and fewer people feel compelled to continue relationships that don't provide the opportunity for new experiences. There is now the view that rather than seeing the selection of a love partner as a once-and-for-all choice, one ought not to be committed to any relationship that seriously interferes with one's own growth and self-actualization. While such a changing ideal does open the possibility for new, deeper, richer, love relationships, it also has the result of lessening the strength of the ties that bind lovers, spouses, and the family together.

Closely related to changes in the ideal of commitment are those concerning attachment. In the traditional view, the ideal of attachment was realized through the progression from love to marriage and thereby to permanent involvement and obligations. In the contemporary world, however, such attachments are often viewed as dangerous or destructive. This fear of binding attachments may, as Swidler suggests, allow for a redirection of emotional energy toward new challenges.[103] But, on the other hand, the emphasis on "keeping your options open," "playing it cool," and "staying loose," seems to represent a conviction that society sets all sorts of booby traps that rob the individual of the possibility for self-realization and continuous change. An important consequence of this emphasis on keeping oneself flexible and open to new experiences is that it precludes those sorts of social attachments necessary for establishing a stable and coherent sense of personal identity.

The ideal of self-sacrifice is also undergoing serious modification.

[103] Swidler, "Love and Adulthood," p. 134.

The traditional ideal was achieved when the individual fulfilled him- or herself through the love of another. In this view, self-sacrifice was an important component of one's realization of a permanent sense of self. Certainly an earlier ethic of sacrifice did much to bind husband and wife, parents and children, and parents and their parents. But, at the same time, this ethic also frequently compelled individuals (especially women) to surrender their own happiness and possibilities of development for the sake of others. Today, it is no longer widely believed that someone's life can be meaningfully defined by the sacrifices he or she makes for spouse, children, or parents. Instead, as Swidler observes, there is "a new concern with the survival, wholeness, and autonomy of the self that makes self-sacrifice seem weakness."[104] For many today, sacrifice is a con job, a loss with no benefits.[105]

Like the other values discussed above, intimacy, too, has undergone important changes. Traditionally, love was intensified and strengthened by the tension between sexual expression and restraint. "Sexuality sealed the intimacy of lovers"; notes Swidler, "sexual restraint made their bond exclusive and inviolable."[106] In the contemporary period, as we know, there is an increasing emphasis on the desirability of nonexclusive sexual expression. And, in fact, the possibilities for greater sexual expression and experimentation have indeed increased. As a consequence, the ideal of sexual restraint has been seriously weakened. Sexuality was once a symbol of intimacy, and sexual exclusivity was a seal of emotional bondedness to one's partner or spouse. Undoubtedly, such exclusivity and fidelity exacted a serious price for many (again, especially women) who upheld this ideal. Even where deep emotional and sexual gratification were lacking, allegiance to the ideal of restricting sexual relations to one's marital partner effectively prevented many individuals from exploring new possibilities for sexual enjoyment and satisfaction. Still, the capacity for sexual restraint and fidelity did serve to constitute evidence for the integrity of the self. Today, however, there is a widespread rejection of the ideal of sexual restraint, fidelity, and exclusive devotion to a single partner. In their desire to keep their sex life continually gratifying, many persons are constantly in search of new sexual experiences, new partners, and new ways of realizing self-actualization through

[104] Ibid., p. 139.

[105] Russell Jacoby, "Narcissism and the Crisis of Capitalism," *Telos* 44 (Summer 1980): 58–65; Kovel, "Narcissism and the Family."

[106] Swidler, "Love and Adulthood," p. 139.

means of sexual and emotional relations. The trust and continuity necessary for real intimacy and mutuality, and thus for the wholeness and unity of one's personal identity, are increasingly absent among those who embrace the new ideology.

These changes as regards the ideals of commitment, attachment, self-sacrifice, and intimacy have had important consequences for the identity formation of those growing up in recent decades. Living among persons who are themselves frequently uncertain and ambivalent about the above named ideals, it is difficult for the young to conceive of love—and all that it has traditionally implied—as a firm basis for establishing a sense of one's personal identity.

When marriage comes to be viewed as a tentative affair, when it is perceived as an obstacle to the realization of new experiences, when its obligations and responsibilities are seen as burdensome and unrewarding, it is difficult to imagine that love—at least as it is found in marital and familial relations—can serve as an effective source of personal identity for either the adult partners or for their children.

Much the same can be said about work, the other important source of personal identity considered earlier. In the early bourgeois family, work was viewed as an activity that purified and ennobled the individual; it was both a virtue and a remedy. As I observed in my initial contrast of work and labor, work as an ideal promised the possibility of challenge, exploration, autonomy, and fulfillment. Undoubtedly, such an ideal was not always realized in the individual's actual experience. And it is certainly true that there was sometimes an almost pathological quality to some people's involvement in work. Nevertheless, work as an ideal was crucial for many person's sense of who and what they were.

Work has obviously become problematic for most persons today. There is, in fact, a general lack of work in the economies of postmodern societies. Both labor and work are, of course, less fatiguing and of shorter duration than was the case in past decades. But, on the other hand, work as a source of challenge, responsibility, and achievement is rapidly disappearing. Most work has taken on the characteristics of labor. It is experienced as an aimless, useless, and callous activity, where one is tied to a clock and to bureaucratic rules and regulations, and where the individual is no longer responsible for what he or she does. When work is not fulfilling, when it allows little room for autonomy, exploration, and establishing a sense of personal identity, when it is experienced as simply something that one must do to earn a living, there is little reason to expect that it will provide a firm basis for identity formation.

The social commitment that was once expressed through work by the more privileged segment of the work force in Western societies is largely something of the past. Swidler expresses it nicely:

In the modern economy, those occupations with the greatest prestige and interest are also those which require the greatest readiness for continuing change. Innovation in the economy requires flexibility in elite workers; an occupation in which one can "settle down" is an occupation which represents a "dead end." Only the person who is always ready with a new idea, who can move from one organization or role to another, can succeed. We therefore find a new tentativeness about the meaning of work. Finding one's "right place" in the social world . . . now becomes a contradiction in terms. The right place is inevitably wrong, a chimera. The only right solution is to have a set of ideas and talents, completely contained within the self, perpetually renewed, continually shifting into original patterns. One's self is one's only resource, but that self cannot look for "proof" of its worth . . . in a fixed calling.[107]

Thus, work cannot effectively serve as a means of establishing and proving who one is for the many persons who must remain flexible and continually ready for new demands. As with love, serious commitment and entanglement are to be avoided. One's sense of identity, then, is not likely to be formed by a deep-seated commitment to love and work among persons in the post-industrial society.

If, as I suggested earlier, a coherent personal identity requires the availability of appropriate cultural models, then it follows that most individuals in the contemporary age will not achieve such a single, conscious sense of self, of sameness over an extended period of time. Given the absence of the required cultural models both within the family and elsewhere, identity formation is extremely problematic for many persons today.

This means, of course, that moral socialization within the family is also strongly affected. As the course of marriage, love, and work become less continuous, it becomes increasingly more difficult for the family to provide the kind of stable and socially coherent surroundings that are necessary for the child's acquiring a sense of

[107] Ibid., pp. 133–34.

personal identity informed by moral principles and standards. This is certainly not to claim that the bourgeois nuclear family of the past was ideal, for it obviously was not. Among other things, the imposition and internalization of normative, parental authority too often created psychically repressed and crippled individuals.[108] On the other hand, that type of family constellation does appear to have been better able to assure an internalized code of morality when compared to the contemporary family. Whatever the advantages and disadvantages of bourgeois family life as contrasted with the dominant patterns of the family today, my emphasis in what follows is on a comparison between persons whose actions are guided by moral considerations (who, in actual fact, are probably small in number but constitute an ideal) and those whose conduct is governed entirely by a new conception of identity, which lays heavy stress on authenticity.

My intention here is threefold: first, to indicate just how far removed morality today is from the kinds of requirements that I have sketched out earlier in this chapter; second, to make clear the concrete difficulties encountered in attempting to encourage moral development and the educating of moral emotions; and, finally, to suggest why personal identities and conduct based on morality are superior to those based on authenticity.

Morality, Authenticity, and the Just Social Order

Morality, as we know, concerns the good and the right way of living in the world as human beings. It includes insight and action: insight into the nature and likely consequences of our observing or violating those standards and principles that specify what is permissible; and action to help assure the right, the good, and the just, while avoiding their opposites. Such standards and principles specify what we may and may not do to one another, and are necessary for structuring our social relationships.

I have argued that a just social order requires that all persons come to recognize and act in accord with everyone's generic rights to freedom and well-being, and that it further requires that they acquire the disposition to feel guilty (or, when appropriate, ashamed) whenever they violate those rights. Along with moral principles and emotions, morality also includes the *virtues* that are admirable both in themselves and because they facilitate morally

[108] John Alt and Frank Hearn, "The Cortland Conference on Narcissism," *Telos* 44 (Summer 1980): 50.

right conduct.[109] As with moral principles and emotions, the various virtues must be acquired by teaching and practice. Together with the moral emotions, these virtues help assure that people's conduct will be in line with the dictates of morality.

The Greeks seemed to have conceived of morality almost entirely in terms of the virtues and the virtuous, rather than in regard to what is right or obligatory. They gave primary attention to the four cardinal virtues of wisdom, courage, temperance, and justice. Although these can all be among the excellences of human beings and are usually admirable in themselves, the possession of such qualities is not a sufficient condition for morally correct behavior. With the exception of justice, which is a true moral virtue, these virtues—as well as those of sincerity and kindness—are not really moral virtues at all. Ordinarily, they are to be encouraged and desired, but they are not necessarily associated with morally praiseworthy conduct.

An individual can, for example, serve an evil cause with tremendous courage and complete sincerity, and can show unusual kindness and sympathy toward those who support the same cause. What this means is that the display of these virtues can be associated with widespread cruelty, torture, killing, and a general inhumanity toward those who oppose the cause. Hitler and Stalin are only two among the many tyrants of our time who may have possessed these virtues to a high degree.

Thus, excepting justice, none of the above virtues is unqualifiably good, since someone who acts according to them may violate the dictates of morality. One cannot, then, construct a moral view from these virtues alone. But if they are joined to the appropriate moral viewpoint, they can have considerable importance for morality. In order for courage, wisdom, and the like, to be moral virtues, they must be guided by the supreme moral virtue: justice.

While someone could be courageous and sincere and a Nazi or a Stalinist, no one whose conduct is guided by a concern with justice could have accepted Hitler's and Stalin's views. Similarly, today a thief or a kidnapper may show considerable courage in his actions, and an expert at impression management may exhibit great sincerity in manipulating others to achieve his own selfish ends. But someone whose conduct is guided by a recognition of the rights

[109] For excellent discussions of virtue, see Lawrence C. Becker, "The Neglect of Virtue," *Ethics* 85 (1975): 110–22; Philippa Foot, *Virtues and Vices and Other Essays in Moral Philosophy* (Berkeley: University of California Press, 1978); and James D. Wallace, *Virtues and Vices* (Ithaca, N.Y.: Cornell University Press, 1978).

of others will either refrain from stealing, kidnapping, and the like, or will experience feelings of true guilt when acting wrongly.

Hence the moral virtue of justice, guided by a recognition of everyone's generic rights, is primary; other virtues are secondary. Nevertheless, the morality of principle and the morality of virtue are complementary. The virtues, as I noted, are virtues of form only. They do not become moral virtues until they are guided by moral principles. But similarly, principles without the appropriate virtues may be impotent. Only if people have the disposition to *act* on the basis of moral principles can those principles come to influence our relations with one another. For the moral life, then, moral principles, moral emotions, and virtues of character are all required to help assure that people act in the ways that morality demands.

Among people whose conduct is guided by considerations of morality, the coherence of social life rests on the convictions they share about its moral meanings. Such persons make sense of their lives, and of one another, partly through *discourse* about what is good, which actions are right, and who is virtuous.[110] This means that what individuals ought to do is distinguished from what they want to do, and their actions are evaluated on the basis of whether or not they are in line with the requirements of morality. In judging their own and other people's conduct, these individuals appeal to notions of blame and responsibility, guilt and shame, respect and moral indignation. How important, then, is moral discourse in the lives of people in the contemporary Western world?

It seems to me that moral discourse plays a rather insignificant role in terms of people judging one another's actions today. And it is undoubtedly less often utilized or appealed to than in past decades. We are living at a time when moral precepts are seldom used as inciters to desirable conduct. Parents, friends, teachers, colleagues, therapists, and even the clergy, only infrequently speak of someone's being good or bad, just or unjust, morally praise-worthy or morally lacking. Instead, people talk of being self-ful-filled or unfulfilled, psychologically healthy or disturbed, self-ac-tualizing or the opposite.

It is curious, to say the least, that many people today who pride themselves on their willingness to talk openly about their sexual life and other personal matters, should seem almost embarrassed

---

[110] Stephen M. Tipton, "The Moral Logic of Alternative Religions," *Daedalus* 3 (Winter 1982): 185.

by references to morality. Not only does the use of such terms as *evil* and *wicked* make people uneasy, but even talk about right and wrong, good and bad, blame and responsibility, is studiously avoided among those who are quite ready to speak of their own desires, wants, fantasies, aggressions, fears, hang-ups, and uncertainties. Rarely, nowadays, do we hear anyone characterized by reference to such old-fashioned virtues as wisdom, temperance, or justice. Rather than being evaluated on the basis of their goodness, responsibility, wisdom, or sense of justice, people today are more often judged in terms of their being frank, spontaneous, outgoing, and the like.

In the modern age of enlightenment, psychology is often seen as encouraging people to psychologically undress themselves and others in order to shed their inhibitions and discover their "true selves." And sociology and anthropology, whatever else they may or may not contribute, do seem to successfully convey to students and others the relativity of moral principles and standards. That is, these disciplines encourage the view that right and wrong, good and bad, depend entirely upon the norms in the society where one happens to live. Taken a step further, many persons conclude from studying the social sciences that right or wrong, and the like, do not depend even on widely held societal norms, but are fully determined by the norms within one's own particular group. And taken still further, many people today conclude that each individual makes his or her own morality, i.e., that there are no standards of morality external to oneself.

But, of course, this emphasis on relativity cannot be attributed entirely to the influence of sociology and anthropology. For example, the English philosopher, Anthony Skillen, notes that his students "tend to hover between a merely formal libertarianism ('Live by your own values') and a purely formal collectivism ('It depends on what is right in your own society')."[111] He goes on to say: "So 'liberal' are many of my students, indeed, that they hold that it is immoral to pass judgments on people."[112] This echoes what I have heard offered as the highest expression of praise for another: "He is non-judgmental."

Whatever the influence of the various academic disciplines in this regard, it seems obvious that traditional moral ideals and stand-

---

[111] Anthony Skillen, *Ruling Illusions: Philosophy and the Social Order* (Hussocks, Sussex: Harvester Press, 1977), p. 128.
[112] Ibid., p. 127.

ards have been very much undermined and unmasked. This, in itself, is not always to be regretted. After all, there is much, especially in some religiously based moralities, that needed to be revealed for what it was (for example, sexism, racism, and other elements that deny our common humanity). But one result of this unmasking of particular moral values and standards has been that the very possibility of there being *any* moral values and standards that might call for (or demand) our attention and allegiance is for many persons today a moot question.

Given the general situation both inside and outside the academy, it is probably not surprising that talk of good and bad, right and wrong, and the like, seldom appear in the discourse of "sophisticated" persons. For who is to say, many ask, that someone's actions are morally wrong or that he should feel guilty for what he has done? After all, we are told, I might consider a person's conduct wrong, but that is only in terms of what I personally consider to be right and wrong, and I know that other persons think differently about such things. So even if I think that someone has done something that is morally unacceptable, it's only my opinion ("Thou shalt not commit a value-judgment"). If God is dead, then, as Ivan Karamazov concluded, everything is permitted.

What this means is that there is not only a general absence of moral terminology in people's discourse, but that their *actions* are also seldom guided by moral considerations. The concern is far more with one's inner emotional life than with one's moral life. For many persons today, it is the degree of allegiance to one's internal desires and impulses that is important and not adherence to moral principles and standards. In fact, people nowadays are increasingly encouraged to be open and forthright about their wants and desires, and to seek authenticity in their lives through the unmasking of pretense and the searching out of covert motivations. An emphasis on openness and spontaneity, a frankness about sexual behavior and sexual problems, and a concern with self-actualization and being oneself, are all characteristic of life in the contemporary age. Phrases like "going with the flow," "letting it all hang out," and their equivalents are highly valued as ways of demonstrating that one has liberated oneself from the constraints of traditional values and standards. In short, it is "authenticity" and not morality that constitutes the standard of human adequacy for many persons in the post-industrial age.

Such individuals view authenticity as the chief "virtue" to which they should aspire. In a very limited sense, authenticity resembles the old Greek doctrine of living according to one's nature, of "knowing thyself" and "becoming what you are." But for the Greeks, man was regarded as essentially a rational being who was susceptible to moral education and improvement in terms of the development of his own ideal possibility. Every person was expected to discover and know this ideal possibility (or *claimon*). Today, by contrast, many people no longer view man as essentially a rational being whose reason is the master of his soul. Thus, authenticity is now pursued in the absence of any ideal concerning what reason or rationality requires. That is, the present emphasis on authenticity requires man to follow his own nature without his knowing what that nature is.

As many observers have noted, the contemporary age is therapeutic, not religious.[113] People nowadays, in the words of Christopher Lasch, hunger not for personal salvation but "for the feeling, the momentary illusion, of personal well-being, health, and psychic security."[114] With the loss of authority, especially that of religion and, more recently, that of the family, the individual stands—in a very real sense—alone: uncertain, insecure, and lacking any inner sense of standards and direction. Whatever problems he or she may have are defined as arising not from weaknesses of character or lack of inner control, but increasingly as "psychic" difficulties. For many today, evil and morally wrong actions are dissolved into sickness and social maladjustment.

This new personality type with new problems is referred to as "psychological man" by Rieff,[115] as "protean man" by Hendin,[116] and is described in terms of "narcissism" by Sennett and Lasch.[117] Lacking the forms of authority formerly (and certainly ideally) represented by parents, teachers, and the clergy, this new personality type lacks an internalized ego-ideal concerning a code of moral conduct. In place of the internalized standards that once (again, ideally) helped to guide an individual's actions, it is today the therapists—of one or another stripe—who help achieve the modern equivalent of salvation: authenticity or self-actualization.

With the new therapies, restrictions and inhibitions are to be

[113] Rieff, *Fellow Teachers*; Philip Rieff, *The Triumph of the Therapeutic* (New York: Harper & Row, 1966); Lasch, *The Culture of Narcissism*.

[114] Lasch, *The Culture of Narcissism*, p. 7.

[115] Rieff, *Triumph of the Therapeutic*.

[116] Herbert Hendlin, *The Age of Sensation* (New York: McGraw-Hill, 1975).

[117] Lasch, *The Culture of Narcissism*; Richard Sennet, *The Fall of Public Man* (New York: Random House, 1978).

eliminated in the name of realizing authenticity. In essence, as Alt points out, the therapeutic ideal "deems individuals incapable of guiding their own relationships and seeks to replace their judgment with behavioral canons derived from psychiatric and social science."[118] Older ideas of moral limits and personal responsibility are replaced by an emphasis on acquiring the correct technique for emotional and relational management. Whereas the moral life begins with renunciation ("Thou shalt not . . ."), the therapeutic life begins with the renunciation of renunciation ("Thou shalt not commit a 'shalt not' ").

Some persons nowadays turn to "assertiveness therapy" in order to rid themselves of all "feelings of anxiety, ignorance, and guilt that . . . are used efficiently by other people to get us to do what they want."[119] Other persons are busy learning to exert control, exercise power, and extend their influence over the actions of those with whom they come into contact. Since everyone else is presumed to be guided by a similar concern with control, power, and influence, they must master the techniques of manipulation in order to avoid becoming a victim of the desires of the rest. This sort of therapeutic sensibility is based on the view, remarks Lasch, "that success depends on psychological manipulation and that all of life . . . centers on the struggle for interpersonal advantage, the deadly game of intimidating friends and seducing people."[120] Needless to say, such a view encourages a shallow and exploitative approach to human relationships.

This is not to claim that therapists never recognize the need for "love" and "meaning." But many therapists in the contemporary world, as Lasch observes, "define love and meaning simply as fulfillment of the patient's emotional requirements. . . . 'Love' as self-sacrifice, as self-abasement, 'meaning' as submission to a higher loyalty—these submissions strike the therapeutic sensibility as intolerably oppressive, offensive to common sense and injurious to personal health and well-being."[121]

Still, many of those guided by considerations of authenticity rather than morality find that even one or another type of therapy— Freudian, Reichian, Gestalt, sex, Silva Mind Control, Esalen, or whatever—is not enough. Authenticity is also sought in mysticism,

---

[118] John Alt, "Authority, Reason, and the Civilizing Process," *Theory and Society* 10 (May 1981): 393.
[119] Lasch, *The Culture of Narcissism*, pp. 65–66.
[120] Ibid., p. 66.
[121] Ibid., p. 13.

meditation, scientology, astrology, the occult, drugs, and even madness by a wide variety of religious groups. These, too, reflect the therapeutic ideal of finding one's self through commitment to one or another method or movement that promises comfort and psychic relief.

Plagued by uncertainty, anxiety, and what is often described as an inner emptiness,[122] those in search of authenticity often embrace the therapeutic sensibility. Thus, the emphasis is on psychological and social engineering rather than moral principles and the virtues of character. As a consequence, what was once thought to be within the control of the individual is now to be regulated by technology. Many persons today, in fact, look with happy anticipation toward the day when moral character will be totally superceded by psychological and sociological know-how. Yet, despite the self-professed need to establish their own unique, personal identity, those in search of authenticity all too often surrender themselves to whatever causes appear to promise gratification and relief. In their pursuit of authenticity, an increasing number of persons find themselves more and more dependent on one or another mode of therapeutic thought and practice. The result, of course, is to remove the individual from critical judgment and relieve him of responsibility for his actions. Without such responsibility, there is little likelihood that people's conduct will be in line with what is required for a just social order.

Although I may have drawn a somewhat one-sided picture as regards authenticity, it seems clear that the kinds of moral thinking, actions, and experiences necessary for a just social order are generally absent in post-modern societies. Few people today (even fewer, I believe, than in past decades) accept that there can be rationally justifiable measures of difference between those actions that are right and wrong, or morally permissible or impermissible. As a consequence, moral discourse does not occupy a dominant place in people's lives and their actions generally rest far less on what they ought to do than on what they want to do.

Understandably, then, there is little concern with the kinds of feelings that ought to accompany the violation of certain norms and standards. An expectation that individuals who transgress moral dictates ought to feel guilty or ashamed does not have widespread currency. More importantly, the *moral structure* that underlies the judgments and actions of people who are guided by

---

[122] Kovel, "Narcissism and the Family."

considerations of morality is lacking among those for whom authenticity is the chief consideration. Given the predominance of the latter today, it is not surprising that there is less talk about guilt, shame, moral indignation, and the like, than in past decades. Nor is it surprising that there is probably a decrease in the extent to which people actually do experience guilt, shame, and moral indignation. Whatever the comparisons with the past, the contemporary age can hardly be characterized as one where morality reigns supreme.

As I said earlier, I do not want to romanticize the virtues of the classic bourgeois family of the past. Nor, on the other hand, do I want to identify with those persons who see the family as an obsolete social institution. To the contrary, I have tried to emphasize that the learning of moral values and principles, the ability to exert inner controls, the emergence of a conscience, and the acquisition of a coherent sense of personal identity are possible *only* on the basis of highly stable, intense, direct, and prolonged personal relations with meaningful others.

For better or worse, the family appears to be the only form of social organization that even begins to meet these requirements. Whatever the various viewpoints regarding its desirability or inevitability, the family seems to be a universal human grouping, predominating in all known societies throughout history.[123] "Most of the time," Elshtain points out, the family remains "the locus of the most powerful, ambivalent, and meaningful emotional ties . . . [and] thus far it has stubbornly refused to blow away, despite the chill winds of apocalyptic social criticism and abominable social policies."[124]

As she also observes, "One of the signs of hope today is the attempt by men and women to form and sustain strong family ties, to reassert their primacy in the rearing of children, to catalyze identification on the basis of love and respect, authority and reasonable discipline rather than unthought-out, irrational, and primal fear and terror."[125] If we are to assure successful socialization for the just social order, it is this sort of conception of the family that morality demands.

---

[123] See, for example, Ferdinand Mount, *The Subversive Family: An Alternative History of Love and Marriage* (London: Cage, 1982).

[124] Jean Bethke Elshtain, "The Self: Reborn, Undone, Transformed," *Telos* 44 (Summer 1980): 108.

[125] Ibid., p. 109.

V

It should by now be clear that a just social order is better assured by morality than by authenticity. But it needs to be emphasized that morality is also preferable—both morally and sociologically—to another mechanism that is often utilized to help assure social order: control by the community. Although I will give detailed consideration to the law as a form of social control in Part III, it is useful to briefly examine here the alternatives of morality and community control.

Under normal circumstances, the following sorts of acts are morally wrong in all societies and in each and every historical epoch: lying, stealing, extortion, kidnapping, rape, and killing. In certain instances, as I noted in an earlier chapter, some of these acts might not constitute morally wrong conduct. In a situation of war, as already mentioned, the taking of a human life might be morally justifiable. But with other acts it is inconceivable that they could ever be morally justified. I can, for instance, conceive of no possible situation where there could ever be a moral justification for rape.

The above kinds of acts, then, are morally wrong and ought not to be done. Even those persons who reject the application of moral labels would generally agree that such acts are socially "disruptive." But since my own concern is with the moral standing of various actions, I will continue to utilize moral terminology in what follows. In any case, the main burden of preventing such morally wrong (or disruptive) conduct obviously falls on those individuals who might be tempted to engage in such actions; they ought themselves to exercise control and responsibility in order to avoid moral wrongdoing. But because these acts are morally wrong (and certainly disruptive) for everyone, the burden of preventing them also falls to some extent on the rest of the community. The wider society has a vested interest in discouraging such morally wrong conduct.

To the extent that stealing, rape, extortion, and the like, do not occur, this is largely the result of some combination of the affects of individual responsibility and of the wider community. Simplifying greatly, it can be said that the absence of wrongful conduct will be the result of either (1) the ability of the community to create and maintain various sanctions and pressures that deter and punish morally wrong conduct; or (2) the willingness of individuals to exercise control and responsibility in regard to their own actions. In reality, of course, both of these ways of assuring social order are found—in varying combinations—in all societies.

Consider, first, how the community could discourage wrongful conduct. Let us begin with *shame*. As I observed earlier, shame is no longer a very effective means of enforcing desired conduct since so many people live much of their lives among persons to whom they have no close personal ties. But it could be otherwise. The community, i.e., the state or government, might decide to severely limit the right of people to live where they choose, and to also impose heavy restrictions on the kinds of work that people are allowed to do (think of China or the Soviet Union in this regard). By assuring that most people will spend all their lives in the towns or villages where they were born (or be returned there from the places where they now live) and by stipulating that they will be unable to choose (or change) their occupations, the community could increase the extent to which people are able to exercise close surveillance over one another. This would help create an atmosphere where shame might be utilized to discourage morally wrong conduct.

The community could also employ *fear* as a means of preventing wrongful acts. Everyone could be obliged to inform on people who engage in, or are thought to be planning to engage in, certain wrongful actions. Parents, children, friends, and colleagues would be reported to the central authorities in such circumstances. And there might be, literally, a policeman on every street corner, in every factory, in every classroom, and even in every home. Under such conditions, the community could do much to assure that wrongful conduct was discouraged or eliminated. But, obviously, these conditions would also help constitute the worst sort of repressive and closed society.

In fact, even in contemporary nontotalitarian societies, there is much today that evidences the community's attempts to discourage morally wrong actions. In New York City, for example, there are policemen in many schools, in apartment complexes, on subway cars, and in public buildings. To prevent robbery, passengers on public buses are required to have the "correct change" for the driver; and to prevent stealing, customers are required to check their bags upon entering many shops. In large department stores, certain expensive goods are chained so as to prevent their unauthorized removal. Cameras are an increasingly common feature in stores, schools, public buildings, and on the streets so as to monitor people's activities. All of these measures are intended, in one way or another, to discourage wrongful conduct among New Yorkers.

239

Many of them are, of course, in use elsewhere as well—other large American and European cities being no exception.

It is not only what we might term the "grand" moral wrongs (stealing, murder, rape, and the like), however, that represent a violation of moral standards. Allowing one's dog to foul the streets, sneaking in ahead of others who stand in front of one in the bakery or butcher shop, not paying for one's ride when using public transportation, and not doing the work for which one is paid, also represents a failure to respect certain moral standards and the status of other persons as full-fledged moral beings. And, as we know, the community frequently steps in to exercise external control in order to assure that people do not abuse these standards. Thus, in New York City the police are expected to levy a fine on those persons whose dogs befoul the streets. Many shops nowadays require customers to take a numbered ticket upon entering so as to assure that no one sneaks in ahead of others who have been waiting. Controllers ride the buses and streetcars in European cities in order to apprehend people who have not paid their fares. And in the University of Amsterdam, where I teach, the scientific staff has been threatened with the requirement of punching a time clock on the assumption that this will have a positive affect on those persons who otherwise don't fulfill their responsibilities. Obviously, such examples of the imposition of various community controls could be multiplied many times over.

One way to discourage wrongful conduct, then, is through various pressures, sanctions, and controls imposed by the wider community. But this means of discouragement is enormously costly. It is costly not only in financial terms but, more importantly, it is costly in terms of infringements of our liberties, invasions of our privacy, and losses of our human dignity. Such costs are, in fact, inevitable so long as various formal mechanisms of social control are widely employed to discourage wrongful conduct. Unfortunately, many persons today are unable to even recognize the costs we are now paying in terms of losses of liberty, privacy, and dignity. For them, surveillance cameras, the widespread presence of police personnel, and body searches (in the case of air travel) are accepted as "normal" features of the human environment.

Consider now the alternative means of discouraging misconduct and helping to assure a just social order: the exercise of individual control and responsibility. In the ideal situation, where all persons recognized and respected everyone's generic rights to freedom and well-being, generally acted in accordance with them, and had the

240

disposition to feel guilty when violating the rights of others, there would be little need for community sanctions and pressures to discourage morally wrongful conduct. Under these conditions, we would no longer have to live among various safeguards against theft and other crimes, with cameras filming our activities in public places, and with a wide variety of other mechanisms designed to discourage and control misconduct. In such a society, we would be better able to exercise our liberties, enjoy our privacy, and cherish our human dignity.

If we aspire to the achievement of a just social order, then people's actions must be governed by *internal* rather than *external* mechanisms. For me this means that we must reject the pursuit of authenticity and embrace morality as the timeless and universal standard of human adequacy. We must recognize the crucial importance of socialization in helping to inculcate moral principles, educate the moral emotions, and develop the virtues. More than anyone else, then, it is parents and other child-rearers who must see to socialization for the just social order.

III

Social Control

IF socialization were to assure that every individual accepted and acted in accordance with the dominant social norms and values in a society, there would be social order. Were everyone's actions guided by recognition and respect for the generic rights to freedom and well-being for himself and others, then this would assure a *just* social order. In fact, however, it is never the case that everyone is successfully socialized. For a variety of reasons, socialization doesn't always "take," and there are always persons who are not ready to act in accord with society's norms and values. Therefore, the ideal of successfully socializing everyone for a just social order is almost certainly unrealizable.

Because socialization is seldom sufficient by itself to assure conformity with the prevailing norms and values, various social control mechanisms are necessary for those "deviants" who violate these norms and values.[1] Such mechanisms are concerned with the prevention of deviance, on the one hand, and its containment and control, on the other. As is known, social control is exercised in (and by) the family, the neighborhood, the village, the church, and the school. Etiquette and psychotherapy are also sources of social control, and so are customs, ethics, and the law. Whenever and wherever people hold one another to standards, social control is to be found.

My major focus in the next two chapters will be on the *law* as a mechanism of social control. Although I will not attempt to argue it here, I assume that there has been a weakening of social control in the family, neighborhood, church, and school in modern societies, and that everywhere the law has correspondingly increased as a social control mechanism. My concern in the following chapters is mainly with the normative or prescriptive character of the law.

There exists an enormous disparity in the various definitions of the term *law*, and different schools of jurisprudence have been built on these definitions. What the law is, and what distinguishes it from other normative systems, is a matter of considerable disagreement.[2] H. L. A. Hart says of the question, What is Law?, that "nothing concise enough to be recognized as a definition could provide a satisfactory answer to it."[3] Acknowledging the futility of

---

[1] See, for example, Talcott Parsons and Edward Shils, eds., *Toward a General Theory of Action* (Cambridge, Mass.: Harvard University Press, 1951).

[2] See the general discussion in Iredell Jenkins, *Social Order and the Limits of Law* (Princeton: Princeton University Press, 1980).

[3] H. L. A. Hart, *The Concept of Law* (Oxford: The Clarendon Press, 1961), p. 16.

providing a concise and definitive answer to the question, Jenkins suggests that it is more fruitful to ask the question, *Why is law?*[4]

This sort of question demands an explanation for the existence of law; it asks why law is necessary. Jenkins canvasses the views of a large number of authorities and concludes that there is general consensus that "law is a principle of order."[5] Law is a principle that defines and guarantees a rule of order, a uniformity and regularity, that would not otherwise exist. This is quite similar to Weber's view that " 'Law,' as understood by us, is simply an 'order system' endowed with certain specific guarantees of the probability of its empirical validity."[6] And elsewhere he states that an order system "will be called *law* when conformity with it is upheld by the probability that deviant actors will be met by physical or psychic sanctions aimed to compel conformity or to punish disobedience, and applied by a group of men especially empowered to carry out this function."[7] Law can be distinguished from other normative systems, then, by its primary emphasis on order and on the use of secular sanctions to compel conformity or penalize deviant conduct.

Law is a necessary but not sufficient condition for social order in most societies. That is, it supplements but never replaces the order that is expressed and supported by other social institutions. The essential features of a legal system are largely determined by the successes and failures of these other institutional arrangements, especially by the extent to which they are able to successfully exercise social control. This means, as is clear from the anthropological literature, that there is a vast range of legal systems consistent with the existence of social order.[8] In industrialized Western societies, a legal system meets three different, although interrelated, demands.[9] First of all, it establishes and maintains

[4] Jenkins, *Social Order*, p. 3.

[5] Ibid., p. 10.

[6] Max Weber, *On Law and Economy in Society*, trans. Max Rheinstein (Cambridge, Mass.: Harvard University Press, 1954), p. 13.

[7] Max Weber, *General Economic History* (New York: Collier Books, 1966), p. 127.

[8] See, for example, Max Gluckman, *The Judicial Process Among the Barotse of Northern Rhodesia* (Manchester: Manchester University Press, 1967); Lloyd A. Fallers, *Law Without Precedent* (Chicago: University of Chicago Press, 1969); and Martin Krygier, "Anthropological Approaches," in Eugene Kamenka and Alice Erh-Soon Tay, eds., *Law and Social Control* (London: Edward Arnold, 1980), pp. 27–59.

[9] See, Jenkins, *Social Order*; Roberto Mangabeira Unger, *Law in Modern Society* (New York: Free Press, 1976); Eugene Kamenka and Alice Erh-Soon Tay, "Social Traditions, Legal Traditions," in Kamenka and Tay, *Law and Social Control*, pp. 3–26.

rules of behavior: prescribing and prohibiting certain modes of conduct, defining people's legal rights, and allocating social duties, functions, and privileges. The creation of a body of civil, criminal, and public law assures a higher level of social harmony and peace-keeping than would otherwise be the case. Second, the law provides principles and procedures for the resolution of conflicts between individuals and groups within society. The resolution, or at least the regulation, of conflict requires techniques for ascertaining the relevant facts, determining the applicable rules, and imposing and enforcing sanctions. Finally, the law sees to the distribution of resources. Sometimes this involves the guarantee and protection of existing relationships and ways of distributing resources. At other times, the law provides for actual intervention by the state to assure the implementation and enforcement of certain fiscal and monetary policies, social welfare programs, and other ways of consciously altering the society. Thus, a legal system must meet three demands: the keeping of the peace, the resolution and regulation of conflict, and the allocation of resources. The law is indispensable because it helps assure a continuity and predictability in human conduct that is (at least in Western societies) otherwise absent or inadequate.

Sociologists have long had an interest in the law, and it has been a topic of inquiry for Weber, Durkheim, and Parsons, among others.[10] Many sociologists have looked at the functions of law, most especially in the broader perspective of its place in the society and its relation to other social institutions. Today, the sociology of law is a well-developed specialty, and its practitioners study a variety of legal phenomena from a sociological perspective: among them, the effectiveness of various laws, policies, and legal decisions; the influence of judge's backgrounds on their judicial decisions; discrimination in the application of the law; and the law's impact on persons who differ by sex, age, race, socio-economic status, and so forth. These kinds of studies are referred to by Donald Black as examples of the "applied sociology of law," and he differentiates them from a sociological concern with a "general theory of law."[11] Such a theory, he says, "seeks to discover the

---

[10] Weber, *Law and Economy*; Émile Durkheim, *The Division of Labor in Society* (New York: Free Press, 1964); Talcott Parsons, "The Law and Social Control," in William M. Evan, ed., *Law and Society: Explanatory Essays* (New York: Free Press, 1962), pp. 56–72. See also Philippe Nonet and Philip Selznick, *Law and Society in Transition* (New York: Harper Torchbooks, 1978).

[11] Donald J. Black, "The Boundaries of Legal Sociology," *Yale Law Journal* 81 (1972):

principles and mechanisms that predict empirical patterns of law, whether these patterns occur in this day or the past, regardless of the substantive area of law involved and regardless of the society."[12]

But whether sociological research is applied or general, empirical or theoretical, most sociologists of law are in agreement that the investigator must maintain the distinction between what is and what ought to be. That is, the concerns of the sociologist must be wholly descriptive and explanatory and not normative or prescriptive. As Weber emphasized, it is not for the social scientist to make any judgments as to the validity or the moral standing of a system of law.[13]

Even though I am a sociologist, my primary concern *is* with the moral standing of legal systems and, of course, with the character of a legal system that would be in accord with the recognition and respect for everyone's rights to freedom and well-being. Of particular importance here is the relation of law and morality, especially with regard to the legitimate authority of a legal system and the moral obligation of citizens to obey its dictates. Just as I argued in Part II that justifiable moral principles have both a privileged moral status and are also superior to unjustifiable principles in their capacity for assuring normative consensus and social order, so does legitimate authority have both a special moral standing and a superior capacity for securing compliance with its demands. A legal system whose legitimate authority is rationally justifiable creates more reliable conformity with its dictates than does a legal system that rests entirely on tradition or on its ability to coerce a society's citizens. When the legitimate authority of a legal system is rationally justifiable, it will impose a moral obligation on citizens to support and comply with it. Because of the general acknowledgment that everyone "ought" to obey legitimate authority, the need for the legal system and its apparatus to maintain means of coercion in constant readiness is minimized.

In Chapter 6, I will consider the general relation between law and morality as it is conceived of in four traditions of legal theory:

1086–100. See also, Theodore M. Benditt, *Law as Rule and Principle* (London: Harvester Press, 1978).

[12] Black, "The Boundaries," p. 1096. Also see Donald J. Black, *The Behavior of Law* (New York: Academic Press, 1976).

[13] Weber, *General Economic History*. Of course, some sociologists do take value positions, but usually without attempting to provide a rational justification for their own normative preferences and commitments.

natural law theory, legal realism, legal positivism, and Ronald Dworkin's "liberal theory of law." The latter is the best known of recent theories of law, and will receive an especially detailed examination. My general discussion of these different legal theories sets the stage for my consideration in Chapter 7 of law in the just social order. My concern there is with the general character of the legal system that ought to arise from, and be consistent with, everyone's generic rights to freedom and well-being. Thus, Part III focuses on the law as a mechanism of social control.

SIX

The Law and Moral Values

IN this chapter, I examine four modern approaches to legal theory. These approaches will be explained and critically evaluated, with special attention given to the relationship between law and morality. Of particular concern here is the way that different legal theories deal with questions about the justifiability of a legal system and the moral obligation of citizens to obey the law.

Since it is the *source* rather than the *content* of a legal system that endows it with legitimate authority, I will be asking: What justification is provided for the authority of law? And related to this is the question: Are people morally obligated to obey the dictates of the law? If so, what is the source of the law's obligatory character? These questions regarding authority and obligation are obviously related; citizens have an obligation to obey the law only when the authority of the legal system itself is sufficiently justified. When it is not, we usually speak of "de facto" authority, meaning that we recognize the authority of a legal system and yet deny that it is justifiable. Thus, many of us would deny that citizens have a moral obligation to obey the laws of a tyrannical government.[1]

Let us turn, then, to an examination of the various approaches to legal theory, keeping in mind my special concern with questions about the legitimate authority of the law and a citizen's obligation to obey it.

---

[1] There are those, however, who argue that citizens have a prima facie obligation to obey all incumbent state authorities. R. M. Hare, for example, claims that there is a moral obligation to obey the laws of one's polity. Such an obligation arises, he says, "only because there is a state with laws." Simply by virtue of the existence of an enforced set of laws, all citizens have a moral obligation to obey the law. R. M. Hare, "Political Obligation," in Ted Honderich, ed., *Social Ends and Political Means* (London: Routledge & Kegan Paul, 1976), p. 5. But contrary to what Hare claims, legal obligations do not necessarily impose moral obligations on a society's citizens. People may have the legal obligations imposed by the legal system operative within the state, and are certainly apt to run afoul of the law if they do not meet certain legal requirements, but the moral obligation to obey the law can be justified only by appeal to some principles of morality beyond the law itself. This will be clarified, I believe, in my discussion of the various legal theorists.

I

Natural Law Theories

Although there is no one view that is *the* natural law position, all the various natural law theories share the view that at least some nonconventional directives for human behavior can be found.[2] Such directives are moral principles that combine description with prescription, and apply universally to all societies. They have absolute and objective validity, and are discoverable by reason or intuition. Blackstone provides an excellent summary statement of the natural law doctrine: "This law of nature being coeval with mankind and dictated by God himself is of course superior in obligation to any other. It is binding over the whole globe, in all countries and at all times. No human laws are of any validity if contrary to this. . . ."[3]

A distinctive feature of the natural law doctrine has been the central place given to moral values. If the law of nature is to have any relevance to the laws that human beings make for the regulation of themselves and others, it must contain guiding principles. The Stoics were probably the first to search for an absolute law of nature against which the laws made by men could be appraised. Their view of the law of nature was based on a conception of human reason as both part of nature and as a capacity for volition, insight, and discovery. This was developed into the general principle that reason governs all parts of the universe. Since man, as part of universal nature, is governed by reason, he lives "naturally" if he lives according to his reason. It is, in fact, his moral duty to do this. Under the guiding hand of the Roman advocate, Cicero, the Stoic law of nature took root in the philosophy of the Romans. "True law," Cicero taught:

> is right reason consonant with nature, diffused among all men, constant, eternal; which summons to duty by its command and hinders from fraud by its prohibition, which neither commands nor forbids good men in vain nor moves bad ones by either. To make enactments infringing this law, religion forbids, neither may it be repealed even in part, nor have we power through Senate or people to free ourselves from it. It

[2] For an excellent discussion of natural law theories, see Theodore M. Benditt, *Law as Rule and Principle: Problems of Legal Philosophy* (London: Harvester Press, 1978), chap. 5.

[3] Quoted in John Mackie, "The Third Theory of Law," *Philosophy and Public Affairs* 7 (Fall 1977): 3.

needs no interpreter or expounder but itself, nor will there be one law in Rome and another in Athens, one in the present and another in time to come, but one law and that eternal and immutable shall embrace all people and for all time, and there shall be as it were one common master and ruler, the god of all, the author and judge and proposer of the law.[4]

This is the conception of natural law that dominated Western political thought for more than eighteen hundred years. Natural law was distinguished from laws that are made by men, with the latter being genuine law only when they are consistent with the natural law.

The discovery of this "higher" (natural) law serves, then, as a sort of Archimedean point from which existing laws and legal systems can be evaluated. Further, according to the natural law doctrine, there is always an obligation to obey the law. This is because everything that *really* is law is in accordance with (correct) morality. And since everyone certainly has an obligation to act in accordance with morality, everyone has an obligation to obey the law.[5]

A modern natural law standpoint is defended by Fuller in his book, *The Morality of Law*. His position, he writes, has been shaped by "a dissatisfaction with the existing literature concerning the relation between law and morality."[6] Fuller argues that the purpose of the institution of law is to subject human conduct to the guidance and control of several rules. Instead of seeing the law as merely "there," as a manifested fact of social power, as an established lawmaking activity, he claims that it must be recognized as a particular kind of activity that is the "product of a sustained purposive effort."[7] A legal system, states Fuller, must be both created and maintained, and there are eight conditions that are necessary to assure this. Among these eight are the following: (1) there must be rules; (2) the rules to be observed must be publicized; and (4) the rules must be understandable.[8]

---

[4] *De Re Publica*, 3: 22, quoted in C. H. McIlwain, *The Growth of Political Thought in the West* (New York: Macmillan, 1932), pp. 111–12.

[5] Benditt, *Law as Rule*, p. 92.

[6] Lon L. Fuller, *The Morality of Law* (New Haven: Yale University Press, 1969), p. 3.

[7] Ibid., p. 106.

[8] Ibid., p. 39. These eight conditions constitute what Fuller calls the "internal morality" of law. This is in contrast to the external morality of law, which is concerned with specific topics of lawmaking. The conditions form, then, a procedural version of natural law. They are procedural in that Fuller says nothing about the

Fuller claims that his eight conditions represent a variety of natural laws.[9] He says that he has tried to discover and articulate the natural laws of a particular kind of human undertaking, which he describes as "the enterprise of subjecting human conduct to the governance of rules."[10] These natural laws, he remarks, have nothing to do with any "brooding omnipresence in the skies," nor with God's or other "higher" laws. Nevertheless, he says, they are natural laws. But, like many of Fuller's critics,[11] I fail to see this supposed connection between law and morality. Of course, he does assert that his eight conditions constitute a morality of law. But, it must be asked, what kind of morality?

Since the eight conditions are procedural, or content-neutral, they appear to be compatible with a variety of legal systems, some of which might (from some other natural law standpoint) be considered substantially evil or unjust. In fact, a non-democratic legal order, based on racial and sexual inequalities and persecution, may conform to Fuller's eight principles better than any of the legal systems of the more enlightened Western democracies. It seems obvious to me that Fuller has a natural law position only in so far as the eight conditions are themselves moral requirements. He stipulates that they are the moral requirements that must be satisfied if there is to be law at all. But are they indeed moral requirements? Leaving aside the questions of their adequacy as a set of requirements, I have doubts about their status as "moral" requirements. Consider the following example.

According to the second of Fuller's eight principles of legality, "the rules to be observed must be publicized." Suppose that someone were punished for violating a particular law, and that he is able to show that the law was not given adequate publicity and that, therefore, he and most other people did not know about it. Such punishment would be clearly unjust. But does this show that the legal principle ("the rule must be publicized") is itself a moral principle? I think not. The judge who imposed the punishment

---

substance of the rules. They are a version of natural law, *ibid.*, because "A total failure of any one of these eight conditions does not simply result in a bad system of law; it results in something that is not properly called a legal system at all, except perhaps in the Pickwickian sense in which an invalid contract can still be said to be one kind of contract."

[9] Ibid., p. 96.

[10] Ibid.

[11] See, for example, the review by Ronald Dworkin, "Philosophy, Morality and Law—Observations Prompted by Professor Fuller's Novel Claim," *University of Pennsylvania Law Review* 113 (1965): 668–90.

has, I agree, acted in an unjust manner. This does not mean, however, that every time the legislature fails to adequately publicize a rule that it has done something immoral. They might be accused of carelessness or irresponsibility, but not of immoral actions (or inactions). There is certainly an injustice (and a violation of some other, genuine, moral principle) in the action of the judge, but this injustice is not derived from the violation of the publicity rule. It seems to me that principles like Fuller's are not moral principles at all, but rather are designed to minimize the danger created by the law itself.[12] There are good reasons, then, for being skeptical about the success of Fuller's attempt to establish a necessary connection between law and morality.

Natural law theories, especially the older ones, hold that the laws operative in nature are either self-evident or discoverable by our intuitive capacities unguided by particular ethical criteria. The major criticism of this view is well known; different people see different laws or principles as self-evident, and different people's intuitions also reveal different and sometimes conflicting things to them. Natural law was invoked, for example, on both sides of the slavery question in the United States, i.e., to "prove" both the equality and the inferiority of blacks. In fact, as noted by Wright, natural law has been called upon to support an almost infinite list of causes:

> [N]atural law has had as its content whatever the individual in question desired to advocate. This has varied from a defence of theocracy to a defence of the complete separation of church and state, from revolutionary rights in 1776 to liberty of contract in recent judicial opinions, from the advocacy of universal adult suffrage to a defence of rigid limitations upon the voting power, from philosophical anarchy in 1849 with Thoreau to strict paternalism five years later with Fitzhugh, from the advocacy of the inalienable rights of succession to the assertion of the natural law of national supremacy, from the right of majority of rule to the rights of vested interests.[13]

Because there are no natural laws that impress themselves in the same way on everyone, there is no way of drawing conclusions

---

[12] The same point is made by Joseph Raz, *The Authority of Law: Essays on Law and Morality* (Oxford: Clarendon Press, 1979), p. 224.

[13] B. Wright, quoted in John Hart Ely, *Democracy and Distrust: A Theory of Judicial Review* (Cambridge, Mass.: Harvard University Press, 1980), p. 51.

from the enormous variety of perspectives and intuitions concerning such laws. Consequently, natural law arguments cannot be used to justify the legitimate authority of a legal system or to ground the moral obligation for citizens to obey the law.

This results in a rather unsatisfactory conclusion in regard to the connection between natural law and human law. Such a conclusion is also linked to the fact that for natural law theorists there is no special notion of legal validity. The only concept of validity is validity according to natural law, i.e., moral validity.[14] Human law, therefore, derives its validity entirely from natural law. Statutes, court decisions, etc., that are contrary to natural law are not valid. Thus, they are not law at all. The upshot of all this is that the inability of natural law theorists to justify any valid moral principles forces them to conclude that there exist no (valid) legal systems at all.

II

Legal Realism

Perhaps the most distinctive American contribution to legal philosophy in the twentieth century comes from the group of legal writers called legal realists. In their view, there is no such thing as a distinctive realm of legal reasoning. Instead of seeing the law as an ideal and judicial decisions as the products of informed reason, they argue that the law is nothing more than the rules for decision that the courts lay down. It is the fact that courts apply rules that makes these rules law.

In other words, judges are creators of the law. The legal realists criticize as naive the belief that the task of a judge is to find the law and apply it to the particular circumstances of the cases he is judging. In fact, they reject the idea that the rules of law, or objective principles transcending the will of the judge, play a central role in legal reasoning. The weakness of such a standpoint is clearly demonstrated, they say, by the fact that there is frequently a considerable diversity of judicial opinion in the same and similar cases. In many instances, there are no unequivocal rules available for application and, in other cases, there are conflicting rules. Thus, judges must decide on their own when no applicable rules exist and they are free to choose among conflicting rules where more than one applies. From the perspective of the legal realists, then,

---

[14] Raz, *The Authority of Law*, p. 131.

the judge is an independent operative, perhaps consulting but not in reality bound by rules in arriving at his decisions.[15]

The legal realists minimize the normative or prescriptive nature of law, emphasizing instead an insistence on a strictly empirical approach to law. This means that they have no real concern with justifying the authority of the law. Consider the remarks of Justice Oliver Wendell Holmes, Jr., the most famous adherent of the realist position: "The prophecies of what the courts will do in fact, and nothing more pretentious, are what I mean by the law."[16] This statement reflects his concern—common to other legal realists—with achieving some sort of control over things by being in a position to predict what is going to happen. It is the meaning of the law to the people subject to it and its significance to the ordinary person seeking legal advice that are important. The best way of assuring that we are in a position to say what the law is, Holmes taught, is to take the view of the "bad man"—someone whose only concern is what is likely to happen to him if he does one thing rather than another.

> What constitutes the law? You will find some text writers telling you that it is something different from what is decided by the courts of Massachusetts or England, that it is a system of reason, that it is deduction from principles of ethics or admitted axioms or what not, which may or may not coincide with the decisions. But if we take the view of our friend the bad man we shall find that he does not care two straws for the axioms or deductions, but that he does want to know what the Massachusetts or English courts are likely to do in fact. I am much of his mind. The prophecies of what the court will do in fact, and nothing more pretentious, are what I mean by the law.[17]

With the "bad man's" notion of law, laws do not entail any sort of obligation. From this standpoint, every decision is a correct decision. It is not the content of a decision or the fact that it is arrived at in consistency with certain rules that make it law, but rather the source from which it emanates. And it is not respect for the law or considerations of justice that underlie and support the sanctions for disobedience, but simply fear and force. Not sur-

---

[15] Benditt, *Law as Rule*.

[16] Oliver Wendell Holmes, "The Path of the Law," in Max Lerner, ed., *The Mind and Faith of Justice Holmes* (Boston: Little, Brown, 1943), p. 78.

[17] Ibid., p. 75.

prisingly, then, Holmes and other realists were particularly critical of what they saw as the "danger, both to speculation and to practice, of confounding morality with law."[18]

More recently, there has emerged a group of radical legal scholars who represent a neo-realist approach to the law.[19] Like earlier legal realists, they hold that there is no such thing as distinctly legal reasoning. Instead, they argue, the choices confronting courts and legal systems are not really questions of law at all. They can, rather, better be recognized as questions of politics and political theory. Informed by the ideas of the Frankfurt School, some of these neo-realist scholars emphasize that legal rules cannot be understood independently of the way they have arisen in a particular society. In fact, they believe that the historic function of the law has been to protect the social, economic, and political structures that serve and legitimate the class interests of a privileged elite.[20]

These neo-realists have much in common with other recent radical critiques of Western societies.[21] They draw on the conclusions of both legal and sociological research concerning the relationship between different kinds of judicial decisions and the economic interests of various groups and social classes. From their perspective, the results of such research are fully compatible with their own standpoint.

There are, in my view, several serious problems with the legal realist and neo-realist doctrines. First of all, the realists' view that so-called rules of law are merely predictions of judicial behavior is overly simple. If a lawyer accepts a proposition of law, he is, according to the realists, simply predicting what the courts will do in particular cases. If this prediction is correct, then what he said was true; otherwise, it was false. But this line of reasoning cannot be accepted as a useful explanation of how lawyers and other legal officials *use* such propositions.[22] When a lawyer advises his client

---

[18] Ibid., p. 78.

[19] Robert Mangabeira Unger, "The Critical Legal Studies Movement," *Harvard Law Journal* 96 (1983): 561-75; and David Kairys, ed., *The Politics of Law: A Progressive Critique* (New York: Pantheon Books, 1982).

[20] See, for example, Donald Kennedy, "Legal Education as Training for Hierarchy," in Kairys, *Politics of Law*; and Mark Tushnet, "Corporations and Free Speech," Ibid.

[21] See, for example, Maureen Cain and Alan Hunt, *Marx and Engels on Law* (London: Academic Press, 1980); P. Q. Hirst, *On Law and Ideology* (London: Macmillan, 1979); and Hugh Collins, *Marxism and Law* (New York: Oxford University Press, 1982).

[22] H. L. A. Hart, *The Concept of Law* (Oxford: Oxford University Press, 1961).

about a particular legal matter, he is not usually predicting what the court will decide, but is expressing his view that it would be right for the court to reach that decision. And when a judge hands down a decision, he offers a justification for his decision. This decision is certainly not a result of his own prediction. "In saying that something *is* the law," Benditt points out, a court "is not predicting how it is going to decide the case: an observer may predict what a judge is going to do, but a judge cannot, in deciding a case, merely be predicting what he is going to do; he is doing it."[23]

Second, by emphasizing the point of view of the bad man, legal realists totally ignore the good man. Since there are good men and women who sincerely want to know what they ought (legally) to do so that they can act in conformity with these legal obligations, one would expect that the law should also be considered from their point of view. The fact that their point of view is ignored arises from the undue weight that is placed on predicting and exposing judicial decisions, and from the general lack of attention given by legal realists to the internal coherence and values of a legal system.

Third, both the realists and neo-realists are extremely nihilistic with regard to the possibility of providing a rational justification for judicial decisions. Although they claim that the law is basically only a struggle for power, they have no way of grounding their own conclusion that this is morally unacceptable, outrageous, or whatever. If judges are in a position to bring about any results they want (in that they "make" the law), and if there exist no valid moral standards that allow for the assessment of these results, then questions about the justification of the legitimate authority of a legal system, about an individual's moral obligation to obey judge-made law, or about the fairness or justice of judicial decisions can never be answered. This is a conclusion many persons are unwilling to accept. By assuming that judges often make up new rules and apply them retroactively, legal realists suggest that the idea of the law as largely a rule-following activity is totally false.

But this forecloses a consideration of different sorts of justification for legal rulings. When the Supreme Court overturns precedent and orders the desegregation of schools, for example, legal realists claim that the Court is deciding the case entirely in accordance with its own moral and political beliefs. In fact, the late William O. Douglas reports that at the start of his own career on the Supreme Court, Chief Justice Charles Evans Hughes told him;

[23] Benditt, *Law as Rule*, p. 13.

"Justice Douglas, you must remember one thing. At the constitutional level where we work, ninety percent of any decision is emotional. The rational part of us supplies the reasons for supporting our predilections."[24]

There is obviously an alternative explanation to that set forth by Chief Justice Hughes and the legal realists: the Court may be following general and abstract rules resting on an appeal to some justified authority or rules and procedures. These rules may be widely recognized and accepted (or are, at the very least, viewed as justifiable) and are, therefore, something other than the expression of the Court's own, personal, subjective, emotional judgments. Thus, realists and non-realists ignore the possibility that jurisprudential issues may be, at their core, issues that are resolvable in accordance with justifiable rules and procedures.

III

Legal Positivism

Legal positivists, like the realists, place an emphasis on the separation of law from morality. What the law *is* and what it *ought* to be are viewed as two distinct issues. But they do not deny that there are linkages between law and morality. They recognize that moral conceptions may influence legislation, provide standards for the criticism of existing law, and may be taken into account in interpreting the law. Their claim, however, is that there is no *logical* connection between law and morality. There are, they argue, no moral criteria for the validity of law. From the positivist perspective, questions about the "justice" of law cannot even be raised. According to Kelsen, "Just is only another word for legal or legitimate."[25] The focus must be on the constitutionality of an act of legislation, while the character of the rules laid down must be ignored. Thus Kelsen maintained that "from the point of view of the science of law, the law (*Recht*) under the Nazi-government was law (*Recht*). We may regret it but we cannot deny that it was law."[26]

Legal positivists hold that there is always a single ultimate fundamental test for law. Since the law of a society is constituted by a set of rules used for determining what behavior will be punished

[24] Quoted in Ronald Dworkin, "Dissent on Douglas," *The New York Review* 28 (19 February, 1981): 4.

[25] Hans Kelsen, "The Pure Theory of Law," *Law Quarterly Review* 50 (1934): 482.

[26] Hans Kelsen, *Das Naturrecht in der Politischen Theorie*, ed. F. M. Schmoelz (Salzburg, 1963), p. 148.

or coerced by the public power, there must be specific criteria for identifying and distinguishing these special rules. Such criteria do not pertain to the content of the rules but to their *pedigree*. In the view of legal positivists, the legal validity of a law is established by showing that it conforms to tests of validity laid down by some other rules of the system.[27] A law is valid if and only if it was enacted by the sovereign of the system (Austin),[28] or if and only if it was authorized by the basic norm of the system (Kelsen),[29] or if and only if it ought to be recognized according to what Hart calls the "rule of recognition" of the system.[30] Thus, the norm supplying the criterion of legal validity is always itself a social (i.e., non-legal) norm.

AUSTIN'S THEORY. According to John Austin's 1832 work, *The Province of Jurisprudence Determined*, the fundamental test of pedigree that a rule must meet to count as a rule of law is that it must emanate from the sovereign. Laws are commands of the sovereign that are backed up by the threat of force.[31] A law in the proper sense is a species of command; it is a desire directed from one rational being to another, regarding something that the latter is to do (or refrain from doing), and backed up by a threat of force in the event of disobedience.

In every political community, Austin claimed, one will find a sovereign—a person (or group of persons) who is habitually obeyed by everyone else in the society, and who himself obeys no other person or group. Valid legal rules of a community are the general commands deployed by its sovereign. Since the sovereign cannot provide for all contingencies, he delegates to the judicial system the discretion to issue new commands (that is, create new laws) whenever necessary. It is, of course, up to the sovereign to accept or reject these new laws. Law, then, is what is commanded by a definite body of political superiors, whatever these commands might be. Law as a whole is the aggregate of individual laws or commands. It is the form of the law, not its substance, which is the distinguishing element of law.

[27] Raz, *The Authority of Law*; Ronald Dworkin, *Taking Rights Seriously*, New impression with a Reply to Critics (London: Duckworth, 1978).

[28] J. L. Austin, *The Province of Jurisprudence Determined* (London: Weidenfeld and Nicolson, 1968). Originally published in 1832.

[29] Kelsen, "The Pure Theory."

[30] Hart, *The Concept of Law*.

[31] Austin, *The Province*.

Among the objections raised against Austin's theory two are especially worthy of mention. First, criticisms have been made against his argument that in every community a determinate group or institution can be found who have a monopoly on the use of force. This is a problem that is also associated with Weber's definition of the state as that entity within a geographical area having monopoly on the use of force. It seems obvious that the state is not the only institution actually using force. As Dworkin points out: "Political control in a modern nation is pluralistic and shifting, a matter of more or less, of compromise and cooperation and alliance, so that it is often impossible to say that any person or group has that dramatic control necessary to qualify as an Austinian sovereign."[32] Second, critics have noted that Austin's account fails to recognize certain attitudes people actually take toward "the law." He failed to give an adequate account of the reasons for the commands of the sovereign to be recognized as authoritative. No attempt was made to justify the legitimate authority of the sovereign's rule.

Austin claimed that laws obligate us, and that the notion of being obligated is connected with the idea of a command. To be commanded is to be threatened with a sanction if one disobeys, and, consequently (Austin believed), to be placed under a duty. But surely someone's ability to harm those who disobey does not by itself place them under a duty to follow his commands. Complying with a gunman's command may be prudent, but there is no duty to do so. Austin's analysis allows no place for the distinction between our duties to the gunman and those to the strictures of the law. What he provides is an account of being "obliged," not an account of being "obligated." Being obliged may mean being forced or physically coerced, while being obligated means that there are certain legitimate requirements that apply to people in a particular situation.[33] Actually Austin had no theory of legal obligation; he assumed it as a fact but did not explain it. Given his failure to provide any justification for people's presumed legal obligation to

[32] Dworkin, *Taking Rights Seriously*, p. 18.

[33] Benditt, *Law as Rule*, p. 78, makes the distinction nicely: "First, one can be under an obligation even if there is no chance of being caught and penalized. And second, a statement that someone has or is under a legal obligation functions as a reason or justification for his acting in a certain way and also for the imposition of a sanction if he fails to do so, whereas a statement that someone was obliged to do something is never a justification, but may be an excuse."

obey the dictates of the law, he also ignored questions about any moral obligation to obey the law.

KELSEN'S THEORY. In an effort to establish a "pure" science of law, Hans Kelsen sought to find the *a priori* principles that underlie all law, regardless of its content.[34] Kelsen held that it is logically necessary that in every legal system there exist one basic norm. It is this one basic norm that authorizes all the constitutional laws, but its own existence is not dependent upon any law-creating organ or agency. It is, rather, a logical necessity.[35] "This basic norm is not created by the organs of the legal order," according to Kelsen, "but is presupposed by legal cognition: the basic norm is therefore not a positive but a hypothetical norm."[36]

Thus, laws are valid insofar as they have been created in the way prescribed by the basic norm. As to specific legal norms, Kelsen stated:

> To the question why this individual norm is valid as part of a definite legal order, the answer is: because it has been created in conformity with a criminal statute. This statute, finally, receives its validity from the constitution, since it has been established by the competent organ in the way the constitution prescribes. If we ask why the constitution is valid, perhaps we come upon an older constitution. Ultimately we reach some constitution that is the first historically and that was laid down by an individual usurper or by some kind of assembly. . . .
> It is postulated that one ought to behave as the individual, or the individuals, who laid down the constitution have ordained. This is the basic norm of the legal order under consideration.[37]

Ultimately, then, all positive laws owe their validity to a non-positive law, a law not created by human action, the basic norm. This basic norm, Kelsen argued, is not itself created. Nevertheless, it can be said to exist, for it is valid.

According to Kelsen, the existence of a norm is the same as its validity, and this validity is determined by its logical derivability from a *hypothetical* basic norm. Consequently, no distinction can

[34] Kelsen, "The Pure Theory."

[35] Hans Kelsen, "Centralization and Decentralization," in *Authority and the Individual* (Cambridge, Mass.: Harvard University Press, 1937), p. 213.

[36] Ibid.

[37] Hans Kelsen, *The General Theory of Law and State* (New York: Russell and Russell, 1945), p. 115.

be drawn between a legal system in which the powers of authority are wholly unlimited and one in which there are definite limitations set on the wielding of authority. In fact, his assertion that all valid law is set (positive) law is made good by redefining "set" as "made valid" and "made valid" as "in fact enforced by authority."[38] The rules of positive law, he wrote, "are derived from the arbitrary will of a human authority."

Like Austin, Kelsen maintained a connection between law and force:

> Legal norms are coercive norms. In order to bring about the desired behavior, the norm threatens the person disobeying it with a coercive act which he deems as evil. . . . Thus the specific structure of a legal norm is revealed as the typical rule of law; it connects two facts; a certain fact, as the condition, with another fact—the coercive act—as the consequence.[39]

Kelsen claimed that the law imposes duties only on legal officials, and not on ordinary citizens as such. The latter can determine what they are to do by looking at the conditions under which officials are to impose sanctions.[40] His concern was with the validity of positive law from the point of view of a hypothetical legal person, and not from the point of view of the community's citizens.

Kelsen's theory, he emphasized, was concerned with neither actual nor tacit recognition by a community's citizens; it had no interest at all with the attitudes or beliefs of the population of the law. For him, a legal system exists if it is effective. The norms of a legal order regulate behavior, and they are only valid norms to the extent that they do so effectively.[41] In Kelsen's words: "A general legal norm is regarded as valid only if the human behavior that is regulated by it actually conforms with it, at least to some degree. . . . A minimum of effectiveness is a condition of validity."[42]

Kelsen's definition of the law as the only possible and significant definition has the consequence that it is illegitimate to use the term "law" in any different sense than the one he stipulates. There are no tests other than the basic norm idea, which can be used to

[38] This is a point made by F. A. Hayek, *Law, Legislation and Liberty*, vol. 2, *The Mirage of Social Justice* (London: Routledge & Kegan Paul, 1976), p. 52.

[39] Kelsen, "Centralization and Decentralization," p. 212.

[40] See the discussion in Benditt, *Law as Rule*, p. 55.

[41] Hans Kelsen, *The Pure Theory of Law* (Berkeley: University of California Press, 1967), p. 31.

[42] Ibid., p. 11.

determine whether a law is valid or not. The content of the law may be good or evil; it may be supplied by the parliament, the despot, or the absolute monarch—these are matters of complete indifference to Kelsen.

For Kelsen, as for many other persons emphasizing the separation of law and morality, moral judgments are simply matters of individual preferences. Of course, he recognized that some people do assess the law by moral standards. But since these standards themselves cannot be rationally justified, such an assessment is totally a matter of personal or political subjectivity.[43] Thus, he writes about the criterion of justice: "He who denies the justice of such, i.e., any positive 'law' and asserts that the so-called law is not 'true' law, has to prove it; and this proof is practically impossible since there is no objective criterion of justice."[44]

In short, Kelsen provided a definition of law under which every state is a state of law. This means that nothing can be said with regard to justifying the legitimate authority of a legal system, or about people's moral obligations to obey one or another system of law. For Kelsen, law and morality were totally unrelated.

HART'S THEORY. H. L. A. Hart, the best known of contemporary legal positivists, attempts to formulate a theory that comes to grips with some of the difficulties found in earlier accounts of the law.[45] Whereas Austin located the validity of a law in its having emanated from the sovereign, and Kelsen found it in the basic norm of the system, Hart gives predominance to the attitudes toward the rules of the legal system of those who are subject to it, most especially its officials. Like Austin, he says that valid rules of law may be created through the order of officials and public institutions. But while Austin (and Kelsen) held that the authority of these institutions lay only in their monopoly of force and power, Hart locates their authority in a fundamental "rule of recognition."

In arguing for this rule, Hart distinguishes two kinds of rules, primary and secondary, the union of which explains the nature of law. Primary rules are the duty-imposing rules in a society, under which "human beings are required to do or abstain from certain actions, whether they wish or not."[46] They are meant to

---

[43] Ibid., p. 68.

[44] Hans Kelsen, *What is Justice?* (Berkeley: University of California Press, 1957), p. 295.

[45] Hart, *The Concept of Law.*

[46] Ibid., p. 78.

guide the conduct of individuals. Such rules might be the only kind of rules in a small, simple society without a legislature, courts, or officials of any kind. But they may not suffice even there, and certainly not in a more complex society. It is plain, Hart says, "that only a small community closely knit by ties of kinship, common sentiment, and belief, and placed in a stable environment, could live successfully by such a regime of unofficial rules. In any other conditions such a simple form of social control must prove defective and will require supplementation in different ways."[47] If primary rules are binding entirely because of practices of acceptance, this may lead to situations in which there is uncertainty about what the rules are or what their scope is. Since the rules are unofficial, there is no institutionalized way of altering them or creating new rules. And a reliance entirely on such primary rules may be extremely inefficient, since there is no agency invested with the responsibility of ascertaining when they have been violated.

To remedy these defects, Hart says, the primary rules are supplemented with secondary rules. These are rules about how primary rules are to be created or recognized. Herein, according to Hart, lies the step from the pre-legal to the legal world. When a community has developed a fundamental secondary rule that specifies how legal rules are to be identified, a legal system is born.[48] It is such a fundamental secondary rule that Hart terms a "rule of recognition." The rule of recognition settles the question about the existence and scope of the rules, introduces procedures for changing the rules, and eliminates inefficiency by the introduction of rules of adjudication. Hart's thesis that a rule of recognition exists in every legal system is the central feature of his positivist theory of law, for it is this rule that distinguishes what is and is not valid law.

The rule of recognition may be relatively simple. In the English legal system, according to Hart, it might be that whatever the Queen in Parliament enacts is law. Or it might be more complex, as seen in the United States Constitution and its many problems of interpretation. To demonstrate that a particular law is valid may require tracing a chain of validity, as did Kelsen with the basic norm, back from that law to the fundamental rule of recognition. But whereas Kelsen's "basic norm" is hypothetical, the existence of a rule of recognition legitimates the decisions of the government

[47] Ibid., pp. 89–90.
[48] Ibid.

and gives them the sense of obligation that is lacking in the naked commands of Austin's sovereign and Kelsen's idea of the basic norm, which directs an official to apply force.

Hart's theory is superior to those of Austin and Kelsen in that he recognizes that it is the different motives and attitudes that may have nurtured obedience that are decisive in conferring legitimacy on a power. He emphasizes that we can understand legal concepts like obligation and sanction only by paying attention to what he calls the *internal* point of view. Someone who takes the internal point of view with respect to a social rule, will express his or her attitude toward the rule by saying such things as, "I ought to do . . ." or, "You have a duty to. . . ."[49] This is in contrast to the external point of view, where someone is concerned only with the probable consequences of a particular behavior. When most persons take the internal point of view toward a particular directive, Hart says, it can be said that a social rule exists. Obligation and duty, then, can be explained by referring to the internal aspect of primary rules; while legal powers, obligations, and sanctions are explained by referring to the internal aspect of secondary rules, and in particular to the point of view taken by legal officials.

While Austin claimed that law exists whenever a population habitually obeys the commands of a sovereign, and Kelsen affirmed that law exists when people recognize a basic norm stipulating sanctions, Hart argues that law exists only when the population accepts a particular secondary rule—a rule of recognition—which gives those who exercise power the authority to do so. Authority is legitimate, Hart says, only when it is exercised in accordance with some accepted constitutional rule.

Despite the superiority of Hart's theory over those of Austin and Kelsen, it has several important weaknesses. First of all, there are problems with the notion of the rule of recognition. Hart insists that the existence of the rule of recognition is of an "essentially factual character" and can "neither be valid nor invalid but is simply accepted as appropriate for use in this way (i.e., to determine the validity of rules *within* a system)."[50] He goes on to say that "the rule of recognition exists only as a complex, but normally concordant, practice of the courts, officials, and private persons in identifying the law by reference to certain criteria. Its existence is a

[49] Ibid., pp. 55–56, p. 88.
[50] Ibid., pp. 106 and 105, respectively.

matter of fact."[51] In other words, the legal order is founded upon the rule of recognition, and it is this rule that determines the validity of rules within the system. But the only argument for the rule of recognition itself is the external "fact" that people generally accept it as a standard and act in accord with it. Consider the following statements by Hart:

> The ordinary citizen manifests his acceptance largely by acquiescence in the results of . . . official operations. He keeps the law which is made and identified in this way, and also makes claims and exercises power conferred by it. But he may know little of its origins or of its makers: some may know nothing more of the laws than that they are "the law."[52]

Thus, the fact that the ordinary citizen passively accepts the law that is "effectively accepted"[53] by lawyers and other legal officials is all that is necessary to establish the rule of recognition. It seems obvious, then, that the brute fact of the existence of the law of recognition is not one that Hart sees as demanding justification. Remarking on this, Jenkins in his *Social Order and the Limits of Law* observes that "a legal system with no better foundation than this would never be acknowledged as binding, as creating duties and obligations, as meriting to be observed."[54]

Hart fails to distinguish between a legal system that people accept because they believe its authority is rationally justifiable, on the one hand, and a legal system that rests on inertia, disinterest, fear, or prudence, on the other. According to Hart, officials must take the "internal" point of view toward the rules for official behavior, but this is not necessary for ordinary individuals. They may take either the internal or the external point of view toward the rules that apply to them. Hart writes:

> In an extreme case the internal point of view with its characteristic normative use of legal language ("This is a valid rule") might be confined to the official world. . . . [O]nly officials might accept and use the system's criteria of legal validity. The society in which this was so might be deplorably sheeplike; the sheep might end in the slaughterhouse. But there is little

[51] Ibid., p. 107.

[52] Ibid., p. 60.

[53] Ibid., p. 113.

[54] Iredell Jenkins, *Social Order and the Limits of Law* (Princeton: Princeton University Press, 1980), p. 180.

reason for thinking that it could not exist or for denying it the title of a legal system.[55]

But would we really want to recognize this as a *valid* legal system? I think not.

What is required for a system of laws to constitute a valid legal system is that the system of laws be one toward which ordinary individuals also take an internal point of view, i.e., accept it as valid.[56] In this connection, Hart says, "So long as the laws which are valid by the system's tests of validity are observed by the bulk of the populace this is surely all the evidence we need in order to establish that a given system exists."[57] Surely, though, the mere "observance" of the law by most citizens is not enough to establish its validity. For a system of laws to be legally valid, ordinary citizens, as well as legal officials, must take the internal point of view.

Given Hart's position regarding the relation between law and morality, however, he must avoid this conclusion. A society's citizens can have an internal point of view toward the law only if they have a certain attitude toward the political system as a whole. Thus, they must first accept that an adequate justification is provided for the legitimate authority of the political system of which the law is a part. And the reasons people have for accepting the justified authority of the political system itself are largely moral, i.e., they concern rights, justice, the good, and the like. But Hart rejects the view that there is any *logical* connection between law and morality. He acknowledges that there may be a connection and overlap of laws with moral principles, but denies that there are any specific standards of morality that must be adhered to in order for a set of rules to count as a valid legal system. Like other legal positivists, he holds that there are more or less mechanical tests that provide necessary and sufficient conditions for the truth of propositions about what the law is. The propositions of law are seen as being independent of any theory of moral ontology.

Were Hart to accept the above suggestion that a belief by ordinary citizens in the rational justifiability of the wider social order is necessary for acceptance of the constitutional rule or other rule of recognition that provides for the validity of law, he would have to agree that it is doubtful whether there was "law" in Nazi Germany or whether there is today law in South Africa. But Hart denies that

[55] Hart, *The Concept of Law*, p. 114.
[56] Benditt, *Law as Rule*, makes the same point.
[57] Hart, *The Concept of Law*, p. 111.

the law in the Nazi regime was not valid law.[58] Although it was clearly evil, says Hart, we cannot claim that evil things are not law. Rather, "We say that laws may be law but too evil to be obeyed."[59] From this it seems to follow that the officials and citizens who themselves considered the Nazi system of laws evil and unjust, but nevertheless accepted the constitutional rule concerning who had authority to govern, were very much like the fearful command-followers in Austin's theory. If this is so, then the difference between Hart's and Austin's theories are much less than Hart claims.

Even though Hart employs the moral vocabulary of law—"ought," "duty," "obligation"—as against the coercive vocabulary utilized by Austin, he makes no serious attempt to provide an extra-legal basis for the authority of the law and for our obligation to obey it. This is not to say that he ignores moral considerations altogether, for he certainly does not. He emphasizes that if the law is to be "efficient" (a central value for Hart as for Kelsen), it cannot ignore certain basic principles of morality. The law, he says, must provide for several "natural necessities"; he mentions the protection of persons, property, and promises.[60] And it must meet such familiar "virtues of justice" as neutrality and impartiality, intelligibility, certainty, and adherence to principles. He goes on to say:

> What surely is most needed in order to make men clear sighted in confronting the official abuse of power, is that they should preserve the sense that the certification of something as legally valid is not conclusive for the question of obedience, and that however great the aura of majesty or authority which the official system may have, its demands must in the end be submitted to moral scrutiny.[61]

As Jenkins points out, it does seem that Hart "fully recognizes the dependence of the authority of the legal order on these extralegal considerations of justice and morality."[62]

An important consequence of this recognition is that the conditions of legal validity spelled out by Hart are not themselves sufficient to justify a *moral* obligation to obey the law. This is clear from his statement that there can be occasions when "we should

[58] H. L. A. Hart, "Positivism and the Separation of Law and Morals," in Ronald Dworkin, ed., *The Philosophy of Law* (Oxford: Oxford University Press, 1977), p. 34.
[59] Ibid.
[60] Hart, *The Concept of Law*, pp. 200, 202.
[61] Ibid., p. 206.
[62] Jenkins, *Social Order*, p. 182.

say: 'This is law; but it is too iniquitous to be applied or obeyed.' "[63] And he goes on to add, in this connection, that "there is something outside the official system, by reference to which in the last resort the individual must solve his problem of obedience."[64] Thus, Hart recognizes that the law may be valid and hence legally obligatory (at least by his definition of legal validity) and yet impose no moral obligation on its recipients to obey it.

But Hart himself never pursues the issue of what the "something" is outside the official system that needs to be appealed to in deciding about whether or not one is morally obligated to obey the dictates of the law. Although he apparently acknowledges that it concerns moral principles and standards, he does not go on to show how a legal system—and the wider political system it serves—might be grounded in a set of rationally justifiable moral principles. As his theory stands, then, Hart provides no justification for the legitimate authority of a legal system or for the moral obligation of a society's citizens to obey the law. More generally, the right of the government to govern and the acknowledgment of that right by the governed are never established. This failure to deal satisfactorily with questions about legitimate authority and obligation follows, of course, from Hart's general acceptance of the positivist thesis that legal rights and moral rights are always conceptually distinct.

IV

Dworkin's "Liberal Theory" of Law

Among recent theories of law, the best known is Ronald Dworkin's "liberal theory," a broad theory, which includes distinct theories of legislation, adjudication, and compliance.[65] His theory is normative as well as conceptual, and is embedded in a more general political and moral philosophy. In opposition to most other modern legal theorists, Dworkin argues *for* the logical connection between law and morality. Since his theory is widely regarded as an important alternative to the dominant legal positivism, it is deserving of detailed consideration and careful examination.

To a large extent, Dworkin's theory takes the form of a strong attack on several of the central aspects of Hart's influential positivist

[63] Hart, *The Concept of Law*, p. 212.
[64] Ibid., p. 205.
[65] Dworkin, *Taking Rights Seriously*.

theory of law.[66] In particular, he calls into question three important tenets of the positivists' position: that there is a single ultimate or fundamental test for law, such as Hart's rule of recognition; that in deciding hard cases judges must utilize extralegal standards; and that having a legal obligation is a matter of a valid legal rule applying to an individual in certain circumstances.[67] His criticisms of these three tenets follow directly from his own central argument that the law consists not only of rules but also of principles. The distinction between them, Dworkin says, is logical: "Rules are applicable in an all-or-nothing fashion,"[68] while principles have the extra dimension of weight.[69] Dworkin uses the term "principle" generically to refer to the whole set of standards other than formal rules.[70]

A principle, Dworkin writes, is "a standard that is to be observed, not because it will advance or secure an economic, political, or social situation deemed desirable, but because it is a requirement of justice or fairness or some other dimension of morality."[71] An example of the principle is: "No man may profit from his own wrong." This, Dworkin contends, is not just a moral principle; it is a principle of law. He cites a case where the court refused to allow a murderer to inherit under the will of the man he had murdered, and justified its decision by reference to the principle that a man should not profit from his own wrong. Such a principle is substantially different from a rule like "The maximum speed limit is sixty miles per hour." Since principles have weight, this means that in those cases where different principles intersect, whoever must resolve the conflict must take into account the relative weight or importance of each.

According to Hart, the rule of recognition of a given community is identified by the fact that its province is the operation of legislatures, courts, policemen, and the rest of the government apparatus.[72] Dworkin, on the other hand, argues that there is no one "master rule" that distinguishes the law of a community from other social standards. He recognizes, of course, that some parts of the

[66] Hart, *The Concept of Law*. It is also, of course, intended to be an alternative to the theories of natural rights theorists and legal realists.

[67] Ibid.

[68] Dworkin, *Taking Rights Seriously*, p. 24.

[69] Ibid., p. 26.

[70] Ibid., p. 22.

[71] Ibid.

[72] Hart, *The Concept of Law*.

law in a certain jurisdiction may be settled and relatively uncontroversial. But these must themselves be seen as explainable in terms of rights and principles which justify them. A principle such as "No one may profit from his own wrong" is often, Dworkin says, one that a judge must take into account in deciding certain cases. It may, however, sometimes be outweighed by other principles. But this weighing of principles does not itself involve "rules" as to how much weight one or another principle is to have in a given case. This is an area where judges are frequently viewed as exercising "discretion." While the positivists argue that when a case is not controlled by an established rule, the judge must decide on the basis of his discretion, Dworkin claims that judges never have discretion, in the sense of having no *duty*, to decide a case one way rather than another. To the question, What is the law on this issue?, Dworkin says that there is always a "right answer."

He argues that judges (and other legal officials) never exercise judicial discretion in the strong sense of being "not bound by standards set by the authority in question."[73] Dworkin agrees that when no clearly applicable rule can be found, the judge may appeal to principles or standards that are more general than legal rules. But contrary to the positivists' views, he holds that these are legal principles and, consequently, part of the law. Judges must legally (and not just morally) appeal to these principles and are, in fact, legally bound by them. And a party in a given case is himself legally (and, again, not just morally) entitled to a decision in accordance with the weight of the applicable principles. Against the positivist view of discretion, Dworkin argues that one party may have a *right* to win, even when there is no settled legal rule for disposing of the case. He distinguishes here between two sorts of arguments that may be involved in deciding "hard cases" in the law—situations where a particular lawsuit cannot be brought under a clear rule of law laid down by some institution in advance—arguments of policy, and arguments of principles. With arguments of "policy," a decision is justified by showing that it advances or protects some collective goal of the community or society as a whole.[74] With arguments of "principle," a decision is justified by showing that it respects or secures some individual or group right.[75]

Dworkin contends that judicial decisions, especially in civil cases

[73] Dworkin, *Taking Rights Seriously*, p. 32.
[74] Ibid., p. 22.
[75] Ibid.

involving rights against fellow citizens, "characteristically are and should be generated by principles not policy."[76] If the rights thesis, i.e., that judicial decisions enforce existing political rights, holds, then "the institutional history acts not as a constraint on the political judgment of judges but as an ingredient in that judgment, because institutional history is part of the background that any plausible judgment about the rights of an individual must accommodate."[77]

As to the positivists' third tenet—that someone has a "legal obligation" only when an established legal rule imposes such an obligation—that, too, is called into question by Dworkin. By abandoning the second tenet, where discretion means that a judge is free to use extralegal principles, and by treating principles as law, says Dworkin, "we raise the possibility that a legal obligation might be imposed by a constellation of principles as well as by an established rule."[78] Thus, it is not only legal rules that impose legal obligations on judges, but genuine moral and/or political principles as well. Though frequently unwritten, they are nevertheless part of the law.

While legal positivists hold that individuals have rights only insofar as these have been created by explicit political decisions or explicit social practices, Dworkin views rights as political trumps held by individuals.[79] "Individuals have rights," Dworkin states, "when, for some reason, a collective goal is not a sufficient justification for denying them what they wish, as individuals, to have or to do, or not a sufficient justification for imposing some loss or injury upon them."[80]

Dworkin distinguishes two types of political rights: background and institutional rights. Background rights are the rights that provide a justification for political decisions by society in the abstract, while institutional rights provide a justification for a decision by some particular and specified political institution.[81] Legal rights, then, are institutional rights. Dworkin also makes a distinction between abstract and concrete rights. An abstract right is, in his words, "a general political aim the statement of which does not indicate how that general aim is to be weighed or compromised in

---

[76] Ibid., p. 84.
[77] Ibid., p. 82.
[78] Ibid., p. 44.
[79] Ibid., p. xi.
[80] Ibid.
[81] Ibid., p. 93.

particular circumstances against other political aims."[82] Abstract rights take no account of competing rights. The right to freedom of speech is an example of such an abstract right. Concrete rights, Dworkin says, are "political aims that are more precisely defined so as to express more definitely the weight they have against other political aims on particular occasions."[83] Thus a concrete right to freedom of speech may specify the circumstances under which it can and cannot be exercised.

According to Dworkin's rights thesis, judges decide cases by confirming or denying concrete rights. In hard cases, legal argument must consider the "intention" or "purpose" of a particular statute or statutory clause, and the principles that "underlie" or are "embedded" in the positive rules of law.[84] Since some parts of the law in any given jurisdiction are settled and relatively uncontroversial in the constitutions, statutes, or precedents, these must be used in formulating a theory, in terms of further rights and principles, that best explains and justifies this settled law. To demonstrate how a judge might ideally develop theories of what legislative purpose and legal principles require, Dworkin invents a judge of superhuman skill, learning, patience, and acumen, whom he calls Hercules.[85]

In a case where there exists a written constitution, the words of the constitutional provision might support either of two competing views. Thus, Hercules, as judge, is faced with a hard case. In reaching a decision, he must do several things in seeking guidance from the constitution.

> He must develop a theory of the constitution, in the shape of a complex set of principles and policies that justify . . . [a particular] scheme of government. . . . He must develop that theory by referring alternatively to political philosophy and institutional detail. He must generate possible theories justifying different aspects of the scheme and test the theories against the broader institution. When the discriminatory power of that test is exhausted, he must elaborate the contested concepts that the successful theory employs.[86]

It may be that Hercules utilizes not the constitution, but a particular statute. In some instances, that statute might be so vague

---

[82] Ibid.
[83] Ibid.
[84] Ibid., p. 105.
[85] Ibid., pp. 105–06.
[86] Ibid., p. 107.

or broadly worded that it is unclear whether it does or does not apply to the specific case at hand. In reaching a decision in such a hard case, Hercules may have to construct a special political theory justifying this statute, in light of the legislature's more general responsibilities, that is better than any alternative theory.[87] Whereas statutory interpretation depends on the availability of a canonical form of words, this may not be so when Hercules turns to the common law in reaching a decision in a hard case. Frequently, judicial decisions offer reasons, in the form of principles and policies, to justify a decision, without laying down a specific rule of law. Nevertheless, Dworkin says, these earlier decisions may constitute precedents, that is, they have enactment force. They may exert what Dworkin calls a "gravitational force" on later decisions.[88] "The gravitational force of a precedent may be explained by appeal, not to the wisdom of enforcing enactments," Dworkin argues, "but to the fairness of treating like cases alike. A precedent is the report of an earlier political decision; the very fact of that decision, as a piece of political history, provides some reason for deciding cases in a similar way in the future."[89] In deciding on the gravitational force of a particular precedent, Hercules must take account of the (sometimes competing) principles that may or may not justify that precedent.

It is clear why Dworkin calls his judge Hercules. This mythical judge has the task of constructing a scheme of abstract and concrete principles that provides a coherent justification for all common law precedents, and for all constitutional and statutory provisions that can be justified as principles.[90]

In requiring Hercules (and any other judge in hard cases) to find the *morally* best function for the constitution, statutes, and precedents in the common law, Dworkin is clearly rejecting the traditional positivist separation of law from morality. Of course, some positivists do recognize that law and morality are often linked. For example, Hart writes that "judicial decisions, especially on matters of high constitutional import, often involve a choice between moral values. . . ."[91] But Dworkin *requires* that decisions about hard cases be made on the basis of arguments that include considerations of moral and/or political elements. It is part of his program, in a sense,

---

[87] Ibid., p. 108.
[88] Ibid., p. 111.
[89] Ibid., p. 113.
[90] Ibid., pp. 16–17.
[91] Hart, *The Concept of Law*, pp. 199–200.

that the moral dimension must be included as a consideration in deciding what the law is. The rights thesis, Dworkin says, "encourages a connection between law and political and moral philosophy that must be for the benefit of both."[92]

The "Right Answer" Thesis

As I noted at the outset of this discussion of Dworkin's theory, it is both descriptive and prescriptive. On the one hand, he claims that his theory of law gives a better understanding than do other theories of the legal procedures and reasoning actually at work in such systems as those in the United States and England. On the other hand, he argues that his theory should be more explicitly accepted and consciously followed. Dworkin's description of the way the law actually works constitutes a particular conception of law and legal rights. All lawyers and legal theorists share a concept of law and legal rights. Natural law theorists, legal realists, and legal positivists each defend a particular conception of that concept. Dworkin, as we have seen, defends a competing conception. These various theories fundamentally disagree about what the *practice* of law comes to, that is, about which theoretical account of the practice is superior. I acknowledge that Dworkin's liberal theory of law may be superior to other theories as a description of the legal procedures and legal reasoning actually at work in the United States and England. Nevertheless, there are serious problems with his theory—most especially with regard to the prescriptive elements contained therein.

There are two such elements in Dworkin's liberal theory of law that require careful scrutiny. These involve the requirement that a judge accept some general political theory that justifies the settled practices of his legal system (the requirement of "institutional fit"), and the requirement that the judge utilize a broader moral and political theory (the requirement of "moral acceptability") in making his decisions.

According to Dworkin's "right answer" thesis, in every legal dispute brought before a court one party or the other has a pre-existing right, which the court must vindicate. The right answer is the proposition of law that, of competing propositions, has the best fit with the soundest theory of law.[93] Soundness of a theory of law depends, in part, on the theory's "fit" with the institutional history

---

[92] Dworkin, *Taking Rights Seriously*, p. 313.
[93] Ibid., p. 283.

of a jurisdiction as found in precedent, statute, and the like. Institutional fit is never exact, but concerns the extent to which a legal theory adequately accounts for earlier decisions or other legal materials.[94] Dworkin believes that there are criteria that determine the adequacy of fit as regards a legal theory's account of particular legal judgments that are themselves independent of that theory. These theory-independent criteria allow for the judgment that one legal theory is better than another, i.e., has a better fit, in the sense that it requires less of the material to be "mistaken."[95] A theory has a better fit than other theories when it is better able than they are to show, in Dworkin's words, "the consequences for further arguments of taking some institutional event to be mistaken" and to "limit the number and character of the events that can be disposed of in this way."[96]

But since it is possible, says Dworkin, that different theories may all show adequate institutional fit with settled law, the soundest theory of law is the one with the greatest degree of moral acceptability, that is, the one that is most defensible in terms of a broader political and moral theory.[97] Assessments of alternative possible theories of law involve, then, two different dimensions: institutional fit and moral acceptability.

Dworkin points out that a theory may vary along these two dimensions:

> If a theory containing one principle is better on the dimension of fit, but a theory containing a contrary principle is better on the dimension of morality, then the jurisprudential question is raised as to which dimension is more important in determining institutional rights in cases of that sort. One answer to that jurisprudential question (stated in a crude and simple form) would be this: No theory can count as an adequate justification of institutional history unless it provides a good fit with that history; it must not expose more than a low threshold number of decisions, particularly recent decisions, as mistakes; but if two or more theories each provide an adequate fit, on that test, then the theory among these that is morally the strongest provides the best justification, even though it exposes more decisions as mistakes than another.[98]

[94] Ibid., p. 340.
[95] Ibid.
[96] Ibid., p. 121.
[97] Ibid., p. 360.
[98] Ibid., p. 340.

Clearly, then, Dworkin sees fit and moral acceptability as two different dimensions along which legal theories may be evaluated. Further, in the situation where one theory is better than its competitors on the dimension of fit and a competing theory is better on the dimension of morality, Dworkin appears to give heavier weight to the fit dimension. It is only when competing legal theories each provide an adequate fit that the dimension of moral acceptability comes into play in choosing between them.[99] The right answer in hard cases is the one provided by the legal theory that is at the highest point on the moral acceptability dimension among those legal theories beyond a threshold point on the fit dimension.

Dworkin's emphasis on institutional fit and moral acceptability gives rise to a trio of important questions, which I want to consider in some detail. First, what does he provide as a *justification* for the requirement that a judge accept the settled practices of his legal system and the constitution as a whole? What, that is, justifies the legitimate authority of the legal system and the wider political system that it serves? Second, and related, does Dworkin show why a society's citizens (including judges and other legal officials) have a *moral* obligation to support and comply with the common law, particular legal statutes, or the constitution and the political scheme set forth therein? Is Dworkin successful, I am asking, in demonstrating that legal obligations are backed up by some more basic moral principle? And third, what does he provide in the way of a *justification* for those principles of morality relevant to legal decisions and the validity of law?

Although Dworkin rejects both the positivists' contention that often the law does not provide a right answer and the natural lawyers' contention that the law is what is morally required, he does accept the former's claim that what is legally required is not necessarily what is morally required and the latter's claim that there is a legally correct (right) answer to every legal dispute.

Dworkin acknowledges the possibility that a legal system may be grossly unjust, and that the dimension of institutional fit and moral acceptability may pull strongly in opposite directions.[100] That is to say, there may be situations where institutional rights are clearly established by the fit with various legal materials and yet are in conflict with important background moral principles. In such a case, a judge is faced with a conflict between the moral considerations underlying recognition of rights generated by the insti-

[99] Ibid., pp. 340, 360.
[100] Ibid., p. 326.

tutional materials and moral principles that support unacknowl-
edged background rights.

INSTITUTIONAL FIT. In my view, it is not at all surprising that there
should be conflicts between institutional fit and moral acceptability.
Such conflicts are an almost inevitable consequence of Dworkin's
emphasis on what he calls "the doctrine of political responsibility,"
which stipulates that a judge must accept some general political
theory that justifies the *settled* practices of his legal system.[101] With
the doctrine of political responsibility, a judge has the obligation
to distinguish the rights of the parties that are generated by the
institution. He does this by formulating a coherent general political
theory that justifies (a significantly large portion of) both past and
future decisions. This emphasis on coherence or consistency in
official decision-making, Dworkin several times states, is imposed
by the requirement of "fairness."[102] This is the assumption "that
it is unfair for officials to act except on the basis of a general public
theory that will constrain them to consistency, provide a public
standard for testing or debating or predicting what they do, and
not allow appeals to unique intuitions that might mask prejudice
or self-interest in particular cases."[103]

As Postema has recently pointed out,[104] Dworkin's doctrine of
political responsibility and his general emphasis on considerations
of fairness are themselves the principles that constitute the moral
foundations for a judge's obligation to construct a specific theory.
This theory must, as already noted, explain the part of his community's morality encapsulated in its existing legal system.

In discussing how Hercules might develop a theory of what
legislative purpose and legal principles require, Dworkin describes
how Hercules formulates a general political theory that justifies
these practices. Hercules's task is to "construct a scheme of abstract
and concrete principles that provides a coherent justification for
all common law precedents and, so far as these are to be justified
on principle, constitutional and statutory provisions as well.[105] Hercules must undertake this task from a starting point of *accepting*
"the main uncontroversial constitutive and regulative rules of the

[101] Ibid., p. 105.
[102] Ibid., pp. 106, 120.
[103] Ibid., pp. 162–63.
[104] Gerald J. Postema, "Bentham and Dworkin on Positivism and Adjudication,"
Social Theory and Practice 5 (1980): 373.
[105] Dworkin, *Taking Rights Seriously*, pp. 116–17.

law in his jurisdiction."[106] But these are not themselves called into question. In other words, Hercules's task is to construct a theory that justifies most of the settled rules of law and common law decisions of the jurisdiction. It is *not* part of his task to raise questions about the legitimacy or moral standing of the constitution and the scheme of government itself. Let us now consider the implication of this.

In a review of Robert M. Cover's book, *Justice Accused*, Dworkin applies the notion of "institutional fit" to cases that arose under the Fugitive Slave Acts before the Civil War.[107] He notes that certain judges enforced these acts, even though they themselves were strongly opposed to slavery. By so doing, they sent the alleged runaway slaves back from states in which slavery was not permitted to states where it was still allowed and from which they were alleged to have escaped. The judges viewed their decisions as fully in line with what the law required. They were simply doing their legal duty in enforcing the law of the land. They enforced the law, as noted above, despite the fact that it conflicted with their own moral values. For a positivist, who sees the law as consisting entirely of rules that are applicable in an all-or-nothing fashion, no other decision was possible. The matter was simple.

For Dworkin, however, it is not so simple. He argues that the reasoning of the judges was a "failure of jurisprudence."[108] In his view, slavery cases were hard cases, not to be decided in advance by the plain meaning of constitutional provisions and statutes. Had the judges been advocates of Dworkin's theory, rather than of positivism, they could have found in the general structure of the American Constitution "a conception of individual freedom antagonistic to slavery, a conception of procedural justice that condemned the procedures established by the Fugitive Slave Acts, and a conception of federalism inconsistent with the idea that the State of Massachusetts had no power to supervise the capture of men and women within its territory."[109] These principles, Dworkin argues, were "more central to the law than were the particular and transitory policies of the slave compromise."[110] Thus, Dworkin claims that the better legal argument (his own) justifies a decision

---

[106] Ibid., pp. 105–06.
[107] I rely here on the discussion in John Mackie, "The Third Theory of Law," *Philosophy and Public Affairs* 7 (Fall 1977).
[108] Ibid.
[109] Quoted in Ibid., p. 11.
[110] Ibid.

against the slave catchers and in favor of the alleged slaves, though the judges actually reached the opposite conclusion.

We can acknowledge the correctness of Dworkin's argument and admit that the judges should have (prescriptively) reached the decision that Dworkin himself advocates. The judges, we can admit, could have found in the general structure of the American Constitution conceptions of individual freedom, procedural justice, and federalism that were "more central to the law than were particular and transitory policies of the slave compromise." Based on moral principles underlying or embedded in the American Constitution, the judges should have ruled in favor of the alleged runaway slaves. So far as Dworkin's example of the slaves is concerned, it is not difficult to be fully satisfied with the outcome of his argument. If we are ourselves morally opposed to slavery, we will be pleased with the conclusion reached by Dworkin's theory.

But we must recognize just *how much* of his argument rests on the general structure of a particular constitution—the American Constitution—and on the principles that underlie and are embedded in it. It is not at all difficult, however, to imagine an entirely different constitution, with widely different conceptions of individual freedom and procedural justice. Would we want a judge, even Hercules, to begin by accepting "the settled practices of his legal system and the constitution as a whole" if the constitution contained conceptions of individual freedom and procedural justice that were abhorrent to us (e.g., where blacks were not seen as citizens, and had rights only insofar as these were agreed to by whites)? I think not.

Dworkin's argument has the consequence that a judge in South Africa or Nazi Germany, having to decide in a hard case, may labor like Hercules in order to arrive at the "right answer" and find that such an answer is morally abhorrent. That is, it may be that the theory that provides the best fit—in that it accounts for more of institutional history than any competing theory—leads to a morally obnoxious answer. In some hard cases, at least, Dworkin's right answer thesis leads to a denial of the opportunity to provide the morally best answer. So long as institutional fit and moral acceptability are viewed as separate dimensions, with heavier weight being given to the fit dimension, the theory utilized by Hercules (or any other judge) in arriving at the right answer always has the potential for providing an answer that is morally abhorrent. If a legal theory has a close "fit" with institutional history and the general sense of the legal community, the judge must use this theory—even though there may be important arguments of morality that could be seen as counting against it.

Because of Dworkin's requirement that the constitution, settled rules of law, and common law decisions are systematically relevant to the truth of propositions about legal rights, application of his theory has the consequence of sometimes denying legal rights, which—on the basis of independent arguments of morality—we believe to exist. This is obviously a serious weakness in his overall theory.

If Dworkin's theory of law is intended to be a general theory, and certainly his emphasis on the logical connection between law and morality suggests that this is his intention, then he must recognize that there exist differences in the constitutions, statutes, and common law decisions in different societies, and in the same society at different times. This necessarily raises questions about the moral standing or justifiability of one or another constitution, statute, or system of common law. But Dworkin never attempts to provide a rational justification for the authority of a legal system and the wider political system it serves.

Because of his failure to specify the criteria to be used in deciding which particular constitutions and legal systems "ought" to be accepted by a judge in his quest to discover the rights of a society's citizens, Dworkin is also unable to establish that a society's citizens (including Hercules and other judges) have a *moral* obligation to accept and obey the common law, particular legal statutes, or the constitution and the political scheme set forth therein. As it now stands, then, his emphasis on the importance of a theory's "fit" with the institutional history of a jurisdiction will often result in legal decisions to which morally sensitive persons cannot subscribe and to which they will feel no moral obligation of obedience.

MORAL ACCEPTABILITY. Having considered the problem of a lack of justification for the legitimate authority of the legal system and the (related) lack of justification for a society's citizens to be morally obligated to support and comply with the law, I turn now to the third problem under consideration: Dworkin's thesis that legal principles are genuine moral and/or political principles that judges must take into account in reaching their decisions. My focus here is on the question of how principles of morality relevant to legal decisions, and the validity of law, are themselves to be rationally justified and defended.

Dworkin acknowledges that "if a social practice makes morality

283

systematically relevant to legal issues . . . then the truth of propositions of law will systematically depend upon the truth of propositions of morality. The truth of the former will consist, at least partially, in the truth of the latter."[111] What, then, does Dworkin provide in the way of justification for those moral propositions upon which the truth of the propositions of law are so dependent?[112]

For Dworkin, the most fundamental right is that to equal concern and respect, a right against the government, which he does not attempt to derive from his general theory. "If someone has a right to something," he says, "then it is wrong for the government to deny it to him even though it would be in the general interest to do so."[113] Rights, then, are legal and moral considerations that cannot be denied on mere utilitarian grounds. The right to equal concern and respect is not, Dworkin emphasizes, the right to receive the same distribution of some burden or benefit, but the right to be treated with the same respect and concern as anyone else.[114] Fundamental liberties like freedom of speech are, in his view, important because they protect people's rights to be treated as equals.[115]

> These rights will function as trump cards held by individuals; they will enable individuals to resist particular decisions in spite of the fact that these decisions are or would be reached through the normal workings of general institutions that are not themselves challenged. The ultimate justification for these rights is that they are necessary to protect equal concern and respect. . . .[116]

But how are the principles of morality relevant to legal decisions and the validity of law to be justified and defended? If, as Dworkin

[111] Ibid., p. 348.
[112] I also draw here on Ronald Dworkin, "Liberalism," pp. 113–43, in Stuart Hampshire, ed., *Public and Private Morality* (Cambridge: Cambridge University Press, 1978).
[113] Dworkin, *Taking Rights Seriously*, p. 269.
[114] Dworkin, "Liberalism," p. 125.
[115] Ibid., pp. 124–45. It is the right to equal concern and respect, and not to liberty and freedom, that is most basic for Dworkin. He denies that people have a right to liberty, saying that it is "absurd to suppose that men and women have any general right to liberty at all." (Dworkin, *Taking Rights Seriously*, p. 267.) Although I disagree with Dworkin's position regarding the right to liberty or freedom, I will not pursue that disagreement here.
[116] Dworkin, "Liberalism," p. 136.

emphasizes, the truth of propositions of law depends upon the truth of propositions of morality, has Dworkin provided an adequate justification for the latter? Since the liberal state Dworkin advocates is organized, as far as possible, to protect each citizen's right to equal concern and respect, then this principle of equality appears to constitute the most fundamental moral principle in Dworkin's theory. It is, in turn, the principle upon which the propositions of law depend. The principle of equality, as already noted, gives rise to the rights that function as trump cards.

Although Dworkin takes "rights seriously," I want to consider whether he takes them seriously enough. He notes that the American Constitution provides a set of individual *legal* rights in the First Amendment, and in due process, equal protection, and similar clauses. "The Constitution fuses legal and moral issues," Dworkin observes, "by making the validity of a law depend on the answer to complex moral problems, like the problem of whether a particular statute respects the inherent equality of all men."[117]

American citizens have certain moral rights made into legal rights by the Constitution, and these rights are what Dworkin refers to as "strong rights."[118] We say that someone has a strong right to something, explains Dworkin, when it would be wrong to interfere with his doing it, or when some special grounds are needed for justifying any interference. Anyone who professes to take rights seriously, and expects the government to respect them, Dworkin writes, must accept, at the minimum, one or both of two important ideas: the idea of human dignity, and the idea of political equality.[119] "It makes sense to say that a man has a fundamental right against the Government, in the strong sense, like free speech," argues Dworkin, "if that right is necessary to protect his dignity, or his standing as equally entitled to concern and respect, or some other personal value of life consequence. It does not make sense otherwise."[120] Violations of dignity and equality (the principle of equal concern and respect) must be treated as "special moral crimes, beyond the reach of ordinary utilitarian justification."[121]

Much of Dworkin's argument is directed against utilitarian justifications for political decisions, especially those where such decisions are justified by some appeal to the general welfare, under-

[117] Dworkin, *Taking Rights Seriously*, p. 185.
[118] Ibid., p. 190.
[119] Ibid., p. 198.
[120] Ibid., p. 199.
[121] Ibid.

stood as an appeal to a utilitarian maximization of preferences.[122] It is most especially in those communities where political decisions are justified on utilitarian grounds, that rights function as trumps against some collective justification. Thus, Dworkin appears to have an anti-utilitarian conception of a right; if someone has a right to something, then it is morally wrong for the government to deny it to him or her—even though it might be in the general interest to do so.

It is at this point that a serious weakness reveals itself in Dworkin's liberal theory of law. This weakness concerns two related issues: first, his vague and ungrounded notion of rights; and, second, his lack of clarity about what particular morality ought to "count" in legal decisions.

Rights

Consider, first, Dworkin's conception of rights. He remarks that in the United States "certain moral rights are made into legal rights by the Constitution."[123] "Our constitutional system," he says, "rests on a particular moral theory, namely that men have moral rights against the state."[124] But what is the status of these moral rights, and where do they come from? Dworkin denies that his view of rights rests on any "ontological assumptions," such as that men have rights in the same sense that they have tonsils.[125] But he nowhere makes clear what standing these rights have. The closest he seems to come is in his statement that "a claim of right is a special, in the sense of restricted, sort of judgment about what is right or wrong for governments to do."[126] In other words, law and government do not create rights but merely recognize and enforce them.

There are two broad views about the standing of rights.[127] One view holds that rights have a real metaphysical or moral status: they are extra- and supralegal. With this view, rights derive directly from the ultimate structure of things—and they belong to man as part of his intrinsic nature, as much as his body, his mind, and his various powers. Gewirth, of course, represents this view. Law

[122] Ibid., p. 364.
[123] Ibid., p. 190.
[124] Ibid., p. 147.
[125] Ibid., p. 139.
[126] Ibid.
[127] See, for example, Jenkins, *Social Order*.

286

merely recognizes these rights and enforces respect for them.[128] According to the other view, rights are strictly legal entities or notions; rights are conceived and created by law. Regarded substantively, then, rights are either legal or metalegal.[129]

For Dworkin, rights are clearly metalegal, i.e., extra- and supralegal. Given his emphasis on the metalegal character of rights, one would expect him to say something about their ontological basis. But he never does so. The central conception in his argument, he stresses, is "the concept not of liberty but of equality."[130] The right to be treated as an equal, "to be treated with the same respect and concern as anyone else," is the most fundamental of all rights for Dworkin.[131]

This certainly seems to imply that everyone *has* this right. But where does it come from, how is it to be justified? Philosophers like Hobbes, Locke, and Rousseau, as well as various leaders of the American and French revolutions, all saw rights as belonging to the individual in his naked condition, prior to any form of social or political organization.[132] Nozick apparently holds the same view.[133] And while the theoretical bases provided for natural rights by these various thinkers have been called into question, they did at least attempt to justify their rights-claims. Rawls and Habermas, in different ways, justify moral principles—including those regarding rights in the case of Rawls—in terms of what would be agreed to by individuals under certain specified conditions.[134] And Gewirth shows that rights can be rationally justified from the nature of human action.[135] Despite his own strong emphasis on taking rights seriously, however, Dworkin never attempts to provide a

---

[128] This is also the position of Nozick, although he never provides a satisfactory justification for rights. Robert Nozick, *Anarchy, State, and Utopia* (New York: Basic Books, 1974).

[129] Jenkins, *Social Order.*

[130] Dworkin, *Taking Rights Seriously*, p. 272.

[131] Ibid.

[132] See, for example, Thomas Hobbes, *Leviathan*, edited with an introduction by Michael Oakeshott (New York: Oxford University Press, 1947); John Locke, *Two Treaties of Government*, ed. Peter Laslett, 2nd ed. (Cambridge: Cambridge University Press, 1970); J. J. Rousseau, *The Social Contract*, trans. G. D. H. Cole (New York: Dutton, 1950).

[133] Nozick, *Anarchy, State, and Utopia.*

[134] John Rawls, *A Theory of Justice* (Cambridge, Mass.: Belknap Press of the Harvard University Press, 1971); Jürgen Habermas, *Legitimation Crisis*, trans. Thomas McCarthy (Boston: Beacon Press, 1975); Jürgen Habermas, *Communication and the Evolution of Society*, trans. Thomas McCarthy (Boston: Beacon Press, 1979).

[135] Alan Gewirth, *Reason and Morality* (Chicago: University of Chicago Press, 1978).

justification for those rights that are so crucial to his theory. He does say that "no one who believes in a moral idea can honestly and consistently regard that idea as having no more independent objective validity than his tastes in food and drink."[136] And he appears to endorse the view "that individuals have certain moral rights against their government that are prior to all law including the Constitution."[137] But, of course, rights are claimed against other persons and not against governments. The main justification of government is, in fact, usually the protection of people's basic rights. Thus, the normative existence of rights is prior to the government that is appealed to for their protection.

Dworkin's failure to provide any rational justification for the right to be treated as an equal might not by itself be so terribly important were it not for the fact that a major element in his general thesis is that legal validity is partly a function of a theory's fit with moral principles. But these moral principles are apparently not to be regarded as universal, i.e., they are not principles specifying, for example, that within each and every society and in each and every historical period everyone has the basic right to be treated as an equal. In contrast to a view that sees principles as universal, Dworkin emphasizes that judges have the task of discovering and taking into account those principles of political morality (some of which involve consideration of rights) that have currency in the community.[138]

Moral Principles

But Dworkin's line of argumentation leads directly to the second problem mentioned above: What, if anything, can be said about the moral standing of these various moral principles, and how does a judge choose among them? Dworkin asserts that "in the United States, at least, almost any law which a significant number of people would be tempted to disobey on moral grounds would be doubtful—if not clearly invalid—on constitutional grounds as well. The Constitution makes our conventional political morality relevant to the question of validity."[139] Assuming that his use of the term "moral" refers to people's strong convictions about what is right and wrong, good and bad, and what it is proper and improper for the government to do, a question arises concerning "our" conven-

---

[136] Dworkin, "Dissent on Douglas," p. 7.

[137] Ibid., p. 4.

[138] Dworkin, *Taking Rights Seriously*, p. 344.

[139] Ibid., p. 208.

288

tional political morality. In the first place, there may be (in fact, there are in the United States) a large number of conventional moralities. Which of these should be singled out as the one constituting "our" conventional morality relevant to legal validity? Even if moral beliefs and standards did not differ by age, class, education, or region of the country, so that "our" conventional morality was one embraced by almost everyone, why should *that* be the morality to be considered in deciding questions of legal validity?

Because it is Dworkin's thesis that the institutional practices and history of each particular society are relevant to the truth of propositions about legal rights, this means that these legal rights are dependent upon the moral rights that are recognized within a particular society. Assuming, as Dworkin seems to, that there is one dominant background morality within a society, recognized legal rights may be either consistent with or at variance with this background political morality. But the absence of any absolute rights in Dworkin's scheme means that the *linkage* or relationship between background moral principles (including those regarding rights) and legal rights is crucial to determining what legal rights people do, in fact, have.

Even though the right to treatment as an equal does resemble an absolute right in Dworkin's formulation, the legal rights to which it gives rise may, he says, be denied in certain circumstances. Despite its status as a strong "moral right,"[140] it is plausible to allow the government to deny the right to free speech "when necessary to protect the rights of others, or to prevent a catastrophe, or even to obtain a clear and major public benefit. . . ."[141] Apparently, then, the right to free speech is not an absolute right. In fact, Dworkin states that "even the grand individual rights are not absolute, but will yield to especially powerful considerations of consequence. . . ."[142] Thus, the relation between morality and law, which Dworkin emphasizes so strongly, does *not* require that legal rights be consistent with any specific right or set of absolute rights. It requires only that legal rights be consistent with whatever background moral rights exist as part of the conventional morality in a given society. The implication of this for Dworkin's theory, as a

[140] Ibid., p. 191.
[141] Ibid.
[142] Ibid., p. 354.

legal theory with application outside the American context, needs to be seriously considered.

Background Morality

If one believes, as Dworkin does, that a liberal society like the United States has a background morality that requires the specific legal rights that Dworkin espouses (free speech, and the like), then this emphasis on the relationship between background morality and legal rights may not be very troublesome. But it needs to be recognized that the background morality of, say, a totalitarian society, may be such as to deny legal rights, which we believe (morally speaking) should be the rights of citizens in *any* society.

Dworkin is very explicit in stating that "even the content of rights may vary with background justification, or with the structure of political institutions designed to enforce different background justifications."[143] Thus, particular legal rights cohere with the particular background justification of paramount importance in a given society. Replying to his critics, Dworkin suggests that in the United States

> particular political rights, *and* the idea of the collective welfare, *and* the idea that these function as antagonists at the level of political debate, are all consequences of the fundamental ideal of a political community as a community of equals. I did speak [in *Taking Rights Seriously*] of a "right" to be treated as an equal, with equal concern and respect, but I pointed out that this is "a right so fundamental that it is not captured by the general characterization of rights as trumps over collective goals, except as a limiting case, because it is the source both of the general authority of collective goals and of the specific limitations on their authority that justify some particular rights.[144]

In other words, the right to be treated as an equal is so fundamental in the United States that it is the *source* of various ideas about both political rights and about the general welfare. The fundamental idea of a political community as a community of equals constitutes the moral background that is relevant to legal decisions and the validity of law in the United States. When the moral background of a society is constituted by this emphasis on equal treat-

143 Ibid., p. 365.
144 Ibid., p. 368.

ment, Dworkin's theory requires that propositions of law in that society be consistent with this emphasis.

But what if the moral background is otherwise? What if the fundamental idea of a society is not that of treatment as an equal but one that demands natural privileges for the natural leaders, that requires each person to keep his or her own station, that sees the purpose of the individual as mainly to maintain the stability of the state? What, in short, if the background morality is such as to hold totalitarianism as the preferred moral ideal? Surely, Dworkin does not intend that the legal rules of such a society should follow from *whatever* conceptions of individual freedom and procedural justice are dominant in that society. It is not simply that a totalitarian society holds different conceptions of concepts like freedom and justice than the ones we perhaps prefer, but we might be convinced that those conceptions are morally wrong or indefensible. Dworkin certainly recognizes this and has much to say in opposition to such conceptions of individual freedom and justice.

My point is that, contrary to what Dworkin seems to suggest, it is not sufficient to argue that people's legal rights are and should be a function of the moral background and history of a society. The consistency or lack of consistency between legal rights and the principles of morality in a society says nothing about the moral standing of a legal or political system. In a society like the United States, it may be that the moral background and social practices are in some ways superior, more humane, of a higher moral standing, or whatever, than the propositions and practices of law. If so, then it certainly makes sense to argue that the propositions of law should be in line with this background morality. Of course, it should be remembered that Dworkin sees background morality as entering into the calculations of what legal rights people have only when "the standard materials provide uncertain guidance."[145] He recognizes that there may be other situations where there is a conflict between background moral rights and what is clearly settled by established legal materials. Speaking specifically of those cases where the institutional rights conflict with background moral rights, he states:

> In these cases the judge seeking to do what is morally right is faced with a familiar sort of conflict: the institutional right provides a genuine reason, the importance of which will vary with the general justice or wickedness of the system as a whole,

[145] Ibid., p. 326.

for a decision one way, but certain considerations of morality present an important reason against it. If the judge decides that the reasons supplied by background moral rights are so strong that he has a moral duty to do what he can to support these rights, then it may be that he must lie, because he cannot be of any help unless he is understood as saying, in his official role, that the legal rights are different from what he believes they are.[146]

Dworkin is speaking here only of those "hard cases" where the background moral rights are themselves taken as unproblematic. In the situation described above, the judge may be unable to give certain considerations of morality the attention they seem to deserve because the law is clear about the case in question. But it might seem, therefore, that there are good reasons for insisting that background rights ought to enter into the calculation of what people's rights are even when the standard materials *do not* provide uncertain guidance. This would, of course, require us to have some clear criteria for justifying the acceptance of those background rights.

Dworkin says that the soundest theory of law—i.e., the one that a judge ought to utilize—is the one with the greatest degree of moral acceptability in terms of a broader moral and political theory. The problem is that Dworkin does not clearly identify this broader theory. In the first edition of *Taking Rights Seriously*, he seemed to conceive of this broader moral and political theory as the one to which the political community is committed by its "conventional morality."[147] He said, for example, that Hercules's theory of adjudication in hard cases must identify "a particular conception of community morality as decisive of legal issues; that conception holds that community morality is the political morality presupposed by the law and institutions of the community."[148] But in his more recent "A Reply to Critics," Dworkin suggests that the broader moral and political theory is the "soundest" theory.[149] One justification may be better than another on the dimension of moral acceptability, he says, because "it comes closer to capturing sound political morality."[150] These two alternative conceptions of moral

[146] Ibid., pp. 326–27.
[147] Ibid., pp. 40–41.
[148] Ibid., p. 126.
[149] Ibid., pp. 340, 343.
[150] Ibid., p. 340.

and political theory have very different consequences for decision-making in hard cases.

If it is Dworkin's position that law is tied to the conventional morality of the community, as he seems to hold in *Taking Rights Seriously*, then this has the consequence that a hard case under Nazi law must be decided by recourse to Nazi morality. This certainly would not support Dworkin's general thesis that there are right answers in every case and that such answers are based on pre-existing rights. If, on the other hand, he holds that law is tied to "sound" political morality, then it is this sound (i.e., rationally justifiable, or "critical") morality that judges ought to utilize in reaching their decisions. Thus, under Nazi law a judge ought to decide a hard case by recourse to this critical morality. In such a situation, the right answer might indeed (depending, of course, on the specifics of the critical morality) be based on pre-existing rights.

But, as I noted above, Dworkin is very unclear as to which conception of morality he has in mind. In his earlier work he suggests that the "moral standards of the community" are the "moral principles that underlie the community's institutions and laws, in the sense that these principles would figure in a sound theory of law . . ."[151] Here a theory of law is obviously to be assessed in terms of its defensibility with regard to the conventional morality of the community. But in his more recent writings, Dworkin seems to point more in the direction of an emphasis on critical morality. Speaking specifically about rights, he notes that "many rights are universal, because arguments are available in favor of these rights against any collective justification in any circumstances likely to be found in political society. It is these that might plausibly be called human rights."[152] Apparently, then, Dworkin does conceive of some broader political and moral theory that can be rationally distinguished from the conventional morality of a community. If so, then the conventional morality of a jurisdiction can be assessed in terms of this broader theory. This would mean that a judge could reach a right answer based on pre-existing rights as justified by the broader political and moral theory. As already noted, however, Dworkin never attempts to spell out such a theory.

Although Dworkin is very inconsistent about this, it seems to me that in the final analysis he is wedded to an emphasis on

[151] Ibid., p. 79.
[152] Ibid., p. 365.

conventional, and not critical, morality. This may be a consequence of his need to distinguish his own position from that of the positivists' contention that often the law does not provide a right answer, and from the natural lawyers' contention that the law is what is morally required. Both of these extreme views, he argues, are wrong.[153]

Thus, if we adopt Dworkin's position, we encounter the following situation: When the test of institutional fit and moral acceptability "is applied to a wicked legal system, it may be that no principle we would find acceptable on grounds of morality could pass the threshold test. In that case the general theory must endorse some unattractive principle as providing the best justification of institutional history, presenting the judge with a legal decision and also, perhaps, a moral problem."[154] That is, the judge might conclude that the legal principle that best decides what the law is may be, in Dworkin's words, an "unjust"[155] or "incorrect"[156] moral principle. While holding to the view that "legal principles are always moral principles in form (whether they are sound or unsound, compelling or despicable as moral judgments)," Dworkin rejects the idea that legal principles are always "sound or correct moral principles."[157]

In other words, Dworkin does recognize the importance of both the conventional morality of a community and a broader (critical) morality that allows for judgments about unjust or incorrect moral principles. But with regard to the judge's duty to find the right answer in any case, Dworkin stipulates that he is bound by the conventional morality of his jurisdiction; it is the "moral principles that underlie the community's institutions and law" that must prove decisive in hard cases.[158] When a judge faces a moral problem because of what he sees as a conflict between the conventional morality of the community and a broader moral theory (involving considerations of justice and the like), then, Dworkin says, he must either (a) resign, (b) lie, or (c) make his argument for a decision contrary to the prevailing law on moral grounds.[159] Dworkin himself favors the lie strategy:

[153] Ibid., p. 342.
[154] Ibid.
[155] Ibid.
[156] Ibid., p. 343.
[157] Ibid.
[158] Ibid., p. 79.
[159] Ibid., p. 327.

If the institutional legal right does conflict with morality, in spite of the influence that morality must have on the right answer in a hard case, then jurisprudence must report that conflict accurately, leaving to the judge both the difficult moral decision he must make and the lie he may be forced to tell.[160]

While the natural lawyer would give preference to moral rights when legal and moral rights are in conflict, Dworkin's account brings him very close to the positivist position that what is legally required is not necessarily what morality demands.

In examining Dworkin's liberal theory of law, I have pointed to three major weaknesses: First of all, he provides no justification for the legitimate authority of a legal system and the wider political system it serves. This means that the requirement for a judge to accept the settled practices of his legal system and the constitution as a whole is not rationally justified in terms of a wider political and moral theory. Thus—and this is the second weakness—neither judges nor other citizens have a moral obligation to accept the dictates of the law. Finally, Dworkin fails to deal satisfactorily with the question of how the principles of morality relevant to legal decisions are themselves to be identified and defended.

Unless these weaknesses are remedied, both the requirement that a judge must accept some general political theory that justifies the *settled* practices of his legal system (the requirement of "institutional fit") and the requirement that the judge must identify and utilize the *conventional morality* of the community (the requirement of "moral acceptability") can easily lead to what we may consider morally obnoxious right answers.

A judge in a society with a totalitarian legal system and/or a conventional morality characterized by totalitarian moral principles may labor like Hercules on a hard case to arrive at the "right answer" and deliver a decision that is, from the standpoint of a critical morality, morally abhorrent. That is, a judge who utilizes a theory of law that provides an adequate fit with institutional history and is the morally most acceptable within that society may well find a right answer that is considered morally wanting in terms of some *independent* set of moral principles, i.e., critical morality. What is totally missing in Dworkin's work is a concern with the moral legitimacy of a particular social order, or with the moral justification (or justifiability) of a particular set of legal and moral standards found within one or another society.

[160] Ibid.

295

One of the factors that gives rise to this conclusion is Dworkin's lack of clarity concerning the relation between the legal order and the moral order. His inclusion of the fit dimension (which emphasizes such institutional constraints as past decisions and settled explanations) seems to indicate that he views the legal order as at least partially autonomous from the moral order. At the same time, however, his inclusion of the dimension of moral acceptability as the second of the two dimensions involved in choosing the best legal theory suggests that the legal and moral orders are not totally independent. Rather, Dworkin appears to conceive of the legal order as part of the moral order. But if he really does see the legal order as part of the moral order, then he might be expected to utilize the principles found in the conventional morality to determine the degree of fit that particular legal decisions must display with other legal materials.[161] This, he does not do.

Things are complicated still further if we include the distinction between conventional and critical (what Dworkin calls "sound") political morality. Dworkin views institutional rights as a species of moral rights, which are themselves derived from the conventional political morality of the community. But if one also assumes that there is a critical (rationally justifiable) political morality that contains moral principles superior (that is, more universal or better justified) to those found in the conventional morality of a community, then it is appeal to this critical morality that ought to be decisive in regard to right answers in hard cases. This would allow for the judgment that *both* the legal and moral orders of a particular society are morally flawed. It would also, of course, allow a judge to find a morally right answer that is independent of the two dimensions of institutional fit and (conventional) moral acceptability. But this would completely undermine Dworkin's whole argument concerning the importance of these two dimensions. It would also make his position almost indistinguishable from that of the natural lawyers who contend that the law is what is morally required.

Despite the many ambiguities in Dworkin's liberal theory of law, it does seem to lead—at least, as it now stands—to a conclusion avoided by both positivists and lawyers in the natural law tradition, i.e., that there is always a legally right answer in hard cases, which sometimes it may be morally wrong to embrace. With regard to

---

[161] The same point is made by Lawrence Alexander and Michael Bayles, "Hercules or Proteus? The Many Theses of Ronald Dworkin," *Social Theory and Practice* 5 (1980): 296.

my own concern with the law as a mechanism of social control, it seems clear that if a legal system is to be morally justifiable and if it is to impose a moral obligation on its citizens to obey its dictates, then it requires more serious attention than is given by Dworkin (and others) to questions concerning the moral legitimacy of one or another social order and the justifiability of the legal and moral standards that help to regulate it. I turn to a consideration of just these issues in the next chapter.

SEVEN

Law, Obligation, and Legitimacy

It is a serious shortcoming of all existing legal theories that they fail to successfully come to grips with the twin problem of legitimacy and obligation. Moreover, this failure has obvious implications for the ideal of a just social order. For it violates the demand that the legal system, like other institutional arrangements, be predicated on recognition and respect for everyone's generic rights to freedom and well-being and on the obligations to which these rights give rise.

If we accept the conclusion reached thus far, then—i.e., that there appears to be no rational justification for the legitimate authority of a system of laws and for whatever obligations it imposes on citizens—we must aknowledge that the ideal of a just social order is not realizable. Since such a conclusion is clearly unacceptable, it is necessary to explore further the crucial issues of legitimacy and obligation. At issue here are two separate, but interrelated, questions: Can we rationally justify the legitimate authority of the legal system that helps to regulate the just social order? and, Can we rationally justify the moral obligation of all citizens to obey the dictates of such a system?

I

Legitimate Authority

Every legal system does, of course, claim authority, and certainly it can be said that a system of laws is authoritative if its existence is a reason for people to conform their actions to its dictates. All of the various legal theories examined in the previous chapter are in agreement that every society has a legal system that does exercise *de facto* authority. But they are unable to provide an adequate justification for the legitimate, *de jure* authority of a particular legal system.

The nature of the authority of a legal system, and of the state it serves, has long been a central question of legal and political philosophy. Hobbes, for example, held a *de jure* conception of authority; the term authority indicates that someone has a right to certain kinds of things, that a particular individual or group is justified in doing certain things. "Done by authority," Hobbes says, means "done by commission, or license, from him whose right it is."[1] De Jouvenel, on the other hand, favors a *de facto* conception of authority: "What I mean by 'authority' is the ability of a man to get his proposals accepted."[2] The *de jure* sense of authority, then, proclaims that an individual or a particular group of persons has a right to exercise authority; while the *de facto* sense states that the individual or group does, as a matter of fact, exercise authority. *De facto* authority is illegitimate authority, meaning that we recognize the authority of a practice and yet deny that it is justified.

Among sociologists, too, much has been written concerning the various types of authority and the relations between authority and power. In his book, *Power*, Dennis Wrong argues that authority is one particular form of power (other forms being force, manipulation, and persuasion.[3] He notes that Max Weber defined authority, (or domination, as most translators have rendered the German term *Herrschaft*) as a special case of power. "Domination," writes Weber

will thus mean the situation in which the manifested will (*command*) of the *ruler* or rulers is meant to influence the conduct of one or more others (the ruled) and actually does influence it in such a way that their conduct to a socially relevant degree occurs as if the ruled had made the content of the command the maxim of their conduct for its very own sake. Looked upon from the other end, this situation will be called *obedience*.[4]

As Wrong points out, this definition does not exclude a relationship in which an individual obeys a superior out of prudence, or the threat of force, should he resist obedience.[5] Weber himself says that "every genuine form of domination implies a maximum of voluntary compliance, that is, an *interest* (based on ulterior motives or genuine acceptance) in obedience."[6] And he goes on to observe

[1] Thomas Hobbes, *Leviathan*, ed. and introduction Michael Oakeshott (New York: Oxford University Press, 1947), p. 106.

[2] Bertrand de Jouvenel, *Sovereignty* (Chicago: University of Chicago Press, 1957), p. 31.

[3] Dennis Wrong, *Power: Its Forms, Bases, and Uses* (New York: Harper & Row, 1979), pp. 23–24.

[4] Max Weber, *Economy and Society*, trans. and ed. Guenther Roth and Claus Wittich, 3 vols. (Totowa, N.J.: Bedminster Press, 1968), 3: 946. Italics in original.

[5] Wrong, *Power*, p. 36.

[6] Weber, *Economy and Society*, 1: 212.

that with authority, or domination, "in addition there is normally a further element, the belief in legitimacy."[7]

Weber's views concerning legitimate authority have had a strong influence on the treatment of legitimacy by many modern social and political theorists. He argued that the term has both a "normative" and an "empirical" meaning, and cautioned the social scientist to use only the latter.[8] While Weber is never explicit about the normative meaning, the empirical or social scientific meaning of legitimacy refers to "the prestige of being considered exemplary or binding."[9] A law is valid or a political system legitimate to the extent that people's actions are "oriented toward" that law or that system. "Action, especially social action which involves social relationships," Weber writes, "may be oriented by the actors to a *belief (Vorstellung)* in the existence of a 'legitimate order.' "[10] Every sphere of domination, he asserts, "attempts to establish and cultivate the belief in its legitimacy."[11] He says that "the legitimacy of a system of authority may be treated sociologically only as the probability that to a relevant degree the appropriate attitudes [toward the system] will exist, and the corresponding practical conduct ensue."[12]

Legitimacy, then, is completely a matter of belief or opinion. Similarly for Lipset, who says, "Legitimacy involves the capacity of the system to engender and maintain the belief that the existing political institutions are the most appropriate ones for the society."[13] In other words, if people come to believe (for any reason) that the existing political institutions are legitimate, then they *are* legitimate.

According to Weber, those acting subject to an order may ascribe legitimacy to it in several ways: (1) on rational or legal grounds, "resting on a belief in the 'legality' of patterns of normative rules and the right of those elevated to authority under such rules to

[7] Ibid., p. 213.

[8] Max Weber, *Basic Concepts in Sociology* (New York: Citadel Press, 1962), p. 73.

[9] Ibid., p. 72.

[10] Max Weber, "The Concept of Legitimate Order," reprinted in Talcott Parsons, et al. *Theories of Society*, vol. I (New York: Free Press, 1961).

[11] Weber, *Economy and Society*, 1: 213.

[12] Max Weber, *The Theory of Social and Economic Organizations* (New York: Oxford University Press, 1947), p. 299.

[13] Seymour Martin Lipset, *Political Man* (Garden City: Doubleday, 1960), p. 77. In *The First New Nation* (New York: Doubleday Anchor, 1967), p. 330, Lipset speaks of legitimacy in terms of a "believed-in-title-to-rule."

issue commands";[14] (2) on traditional grounds, in "a belief in the legitimacy of what has always existed";[15] (3) on charismatic grounds, by virtue of devotion to the specific and exceptional sanctity, heroism or exemplary character of an individual person, and of the normative patterns or order revealed or ordained by him;[16] and (4) "by virtue of a rational belief in an absolute value (*Wertrational*), thus lending it the validity of an absolute and final commitment,"[17] an example of which is an absolute value in "Natural Law."[18]

Although Weber speaks of four ways in which claims to legitimacy may be grounded, in subsequent analyses he excluded (4) above, and developed his three well-known "pure" types of legitimacy: rational, traditional, and charismatic. Even had he continued to consider all four types of belief as ways to legitimate a social order, however, he would have been subject to the criticism that his concept of legitimacy is, in one sense, incomprehensible. This is because it makes it impossible (or meaningless) to pose the important question, Is this government (legal system, or whatever) legitimate? Weber has already assimilated this question into the, for him, primary question, Is this government (legal system, etc.) believed to be legitimate?

For Weber, and for those who follow him, questions about the legitimacy of the government or a particular political institution are purely "empirical" questions; to answer them, we merely have to observe whether or not people "believe" in them or obey their dictates. Thus, in the Soviet Union, for example, if the government engenders and maintains this belief through the use of secret police and propaganda, it can still be considered legitimate. If government decisions, no matter how arbitrary or unrelated to specifiable rules, are accepted by citizens, they are legitimate. Since legitimacy is defined in terms of belief or acquiescence, no "normative" considerations need be involved. In fact, Weber himself distinguishes between the legal legitimacy of an order and its moral standing, stating that not all "legally guaranteed forms of order . . . claim the authority of ethical norms."[19]

Although Wrong does not criticize Weber on the above grounds,

---

[14] Weber, *Social and Economic Organizations*, pp. 300–01.
[15] Ibid.
[16] Ibid.
[17] Ibid.
[18] Ibid.
[19] Weber, *Economy and Society*, 1: 36.

he does emphasize the need to distinguish between "coercive" and "legitimate" authority. With coercive authority, compliance is obtained through the threat of force. For this to be successful, of course, those threatened must believe that those doing the threatening are both capable and willing to use force against them.[20] "With the exception of the actual use of force," says Wrong, "coercion is potentially the most extensive form of power of all because it requires a bare minimum of communication and mutual understanding between the power holder and power subject to compel the latter's obedience."[21] Coercion is, with legitimate authority, one of the two major forms of political power. In fact, states Wrong, political institutions are "most clearly differentiated from other institutions by virtue of their monopolistic control of the means of coercion."[22]

But obviously, as Wrong recognizes, coercive authority totally omits any normative considerations. It ignores questions about the right of individuals or political or legal institutions to rule and about the sense of obligation for a society's citizens to comply with their demands. Therefore, Wrong distinguishes legitimate authority in the following way:

> Legitimate authority is a power relation in which the power holder possesses an acknowledged *right to command* and the power subject an acknowledged *obligation to obey*. The *source* rather than the *content* of any particular command endows it with legitimacy and induces willing compliance on the part of the person to whom it is addressed.[23]

Since, as Wrong notes, legitimate authority involves the power holder's acknowledged right to command and the power subject's acknowledged obligation to obey, the question arises as to how this "acknowledgment" is itself to be recognized and justified. After all, actual compliance with the orders of an authority is obviously different than a rational justification for the rights and obligations connected with legitimate authority. Wrong says that legitimate authority involves the "potentiality" of reasoned elaborations, which are invoked to persuade people that an authority has the right to command and the subjects an obligation to obey.[24]

---

[20] Wrong, *Power*, p. 41.
[21] Ibid., p. 42.
[22] Ibid., p. 43.
[23] Ibid., p. 49.
[24] Ibid., p. 77.

He also points out that those who *exercise* authority usually experience "a need to believe that the power they possess is morally justified" and "that the exercise of power is not inescapably at odds with hallowed standards of morality."[25] And he goes on to quote Weber, who regarded claims to legitimacy as arising out of

> the generally observable need of any power, or even of any advantage of life, to justify itself . . . he who is more favoured feels the never ceasing need to look upon his position as in some way "legitimate," upon his advantage as "deserved," and the other's disadvantages as being brought about by the latter's "fault."[26]

Those *subject* to authority or domination, Wrong points out, also have the need to believe that the authority of the power holders is legitimate, saying that the need for legitimation experienced by the powerless is well recognized.

> Helpless to resist coercion, fearful of punishment, dependent on the powerful for satisfaction of basic needs and for any opportunities for autonomous choice and activity, the powerless are inescapably subject to a will to believe in the last analysis of some limits to what he will demand of or inflict upon them, grounded in at least a residual concern for their interests.[27]

In other words, those subject to authority have a disposition to believe that those who dominate them are really benevolent figures. Such a need for legitimation, Wrong says, has "roots in the infantile experience of dependence as understood by psychoanalysis."[28]

But whether or not there is any such psychological need for legitimation, whether or not those exercising and those subject to authority have a need to morally justify the right of the power holders to command and the obligation of those subject to authority to obey, in common with Weber, Wrong ignores the question of whether there can ever be a rational justification for legitimate authority. Instead, somewhat like Weber, he appears to assimilate the question, is this authority legitimate? to the question, Is this authority 'acknowledged' to be legitimate?

It is true that Wrong recognizes that legitimate authority involves the "potentiality" of reasoned elaboration to persuade others with

[25] Ibid., p. 103.
[26] Weber, *Economy and Society*, 3: 953.
[27] Wrong, *Power*, p. 111.
[28] Ibid., p. 122.

303

regard to command and the obligation to obey, that those who exercise authority experience a "need to believe" that their authority is (or can be) morally justified, and that those subject to authority also have a need to believe that the authority of the power holders is legitimate. But none of this concern with people's need to believe that authority can be morally justified ever takes the form of posing the question: *Is* this authority justified or rationally justifiable?

Even though Wrong does distinguish between coercive and legitimate authority, he ignores questions about the ultimate grounding of claims to legitimate authority. So long as the needs of the rulers and ruled alike for the "potentiality" of a reasoned justification of authority are satisfied, an authority *is* legitimate. What this means, then, is that Wrong, very much like Weber, is concerned only with the "empirical" meaning of legitimacy; the normative meaning is totally ignored.

Compare now Weber's and Wrong's use of the term *legitimate* with the most relevant entries in Webster's Seventh New Collegiate Dictionary:

> Legitimate: (1) lawfully begotten . . . (2) real, genuine; not false, counterfeit, or spurious. (3) Accordant with law or with established legal forms and requirements; lawful. (4) Conforming to recognized principles, or accepted rules or standards.

Commenting on the contrast between the above definitions and those operative in current social scientific usage, Schaar remarks:

> The older definitions all revolve around the element of law or right, and rest the force of a claim (whether it be a claim to political power or to the validity of a conclusion of an argument) upon foundations external to and independent of the mere assertion or opinion of the claimant. . . . Thus, a claim to political power is legitimate only when the claimant can invoke some source of authority beyond or above itself. History shows a variety of such sources: immemorial custom, divine law, the law of nature, a constitution.[29]

That is, the normal (dictionary), everyday meaning of legitimacy implies some standard external to the claimant—whether he or she

[29] John H. Schaar, "Legitimacy in the Modern State," in Philip Green and Sanford Levinson, eds., *Power and Community* (New York: Vintage Books, 1970), pp. 283–84. Also see Hannah Pitkin, *Wittgenstein and Justice* (Berkeley: University of California Press, 1975).

be the average citizen, a representative of the government, or a social scientist. To call something legitimate authority is—in normal circumstances—to imply that it ought to be obeyed. That, according to Schaar, is what legitimacy *means*. But for those emphasizing the empirical meaning of legitimacy, the social scientist—like the subjects of his or her inquiry—appears to have no criteria (other than "belief") by which to make decisions about legitimacy and illegitimacy.

But it needs to be emphasized that there are serious weaknesses with this normative view of legitimacy as well. Consider Schaar's listing of some of the sources invoked in claiming legitimacy for a political power: immemorial custom, divine law, the law of nature, a constitution. We can, if we like, accept the argument that a government is legitimate if it has its source in custom or in a constitution. But what is it that justifies custom or a constitution as ultimate sources of support for legitimacy? Should we not be concerned with distinguishing between customs that are widely followed and believed in by free, rational individuals and those that are blindly adhered to by people who have been brainwashed or kept systematically ignorant of the consequences of such adherence to custom? And is it enough to know that a society's citizens (or their ancestors) may have consented to a constitution, which later serves to ground the legitimacy of government? These are, of course, the kind of questions already raised in the previous chapter.

Parsons observes that "in the American system the problem of legitimacy concerns the Constitutional level, in the broadest sense, of the legitimacy of the legal order, its general principles of 'Rights' . . . and the powers of government and limitations of those powers. This sense of the concept legitimation is, I think, essentially the same as Weber's usage."[30] Whether or not this is indeed consistent with Weber's usage, the grounding of legitimacy in a constitution is still open to criticism. Habermas, for example, would argue that people may lend their allegiance to a political power—give it their normative acceptance—simply because they are ignorant about their "true" interests. They may accept historically accomplished "reality"—including the availability of a constitution—as the only source of legitimacy. Consent or the availability of a constitution does not, by itself, distinguish legitimate from illegitimate domination. "Illegitimate domination also meets with consent," Haber-

---

[30] Talcott Parsons, *Social Systems and the Evolution of Action Theory* (New York: Free Press, 1977), p. 358.

mas points out, "else it would not be able to last."[31] It is not sufficient, then, to know either that people "believe" in the legitimacy of a political or legal order or that, in Schaar's words, the claimant to legitimacy can "invoke some source of authority beyond or above itself."

Although normative views of legitimacy, such as Schaar's, are concerned with the grounding of legitimation-claims in some source external to the claimant rather than in people's beliefs, they are unable to deal with arguments revolving around the general idea of false consciousness. Nevertheless, they are far more sensitive to moral considerations than are the many theorists who hold an empirical view of legitimacy.[32]

The Moral Obligation to Obey the Law

We saw earlier that none of the various legal theories is able to show why citizens have a moral obligation to accept and obey the legal system in their society. But perhaps there are other arguments to provide the necessary justification. Let me consider five theories that attempt to provide a rational justification for people's obligation to obey the law: contract theory, consent theory, utilitarianism, Pitkin's theory of hypothetical consent, and the principle of fairness. Strictly speaking, some of these theories are more concerned with political obligation than with legal obligation as such. Although political and legal obligations are not precisely the same thing, they are very closely related. Certainly a large segment of political obligation is the obligation to obey the laws of the state. If political obligation imposes an obligation on people to obey the

[31] Jürgen Habermas, *Communication and the Evolution of Society*, trans. Thomas McCarthy (Boston: Beacon Press, 1979), p. 202.

[32] Some of the difficulties involved in normative theories of legitimacy are to be seen in the discussions arising from Michael Walzer's important work concerning the moral standing of nation-states. See Michael Walzer, *Just and Unjust Wars* (New York: Basic Books, 1977); Gerald Doppelt, "Walzer's Theory of Morality in International Relations," *Philosophy and Public Affairs* 8 (Fall 1978); David Luban, "Just War and Human Rights," *Philosophy and Public Affairs* 9 (Winter 1980): 160–81; Charles R. Beitz, "Bounded Morality: Justice and the State in World Politics," *International Organizations* 33 (1980): 405–24; and Michael Walzer, "The Moral Standing of States: A Response to Four Critics," *Philosophy and Public Affairs* 9 (Spring 1980). Also see the responses to Walzer by three of his critics: Charles R. Beitz, "Nonintervention and Communal Integrity," *Philosophy and Public Affairs* 9 (Summer 1980): 385–91; David Luban, "The Romance of the Nation-State." *Philosophy and Public Affairs* 9 (Summer 1980): 329–97; and Gerald Doppelt, "Statism Without Foundations," *Philosophy and Public Affairs* 9 (Summer 1980): 398–403.

law, then political obligation must itself be justified as a moral obligation.

According to the theory of social contract, the oldest and best-known defense of the obligation to obey the law, someone is obligated to obey the law because he or she is a party to a social contract. His or her obligation arises from having entered into an agreement. Thus, the basis of this obligation is the moral obligation to keep promises. But, of course, not all states are founded in this way. Further, the contract doctrine does not account for *our* obligation (as the descendants of the founders) to obey the law. Except for naturalized citizens who have explicitly promised to obey the law, most citizens of one or another state have made no such promise. Since promises are created by the expressed intention to be bound, it is clear that the ordinary life of most citizens includes nothing amounting to a promise to obey the law. Hence, a moral obligation to obey the law cannot be justified on the basis of the social contract doctrine.

A second theory regarding obligations is consent theory, a weakened version of contract theory. Here, too, the obligation to obey the law is based on the obligation to obey promises. The root idea is that acquiescence amounts to consent. If citizens acquiesce to laws, then they are taken to have consented to them. Mere compliance with the law is taken as consent. This is, of course, the view of Weber and most social scientists. Because people consent to the law, it is wrong to disobey it. But compliance or acquiescence may be due entirely to prudence or the fear of sanctions, and this hardly constitutes a "moral" obligation for obedience. Thus, compliance and acquiescence do not (morally speaking) amount to consent.

A third response to the question of obligation is that of utilitarianism. People have a moral obligation to obey the law because the existence of a stable legal system has great utility. Citizens are obligated to obey the law because the consequences are, on the whole, best in terms of a calculus of pains and pleasures. This, of course, immediately raises the question of *whose* pains and pleasures are to count: your own or those of the majority of persons in the society. Whether they are your own or those of the majority, it is not clear how the maximization of utility will create an obligation for everyone to obey the law. If the individual is obligated to obey only when it is best for her, then her obligation appears to vanish when she believes that the law does not promote her personal welfare. If, on the other hand, people are obligated to obey the law only if the consequences will be best in terms of the greatest good for the greatest number, then they seem to be obligated simply *because* their obedience will promote the greatest good. But, then, why should this criterion be accepted? The common good is, after all, an aggregative principle in that its concern is not with what is owed to individuals or groups as such, but rather with what is beneficial to the whole community.

Since the common good might demand certain sacrifices from some individuals or groups in order to achieve the greatest good, can it be argued that they are morally obligated to obey the law? Utilitarian considerations may require slavery as the best means of achieving the greatest good. Certainly those placed in slavery in order to help achieve the greatest societal good cannot be seriously said to have a moral obligation to obey the law. Thus, utilitarian arguments attempt to justify legal obligations on the basis of considerations of public welfare or the greatest good for the greatest number. But these considerations are not (and cannot be) justified as giving rise to moral obligation.

Pitkin's theory of hypothetical consent is the fourth response to the question of obligation to be considered here. She argues that political obligation turns on the issue of *hypothetical* consent, that is, on whether rational persons *would have* consented to the form of government under which they presently live. According to her argument, "A legitimate government . . . [is] one whose subjects are obligated to obey it, . . . [it is] one to which they *ought to consent*, quite apart from whether they have done so."[33] But this leaves open the question of the criteria for legitimacy. If we require criteria by which a legitimate form of government can be recognized, and a criterion or principle that can be justified in face of competing claims, then hypothetical consent will not—at least by itself—suffice. The problem with the theory of hypothetical consent is that *any* criterion whatsoever could be relevant for some individuals or groups of persons, so that a claim to legitimacy, and thus the moral obligation to obey the law, could never be defeated.[34]

Finally, we come to the "fairness principle" introduced by Hart

[33] Hannah Pitkin, "Obligation and Consent," in Peter Laslett, W. G. Runciman, and Quentin Skinner, eds., *Philosophy, Politics and Society*, fourth series (Oxford: Basil Blackwell, 1972), p. 62.

[34] Each of these attempts at justifying a moral obligation to obey the law is considered in some detail in A. John Simmons, *Moral Principles and Political Obligations* (Princeton: Princeton University Press, 1979).

and also mentioned by Rawls and Dworkin.[35] According to the principle of fairness, the taking of benefits within a cooperative system is by itself sufficient to generate obligations. In formulating this principle, Hart writes:

[W]hen a number of persons conduct any joint enterprise according to rules and thus restrict their liberty, those who have submitted to these restrictions when required have a right to a similar submission from those who have benefited by their submission. The rules may provide that officials should have authority to enforce obedience . . . but the moral obligation to obey the rules in such circumstances is due to the cooperative members of the society and they have the correlative moral right to obedience.[36]

In other words, Hart is claiming that someone is bound to other people's agreements solely because he or she benefits from such arguments—whether or not the individual has expressly or tacitly agreed to cooperate with them. The fact that someone has benefited from the group's activities creates an obligation on his part to do his "fair share," to submit to their rules, or whatever. And the others who have cooperated in the activities have a right to a fair acceptance of the burdens of submission on his part. That is, they have a moral justification for limiting his freedom.

Simmons, however, argues very persuasively against this fairness principle. In his book, *Moral Principles and Political Obligations*, he distinguishes between accepting and receiving benefits from a cooperative scheme. It may be, writes Simmons, "that those who accept the benefits of a cooperative scheme are bound to cooperate."[37] But those who have merely *received* benefits from a scheme are not in any way obligated to do their part (unless, of course, they have otherwise promised to do so). What, then, is the difference between benefits that have been accepted and those that have been merely received?

To say that an individual has "accepted" a benefit, Simmons stipulates, he "must either (1) have tried to get (and succeeded in

---

[35] See H. L. A. Hart, "Are There Any Natural Rights?" *Philosophical Review* 64 (April 1955); John Rawls, "Legal Obligations and the Duty of Fair Play," in Sidney Hook, ed., *Law and Philosophy* (New York: New York University Press, 1964); and Ronald Dworkin, *Taking Rights Seriously*. New Impression with a Reply to Critics (London: Duckworth, 1978).

[36] Hart, "Natural Rights," p. 185.

[37] Simmons, *Moral Principles*, p. 125.

getting) the benefit, or (2) have taken the benefit willingly and knowingly."[38] As an illustration, he contrasts two different types of police protection. With the first type, the benefits received through the efforts of policemen to patrol the streets, capture criminals, and assure general safety are referred to as "open." The only way to avoid them is to leave the area that the police force protects. But if—and this is the second type—someone requests special police protection by asking that his house be watched while he is away, then these are "readily available" benefits.[39] Such benefits can be easily avoided without inconvenience. Obtaining readily available benefits, then, involves going out of one's way or making some special effort to get them. Perhaps it is also necessary, Simmons notes, that the individual be aware that the benefits in question *are* the fruits of a cooperative scheme.[40] It is in those cases where people get readily available benefits, argues Simmons, that the principle of fairness can be said to apply.

In the case of police protection, someone who requests special police protection both gets the benefit and takes it willingly and knowingly. But it is difficult to see how this would work with normal police protection, which is an open benefit. Since police protection is available to everyone, whether they want it or not, there seems to be no way that an individual can be said to *try* to get it (or any other open benefit). Nor can someone be said to accept it willingly and knowingly if he either (a) fails to recognize that the open benefit is provided by a cooperative scheme, or (b) thinks that the benefit is not worth the price he must pay for it. Contrary to the argument of Hart, Simmons concludes that "participants in cooperative schemes which produce 'open' benefits will not always have a right to cooperation on the part of those who benefit from their labors."[41]

What happens, then, when we turn to larger-scale schemes of social cooperation such as political communities? In large-scale cooperative schemes, as in smaller ones, the fairness principle requires people to do their part and not to take advantage of the situation. With regard to political communities, the fairness principle involves all of the things normally thought of as the requirements of political obligation. Although people are born into political communities, it is not clear that they are all necessarily participants

---

[38] Ibid., p. 129.
[39] Ibid., p. 130.
[40] Ibid., p. 131.
[41] Ibid.

in these communities. Applying Simmons's criterion that participants or insiders relative to some scheme or institution are those who "accept" the benefits from the cooperative arrangement, it is difficult to see how very many citizens would qualify as participants. Certainly, most citizens in most states do *receive* benefits from the workings of their legal and political institutions. But is it plausible to claim that they have *accepted* those benefits? It would appear not to be so. Such benefits as the rule of law, protection by the armed forces, and the like, are clearly "open" benefits. And for it to be said that people have accepted such open benefits involves, as noted earlier, their having certain attitudes and beliefs about the benefits they have received.

In order for people to have accepted benefits, they must themselves regard the benefits as the result of a cooperative scheme, rather than seeing them as free for the taking.[42] And they must think that the benefits received are worth the price that must be paid for them. This means that, had they been given the choice, they would have taken the benefits *together* with the burdens involved. But, as Simmons points out, it seems highly unlikely that most citizens do have these requisite attitudes toward or beliefs about the benefits of government.[43] Many citizens barely notice the benefits they receive, and others (faced with high taxes or military service) believe that the benefits received from government are not worth the price they are forced to pay. Furthermore, even in democratic political communities, people commonly regard these benefits as being purchased (with taxes) from a central authority, rather than as accepted from the cooperative efforts of fellow citizens. Most citizens, Simmons observes, will "fall into one of these two classes: those who have not 'accepted' because they have not taken the benefits (with accompanying burdens) willingly, and those who have not 'accepted' because they do not regard the benefits of government as the products of a cooperative scheme."[44] Hence, we are led to conclude that most citizens in actual states will not be bound by the principle of fairness. For that reason, such a principle provides no justification for a moral obligation to obey the law.

It is, I believe, apparent that none of the above approaches to the twin problem of the legitimate authority of a legal system and

[42] Ibid., p. 138.
[43] Ibid., pp. 138–39.
[44] Ibid., p. 139.

the moral obligation of a society's citizens to obey its dictates is satisfactory. None of them successfully comes to grips with the need to provide a rational justification for legitimate authority and moral obligation. Thus, it is necessary to turn elsewhere for possible guidance concerning these two crucial problems.

II

As I noted earlier, most social scientists follow Max Weber in defining legitimacy in terms of the capacity of a system to engender and maintain the belief that existing institutions are legitimate. According to this view, a legal system has legitimate authority when it is established positively (as with Austin and Kelsen) and when those subject to its dictates believe in its legality. Such a view is also represented by Niklas Luhmann who collapses the belief in legitimacy to a belief in legality: "The law of a society is positivized when the legitimacy of pure legality is recognized, that is, in accordance with definite rules."[45] Of course, the problem with these and other standpoints that conceive of legitimacy entirely as an empirical phenomenon is that they ignore questions concerning the rational justification of one or another belief in legitimacy. The widespread recognition of a claim to legal authority does indeed mark it as authority. But by virtue of what other features is it to be considered "legitimate" authority?

Another conception of legitimacy discussed earlier conceives of legitimacy in terms of the availability of some source of authority beyond or above the opinion or belief of the claimant, Schaar mentions immemorial custom, divine law, the law of nature, and a constitution as examples. But, as I remarked before, we need to ask what justifies custom or a constitution as ultimate sources of support for legitimacy. We must distinguish between customs followed and believed in by free, rational individuals and those that are blindly adhered to when freedom and knowledge are lacking.

Sometimes a government is called legitimate when it has acquired its political power through elections and majority consent. But this, too, is unsatisfactory (think of the so-called elections in many totalitarian regimes). In other instances, a government may be considered legitimate when it is recognized as legitimate by other

[45] Niklas Luhmann, quoted in Jürgen Habermas, *Legitimation Crisis*, trans. Thomas McCarthy (Boston: Beacon Press, 1975), p. 98.

312

governments. This use of legitimate is obviously not acceptable, as it confirms the legitimacy of practically each and every government.

In contrast to these other views, and in express opposition to Luhmann's position, Jürgen Habermas argues that a belief in legality is derived from a belief in legitimacy that can be justified.[46] That is, the legal system is part of a system of authority that must itself be legitimized. With regard to the concept of legitimacy, Habermas writes:

> Legitimacy means that there are good arguments for a political order's claim to be recognized as right and just; a legitimate order deserves recognition. *Legitimacy means a political order's worthiness to be recognized*. This definition highlights the fact that legitimacy is a contestable validity claim; the stability of the order of domination (also) depends on its (at least) de facto recognition. Thus, historically as well as analytically, the concept is used above all in situations in which the legitimacy of an order is disputed, in which, as we say, legitimation problems arise. One side denies, the other asserts legitimacy.[47]

The state, Habermas recognizes, provides legitimating support to a social order claiming legitimacy.[48] Whereas most social theorists have either an empirical ("belief," "acknowledgement") or normative (custom, a constitution) view of legitimacy, Habermas introduces a third conception of legitimacy: the "reconstructive."[49] This involves his notion of a rational consensus concerning the legitimacy of a social order. The emphasis here is on specifying the conditions under which an agreement will express the common interest of all involved. Justifiable norms are, as was noted in my discussion of Habermas in Chapter 2, those that have been arrived at in an ideal speech situation. A norm is true or rational to the extent to which it expresses "constraint-free consensus."[50]

Although I have earlier pointed to several weaknesses in Habermas's notion of the ideal speech situation, there is much in his exploration of legitimacy that is extremely important. As I interpret his remarks, he is saying, first of all, that a social order itself requires legitimacy. This means that a legitimate social order would be one that was regulated by norms agreed upon in a situation of con-

---

[46] Habermas, *Legitimation Crisis*, p. 100.
[47] Ibid., pp. 178–79.
[48] Habermas, *Communication*, p. 196.
[49] Ibid., p. 204.
[50] Habermas, *Legitimation Crisis*, p. 198.

straint-free consensus. Given agreement about a legitimate social order, the state provides legitimacy to this (itself legitimate) social order.

With regard to the legal system as part of the state, then, it is legitimate to the extent that it conforms with the norms that underlie and regulate the legitimate social order. This would seem to imply, although Habermas does not say so, that people's political *obligations*—including their obligation to obey the law—depend on the extent to which the state itself is legitimate. Assuming that the state and its legal system cannot be legitimate unless the social order itself is legitimate, it can be concluded that citizens have a moral obligation to obey the law only when the state is legitimate. Thus, from Habermas's view of legitimacy, two important consequences follow with regard to the law: (1) only legal systems that are found in legitimate social orders can be viewed as exercising legitimate authority; and (2) only legitimate legal systems impose a moral obligation on citizens to obey the law.

Of course, as I pointed out in Chapter 2, there are severe problems with Habermas's idea of the ideal speech situation as the appropriate source of consensus about the norms and principles that ought to regulate the legitimate social order and that, therefore, legitimate the legal system. Nevertheless, he is correct in emphasizing the need for a rational justification of a set of moral norms or principles that will allow for the appraisal of particular legal systems from a standpoint independent of these legal systems. In this, he is in agreement with Rawls, Nozick, and Gewirth. All of these theorists are concerned with locating a set of moral principles that can provide the foundation for a legitimate order. All four would agree that the law is not legitimate simply because it *is* the law, but that legitimacy-claims require a rational justification. They would also agree, as a consequence of the fact that legitimacy-claims are contestable, that there is no *prima facie* obligation to obey the law.

Although Habermas seems to be suggesting that a legal system is legitimate to the extent that it conforms to the norms and principles that underlie and regulate a "legitimate" social order, I prefer to speak of the conformity of the law with the principles that define a "just" social order. That is, Habermas's notion of a legitimate social order appears to be identical to my idea of a just social order. As I have argued in earlier chapters, the justice of one or another social order depends on locating a set of rationally justifiable moral principles that can provide the foundation for a just social order.

These principles, as I have shown, are represented by the generic rights to freedom and well-being. Thus, the legal system found in a just social order, i.e., one regulated by recognition and respect for everyone's generic rights, has *legitimate authority*. As such, it imposes a *moral obligation* on all citizens to obey the law.

III

But the above, as is apparent, so far represents only a *claim* that the legitimate authority of a legal system and the moral obligations it imposes can be established on the basis of the justice of a social order. To show how this necessarily follows, I must return to a further consideration of the general idea of a just social order and then examine some of Gewirth's arguments concerning legal and other institutional arrangements.

A just social order, I have argued, is one in which all people's actions are regulated by recognition and respect for everyone's rights to freedom and well-being and by the institutions to which those generic rights give rise. The Principle of Generic Consistency ("Act in accord with the generic rights of your recipients as well as of yourself") thus imposes requirements both on individual agents and on certain institutions. The social rules associated with those institutions, in turn, impose further requirements on the actions of individuals. These social rules are, of course, a means of regulating various interactions, activities, and associations within a society.[51] The moral justification of the social rules resolves itself, in part, into the moral justification of the social activities they serve to regulate. In order for institutions to be consistent with the demands of a just social order, they must be in conformity with the Principle of Generic Consistency. As Gewirth notes: "Humans may associate with one another as governors and governed, as masters and slaves, as employers and employees, as husbands and wives, and in countless other ways, and they may compete or cooperate according to many different rules. The question, then, is: Which of these specific associations, activities, and rules are morally justified, and why?"[52]

According to Durkheim, Parsons, and most other social scientists, all justified moral obligations and duties derive entirely from the requirements of social institutions or of the society as a whole.

---

[51] Alan Gewirth, *Reason and Morality* (Chicago: University of Chicago Press, 1978), p. 273.

[52] Ibid., p. 279.

That is, they hold that the "conventional" moralities of different groups and societies cannot themselves be evaluated in terms of their moral rightness. Dworkin, too, appears to accept that it is the conventional morality of a particular society that must prove decisive in regard to locating the right answer in hard cases in the law. Those who hold this view seem to accept that all moral values and standards are derived entirely from the rules set out by various existing institutional arrangements.

This relativist position concerning moral rules, i.e., that morality is completely a matter of what is upheld as right by the rules within a given institutional setting, is obviously one that I reject. In contrast, as I have argued earlier, it is the generic rights of individuals that serve as the ultimate criteria for the moral rightness of various institutionalized rules and obligations. This being the case, it is useful to now consider Gewirth's treatment of the ways in which people's generic rights can give rise to just institutions—most especially, the institution of law.

Because the freedom component of the principle of Generic Consistency requires that every individual act in accord with the right of his recipients to freedom, he must refrain from involving other persons in transactions unless they unforcedly *consent* to it. But Gewirth argues that the consensual procedures that justify various social rules and institutional arrangements may be either optional or necessary. With "optional" consent, it is up to the free or voluntary consent of individuals to decide whether or not there will be some particular institutional arrangement and whether or not they want to belong to it. Each individual determines whether or not he or she will belong to a voluntary organization and be subject to its rules.

When the procedure is "necessary," on the other hand, the consensual procedure operates only internally to the particular institution. If there is to be a state having legal rules or laws, Gewirth emphasizes, obedience to the state and its specific laws has to be necessary (i.e., obligatory), not optional. Within the political association of the state, there will, however, be a constitution providing for the method of consent to determine the actual contents of the laws, the methods for selecting legislators, executives, and the like.[53] Thus, when the procedure of justification for a particular institutional arrangement is necessary, the consensual procedures operate internally to the political association but are circumscribed

[53] Ibid., p. 283.

by the necessity that there be such an association.[54] It is *not* left to the optional consent of individuals, then, to decide whether or not a state should exist and whether or not they shall obey its laws.

This conclusion is, of course, in direct opposition to the doctrine of consent theory, which holds that no one is obligated to support or comply with any power unless he or she has personally consented to its authority. That is, various social rules and institutional arrangements are to be justified entirely through people voluntarily exercising their individual right to freedom. But, as is widely recognized, the requirement of *unanimous* consent has proved to be a serious obstacle with all varieties of consent theory.[55] If a legitimate government must have the unanimous consent of all its citizens, then the refusal of even one single citizen to give his or her consent to the government will render the government illegitimate. This would result in no one being obligated to the government, since no one can be bound to an illegitimate government. Furthermore, as Gewirth emphasizes, consent theory, with its stress on the exercise of people's right to freedom, makes little provision for rules that protect each person's right to well-being.[56] In fact, Western liberalism has usually ignored people's rights to subsistence and security (well-being). This, as I noted in Chapter 2, is one of the most serious shortcomings of Nozick's entitlement theory of justice.

In order to assure that people's generic rights to freedom and well-being are protected, Gewirth argues, social rules and institutions must be justified instrumentally. Such an instrumental justification derives from the requirements of the Principle of Generic Consistency that every individual act in accord with his or her recipient's right to well-being. Applying this requirement to social rules, particular rules and institutional arrangements are instrumentally justified when they maintain or bring about an equality in people's generic right to well-being. They are also instrumentally justified when they serve to restore or protect people's other generic right: the right to freedom.

The instrumental justification of social rules involves two main phases. One phase is *static*. It assumes that people are already equal with regard to their generic rights, and holds that social rules are

---

[54] Ibid., p. 284.

[55] See Simmons, *Moral Principles*; and Derek L. Phillips, *Equality, Justice and Rectification* (New York: Academic Press, 1979).

[56] Gewirth, *Reason and Morality*, p. 290.

justified when they protect (and, if need be, restore) this equality.[57] The rules of law, as we shall see, are justified in this manner. The other phase of the instrumental justification is *dynamic*. When people are dispositionally unequal in their actual ability to attain and protect their rights to freedom and well-being, social rules are justified when they serve to remove this inequality. Retributive justice is the static phase of this instrumentality; it assigns penalties for various crimes and wrongdoings.[58] It determines penalties solely on the basis of the crime committed and without "respect of persons." Redistributive justice is the dynamic phase; it removes dispositional inequalities that have institutional sources, and seeks to move toward a previously nonexistent equality.[59]

It is, then, the static phase—that of retributive justice—that instrumentally justifies the rules of the criminal law. These rules are justified in that they serve to help uphold such basic goods as liberty and physical integrity, as well as reputation and privacy.[60] To uphold these is to maintain the equality of the generic rights to freedom and well-being. If one person voluntarily and purposively kills, assaults, steals from, rapes, or invades the privacy of another, then he or she obviously violates the other person's rights and creates an inequality between them. "The criminal law," Gewirth says, "provides punishments that rectify this inequality and also serves to protect the equality of rights whereby such harmful acts are eschewed."[61] People's rights can be successfully protected only if other persons are prevented from infringing them. The criminal law is made up of rules intended to prohibit such infringements. It is the institutional arrangements for establishing these prohibitory rules that, for Gewirth, constitute the minimal state.[62]

The criminal law, then, relates to the Principle of Generic Consistency in two different ways. First of all, much of its content is the same as the most basic part of this principle, i.e., it prohibits the infringement of life, liberty, physical integrity, and other basic goods, as well as privacy, reputation, and the like. In this regard, to deny the obligatoriness of the rules of the criminal law would involve exactly the same self-contradictions as would denial of the rights to freedom and well-being (discussed in Chapter 2). Sec-

[57] Ibid., p. 292.
[58] Ibid., p. 293.
[59] Ibid., p. 294.
[60] Ibid.
[61] Ibid.
[62] Ibid., pp. 294–95.

ondly, the criminal law adds to the Principle of Generic Consistency certain enforcement provisions, including the threat and application of punishment for violators. The requirement for the criminal law to bring about an equality of generic rights is an empirical, not a logical one. Nevertheless, the obligatory character of both the content of the law and its enforcement aspect can be denied only at the cost of self-contradiction.[63]

The rules of the criminal law, Gewirth emphasizes, have a stringent logical status.[64] Because any individual's denial of the Principle of Generic Consistency and hence of its obligatoriness is self-contradictory, it is also self-contradictory for him or her to deny the obligatoriness of the rules of law whose content is largely the same as the most basic part of the principle. Similarly with the enforcement provisions of the law; insofar as they are causally (i.e., empirically) required for protecting the equality of generic rights, the obligatoriness of the enforcement must also rationally be granted.

"The basis of the obligation to obey the law, then," writes Gewirth, "is not simply that it is the law but rather that the law is instrumentally justified by the PGC. Hence, indirectly, the obligation to obey the law is a rational obligation, in that to violate the law is to contradict oneself."[65] In other words, it is a *rational obligation* to obey the law when it can be *morally justified* in terms of protecting everyone's rights to freedom and well-being. There is, then, no rational obligation to obey the law when it cannot be morally justified in such a manner. In short, there is no moral obligation to obey unjust laws.

But it might be objected, especially by consent theorists, that a minimal state with its criminal law cannot be morally justified in this manner, since it is not subject to the *voluntary* or *optional* consent of the persons who must obey it. Without voluntary consent to the minimal state and the criminal law itself, they would argue, there can be no moral justification for such institutional arrangements and, hence, no obligation for people to obey them. After all, according to the consent theorists, people are morally obligated to obey only the rules of the associations to which they have freely consented. The question, then, is why the instrumental justification of the law is sufficient without there being any procedural justification.

[63] Ibid., p. 295.
[64] Ibid., p. 300.
[65] Ibid.

Gewirth's answer is as follows: "Since the criminal law directly embodies and enforces basic aspects of the PGC's generic rules, its obligatoriness can no more be contingent on persons' optional consent than can that of the generic rules themselves."[66] Every person values his or her freedom and well-being and wants them to be defended from attack by other persons. This equality of generic rights is inherently morally justifiable, and the criminal law defends the equality of such rights. None of this, Gewirth emphasizes, is subject to optional decisions as in the case of voluntary organizations; the moral correctness of these conclusions does not rest on the optional or voluntary consent of individual citizens.[67]

This does not mean, however, that there is no place for consent in the instrumental justification of the minimal state and the criminal law. There is indeed consent involved, but it is neither empirical, optional, nor contingent. Such consent is, instead, *rational and necessary*.[68] The consent that grounds the state cannot be assimilated or identified with the kind of empirical, optional consent that grounds many voluntary organizations. Rather, all persons *logically* must give their rational consent to the state and its criminal laws because such consent is rationally necessitated by the instrumental relation of the state and the law to the Principle of Generic Consistency.[69]

It is the Principle of Generic Consistency, arising from the rights to freedom and well-being, that ultimately grounds all morally justified obligations. As already noted, the central content of the criminal law is the same as the most basic part of this principle, and acceptance of and obedience to the criminal law is mandatory for all. While other laws required by the state (e.g., rules of the road) may be less directly related to the requirements of the PGC, they too must be in accord with the principle's emphasis on an equality of generic rights. Just as with the criminal law, these laws have a claim to obedience insofar as they are morally justified by the principle of Generic Consistency.[70]

The existence of the state and its institutions of law must depend on rational consent through the arguments of the PGC. Similarly, Gewirth argues that a certain kind of constitution must be made mandatory for the state. This constitution provides for specified

[66] Ibid., p. 302.
[67] Ibid.
[68] Ibid., p. 303.
[69] Ibid., pp. 303–04.
[70] Ibid., p. 305.

consensual decision-procedures. It requires an equal distribution of civil liberties, and sets an important limit on the legitimate powers of the state: it may interfere with the freedom of the individual only to prevent his or her coercing or harming others.[71] The state must respect these civil liberties as the rights of all individuals. And the individuals themselves will utilize civil liberties in participating freely and actively in the political process to help determine who shall govern the state.

Clearly, then, Gewirth's approach to the issue of political obligation differs markedly from traditional contractarian or consensual theories. For the most part, those theories emphasize the necessity for *optional, empirical* consent without distinguishing this from *rational* consent. With optional consent, as already noted, it is up to each individual to voluntarily give or withhold his or her consent. With rational consent, on the other hand, consent is fully determined by rational arguments. Traditional theories treat consent to the political society or state as if it were on a par with consent to a voluntary organization. They assume that decisions like the following must rest on the voluntary consent of those who will be subject to the results: whether or not there should be any state or government at all; whether or not there should be a constitution and, if so, what kind; whether or not to have laws and, again, if so, what kind; and what should be the basic decision-procedures for designating government officials. According to traditional theories of consent, people are morally obligated to obey and support these various institutional arrangements only when they have voluntarily and freely consented to them.

Gewirth avoids the difficulties arising from the requirement of voluntary consent by specifying that some of the above decisions should not be dependent on empirical (i.e., voluntary) consent for their obligatoriness or authority, but solely on rational consent. Thus, as a logical consequence of the Principle of Generic Consistency, there is a *rational justification* for a minimal state, for a constitution, for criminal laws, and for specified procedures for designating government officials. But, on the other hand, decisions about the specific content of laws other than the criminal law and about the actual selection of government officials should rest on the optional, empirical consent of societal members. To repeat a point made earlier, decisions are to be made through people's exercise of their civil liberties. These civil liberties themselves are, of

---

[71] Ibid., p. 308.

course, quaranteed by the constitution and are ultimately justified by people's rights to freedom and well-being and the Principle of Generic Consistency to which they give rise.

The actual selection of public officials and various laws and policies, then, is left to the majoritarian empirical consent of a society's citizens. They will decide who is to be elected to public office and which laws and policies are to be enacted and supported. But Gewirth recognizes that, despite its rational basis, majoritarian consent may sometimes support morally wrong laws and policies. He mentions censorship laws, and the fugitive slave laws, the prohibition amendment, and the segregation laws of the South in the United States.[72] Although he does not say so, I assume that his listing of these morally wrong laws is not meant to imply that the institutional arrangements of the United States are (or were) otherwise consistent with the requirements of his moral theory. In my view, the United States is far from resembling what Gewirth's theory demands or what I call a just social order.

When it is thought that laws and policies are morally wrong, futher use must be made of the procedures of consent to rectify these wrongs; voting to strike an unjust law from the books would be the most obvious example. If such efforts should prove fruitless, Gewirth argues that civil disobedience may be justified in an attempt to bring the injustice of a law or policy to the public's attention.[73] But, of course, the individual who believes that a law or policy is morally wrong must himself be able to provide a rational justification for his beliefs that can be grounded in the Principle of Generic Consistency.

The issue of civil disobedience also bears on the issue of justified limits of legal and governmental interference with individual freedom. Since every person has the generic rights to freedom and well-being, to determine whether an action should be legally interfered with requires a consideration of whether such interference will or will not protect or promote the equality of generic rights. Such considerations of consequences, however, must observe the limitation of the criminal law and the constitution and civil liberties (which are rationally justified as a logical consequence of the principle of Generic Consistency). It is *not* a violation of people's rights to freedom and well-being, therefore, when laws impose limits on individual freedom in certain instances that concern the well-being

[72] Ibid., p. 322.
[73] Ibid., p. 323.

of other persons. For example, Gewirth notes that discrimination in employment on grounds of race, religion, or sex must be prohibited regardless of whether it emanates from employers, from workers, or from their unions. Similarly, there must be a restriction on the freedom to discriminate in the availability of public accommodations.[74]

It is also a justified limitation on individual freedom for the government to require the paying of taxes needed to maintain various state functions connected with the protection and extension of people's rights to freedom and well-being (for example, public education and the legal system). And while there is generally no moral justification for interference with civil liberties, there are certain notable exceptions. Freedom of expression may be legally limited on two counts: when speech directly threatens serious harm (falsely shouting "Fire" in a crowded theater), and when it is used wrongly to attack the dignity or rational autonomy of another (slander, violations of privacy, and the like).

There are instances, then, when governmental or legal interference with people's right to freedom is justified. In general, however, such interference is either to prohibit the infliction of basic and other serious harms or to maintain or extend the equality of generic rights among a society's citizens. As with the minimal state and its criminal law, the constitution, the procedures for designating public officials, and decisions arising from majoritarian empirical consent, legal inteference with people's right to freedom can be rationally justified only as a logical consequence of the Principle of Generic Consistency—whose central point is, of course, that each and every person has rights to freedom and well-being.

IV

Law, Obligation, and Legitimacy

In his discussion of morally acceptable social institutions, Gewirth never explicitly considers the issue of legitimacy. Yet, his arguments concerning the moral justification of various institutions are obviously relevant to the problem of legitimate authority. It may be recalled that I stipulated earlier that a legal system has legitimate authority to the extent that it conforms to the norms and principles that underlie and regulate a just social order. Such a

[74] Ibid., p. 325.

legitimate legal system imposes a moral obligation on all citizens to obey the law.

Combining my own conception of the legitimate authority of a legal system with Gewirth's arguments concerning the justification of the law, it is possible to conclude the following. In a just social order, i.e., a social order in which people's actions are regulated by recognition and respect for every individual's rights to freedom and well-being, and by the institutions to which these generic rights give rise, there must be a legitimate system of laws that protects and secures everyone's rights to freedom and well-being.

Like other social institutions, the law is a relatively stable, standardized arrangement for regulating the activities of societal members and enforcing various social rules and requirements. The law, and especially the criminal law, consists of rules intended to protect and punish infringements of people's rights. Since, in a just social order, the law prohibits the infringement of everyone's rights to freedom and well-being and, at the same time, includes certain enforcement provisions, it is ultimately justified by the Principle of Generic Consistency. Because (as has been shown in Chapter 2) any individual's denial of the Principle of Generic Consistency and hence of its obligatoriness is self-contradictory, it is also self-contradictory for him or her to deny the legitimate authority of a legal system whose content is largely the same as the most basic part of the principle. Thus, the legitimate authority of the law is ultimately justified by the Principle of Generic Consistency. A system of laws has *legitimate authority* when it can be morally justified in terms of securing everyone's rights to freedom and well-being. When the legitimate authority of a legal system can be morally justified, it imposes a *moral obligation* on all citizens to obey its dictates. For an individual to fail to accept such an obligation is to contradict him- or herself.

There is, then, a rational justification for the legitimate authority of a legal system in a just social order and also for the moral obligation of all citizens to obey and uphold it. This legitimate authority of the law is not justified by people's "belief" that it is legitimate (as Weber and most social scientists hold), not by its being able to invoke some source of authority beyond or above itself in the sense specified by Schaar (custom, a constitution), not by the voluntary consent (tacit or explicit) of the society's citizens, not by the fact that the political system it supports has acquired power through general elections, and not by its being considered legitimate by other governments. Similarly, the moral obligation to obey the law is not justified by the principle of fairness, not by a contractual agreement between citizens and the state nor by other types of consent, not by utilitarian considerations, and not by the hypothetical consent that people would have given had they been asked. None of these approaches to the problem of the legitimate authority of a legal system and the moral obligation of a society's citizens to support and comply with the law is satisfactory.

In sharp contrast to all of the above attempts to provide a justification for legitimate authority and moral obligations, the approach taken here provides a rational justification by way of arguments concerning *rational* and *necessary* consent. Drawing on Gewirth, I view the legitimate authority of a legal system as being justified by the fact that it defends the equality of the rights to freedom and well-being. Since the equality of generic rights is inherently morally justifiable, so is the system of criminal law that defends these rights. Therefore, all persons logically have a moral obligation to accept and obey the criminal law. The moral correctness of such conclusions does not, as was indicated earlier, in any way rest on the actual, voluntary, empirical consent of individual citizens.

Decisions about the specific content of laws other than the criminal law must, however, rest on the actual consent of societal members. As a matter of constitutional requirement, people exercise their civil liberties in selecting government officials and in reaching decisions about the content of non-criminal laws. These civil liberties themselves, as already noted, are guaranteed by a constitution and ultimately rationally justified by everyone's generic rights and the Principle of Generic Consistency to which they give rise. Thus, all those laws found in the legal system of a just social order must be in accord with the principle's emphasis on the equality of generic rights. These laws have a claim to obedience only insofar as they are morally justified by the Principle of Generic Consistency.[75]

[75] There does remain, however, the problem of "particularity" raised by Simmons (*Moral Principles*). This concerns those moral principles or requirements "which bind an individual to one *particular* political community, set of political institutions, etc.," p. 31. Simmons shows rather convincingly, I believe, that there is no principle of political obligation that binds the citizen to one particular state (namely, the state in which he is a citizen) above all others. With regard to my own argument that there is a moral obligation to support and comply with the legitimate authority of a legal system in a just social order, it is the fact that the social order itself is *just*— and not that it is *ours*—that imposes an obligation to support it. If we should be lucky enough to live in a just social order, then we would indeed have a moral

In opposition to the standpoint of the legal realists, then, it *is* possible to provide a rational justification for the legitimate authority of a legal system and for people's obligation to obey its dictates. Contrary to what they say, moral values can be justified and are relevant to the questions of authority and obligation. And contrary to the view-point of legal positivists like Hart, a legal system—and the wider political system it serves—can be grounded in a set of rationally justifiable moral principles. The legitimate

obligation to obey the laws and requirements of our own just society. But it is the status of our society as a just society, and not our mere physical presence in it, that accounts for our moral bonds to it. If we do not live in a just social order, of course, we have no moral obligation to support the legal and political institutions found in our society. This means that in the actual societies where we live today, there is, as Simmons concludes, *no* such moral obligation of support and obedience.

The problem that Simmons's particularity requirements raises for my claims about a just social order is as follows. If I am living in an unjust society at war with a just society, can it be said that I have a moral obligation to oppose the efforts of my "own" society and to support the efforts of the "enemy"? Simmons, p. 32, suggests that this cannot be the case. It seems to me, however, that any and all just social orders impose a moral obligation on us to support them.

Insofar as they are truly just, these different societies (almost by definition) cannot come into conflict with one another; all just social orders are organized on the basis of recognition and respect for everyone's rights to freedom and well-being. But if the unjust society, where I happen to live, declares war on a just society, I do believe that I have a moral obligation to support the latter. This is not to say, of course, that such an obligation will necessarily always take precedence over my own "particularized" obligations to my parents, children, friends, and others to whom I may feel morally bound. After all, even within a just social order, moral conflicts may arise between my moral obligation toward the just institutional arrangements of the wider society and toward particular others to whom I feel bound by ties of love and affection. Nevertheless, all individuals do have a moral obligation to support and comply with the legal and political demands of a just social order—whether or not this happens to be the society in which they live.

I am not denying, then, that there may be competing loyalties and moral conflicts both within just societies and when one's own society comes into conflict with another. What I am stressing is that anyone fortunate enough to live in a world with at least one just social order will have a moral obligation to try to comply with the demands of the legal and political systems of that just social order. Should a just social order be one that is 3,000 miles away, with which an individual has no direct contact, there may be no concrete opportunity to fulfill such an obligation. But should one visit or live in such a just social order, then he or she will indeed have a moral obligation (and not just reasons of prudence or avoiding trouble) to support the legal and political institutions.

Simmons is correct, therefore, in concluding that there is no principle of political obligation that morally binds the citizen to the particular state in which he or she is a citizen. But should that society be a just social order, then the individual does have a moral obligation to support it, just as he or she does for any other just social order.

authority of the law and the obligation to obey and support it *does*, despite what Hart argues, involve a logical connection between law and morality.

Natural law theorists and Ronald Dworkin are correct in their insistence on the logical relation between law and morality. But while the natural law theorists claim that there are correct moral principles, they have never managed to provide a rational justification for a particular set of such principles. Their claim that one cannot say that a law is legally valid but morally wrong is also mistaken. In a (non-just) society where the law has authority but not legitimate authority, laws may be legally valid but morally wrong. More generally, there can be (in fact, are) valid legal systems that have illegitimate authority and, therefore, impose no moral obligation on citizens to obey them.

Although the approach followed in this chapter is closer to Dworkin's than to those of other legal theorists, there are clearly important differences. Most importantly, I avoid three major shortcomings of Dworkin's theory. First, Dworkin does not justify the legitimate authority of a legal system and the wider political system it serves, while I am able to provide such a rational justification in terms of a wider moral theory concerning the just social order. Second, Dworkin is unable to show that legal obligations are backed up by some other moral principle so that a society's citizens (including judges and other legal officials) are under an obligation to accept the constitution and the political system set forth therein. My approach, on the other hand, shows why (and when) there is a moral obligation to accept and comply with a legal and political system. Finally, while Dworkin fails to deal satisfactorily with the question of how the principles of morality relevant to legal decisions are themselves to be identified and defended, I have shown that it is the generic rights to freedom and well-being (and the Principle of Generic Consistency to which they give rise) that constitute the rationally justifiable moral principles relevant to legal decisions and the moral standing of the law more generally.

V

Law in a Just Social Order

The idea of a "just social order," as I have emphasized, provides a *standard* against which we can evaluate particular laws and institutions from a moral standpoint independent of those laws and institutions. Let me now briefly consider how a legal system with legitimate authority would function within a just social order.

As I observed earlier, a legal system has to meet three different, though interrelated, demands. First of all, through the creation of a body of civil, criminal, and public law, it prescribes and prohibits certain modes of conduct. Second, it provides principles and procedures for the resolution of conflicts between individuals and groups within a society. And, third, it sees to the enforcement and supervision of principles and policies concerning the allocation of resources.

With regard to the first of these demands, the legal system in a just social order must define and protect people's legal rights consistent with their generic rights to freedom and well-being. By contrast, widespread racism and discrimination in such non-just social orders as Nazi Germany and South Africa represent a blatant disregard for many people's generic rights. The legal systems in such societies, of course, lack legitimate authority. But even though citizens in those societies lack the legal rights consistent with their generic rights, they do have these generic rights. They have them whether or not they are recognized by themselves and others. In such societies, what justice demands is not what the legal system provides. Similarly in the United States; there we find that slaves were treated as chattel, on the same footing as cows and horses, during the almost one hundred years between the adoption of the Constitution and the ratification of the thirteenth, fourteenth, and fifteenth amendments. The law required that slaves who escaped to a free state and were there captured to be returned to their "owners." Certain judges enforced the Fugitive Slave Acts, even though they themselves were morally opposed to slavery. Dworkin, of course, says that this was a failure of jurisprudence. Judges, he argues, could have found in the general structure of the American Constitution conceptions of individual freedom, procedural justice, and federalism that were more central to the law than the transitory policies of the slavery compromise. Based on moral principles underlying or embedded in the American Constitution, the judges should have ruled in favor of the alleged runaway slaves.

But contrary to the conclusion reached by Dworkin's liberal theory of law, judges should have ruled in favor of the slaves *regardless* of what is contained in the Constitution. Because the Fugitive Slave Acts violated people's rights to freedom and well-being, these acts should not have been—morally speaking—enforced. In terms of the theory of legitimate authority developed in the present chapter,

328

the American legal system lacked legitimate authority and, therefore, imposed no obligation on citizens (including judges) to obey its dictates. Similarly with the general denial to women of the right to vote in the United States until the Nineteenth Amendement was ratified in 1920; not only should such gender-based discriminatory laws have been invalidated, but they served as clear evidence of the legal system's lack of legitimate authority. As in Nazi Germany and South Africa, the legal system failed to recognize and respect the equality of generic rights.

Within a just social order, there will be no room for such laws as the Fugitive Slave Acts since there can exist—consistent with the recognition and respect for everyone's rights to freedom and well-being—no category of persons who would occupy the position of slaves. Further, a just social order must contain a system of civil liberties whereby every adult person—black or white, male or female—is entitled to cast his or her vote as he or she pleases. These civil liberties, as we have seen, are ultimately justified by the equality of generic rights.

With regard to the second demand that a legal system must meet, the provision of principles and procedures for resolving conflicts, a just social order must again be regulated by institutions consistent with the equality of generic rights. The legal system must see to impartiality, adjudicative justice, and consistent and predictable legal administration. The public law must recognize that free individuals, with rights and duties, may come into conflict with one another, and the law must attempt to resolve these conflicts in terms of procedures that reflect the recognition of the individuals' status as moral beings. Similarly, the criminal law, which requires that wrongdoers "pay" for their crimes according to a scale of fixed penalties, also rests on the recognition of everyone's rights to freedom and well-being.

In the case of societies like Nazi Germany and South Africa, the notions of equal protection and personal rights as implemented by the requirement of due process are absent. A legal system with legitimate authority requires that all persons be treated in the same manner and have the same access to the services and benefits of society. But blacks in South Africa, as Jenkins notes, "do not enjoy either equal protection of the laws or due process of law, but are subject to special and pejorative legislative enactments and judicial procedures."[76] It is, of course, not only blacks in South Africa and

[76] Iredell Jenkins, *Social Order and the Limits of Law* (Princeton: Princeton University Press, 1980), p. 365.

Jews and gypsies in Nazi Germany who have lacked such protection. Throughout a long period in the history of the United States, for example, blacks did not have equal protection under the law, and many still do not today. Women in the United States and elsewhere also often lack equal protection and do not enjoy due process in the law. In most societies, in fact, large numbers of persons are without the protections that are required in terms of resolving conflicts between individuals and groups in a fair and just manner. In a just social order with a legitimate system of laws, by contrast, all techniques employed for ascertaining the relevant facts in cases at issue, for determining the applicable rules, and for imposing and enforcing sanctions will be utilized in such a way as to protect the equality of generic rights for all persons. The legal system will assure, for example, that qualified legal representation is made available to everyone on a fair and reasonable basis.

The third demand that the legal system must meet—the allocation of resources—is the one that will involve the greatest number of differences in a just social order regulated by a legitimate system of laws. As I noted in Chapter 2, people are able to exercise their generic right to freedom only when their right to well-being is realized. Unless individuals are able to realize a satisfactory level of security and subsistence, they will have no opportunity to enjoy the right to freedom. In most societies of the world today, many persons lack adequate security, food, housing, and medical care, as well as the capacity and/or opportunity to obtain these necessities for well-being. To the extent that they suffer such privations, individuals are unable to enjoy the rights to either freedom or well-being. The extent of such privation differs, of course, from one society to another.

Whether or not the inferior position of those who are unable to enjoy the right to well-being (and, thus, to freedom) is the direct result of harmful actions by other persons, the result is an inequality in the ability to effectively exercise their generic rights. In those instances where it can be clearly shown that the inequalities are the result of exploitation or harmful actions by others, the law must be utilized to help remove or at least reduce these inequalities. Even if those who are victims might be able to remedy their economic and other handicaps through their own efforts, people who have suffered systematic injustices are entitled to one or another type of rectification.[77] Policies of preferential treatment for blacks

---

[77] I discuss rectification at some length in Phillips, *Equality, Justice and Rectification.*

and women in the United States, for instance, may be viewed as attempts to improve the life-chances of persons who have been the victims of widespread prejudice and discrimination.

In other instances where the absence of the necessities for exercising the right to well-being are not the result of exploitation or harmful actions by others, those who are seriously disadvantaged may still be entitled to provision of the required necessities. This is certainly the case with those individuals who suffer handicaps and privations they cannot remedy through their own efforts. Thus, the physically and mentally handicapped, many of the elderly, and those born into extreme poverty have a claim on the rest of us for the provision of (at least) the minimal necessities required for enjoyment of the right to well-being.

Consistent with the principle of Generic Consistency, everyone has the right to be treated in the appropriate way when he or she requires certain basic necessities in order to enjoy the generic rights. Correspondingly, everyone has the duty to help people acquire such necessities when he or she has the ability to do so. As Gewirth points out:

> The PGC's requirement that agents act in accord with the rights of their recipients entails that all prospective purposive agents must refrain from harming one another and that in certain circumstances they must help one another if they can. Hence, limitations on their freedom to abstain from such help are rationally justified. The facts that only some persons may actually be threatened with harm or need help at a particular time, and that only some other persons may be in a position to inflict harm or give help, do not alter the universality of the PGC's provision for the protection of rights.[78]

If there are to be social rules to restore or create a general equality in the condition necessary for the exercise of the generic rights to freedom and well-being, such rules will have to be applied and made effective through the activities of the state, especially through democratically enacted laws that specify the necessary arrangements and also the ways in which such arrangements are to be realized. In a just social order, only the state with its legitimate legal system is able to help assure that the necessities will be securely provided as needed, that these benefits will be equitably and impartially distributed to those persons who need them, and

[78] Gewirth, *Reason and Morality*, p. 316.

331

that the duty to contribute to such arrangements—mainly through taxes—will be equitably distributed among all persons who have the required economic resources.

Contrary to the arguments of Nozick,[79] someone's right to freedom is not violated when he or she must pay taxes to help achieve or restore the well-being of people who are starving or lack adequate security, housing, or medical care. Since (as was shown in Chapter 2) every individual has an unavoidable concern with his or her own well-being, each must hold that he or she has a right to it and that all other persons also have this right. Thus, every individual must acknowledge that one ought to act to protect or secure the well-being of others if this can be done without comparable harm to oneself. If the affluent are taxed to help the needy, then, this is done in order to protect equally the rights of all persons. Of course, those paying such taxes—like everyone else—also have a right to freedom. But this right is relative to the requirement of agency on the part of each person. Since those without a satisfactory level of security and subsistence have no opportunity to enjoy their right to freedom, and since the nonvoluntary payment of taxes in order to help secure the well-being of the needy is far less consequential for the agency of the taxpayers, the needy's right to well-being and the affluents' payment of taxes must take precedence over the interference with the freedom of the persons taxed to use their money as they choose.

In fact, limitations on the affluents' right to freedom that are imposed by taxation do not constitute a loss of any freedom. As a rational agent, the taxpayer must rationally consent to perform this sort of action and hence does not lose any freedom. Should those who now enjoy a high level of well-being someday find themselves in serious need, they have the right to be treated in the appropriate way, i.e., to have their well-being restored through the levying of taxes on the more fortunate. Their present *duty* to help secure the well-being of others who lack the necessities for enjoying the right to well-being is, then, the logical correlate of their own *right* to similar treatment should the need arise; rights and duties are logically connected with being a rational agent.

In a just social order, therefore, the legal system must be concerned not only with peace-keeping and conflict resolution but must also devote considerable attention to meeting the demand of resource allocation. Concretely, this means that the legitimate au-

---

[79] Robert Nozick, *Anarchy, State, and Utopia* (New York: Basic Books, 1974), pp. 30–31, 170, 173, 238.

thority of the legal system must be utilized to assure that the essential services and benefits of society are made available to people on a fair basis. In some instances, as already noted, the legal system must oversee the redistribution of resources—mainly through taxation—so as to help assure that the necessary conditions for enjoyment of the rights to freedom and well-being are assured for everyone.

VI

I indicated in an earlier chapter that moral values that can be rationally justified are not only preferable in a moral sense but also in a sociological sense. That is, rationally justifiable moral values are far more likely to gain consensus than are the moral values people accept and internalize because of ignorance, coercion, tradition, and the like. Exactly the same holds for the legitimate authority of a system of laws. A rationally justifiable legal system creates far greater reliable conformity to its dictates than does a system based simply on a belief that it is legitimate. If that belief can be shown to be consistent with moral principles that justify a legal system's legitimate authority, then there is no problem. But if, as is usually the case, there is no rational justification for the legitimacy of a legal system, then it will have to keep its means of coercion in constant readiness. This will require a level of surveillance and control not necessary for a legitimate system of laws. It is for this very reason, of course, that all legal and political systems seek to clothe themselves in the garments of legitimacy.[80]

If a system of laws is to exercise social control in a just and effective manner, then, it must have legitimate authority. In those cases where socialization fails, i.e., when people either have not successfully internalized the appropriate norms concerning everyone's rights to freedom and well-being, or when they violate those norms, the law as a crucial mechanism of social control must come into play. Thus, it is necessary that a legal system be one to which people can give their obedience and respect.

As is clear from the work of such scholars as Habermas, Bell, and O'Connor, there is a widespread legitimacy crisis in Western societies today.[81] But, as we know, this is true not only for Western societies. All over the world, the ability of the state to justify its

---

[80] Wrong, *Power*, makes the same point.

[81] Habermas, *Legitimation Crisis*; Daniel Bell, *The Cultural Contradictions of Capitalism* (New York: Basic Books, 1977); James O'Connor, *The Corporation and the State* (New York: St. Martin's Press, 1974).

legitimacy in the eyes of its citizens is in jeopardy. In the East and West, alike, there is an increasing concern among the populace for the justice of the various social arrangements—economic, political, legal—that they experience as citizens of a particular society. Large numbers of people feel themselves caught in institutional arrangements they consider unworthy of commitment and allegiance. One consequence of this loss of legitimacy is that many persons today are lacking a sense of a social future they can identify with and can help bring about. More and more, as I argued in Chapter 5, individuals focus on a narrowly conceived "I." The emphasis is on authenticity and on what will bring the individual pleasure and reward, with the result that any possibility of justifying norms, ideals, and limits seems not only unlikely but even undesirable.

Those who believe that social norms and institutional arrangements can never be given a rational underpinning, identify with particular norms and arrangements only when it appears to be in their narrow self-interest to do so. Yet, as I indicated earlier, a sociological conception of social order requires that certain values and principles be internalized in all of a society's citizens. In this connection, George Herbert Mead wrote of the individual "who takes over the institutions of the community into his own conduct" and of social institutions "in which each individual would carry out the response in himself that he calls out in the community."[82]

If the rules, expectations, and laws encountered by people are ever to be voluntarily accepted and observed, they must be rationally justifiable. Otherwise, they will be viewed (as is now often the case) as obstacles to be defeated, circumvented, or simply resigned to. In a just social order, regulated by recognition and respect for everyone's rights to freedom and well-being, individual citizens will identify freely and rationally with its institutional arrangements and collective aspirations. The legitimate authority of its legal system will be rationally grounded and will impose on everyone an obligation to comply with its dictates.

Given my conclusion that we can rationally justify the legitimate authority of a system of laws and the wider political system it serves and, therefore, that there is an obligation of all citizens to obey the law, the next stop is to specify the sorts of institutional arrangements that should be found in a just social order. I turn to this task in the following chapter.

[82] George Herbert Mead in Anselm Strauss, ed., *The Social Psychology of George Herbert Mead* (Chicago: University of Chicago Press, 1958), p. 39.

IV

The Economic Realm

As I emphasized earlier, human beings require a stable and coherent social environment in which they are enabled to anticipate
and rely upon certain regularities and uniformities in the conduct
and expectations of others, to plan securely, and to work to attain
their purposes and realize their personal plans. A general context
of social order provides the necessary matrix for regularized social
relationships among the disparate individuals and groups that constitute a society.

Consistent with the views of many other sociologists, I have
argued that social order is often made possible by consensus about
the relevant normative standards, and that motivation to observe
these standards can be assured through the mechanisms of socialization and social control. But while most sociologists see the
appropriate normative standards as those which will achieve the
greatest degree of social order, I have tried to show—normatively
speaking—that it is necessary to specify and justify the particular
standards or principles that ought to command consensus. A society that is regulated by these rationally justified moral principles
and the institutional arrangements to which they give rise is what
I have termed a *just social order*.

Most of my analysis up to this point has been concerned with
the particular principles that constitute the criteria for a just social
order, with the socialization of children so that they will acquire
and be guided by these principles, and with the legal system the
principles require for their protection. The principles themselves,
i.e., the generic rights to freedom and well-being, and the institutional arrangements they suggest, allow for judgments about the
extent to which one or another concrete society has the general
characteristics of a just social order.

Although a theoretical concern with a just social order as a kind
of ideal in no way requires the providing of *details* about the specific
institutional arrangements to be found in a just society, such an
endeavor is certainly not precluded by this sort of analysis. I have,
in fact, already alluded to some specific arrangements in my discussions of socialization and the law in Parts II and III. Nevertheless, my main focus has been on theoretical rather than practical
questions. This has been necessary for an obvious reason: it is
impossible to even consider the practical questions before settling
the theoretical ones about the nature of a just social order. In the
following chapters, I will continue my concern with theoretical
issues, but will also consider some of the specific *economic* arrange-

ments necessary for helping to asure that everyone will be enabled to enjoy the rights to freedom and well-being.

In Chapter 7, I indicated that a just social order must be a political democracy, characterized by a constitution, specified procedures for electing public officials and enacting non-criminal laws, universal suffrage, fair elections and, of course, extensive liberties for everyone. Political democracy by itself, however, cannot guarantee that all persons will be able to effectively exercise their basic rights to freedom and well-being.

What is also necessary is that everyone have adequate food, clothing, housing, medical care, security, and protection. The absence of these basic goods is frequently accompanied by dependence, disease, and danger. Similarly with an inadequate level of education or income; they, too, hinder the right of people to engage in purpose-fulfilling action. Insofar as individuals lack a satisfactory level of these basic goods, they do not have an effective right to well-being. Further, of course, the effective right to freedom may also be adversely affected by the absence of basic goods. To the extent that an individual lacks adequate food, medical care, or protection, he is unable to voluntarily control his behavior. The lack of the basic necessities may interfere with a number of protected actions associated with the right to freedom: physical movement, speech, privacy, and personal autonomy more generally.

Provision of the basic necessities cannot be left up to the voluntary activity of various individuals and groups, since private charity is unlikely to assure full and adequate benefits for all who require them. Only the state has the ability to assure that these basic goods or benefits are securely provided as needed, that they are equitably and impartially distributed to those who need them, and that the taxes providing them are equitably collected from among those who have the required economic resources. It is for these reasons that, as noted in the previous chapter, the legal system in a just social order must be involved in meeting the demand for resource allocation.

As was shown in Chapter 2, those who lack the basic goods necessary for exercising their generic rights have a claim on the rest of us for the provision of the minimal necessities required for enjoyment of their rights. The legal system must, then, help oversee the distribution and redistribution of certain goods and benefits. More specifically, it must assure that people have the economic means required for obtaining these necessities.

But it needs to be acknowledged that a legal system with legitimate authority—that required for a just social order—cannot possibly exist unless people are already able to effectively exercise their generic rights. Since such effective exercise is itself dependent upon all persons having adequate food, shelter, medical care, etc., a legal system can have legitimate authority only where people do in fact have these basic goods. Assurance of an adequate level of basic goods is, then, a necessary condition for establishing the moral acceptability of a legal system. Whether or not people will have such an adequate level is connected with the manner in which goods and benefits are distributed and/or redistributed within a society. Thus, the provision of the economic goods and benefits that assure everyone of an adequate level of basic goods (necessary for effectively exercising his fundamental rights) has priority over the specification of the sort of legal system that ought to help regulate a just social order.

Exactly the same holds for socialization. Unless people have the necessary preconditions for enjoying their fundamental rights, there is little likelihood for developing in each person a respect for the rights to freedom and well-being of all others, of assuring a disposition to act in accordance with these rights, and of educating people in terms of the virtues and moral emotions. Without an adequate level of basic goods, so that both children and those responsible for their socialization are able to effectively exercise their generic rights, the kinds of processes specified in Chapter 5 cannot occur. Thus, certain basic necessities must be secured before successful moral socialization can take place.

What this means concretely, then, is that practical steps toward achieving a more just social order in the realms of socialization and legal authority can be realized only *after* the necessary economic preconditions have been established. These preconditions must, of course, be specified and justified on the basis of what is required for the effective exercise of the generic rights.

If the theory of justice defended in this volume is to be utilized to suggest ways of improving both the stability and the moral quality of contemporary Western societies, then particular principles and policies for the distribution and redistribution of economic benefits must be advanced and defended. For the concrete realization of a more just social order, these principles and policies in the economic realm have a higher moral priority and political practicality than those considered in regard to the socialization and social control mechanisms considered in Parts II and III. The following chapter will examine the viewpoints of Gewirth and others as they pertain to the distributive arrangements required in a just society. Finally, in Chapter 9, I will consider the sort of production system most suitable for a just social order, and will specify some of the economic principles and policies required for bringing contemporary advanced societies more into line with what justice demands.

EIGHT

Competing Views of Economic Justice:
Their Implications for Freedom
and Well-Being

GEWIRTH, Nozick, and Rawls have introduced theories of justice that have implications for the distributive arrangements required in a just society.[1] For that reason, they require additional consideration before I move on to suggest alternative arrangements for the just social order.

I

Gewirth's View

Gewirth emphasizes that people who labor under economic and other handicaps and privations do not have effective rights to well-being.[2] Thus, there is a justification for the social rules that serve to remove or at least reduce this inequality of effective rights. As I noted in the previous chapter, Gewirth distinguishes between a static and dynamic phase in the institutional justification of social rules and arrangements. In the *static* phase there must be rules to protect an existing equality of generic rights, while in the *dynamic* phase redistributive justice is required to eliminate inequalities and to move toward a previously nonexistent equality. Gewirth discusses this dynamic phase in terms of the "supportive state," under which various procedures for welfare, education, and other basic goods are considered.

Much of Gewirth's consideration of the supportive state concerns the duty of the better-off to help provide for those persons who are unable to effectively exercise their right to well-being. Since action is impossible with the loss of either life or freedom, efforts must be directed at preventing either loss. But in the case where

---

[1] Alan Gewirth, *Reason and Morality* (Chicago: University of Chicago Press, 1978); Robert Nozick, *Anarchy, State, and Utopia* (New York: Basic Books, 1972); and John Rawls, *A Theory of Justice* (Cambridge, Mass.: Harvard University Press, 1971).

[2] Gewirth, *Reason and Morality*, p. 312.

some persons lack adequate food or medical care, for example, other people's right to freedom may have to be justifiably infringed. Thus, in the case of imposing taxes for the protection or satisfaction of the generic right to well-being, the intention "is that of imposing relatively slight costs on some persons only in order to prevent far greater costs from having to be borne by other persons, so that an equality of generic rights for all persons may be more nearly approached."[3]

Gewirth emphasizes that in certain circumstances the requirements of some moral rules justified by the Principle of Generic Consistency (PGC) must be overridden by the requirements of other rules justified by the same principle. Central here is the idea that some goods are more necessary for action than others. In this regard, Gewirth specifies a "lexicographical" arrangement of principles in a serial order.[4] The basis for resolving conflicts among moral rules stems from the PGC as do, of course, the rules and prescribed duties themselves. These are discussed at considerable length by Gewirth, and he shows why one alternative has precedence over another. In the following conflicts between alternatives,

> the alternative listed first must in each case give way to the alternative listed second: . . . when one person's right to occurrent freedom conflicts with another person's right to basic well-being; . . . when a person's right to occurrent freedom conflicts with his own right to basic well-being; . . . when social rules or arrangements of voluntary associations conflict with the right to well-being; . . . when the right to retain one's property conflicts with laws of the supportive state providing for taxation to prevent basic harms such as starvation and to provide public goods. . . .[5]

Although Gewirth provides a long list of conflicts between alternatives justified by the PGC, I have included above only those referring to conflicts where well-being must take precedence over freedom. In every instance, the right to occurrent freedom is overridden by the duty to respect well-being. This overriding of the right to freedom does not mean, of course, that this generic right is violated, i.e., unjustifiably infringed. To the contrary, the right to freedom still preserves its independent status as a necessary

---

[3] Ibid., p. 344.
[4] Ibid., p. 340.
[5] Ibid., p. 341.

good for action. And it must be fully upheld so long as the right to basic well-being is not thereby infringed. But whenever some people's right to basic well-being can be fulfilled only by overriding other people's right to occurrent freedom, the former's right takes precedence insofar as it is more necessary for action.

One of the requirements for the supportive state, Gewirth says, is the specification of social rules for the distribution and redistribution of wealth. The aim of those rules favored by Gewirth is, he emphasizes, "for the most part meliorative rather than conservative or revolutionary."[6] The social rules recommended by Gewirth, then, fall between two extremes. He describes these extremes as follows:

> A certain libertarian extreme would defend the existing distribution of wealth, insofar as it has resulted from voluntary or contractual arrangements that ensue on an initial, presumably just acquisition. The other, egalitarian extreme proposes a drastic redistribution to be guided solely by the aim of maximally benefiting those who are least advantaged. The former extreme does not recognize the independent right to well-being, including additive goods, on the part of those whose initial position in life subjects them to serious disadvantages. The latter extreme does not recognize the independent right to freedom as applied in the production of valued commodities and the consequent earnings in income. Thus the two extreme overlook, respectively, the claims of severe economic need and the claims of desert as based on voluntary effort and accomplishment.[7]

As Gewirth makes clear, he associates these two extremes with Nozick ("conservatives") and Rawls ("revolutionary").

In contrast to the positions of Nozick and Rawls, which are seen as ignoring, respectively, the independent right to well-being and the independent right to freedom, the Principle of Generic Consistency recognizes the claims of both freedom and well-being: "Act in accord with the generic rights of your recipients as well as of yourself." With regard to economic distribution, Gewirth says that the aim of the rules generated by the PGC is a double one: to permit the free exertion of productive effort to reap its rewards,

---

[6] Ibid.
[7] Ibid., pp. 312–13.

and to provide compensating basic goods or benefits for those who lack an adequate level.[8]

Gewirth speaks here of "moderately equalizing and hence re-distributive conditions," and mentions the need for fostering the availability of productive work and assuring the presence of sufficient employment opportunities.[9] There have to be rules, he writes, that "provide for supplying basic goods, such as food and housing, to those persons who cannot obtain them by their own efforts."[10] Rules are also required to improve the "capacities for productive work of persons who are deficient in this respect."[11] Gewirth mentions education as being especially important in this connection. Further, there must be rules that provide for supplying various public goods; for example, unpolluted air, public roads, and fire protection. These public goods not only help everyone in society, says Gewirth, but also serve to increase the opportunities for productive employment.[12] In addition, the state must help to facilitate an increase in the general level of wealth in the society.[13] The maximization of wealth, Gewirth states, will not only make the poor better off, but will also further the distributive aim of maintaining an equality of generic rights whereby the freedom and well-being of the rich and poor alike will be similarly protected.[14]

Although Gewirth emphasizes the need for the state to assure that basic goods are securely provided as needed, he never specifies how this is to be accomplished. His main concern as regards the exercise of effective rights is on the provision of productive work, the maximization of wealth within a society, and the assurance of equality of opportunities.[15] Gewirth continually stresses that persons suffering from economic deprivations must be helped,[16] but he fails to specify the institutional arrangements necessary for this to be accomplished. Despite his strong emphasis on the needs for adequate food, housing, medical care, and other basic goods, Gewirth never speaks of a social minimum or of anything like guaranteed welfare rights. Whatever the many strengths of his work,

[8] Ibid., p. 313.
[9] Ibid.
[10] Ibid., p. 314.
[11] Ibid.
[12] Ibid.
[13] Ibid., p. 318.
[14] Ibid.
[15] Ibid.
[16] Ibid., p. 315.

then, Gewirth has very little to say with regard to how the necessary preconditions for enjoyment of the basic rights to freedom and well-being are to be assured.

Given the general absence of any discussion of specific institutional arrangements in Gewirth and his claims about the conservative and revolutionary consequences of the two extremes represented by Nozick and Rawls, it is appropriate that we consider these two theories anew. My concern here is to see what bearing the application of each of these theories would have on the distribution and redistribution of wealth and income. More specifically, I want to see how their preferred rules for distribution and redistribution would affect the demand of a just social order that everyone have the necesssary preconditions for effectively exercising the rights to freedom and well-being.

Nozick's Conservative View

I have already considered Nozick's entitlement theory at some length in Chapter 2, and have pointed to both its strengths and weaknesses. Nevertheless, the essentials of his argument bear repeating. According to Nozick, individuals obtain absolute control over their holdings (goods, money, property) through historical processes. Through the initial act of acquisition (only vaguely specified by Nozick), the individual acquires unlimited rights to use and dispose of various holdings as he or she sees fit. If someone has acquired holdings in accordance with Nozick's principle of acquisition (which I criticized in Chapter 2), then he may retain or transfer the ownership of them only at his own discretion. All compulsory transferences (for example, taxation), Nozick insists, constitute an infringement on rights. Not surprisingly, therefore, only a laissez-faire economic order satisfies Nozick's normative requirements. And related, of course, is the important moral conclusion that we have no obligation to help the worse off among us.

One of the strengths of Nozick's work, as I noted earlier, is that it reminds us that whatever is to be distributed (equally or not) usually comes already "tied" to particular persons. Further, he demonstrates clearly that there is a general absence of any rational justification for economic equality among social and political theorists. Since Nozick sees entitlement as the ultimate grounding for economic rewards, he is required to provide a justification for the rights he emphasizes so strongly and he must be specific about what constitutes a morally acceptable acquisition of holdings. The fact that he falls short in regard to both requirements constitutes a serious weakness in his whole theory.

But aside from these considerations, both the strengths and weaknesses of Nozick's general notion of entitlement are, as Peter Singer points out, readily apparent.[17] On the one hand, can it be just that one baby comes into the world with a high trust fund, is raised in a family situation where all of life's necessities are in abundance, can look forward to the best possible schooling, and has the certainty of eventually taking over control and ownership of his father's large corporation, while another baby is born to poverty, will not have even the barest necessities, and can anticipate an inadequate education and a life of low-level employment with meager rewards?

On the other hand, if the first father acquired his holdings in a morally acceptable manner, violating no one's rights in the process, doesn't he have the right to give whatever is his to his son or daughter, if he so chooses? And wouldn't the second father have done the same if he had been able to acquire a larger amount of holdings? What if, to complicate matters further, the second father had acquired his very limited holdings in a morally unacceptable manner, violating other people's rights—perhaps through theft or extortion—and therefore passed on to his child various things to which he was not himself entitled? How are we to judge the moral standing of these different scenarios?

If we compare the situation of the rich father, who acquired his vast holdings in a morally acceptable manner, with the poor father who acquired his meager holdings in a manner that is not morally acceptable, then—following Nozick—we must conclude that the first father is entitled to give whatever he wants to his child, while the poor father is not, since he obtained his holdings in an unjust manner. That is, the rich father is entitled to his justly acquired acquisitions and, therefore, can transfer them and their benefits to his child or to anyone else he chooses. The poor father, by contrast, is not entitled to his unjustly acquired holdings, and it is thus not legitimate for him to pass on his ill-gotten gains. Were we to subdivide the fathers of a given society into two groups—the rich and the poor—within each group we would undoubtedly find some men who are entitled to their holdings and some who are not. If

[17] See, for example, Peter Singer, "The Right to be Rich or Poor," *The New York Review of Books* 22, 3 (1975) 19–24; and Jeffrey Paul, ed., *Reading Nozick* (Oxford: Basil Blackwell, 1981).

we had a precise theory of entitlement and exact historical information as to how people had actually acquired their holdings, we could divide all fathers (or breadwinners) into those who are entitled to their holdings and those who are not. But what about the children, wives, and perhaps parents and other relatives who may be dependent on these men for their economic support and survival?

Surely it is not just that the economic situation and life-chances of these other persons should be *totally dependent* on either the extent of the father's holdings or the moral acceptability of the processes through which the holdings were acquired. To see this, let us simplify greatly and classify the fathers of a given society on the basis of whether they are rich or poor *and* in terms of whether or not they are entitled to their holdings. Such a classification yields four separate groupings: rich and entitled, rich but not entitled, poor and entitled, and poor and not entitled.

Let us assume for now that the first group constitutes no moral problem; they have, after all, acquired their holdings in a morally acceptable way and are fully capable of taking care of themselves and their loved ones. But how are we to respond to the situation of the others? According to Nozick's rectification principle, those in the second group—whose highly advantageous socio-economic status results from morally impermissible historical processes—are required to provide rectification to those persons (or their descendants) whose rights they violated. Even assuming that such rectification could be provided, would it be just that the other family relations of someone who has acquired holdings in an unjust manner (or whose father or grandfather or some other distant relative has done so) must now be cast into poverty? If application of the rectification principle requires that one's present holdings be reduced to what they would have been had no historical injustices taken place, then the standard of living of the contemporary beneficiaries of past injustices will be remarkably lowered. Again, the question is whether it is entirely just that these other family members should be made to suffer for the injustices committed by others.

The third group, consisting of poor families where the father (or other breadwinner) has acquired holdings in a just manner, also constitutes a problem. But here it is poverty, and not issues of entitlement and rectification, that raises the moral problem. Even if the father is entitled to some moral credit for having acquired his meager holdings in a just manner, is it just that other family members should suffer simply because he is—for one reason or

347

another—unable to provide for them? In fact, given the father's own moral credit, is there not perhaps an injustice involved in his remaining poor? The "poor but honest" are, as already noted, clearly entitled to their limited holdings. But are they not entitled to something more?

Things are no easier with regard to the fourth group: those who are poor despite the fact that the father (or an ancestor) has violated the rights of others so far as his holdings are concerned and is, therefore, not even entitled to his present holdings. Given the fact that those in this category are already poor, would it be just to apply a rectification principle that would put the family in even more desperate economic straits? Even if we were to agree that the father should in some way be punished for his misdeeds, is it just that other family members should also have to suffer?

Clearly, then, notions of entitlement and rectification on the individual level (i.e., where it is to be paid by one individual to another in order to correct earlier injustices) don't by themselves take us very far in terms of dealing with the inequality of effective rights.[18] Aside from the absence of a full-fledged, systematic theory of entitlement, there is the serious issue of whether it is just to tie the socio-economic standing of other family members entirely to the moral acceptability of the historical process through which the breadwinner has acquired his or her holdings. Is it not morally abhorrent that the poor—whether or not their poverty is a result of unjust acquisitions—should be unable to realize the necessary conditions for the effective exercise of their rights, i.e., adequate food, housing, medical care, and security? Is it not normally distasteful that family members must have their standard of living radically reduced when, in other cases, rectification is required because of someone else's unjust acquisition? And even with the seemingly least problematic group, those rich persons who benefit from the breadwinner's justly acquired wealth, is there not something morally unsatisfactory about their being so very well off compared to others?

In fact, it is difficult to see how Nozick could seriously propose universal moral principles without considering what it would be like if they were universally *applied*. Certainly, when we pass from an abstract to a more substantive description of their applica-

---

[18] I discuss this at length in Derek L. Phillips, *Equality, Justice and Rectification* (London: Academic Press, 1979).

tion, the implausibility of Nozick's principles becomes glaringly apparent.

Just as Gewirth claims, then, Nozick's entitlement theory fails to recognize the independent right to well-being. But furthermore, it also makes it virtually impossible for many persons to exercise their right to freedom. As indicated earlier, a mutual dependence holds between enjoyment of the basic rights to freedom and well-being. People cannot meaningfully exercise their right to freedom unless their right to well-being, i.e., to security, subsistence, and the like, is recognized and respected. And, conversely, enjoyment of the right to well-being itself depends upon exercise of the right to freedom. Unless people have the freedom to demand certain social guarantees as a right, they cannot enjoy their right to well-being. Thus, Gewirth is quite obviously correct in referring to Nozick's theory as "conservative."

Rawls's "Revolutionary" View

But what about the position formulated by Rawls? Is this, as Gewirth claims, really revolutionary in its implications? To answer this question, it is necessary to consider Rawls's "difference principle." This principle, it may be recalled, marks the limit of acceptable inequality. It states that "social and economic inequalities are to be arranged so that they are both (a) to the greatest benefit of the least advantaged consistent with the savings principle, and (b) attached to offices and positions open to all under conditions of fair equality of opportunity."[19] To simplify my discussion, I will omit any consideration of the just savings principle and of section (b) of the different principle.

With the utilization of the difference principle, social and economic inequalities are to be arranged so that they are reasonably expected to be of most benefit to the least advantaged. The principle is not concerned with eliminating all economic inequalities, but with improving the position of the "worst off." An important question, then, is who constitutes the worst off, whose position is to be improved as much as possible? It is not, Rawls makes clear, the individual with the smallest amount of primary goods (economic and social benefits). The reason he gives for this is as follows: "Another thing to bear in mind is that when principles mention persons, or require that everyone gain from an inequality, the reference is to representative persons holding the various social

[19] Rawls, *A Theory of Justice*, p. 302.

349

positions, or offices, or whatever, established by the basic structure."[20] Thus, Rawls assumes that "it is possible to assign an expectation of well-being to representative individuals holding these positions."[21] Although the problem of indentifying the worst-off representative persons is obviously an important one, Rawls gives it very little attention. He offers only two alternatives:

> One possibility is to choose a particular social position, say that of the unskilled worker, and then to count as the least advantaged all those with the average income of this group, or less. The expectation of the lowest representative man is defined as the average over this whole class. Another alternative is a definition solely in terms of relative income and wealth with no reference to social position. Thus all persons with less than half of the median income and wealth may be taken as the least advantaged segment.[22]

Unfortunately, Rawls has little to say about special payments for sickness and unemployment (which are merely mentioned), and concentrates instead on the position of the least advantaged group. Thus, no allowance is made for the particular needs of individuals. Sick people, individuals with many children, blind persons, and the like, are not to be provided with special resources. Since the worst-off representative person is, in Rawls's own examples, the average unskilled worker or someone with less than the median income, his difference principle does not allow us to look behind the distribution of wealth and income to personal circumstances, which would give the same income a radically different significance for different people. The difference principle is insufficiently sensitive to the position of those who are, for example, seriously sick or handicapped. Since worst off is defined economically, such persons will not be seen as constituting a worst-off group. In short, the difference principle is not really concerned with maximizing the position of the worst-off individuals.

With regard to the position of the least advantaged, Rawls considers whether the difference principle can be used to improve the position of the bottom through a tax-transfer structure and other remedies. The difference principle requires a "social minimum." Among the ways of achieving this, Rawls mentions special pay-

[20] Ibid., p. 64.
[21] Ibid.
[22] Ibid., p. 98.

ments for sickness and unemployment, and monetary transfer systems such as a negative income tax.[23] Thereafter, the social minimum is maintained through such mechanisms as taxes and limits on the rights of bequest. But once the social minimum is thus assured, Rawls has no objection to an unequal distribution of economic benefits.[24]

Considering the distribution of income among social classes, Rawls says that large inequalities are permissible if lowering them would make the working class even worse off.[25] Thus, increases in the salaries and wages paid to the more advantaged are acceptable if they improve the position of the least advantaged. Such increases are not acceptable if they in any way adversely affect the position of the least advantaged. Rawls believes that there is a general tendency for the situation of the worst off to be improved by improvements in the prospects of the more advantaged. He writes:

[A]s we raise the expectations of the more advantaged the situation of the worst off is continuously improved. Each such increase is in the latter's interest, up to a certain point anyway. For the greater expectations of the more favored presumably cover the costs of training and encourage better performances thereby contributing to the general advantage. While nothing guarantees that inequalities will not be significant, there is a persistent tendency for them to be leveled down by the increasing availability of educated talent and ever-widening expectation.[26]

Rawls does not, of course, allow that the competitive price system will be totally determinative of distributive shares. This is because it ignores the claims of need and an appropriate standard of living.[27] As noted above, a social minimum will be assured through various transfers. Once a suitable minimum is provided by these transfers, it is perfectly fair that the rest of the total income be settled by the price system.[28] This way of dealing with the claims of need, Rawls says, "would appear to be more effective than trying

[23] Ibid., p. 275.
[24] Ibid., p. 277.
[25] Ibid., p.78.
[26] Ibid., p. 158.
[27] Ibid., p. 277.
[28] Ibid.

to regulate income by minimum wage standards, and the like."[29] Thus, the justice of the distributive shares turns on whether the total income of the least advantaged (wages plus transfers) is such as to maximize their long-run expectations.[30]

The important question here, of course, is: How generous should the social minimum be? It might seem, Rawls observes, that the difference principle requires a very high minimum.[31] This, he quickly adds, is a misconception. Instead, "The appropriate expectation in applying the difference principle is that of the long-term prospects of the least favored extending over future generations."[32] Long-term prospects must be considered because of the requirement that each generation put aside a suitable amount of real capital accumulation. This involves investments in machinery and other means of production, education, training, and the like.[33] Once we know how great such investments should be (which requires a just savings principle), the level of the social minimum is determined. Rawls points out that it is not possible at present to define precisely what the rate of savings should be. Nevertheless, the point is clear.[34]

Say that an existing social minimum is increased by transfers paid for by various sorts of taxes. Raising the minimum then increases the general level of taxation. As this level becomes higher, there comes a point at which one of two things happens:

> Either the appropriate savings cannot be made or the greater taxes interfere so much with economic efficiency that the prospects of the least advantaged in the present generation are no longer improved but begin to decline. In either event the correct minimum has been reached. The difference principle is satisfied and no further increase is called for.[35]

The correct social minimum, then, is that which is achieved without any adverse effects on efficiency or appropriate savings. When the difference principle is fully realized,[36] it is presumably impossible to make any one representative person better off without making

[29] Ibid.
[30] Ibid.
[31] Ibid., p. 285.
[32] Ibid.
[33] Ibid.
[34] Ibid., p. 286.
[35] Ibid.
[36] Ibid., p. 79.

another worse off, namely, the least advantaged representative individual. In such an instance, the difference principle is fully compatible with efficiency. If the taxes paid by the better off are too high, this will result in inefficiency; the situation of the least advantaged can be improved only at the cost of making the better placed worse off. Similarly with investments and appropriate savings; if taxes are too high, the more advantaged will be unable to put aside what is necessary for the future.

All of this points to the central place of "incentives" in Rawls's conception of the difference principle. He believes that high economic incentives are necessary in order that competent people will fulfill the most demanding and important positions, that investments will be stimulated, and efficiency increased. This is, of course, a widely shared assumption in most societies of the world today. Because of its considerable importance for questions of distribution, it deserves special attention. I will examine it in some detail in Section II.

My concern at this point, however, is with the possible consequences of applying Rawls's difference principle to contemporary industrialized societies. The question is whether the transfer and redistributive mechanisms required by Rawls to assure a social minimum would also be sufficient for all persons to effectively exercise their generic rights.

As I showed earlier, such effective exercise requires that everyone have adequate food, housing, clothing, medical care, security, and protection. It is true, of course, that I have not specified precisely (nor does Gewirth) what is intended by "adequate" in this regard. While it might be possible to specify the minimum requirements of food to keep someone alive, an adequate level of food, as I conceive of it here, to some extent depends on the general level of development of the society in which the individual finds himself. In a highly industrialized society like the United States or West Germany, for example, people must have a diet of sufficient nutritional value to allow them to perform normal kinds of physical and intellectual activities. This means that they must not be prevented from attending school, undergoing training, earning their livelihood, or engaging in leisure-time activities by reason of sickness, disease, or long-standing illness, all of which interfere with the effective exercise of their generic rights. Similarly with the other conditions for effective exercise of their rights; there must be an adequate level of the necessities required for enjoyment of these rights within the society where one lives.

In my view, application of Rawls's difference principle would *not* assure an adequate level of the necessary goods and services.[37] The major reason for this concerns Rawls's emphasis on incentives. With the difference principle, as we saw earlier, an unequal distribution of wealth and income is justified if and only if it will maximize benefits to the least advantaged segments within a society. But if, as Rawls assumes, these inequalities must be rather large, than it seems likely that the actual benefits—even if maximized—will not be sufficient to provide an adequate level of the basic goods required for enjoyment of the generic rights. Even if the actual economic benefits are sufficient to provide an adequate level for the least advantaged segment, they will fail to do so for those persons who require extra medical care, protection, or other basic goods. This is a consequence of the fact, noted earlier, that the difference principle makes no allowance for the particular needs of especially disadvantaged individuals.

Very much contrary to what Gewirth claims, then, Rawls's theory of justice hardly constitutes a "revolutionary extreme." Application of the difference principle does not involve, as Gewirth asserts, a drastic redistribution of wealth. It is, rather, the fact that the redistribution is not drastic enough which makes it unlikely that an adequate level of the basic goods needed for all persons to effectively exercise their generic rights would be assured.

If, as Gewirth argues (and I agree), effective exercise of the fundamental rights to freedom and well-being requires an adequate level of medical care, housing, and other basic necessities for everyone, then application of Rawls's difference principle is not a way of assuring this effective exercise. While Gewirth argues that Rawls goes too far in assuring well-being, I believe that he doesn't go nearly far enough.

Be that as it may, Gewirth insists that Rawls is guilty of not giving sufficient weight to the right to freedom. What he intends here, apparently, is not the general generic right to freedom but the exercise of freedom in the economic realm. Rawls, according to Gewirth, "does not recognize the independent right to freedom as applied in the production of valued commodities and the consequent earnings of income."[38] He does not give enough attention to "contributions" and the "free exertion of productive effort to

[37] A similar conclusion is reached by Robert Paul Wolff, *Understanding Rawls* (Princeton: Princeton University Press, 1977); and by Brian Barry, *The Liberal Theory of Justice* (Oxford: Oxford University Press, 1973).

[38] Gewirth, *Reason and Morality*, p. 313.

reap its rewards" and to provide "compensating goods to those who are disadvantaged." But this depiction of Rawls is surely a caricature of his position. He clearly allows free exercise of contributions and productive capacities once the condition of the least advantaged has been (in his view) secured.

Gewirth's real (i.e., deep) objection to Rawls's standpoint is, I believe, a bit different. What he finds totally unacceptable is Rawls's treatment of "desert." The revolutionary Rawlsian extreme, he says, "overlooks the claims of desert as based on voluntary effort and accomplishment."[39] He then quickly adds the following sentence: "The retort that all effort is a product of forces beyond the agent's control ignores that persons with similar advantaged socioeconomic backgrounds may differ drastically in the ways they voluntarily marshal the resources available to them."[40]

It is Gewirth's view, then, that those persons who exert more effort and make a greater contribution are therefore "deserving" of greater earnings. This claim that those who contribute the most are deserving of greater rewards is, of course, a familiar one. In fact, it is probably the major principle of distribution in most societies. Thus, it requires careful examination for two reasons: (1) it is a point of contention between Gewirth and Rawls, and (2) it is at present operative in most societies of the world.

Desert

As noted earlier, Gewirth objects strongly to Rawls's treatment of desert. He says that Rawls overlooks the claims of desert as based on people's voluntary efforts, contributions, and accomplishments. Like many others, then, Gewirth holds that those who contribute more are deserving of higher economic rewards. In capitalist and socialist societies alike, we find the same principle at work: differentials in pay and wages are appropriate rewards for those men and women who have undergone the training or schooling necessary for performing jobs that require unusual skill or talent, who bear responsibility, are highly productive, or contribute more to the social and economic welfare of society. Thus, those who produce or contribute more are, therefore, "deserving" of more in return.

Since the desert principle is central to income distributions in

39 Ibid.
40 Ibid.

capitalist and socialist societies alike,[41] it is worth considering in some detail. I will begin by examining the general notion of desert, and will then turn to the issue of whether or not people can be said to deserve the differential rewards they actually receive.

If someone can be said to be "deserving" of something, it must be *in virtue* of some possessed characteristic, quality, or prior activity.[42] That is, judgments about desert are justified on the basis of certain facts about individuals. "It is because no one can deserve anything unless there is some basis or ostensible occasion for the desert," writes Feinberg, "that judgments of desert carry with them a commitment to the giving of reasons."[43] We cannot claim, for example, that Smith deserves our praise or thanks although he has done "nothing in particular." In asserting that Smith deserves praise or thanks (or punishment, or whatever), we must be ready to answer the question, For what? Unless we can supply a basis for Smith's desert, we are not really using the correct terminology. If someone deserves something, it must be for some particular reason. Thus, the notion of desert requires a basis (a reason).

However, not any old basis will do. Whatever facts serve as the basis of someone's desert must be facts about him or her. If Smith deserves a higher wage than he is now earning, it must be in virtue of his previous training, skill, responsibilities, or something similar, and not because he will be angry or disappointed if he doesn't earn more money. Of course, we might still say that it would be a good thing for Smith if he were given a higher wage (because otherwise, for instance, he will be depressed and unhappy). Although this fact might be a reason for his employer's action, it cannot be the basis of Smith's desert.

"Deserving" something is not the same as being "entitled" to it. Being entitled to something involves a right, claim, or promise. An individual may be deserving of, say, a higher income in virtue of some specific thing that he has done. Or he may be entitled to a higher income on the basis of his having been promised it by his employer, or because he has satisfied clearly defined conditions of his work role. Thus, individuals can be entitled to rewards that

[41] See, for example, Henry Phelps Brown, *The Inequality of Pay* (Oxford: Oxford University Press, 1977); Frank Parkin, *Marxism and Class Theory* (London: Tavistock Publication, 1979); and Frank Parkin, *Class, Inequality and Political Order* (London: Paladin Books, 1972).

[42] See the excellent discussions in Joel Feinberg, *Doing and Deserving* (Princeton: Princeton University Press, 1970); and in Lawrence C. Becker, *Property Rights* (London: Routledge & Kegan Paul, 1977).

[43] Feinberg, *Doing and Deserving*, p. 58.

they do not deserve, or deserving of rewards to which they are not entitled. Imagine that someone is to be selected for promotion to supervisor from among those working in a particular organization. One of the candidates, Smith, is widely recognized as "deserving" of promotion to this post: he is the best trained, most responsible and reliable, and has the greatest skill of all those who apply. But another candidate, Jones, although lacking all the attributes possessed by Smith, is clearly "entitled" to promotion to supervisor on the basis of a long-forgotten rule that makes mandatory the selection of the most senior employee. Clearly, then, desert and entitlement are in conflict there—as they are in numerous real-life situations.

It makes a considerable difference, of course, whether economic rewards are to be linked to desert, on the one hand, or to entitlement, on the other. Since I already considered entitlement in this regard, the following discussion will focus exclusively on desert.

It is apparently the almost universal acceptance of the principle of desert that accounts for the normative acceptability of income differentials in all societies. At least, this is the viewpoint defended in a recent article by Della Fave concerning the legitimation of stratification. "Legitimation," states Della Fave, "refers to a belief on the part of a large majority of the populace that institutionalized inequality in the distribution of primary resources—such as power, wealth, and prestige—is essentially right and reasonable."[44]

Like Weber, Della Fave mentions the need of people to see their advantages or disadvantages as deserved. According to Weber, "He who is more favored feels the never ceasing need to look upon . . . his advantages as 'deserved,' and the others' disadvantages as being brought about by the latter's fault."[45] In fact, says Della Fave, under most circumstances, "Those in power are assumed to be contributing more and are, therefore, seen as deserving of greater rewards."[46]

But do people really deserve the differential rewards they receive, either in capitalist or socialist societies? Della Fave apparently thinks they do, since he takes the populace's belief about institutionalized inequality as the ultimate criterion for its rightness or legitimacy. If, as he argues,[47] the very fact that some persons are

[44] L. Richard Della Fave, "The Meek Shall Not Inherit the Earth," *American Sociological Review* 45 (December 1980): 955–71.

[45] Max Weber, *Economy and Society*, trans. and ed. Guenther Roth and Claus Wittich (Totowa, N.J.: Bedminster Press, 1968), 3: 953.

[46] Della Fave, "The Meek," p. 960.

[47] Ibid., p. 961.

wealthy or powerful is taken as evidence by most people that they are contributing more than other persons and, therefore, are deserving of such high rewards, then those with most of the "spoils" are indeed deserving. The fact that most people accept the ideological standpoint that those with higher incomes and greater power are contributing more, and hence deserve their greater rewards, settles it for Della Fave.

But Rawls, to the contrary, raises serious objections to the general notion of economic desert. It is these objections that Gewirth has in mind when he says that Rawls overlooks the claims of justice arising from people's efforts and contributions. In discussing his two principles of justice, which I examined in Chapter 2, Rawls states:

> [They] seem to be a fair agreement on the basis of which those better endowed, or more fortunate in their social position, *neither of which we can be said to deserve*, could expect the willing cooperation of others. . . . Once we decide to look for a conception of justice that nullifies the accidents of natural endowments and the contingencies of social circumstance . . . we are led to these principles. They express the result of leaving aside those aspects of the social world that seem *arbitrary from a moral point of view*.[48]

Rawls goes on:

> Perhaps some will think that the person with greater natural endowments deserves those aspects and the superior character that makes their development possible. Because he is more worthy in this sense, he deserves the greater advantages that he could achieve with them. This view, however, is surely incorrect. . . . [No] one deserves his place in the distribution of native endowments, any more than one deserves one's initial starting place in society. . . . [His] character depends in large part upon fortunate family and social circumstances *for which he can claim no credit*.[49]

I noted earlier that for someone to be deserving of something, it must be in virtue of some possessed characteristic or prior activity. If people deserve, it is in virtue of those facts about themselves. But, says Rawls, those facts themselves are not deserved. Someone

---

[48] Rawls, *A Theory of Justice*, p. 15. Italics added.

[49] Ibid., p. 103. For the argument that Marx held a very similar view, see Richard J. Arneson, "What's Wrong with Exploitation?" *Ethics* 91 (January 1981): 202–07.

can be said to be deserving of the rewards accruing to greater labor contribution only if he or she is deserving of those facts (greater strength or intelligence, for example) that are responsible for greater contribution. That is, the facts that justify a desert-claim are the ultimate "grounds for deserving." If, therefore, someone claims to deserve his greater economic rewards simply because it "happens" to be true that he is stronger or more intelligent than other people, Rawls would reject such a claim. An individual who deserves something must be able to, in Rawls's formulation, "claim credit" for the ground being true to him. Since no one can claim credit for his strength or intelligence, no one deserves them, and no one deserves the differential rewards that follow from these facts about themselves.

This argument, at least as formulated, leads to an infinite regress. Imagine that Smith claims to deserve his high income in virtue of his greater ability to contribute to labor. Then it has to be shown that he deserves his greater ability. His greater ability, he claims, is deserved in virtue of his having acquired enormous knowledge in the university. But he can deserve his university education only in virtue of some new ground, perhaps his high intelligence. But, again, he must now deserve to have high intelligence. This requires yet another grounding, so that the conditions for deserving are never fully satisfied by anyone. The consequence of this line of argument is that "no one ever deserves anything." What this means, of course, is that the whole notion of desert disappears entirely.

Despite this unhappy conclusion, let us grant that the never-ending sequence of deserving to deserve to deserve . . . is inevitable. Let us accept Rawls's conclusion that the facts about us that ground our desert-claims are "arbitrary from a moral point of view." But even if we accept this, can it not still be said that we deserve something on the basis of what *we do* with those facts: our strength, intelligence, character, or whatever? This is clearly what Gewirth intends when he writes in criticism of Rawls that "persons with similar advantaged socioeconomic backgrounds may differ drastically in the ways they voluntarily marshal the resources available to them."[50]

Rawls says that no one can deserve something in virtue of a ground (e.g., intelligence) that just happens to be true of him or her. The question is whether or not this also holds for effort. Ge-

[50] Gewirth, *Reason and Morality*, p. 313.

wirth believes that it does not. But Rawls says that it does, asserting that "it seems clear that the effort a person is willing to make is influenced by his natural abilities and skills and the alternatives open to him. The better endowed are more likely, other things being equal, to strive conscientiously, and there seems to be no way to discount for their greater good fortune."[51] Thus, the effort that an individual is able to make is influenced by such things as his family background. If, for example, someone is born to parents who emphasize the importance of trying, applying oneself, persevering in the face of difficulties, and the like, he or she will probably be able to exert more effort than someone whose upbringing places less stress on these things. If this argument is correct, then the desert-for-effort argument of Gewirth will fail.

At the very least, it seems apparent that the whole notion of desert is quite problematic. If, as is often claimed, desert *should* depend entirely upon what is within an individual's control, on his own efforts and the choices that he makes, then it is clear that people cannot be said to deserve their native endowments: intelligence, beauty, and perhaps strength and agility. Although Gewirth argues that people are deserving of whatever they are able to achieve on the basis of what they *do* with their native endowments, this is called into question by Rawls. But, for me at least, there is something to be said for Gewirth's position concerning the use of one's resources. Rawls's argument that no one deserves anything is so totally deterministic as to leave no room at all for the exercise of individual initiative, control, and responsibility.[52]

Nevertheless, these considerations of desert do raise serious questions about the general principle that those who contribute more are deserving of higher wages and salaries. If this is to be a genuine principle for the distribution of economic benefits and rewards, then I would think that rewards ought to be proportional *not* to actual contributions but to the part of each person's contributions that can be attributed to those abilities and efforts he or she can be shown to really deserve. As things now stand, however, no one has yet been able to establish what people "really" deserve.

Summarizing my review of the applications of the theories of Gewirth, Nozick, and Rawls, I conclude that *none* of their various principles concerning the distribution and redistribution of wealth

[51] Rawls, *A Theory of Justice*, p. 213.

[52] Gewirth, *Reason and Morality*, p. 331. A similar view is expressed by Nozick, *State, Anarchy, and Utopia*, p. 214.

and income would satisfy the demand of a just social order that everyone be assured of the necessary preconditions for effectively exercising their generic rights.

II

Contributions and Rewards

Rawls and Gewirth differ, of course, in their conceptions of desert as it pertains to the distribution of economic rewards. They also differ about how the needs of the disadvantaged are to be met. Rawls views the distribution of natural talents as a common asset, with an unequal distribution of economic rewards being acceptable only insofar as it benefits the least advantaged. Gewirth has a different view about natural assets, but holds that the wealthy have an obligation to assist those who are unable to effectively exercise their rights.

Despite these differences, it is striking that Rawls and Gewirth are in general agreement about the workings of the economic system and about the general mechanisms that underly it. To a large extent, they also seem to share Nozick's assumptions in this regard.

Gewirth, as already noted, claims that those who produce or contribute more are deserving of greater rewards. Of course, he does emphasize that the means of acquiring wealth and income must be distributed equally. But once that is assured (and he never tells us how), people are viewed as deserving of the unequal economic rewards they acquire on the basis of their differential contributions. Rawls denies that desert plays any role here, but he has no objection to an unequal distribution of rewards (so long as it also benefits the least advantaged). Let us consider what Rawls says in this regard.

The distribution of income and wages will be just, he says, once a workably competitive price system is properly organized and embedded in a just basic structure.[53] In a competitive economy, observes Rawls, wages are strongly determined by contributions.[54] "Experience and training, natural ability and special know-how, tend to earn a premium. Firms are willing to pay more to those with these contributions because their productivity is greater."[55] But also, says Rawls:

[53] Rawls, *A Theory of Justice*, p. 304.
[54] Ibid., p. 311.
[55] Ibid., pp. 305–06.

361

a premium must be paid if those who may later offer their services are to be persuaded to undertake the costs of training and postponement. Similarly jobs which involve uncertain or unstable employment, or which are performed under hazardous and unpleasantly strenuous conditions, tend to receive more pay. Otherwise men cannot be found to fill them.[56]

For sociology readers, this line of argument will be rather familiar. It is an almost perfect rendering of the functionalist's claim that people must be differentially rewarded in order to assure that the most important positions will be filled by competent persons. Rawls says more or less the same. "The function of unequal distributive shares," he writes, "is to cover the costs of training and education, to attract individuals to places and associations where they are most needed from a social point of view, and so on."[57]

Rawls, then, echoes the view of Davis and Moore, who say that social inequality is a device "by which societies insure that the most important positions are conscientiously filled by the most qualified persons."[58] He also agrees with these sociologists that a society must "instill in the proper individuals the desire to fill certain positions, and, once in these positions, the desire to perform the duties attached to them."[59] Rawls shares the view that this is to be accomplished by a system of rewards as individual pecuniary incentives. And he appears to agree with the functionalists' view that the largest rewards must be paid to positions that (a) require the greatest amount of training and education, (b) are the most unpleasant or demanding, and (c) have the greatest importance for society. Gewirth, I believe, also accepts this general line of reasoning. Of course, he does differ from Rawls to the extent that he sees differential rewards as a matter of "desert," while Rawls views them as "incentives." But both appear to accept (a) through (c) above.

The claims of Rawls, Gewirth, and the functionalists, are quite obviously not only theoretical in character; they also intend these to be accurate portrayals of the actual workings of the reward structure in existing societies. It is important to ask, therefore, whether or not there is empirical support for their claims. In at-

[56] Ibid., p. 306.
[57] Ibid., p. 315.
[58] Kingsley David and Wilbert E. Moore, "Some Principles of Stratification," *American Sociological Review* 10 (1945): 243.
[59] Ibid., p. 242.

tempting to answer this question, I will focus mainly on (c) above. Nevertheless, some brief remarks about (a) and (b) are also in order.

While it may be true that many people will not undergo training and schooling unless they are differently rewarded, it is easy to think of many counterexamples to this. Most readers of this book, for example, have probably undergone a long period of university education. Yet it seems highly unlikely that it was the reward structure that initially attracted you to the sorts of intellectual pursuits in which you are currently engaged. When, as is often the case in the United States and elsewhere, other persons with the same or less formal education (for example, engineers, lawyers, many skilled manual workers, and sometimes even policemen and sanitation workers) earn more than many academics, it is simply false to place so much weight on differential economic rewards as incentives or motivating factors.

Or consider the case of elementary schoolteachers in the United States. Despite the fact that their work demands a greater amount of formal education than does the work of plumbers, pipe fitters, tile setters, and stonecutters, the earnings of the latter occupations exceed those of schoolteachers.[60] Further, the range of individual earnings *within* occupations is about as large as the range of average earnings *between* the highest- and lowest-paid occupations.[61] Needless to say, the variance is greater in the higher-paid occupations, given that earnings extend further above the median in these occupations than in others. If, as is clearly the case, a greater amount of education is not necessarily accompanied by higher economic rewards, it is difficult to accept Rawls's claim that such rewards serve as incentives for undergoing longer periods of schooling or training.

This is not to deny that certain occupations and professions that require a long period of formal education are highly paid across different societies. But although they are highly paid, the relative rates offered differ markedly. Consider the situation in two Western industrialized societies. In the United States, physicians earn 3.8 times the average income as compared to a figure of 2.6 for West Germany.[62] But, it might be argued, this difference can be accounted for by the fact that a university and medical school education is much more expensive in the United States than in West

[60] Phelps Brown, *Inequality of Pay*, p. 240.
[61] Ibid., p. 259.
[62] Ibid., p. 38.

Germany. This is, in fact, correct. But given that university education is in general much more costly in the United States than in West Germany, why is it that university teachers earn 1.9 times the average income in the United States as compared to 4.1 in West Germany?[63] And if people require highly unequal salaries as incentives to undergo a long period of formal education, how do we account for the fact that high civil servants earn 3.5 times the average in the United States, while the comparable figure is 6.7 for West Germany?[64] Despite these differences in the reward structure in the two societies, there is no great problem in assuring that a sufficient number of people will be motivated to undergo the schooling and training presumably necessary for filling these positions. Furthermore, there seems to be no difficulty in recruiting people to become physicians in the Soviet Union, even though they earn less than persons working in industry, government administration, transportation, and construction.[65]

As to Rawls's second claim, it is not generally the case that extremely hazardous, unpleasant, or strenuous work receives the highest pay. Mine workers, people doing heavy construction work, and those employed in a variety of other manual occupations, are often exposed to considerable danger, excessive noise, the risk of a disease such as asbestosis, and other unpleasant conditions of work. If, as Rawls asserts, greater pay is necessary in order to attract people to perform demanding jobs, why are the above kinds of work so much more poorly paid than are, for instance, dentists, lawyers, and engineers in Western societies? And why is it that even among manual workers, coal miners and construction workers earn less than plumbers, carpenters, and house painters?[66] It is simply not true that people cannot be found to perform the "dirty work" unless they are paid differentially high wages and salaries.

What, then, of Rawls's claim that the function of an unequal distribution of economic rewards is necessary to assure that the most important positions will be filled? In attempting to answer this question, it is useful to consider two separate assumptions that are implicit in the presumed relation between contributions and rewards: (1) that the relative contributions of different persons or positions (occupations, professions, jobs) can be accurately deter-

[63] Ibid.

[64] Ibid.

[65] Michael Swafford, "Sex Differences in Soviet Earnings," *American Sociological Review* 43 (October 1978): 657–73.

[66] Phelps Brown, *Inequality of Pay*, p. 61.

mined, and (2) that the unequal economic rewards associated with different positions are a function of differential contributions.

Relative Contributions

As already noted, it is sociologists in the functionalist tradition who more than anyone else argue that people must be differentially rewarded in accordance with the "functional importance" of the positions they fill.[67] But even Marx held this view to some extent. During the first stage of post-capitalist society, he said, the governing principle is, "From each according to his capacity, to each according to his contribution." How, then, is the functional importance or relative contribution of various positions to be established?

Perhaps in the paradigm case of the physician it can convincingly be demonstrated that there is a functional requirement for a society to have highly trained specialists who are able to meet people's health needs, and that they contribute greatly to the social welfare of a society's citizens.[68] Probably everyone would agree that the chief of surgery of a large hospital makes a greater contribution than a dishwasher in the same hospital. But the case of the physician is a misleading simple aspect of the question under consideration. After all, the health needs of a society are widely recognized as "basic," and the physician is a clear-cut example of someone who contributes to meeting these basic needs. Yet, even the case of the physician involves considerable difficulties. For example, based purely on considerations of their contributions to a society's health needs, whose contribution is greater: the obstetrician who is involved in seeing that mother and child both survive, the pediatrician who cares for sick children, the internist who ministers to an enormous variety of illnesses and diseases, the heart specialist or the psychiatrist who helps to alleviate mental turmoil and suffering?

The difficulties encountered in the case of medical care pale into insignificance, however, when compared with the problem of judging occupations and professions of a largely *dissimilar* nature. Who contributes more to the social or economic welfare of a society: the chemist who works on developing synthetics for clothing or the

[67] There has, however, been very little progress toward specifying a test of this theory. See, for example, George A. Huaco, "The Functionalist Theory of Stratification: Two Decades of Controversy," *Inquiry* 9 (1966): 212–50.

[68] In the following discussion I draw freely upon my own earlier work, Phillips, *Equality, Justice and Rectification.*

one who works on developing weapons of chemical warfare, the clergyman or the economist, the "pop" entertainer or the construction worker, the philosopher or the policeman, the university teacher or the kindergarten teacher? We need not extend the list to be impressed with the enormity of trying to establish the relative contributions of various positions to a society's social or economic welfare.

There is further the problem—especially in so-called advanced societies—of establishing each individual's *proportional* contribution to jointly made products and to goods and products involving techniques and machines for which the individual him- or herself is not responsible. When, as is often the case nowadays, several persons are involved in producing a common product or result, there is usually no device at hand for measuring the comparative contribution of several different individuals.

Some sociologists do, of course, attempt to establish the functional importance—and, by assumption, the relative contributions—of various positions. The trouble with these studies is that they may not be measuring the respondents' own personal evaluation of the importance or contribution of various positions, but rather their own assessment of what they view as the *existing* or *factual* standing of the different positions. As Parkin points out: "What is often being measured is the perception of the existing status hierarchy, and not our own private evaluations of the way positions *ought* to be socially ranked, if indeed they ought to be ranked at all."[69] But even if, *pace* Parkin, we were able to accurately determine people's "private evaluations," this would not address the question under review here: Can the relative contribution of different positions be accurately determined?

The answer to this question is that we simply do not know how to estimate the relative contributions of tasks employed in different spheres of human endeavor. Although we might reach global agreement when comparing the contributions of say, a brain surgeon and a street cleaner, we encounter great difficulties when it comes to, for example, the artist, clergyman, teacher, and social worker. To the extent that relative contributions can be accurately assessed, this occurs on the basis of comparisons *within* rather than *between* various kinds of jobs or work. That is to say, it is at least sometimes possible to assess the relative contribution of several

[69] Parkin, *Marxism and Class Theory*, p. 40.

bricklayers, football players, art historians, dishwashers, or surgeons. But even here, we know, the problem can be formidable.

With regard, then, to the presumed relationship between contributions and rewards, the first assumption implicit therein is called into question: the relative contributions of different persons or positions, in general, can *not* be accurately determined.

Rewards as a Function of Contributions

If the above conclusion is correct, it has obvious implications for the second assumption implicit in the general principle concerning the distribution of economic benefits, i.e., that the unequal economic rewards associated with different positions are a function of differential contributions. For if, as I have argued, people's relative contributions cannot be accurately determined, then the economic benefits they receive cannot be a function of their actual contributions. If relative contributions cannot usually be accurately determined, then obviously people are not being differentially rewarded *because* of their differential contributions.

This conclusion, I hold, is correct. As the economist Jan Pen notes, it is simply nonsense to claim, as some economists do, that inequalities in income in some way reflect differences in contribution or "marginal productivity."[70] He points out that a secondary schoolteacher may earn more than a primary schoolteacher, but observes that this has very little to do with marginal productivity. What counts is that "society feels that a secondary schoolteacher *ought* to earn more."[71]

> He is further up the ladder, and the number of rungs can be measured by the differences in income. This is a *social evaluation*. The Civil Service hierarchy is reflected by the salary scales, and top incomes in business are set by what the top executives themselves consider right and proper. This explanatory principle does not apply solely to wages and salaries; it also operates in other areas, such as the fees of lawyers and doctors, although in these cases market conditions naturally cut across it.[72]

Thus, it is not contribution or marginal productivity that determines the incomes—or relative salaries of primary school, second-

[70] Jan Pen, *Income Distribution* (London: Allen Lane, The Penguin Press, 1971), p. 40.
[71] Ibid.
[72] Ibid.

ary school, or university teachers, of doctors, lawyers, economists, sociologists, or business executives, but various societal views as to what is appropriate, the influence of tradition and various vested interests, the strength of labor unions and professional organizations, and the influence of the government. (Think of differences in the relative prestige and salaries paid to physicians in the Soviet Union and the United States in this respect.)

Some sociologists, however, interpret the fairly high degree of congruence between the prestige rankings of various occupations and the economic rewards received as evidence that the rewards are a *result* of the prestige rankings of the positions—and of their functional importance or contribution to a society's economic or social welfare. A more correct interpretation, I believe, would reverse the direction of the presumed causal sequence; that is, people perceive that certain positions receive high economic rewards and, for that reason, they rank them highly. Such an interpretation receives support from Della Fave's formulation of the way individuals actually do reason in this regard: the very fact of some people receiving higher economic rewards influences our perception of their contributions and, on the basis of such assessment, we judge those persons worthy of such high rewards.[73]

In fact, as Della Fave points out, most people appear to accept the evaluations of the existing prestige and stratification hierarchies. This generally means that they accept the existing hierarchies upheld by the dominant class in the society in which they live. Parkin is correct when he states: "In so far, then, as there seems to be a general agreement about the factual status order in its day-to-day operation, it would be more realistic to see it as a tribute to the effectiveness of the socialization process than as evidence for some sort of moral consensus independently arrived at by different class members."[74]

At least, when different occupations and professions are being compared, there is no way of adequately accounting for differential

[73] Della Fave, "The Meek," p. 961. This conclusion is supported by a wide variety of studies. See, for instance, Karen S. Cook, "Expectations, Evaluations and Equity," *American Sociological Review* 40 (June 1975): 372–88; Guillermina Jasso and Peter H. Rossi, "Distributive Justice and Earned Income," *American Sociological Review* 42 (August 1977); 639–51; and the excellent survey article by Karol Edward Sołtan, "Empirical Studies of Distributive Justice," *Ethics* 92 (July 1982): 673–91. There is considerable evidence to support the conclusion that people's views about the "rightness" (normative acceptability) of economic inequality are generally a reflection of the existing pattern of economic distribution.

[74] Parkin, *Marxism and Class Theory*, p. 44.

rewards as a function of differential contributions. But even if there were—even if contributions could be fairly accurately measured—there would remain the problem of justifying the differential salaries and wages attached to the different positions. How much, for instance, should an airline pilot be paid relative to the mayor of a large city, and why?

Still, it does appear possible to examine the relationship between contributions and rewards *within* a particular occupational category. Broom and Cushing are among the few to attempt such an examination.[75] For that reason, their research deserves attention here. Recognizing the many problems involved in assessing contributions (and especially those supposedly related to the survival or optimal functioning or society), they specify that the positions to be examined in their investigation should carry high and measurable responsibility (i.e., should be contributing to some specified goal or accomplishment), that there should be a clear way of assessing performance, and that there should indeed be differential rewards.[76] "Senior management positions in capitalist industrial organizations," they state, "come as close to satisfying these criteria as any."[77] Thus, their research focuses on a sample of large, publicly held companies within the private sector of the U.S. economic system.

The logic of their approach required, of course, that they look at companies that are homogeneous with regard to types of business activity in order to control for differences in the scarcity of rewards and of qualified persons.[78] All of their comparisons, therefore, are within and not between types of business activity. The contributions of top management are measured by the "responsibility" of each person. The argument is as follows: "The major responsibility for a company and its success or failure is assumed to rest with the top management of a firm. Clearly, they are responsible to a variety of clients. They are obliged to protect the interests of creditors and shareholders, to maximize profit and growth. They also have obligations to the company's employees. . . ."[79]

---

[75] Leonard Broom and Robert G. Cushing, "A Modest Test of an Immodest Theory: The Functional Theory of Stratification," *American Sociological Review* 42 (February 1977): 157–69.

[76] Ibid., p. 160.

[77] Ibid.

[78] Ibid., p. 166.

[79] Ibid.

The actual "performance" of companies is measured by their profitability, and "compensation" is measured on the basis of the total compensation (salary, bonuses, fees, etc.) received by the chief executive officer in each company.[80] Based on data concerning 859 companies—for example, producers of beer, cosmetics, soft drinks, tobacco, food, steel, and textiles—Broom and Cushing hypothesize that "company performance is positively related to the total compensation of chief executive officers."[81] Consistent with the view that rewards are a function of contributions, they reason that greater compensation should be associated with higher company performance.

> If we accept that organizations providing a product or service have positions that are the loci of responsibility, then if the company is to perform its functions (that is, to do its work and survive), the responsibility inherent in such positions must be competently discharged. Rewards should be related to such competent performances so that the company can retain the service of the competent performer.[82]

In fact, however, they found *no* empirical support for their hypothesis. Contrary to the assumed linkage between contribution and reward, their data showed that company performance is not positively related to the total compensation paid to the chief executive officers.[83]

If the differential rewards received by the chief executive officers within each of a wide variety of types of business are not a function of their differential contributions to the success of their companies, how, then, are these differential rewards to be explained? One answer, Broom and Cushing suggest, is that large companies can provide the greatest amount of compensation with the least visible impact on the balance sheets.[84] The mechanism for this reward pattern, they observe, is simple indeed: "Chief executive officers influence, when they do not determine, their own compensation."[85]

The research of Broom and Cushing shows that even when comparisons are made within similar types of companies, there is no

[80] Ibid., pp. 165–66.
[81] Ibid., p. 167.
[82] Ibid.
[83] Ibid.
[84] Ibid., p. 168.
[85] Ibid.

evidence to support the widely held view that people are unequally rewarded on the basis of their differential contributions. This being the case, it is not surprising that such evidence is also lacking when comparisons are made across different types of tasks. As we cannot estimate the relative contributions of different occupations and professions, we also cannot adequately explain the differential economic rewards associated with these different positions.

Whatever income people receive, it is not a payment in proportionate exchange for a productive contribution. Of course, many persons like to view their own high salaries as the reward of the market for scarce and productive talent. Arrangements where those higher in an organization use their bureaucratic power to enhance the differentials in pay between themselves and others are quite common. One consequence of this is that the compensation paid at different levels in the corporate hierarchy of one organization becomes the standard for others. Often, as Galbraith points out, this inflation of salaries has absolutely nothing to do with any shortage of executive talent; the supply and quality of talent would not be any less at the lower level of compensation.[86] Nevertheless, says Galbraith, it "does serve the fiction that compensation is decided impersonally by outside forces."[87] Hollis and Nell reach a similar conclusion in their book, *Rational Economic Man*:

> Individual incomes do not result from individual hard work but from exercises of power, political decisions, tradition and other social forces, not least the hierarchical organisation of productive work. . . . The clear implication is that there is no natural nor any efficient allocation of incomes. A competitive scramble for incomes is simply a power struggle and there is no hope of basing an "incomes policy" on the nation of "productive contribution" or "efficiency."[88]

With regard, then, to the presumed relation between contributions and economic rewards, the second assumption implicit therein is also called into question: the unequal economic rewards associated with different positions are *not* generally a function of differential contributions.

The above discussion has focused on the empirical standing of

[86] John Kenneth Galbraith, *Economics and the Public Purpose* (London: André Deutsch, 1974), p. 265.

[87] Ibid.

[88] Martin Hollis and Edward Nell, *Rational Economic Man* (Cambridge: Cambridge University Press, 1975).

three claims and two (related) assumptions common to the standpoints of Rawls, Gewirth, and sociologists in the functionalist tradition. These claims are that the largest financial rewards must be paid to persons filling positions that (1) require the greatest amount of training and education, (2) are the most unpleasant or demanding, and (3) have the greatest importance for society. The two assumptions are that the relative contributions of different positions can be accurately determined, and that the unequal economic rewards associated with different positions are a function of differential contributions. Doubt has been cast upon the correctness of all these claims and assumptions.

What, then, can we conclude about the highly unequal distribution of salaries and wages? A minimum conclusion is that we must be extremely skeptical about standpoints that rest on various claims and assumptions concerning the necessity and inevitability of large economic differentials in economic rewards.

But we can also go beyond mere skepticism and conclude that the actual inequalities required to help assure that certain positions are filled and performed in a competent manner are considerably *less* than is widely believed. That is to say, whether it is deserts (Gewirth) or incentives (Rawls) that are seen as the justification for highly unequal economic rewards, there is good reason to conclude that a less unequal distribution of wages and salaries would still ensure that existing positions would be filled by competent persons. Such a conclusion is supported by a wealth of empirical findings.[89]

Thurow, for example, compares the earnings gap between the top and bottom ten per cent of the population in different societies and finds that the West Germans work hard with 36 per cent less inequality than exists in the United States, and the Japanese with 50 per cent less inequality.[90] If income differentials encourage individual initiatives, he remarks, then Americans should be full of initiative, since among industrialized countries only the French have a higher level of inequality. The fact that the extent of income inequality is considerably lower in such highly industrialized so-

[89] See, for example, Robin Barlow, Harvey E. Brazer, and James N. Morgan, *Economic Behavior of the Affluent* (Washington, D.C.: Brookings Institute, 1966); George F. Break, "Income Taxes and Incentive to Work," *American Economic Review* 47 (September 1957), especially pp. 539–41; and David Macarov, *Incentive to Work* (San Francisco: Jossey-Bass, 1970).

[90] Lester C. Thurow, *The Zero-Sum Society* (New York: Penguin Books, 1981), pp. 7–8.

cieties as West Germany and Japan than in the United States and France lends strong empirical support to the conclusion that income differentials need not be nearly so large as they frequently are.

Even if it is true that doctors in the United States and France, for example, must be paid more than schoolteachers in order to encourage young people to undergo the long training required, there is no evidence to show that they must be paid *as much* more than teachers as they now are. There is neither a greater problem in recruitment nor a lesser quality of performance among doctors in Scandinavia and England, where income inequalities are comparatively small, than in those societies (like the United States and France) that are characterized by steep inequalities in income. It appears very likely, then, that there are categories of the highly paid in all societies who would perform their work satisfactorily with smaller incomes than they now enjoy.

III

If it is indeed correct that income inequalities need not always be as large as they usually are, what implications does this have for the application of the theories of Nozick, Rawls, and Gewirth? More specifically, does this conclusion have any direct implications for the problem of assuring a satisfactory level of those basic goods—adequate food, housing, clothing, medical care, security, and protection—necessary for effective exercise of the fundamental rights to freedom and well-being?

Nozick's View

As far as Nozick's theory is concerned, I cannot see that my argument concerning the magnitude of economic inequalities could possibly have any relevance to the problem of providing everyone with an adequate level of basic goods. After all, there is no place in his theory for societal obligations. Consequently, Nozick would reject any and all policies aimed at assuring everyone the necessary basic goods. The extent of inequalities in the distribution of economic rewards would, then, make no difference in this regard.

Gewirth's View

It might be expected that Gewirth would have a great deal to say about the minimum standard of living required to assure the preconditions for enjoying the rights to freedom and well-being. After all, it is central to his theory that all persons have rights to adequate food, shelter, health care, and the like. In fact, Gewirth says that the individual's right to the necessary conditions of action constitute an entitlement that is *logically prior* to all other entitlements.[91] This is because, as he points out, the criterion on which the entitlement is based "consists in the very possibility of engaging in any actions at all and of general success in such actions."[92] Yet, despite his strong emphasis on everyone's entitlement to the rights of freedom and well-being and to the preconditions necessary for exercising these rights, Gewirth never specifies how economic benefits are to be distributed so as to assure that this entitlement is generally honored.

He does specify, as I noted earlier, that there must be social rules that provide for supplying basic goods to those persons who cannot obtain them by their own efforts. But how this might be accomplished is left quite unclear. Gewirth speaks of the responsibility of the government in a just society to remove the dispositional inequalities of well-being that have institutional sources.[93] With what he terms redistributive justice, the attempt is to move toward a previously nonexistent equality of generic rights.[94] Redistributive justice, writes Gewirth, requires that the state make arrangements for applying the necessary equalizing rules.[95] This necessitates the state "prescribing to individual citizens that they contribute to these arrangements by paying taxes in proportion to their ability."[96] But Gewirth never specifies what sort of tax scheme he has in mind here. At any rate, he never speaks of taxation as a means of reducing the extent of inequality between the rich and the poor. Taxation is apparently to be used only to increase the position of the less advantaged, with no attention being paid to a lessening of the advantaged position of the well off.

The above, as already said, concerns redistributive justice. Distributive justice, on the other hand, consists of distribution according to contributions. According to Gewirth, "It is just for A, or A has a right, to receive twice as much of the relevant rewards as B if A contributes twice as much. . . ."[97] Thus, distributive justice requires that rewards be proportional to an individual's contribu-

---

[91] Gewirth, *Reason and Morality*, p. 73.
[92] Ibid.
[93] Ibid., p. 294.
[94] Ibid.
[95] Ibid., p. 314.
[96] Ibid., p. 315.
[97] Ibid., p. 287.

tion; he or she is, Gewirth holds, deserving of such differential rewards. As I pointed out earlier, Gewirth sees a highly unequal distribution of economic rewards as both just and necessary. While redistributive justice may require that people be differentially taxed (how, we are never told) so as to assure the basic goods for everyone, this must not be allowed to take the form of Rawls's "revolutionary" extreme.

Gewirth believes that the notion of distributive justice described above will itself contribute to the equality of generic rights.[98] Allowing people to be rewarded on the basis of contributions will apparently help facilitate the general increase of wealth in the whole society. Measures that increase the wealth of the rich are acceptable, he says, if they can be shown to "further equalize at least the opportunities of the poor."[99] This, quite obviously, sounds a bit like Rawls's difference principle; social inequalities that help improve the position of the least advantaged are perefectly acceptable.

Be that as it may, Gewirth argues that the more national wealth there is in a just society, the more likely it is that persons at the lower end of the economic scale will have a share sufficient for preventing violations of their generic rights. In Gewirth's words:

> It is not only that the poor will be better off, but also that their being better off will further the distributive end of maintaining an equality of generic rights whereby the freedom and well-being of the poorer as well as the richer are equally protected. . . . The expansion of the productive capacity in the society will foster this result not only by making available a greater supply of goods but also by providing greater opportunities for productive and more remunerative labor for all members of society. That the maximization of wealth will have this distributive result is an empirical hypothesis.[100]

It is indeed an empirical hypothesis. In my view, it is a hypothesis easily proven false—especially as it concerns the effective equality of generic rights. There is, by itself, no reason to think that greater national wealth will automatically result in making the poor better off. It is easy to think of situations under which the increased societal wealth accrues only to the already well off, without in any

[98] Ibid., p. 325.
[99] Ibid.
[100] Ibid., pp. 318–19.

way making available a greater supply of basic goods to the seriously disadvantaged. Undoubtedly, a certain level of wealth is a necessary condition for assuring that there is the possibility of an adequate level of basic goods for everyone. But it is not sufficient in and of itself. There must also be specified social mechanisms (minimal incomes, welfare rights, monetary transfer systems, and the like). As is the case with Rawls, Gewirth provides no institutional arrangements that will guarantee everyone the availability of the necessary basic goods for effectively exercising their fundamental rights to freedom and well-being.

Even if, as I have argued earlier, the large inequalities in economic rewards permitted by Gewirth are not required for assuring that certain positions are filled and performed competently, this would have no effect on his views concerning the provision of basic goods. Since, in fact, he regards highly unequal rewards as something deserved and also believes that these contribute to the general wealth of society and ultimately to the improvement of the situation of the seriously disadvantaged, it is unlikely that he would accept a more equal distribution of salaries and wages as something to be desired.

Rawls's Difference Principle

In criticizing Rawls's principle earlier in this chapter, I argued that its application will not provide a sufficient minimum so that an adequate level of the necessary basic goods will be available to everyone. In the absence of these necessary basic goods, the generic rights cannot be effectively exercised. But why is it that application of the difference principle will not provide a sufficient minimum? After all, Rawls's principle is widely regarded as heavily egalitarian in intent. He makes it clear that "the higher expectations of those better situated are just if and only if they work as part of a scheme which improves the expectations of the least advantaged members of society."[101]

The minimum provided by Rawls's difference principle is likely to be extremely low, as indicated earlier, because of his conception of the role of incentive as motivating factors. As I pointed out in my discussion of contributions and rewards, Rawls says that large economic rewards must be paid to assure the filling of positions that require the greatest amount of training and education, are the most unpleasant and demanding, and have the greatest importance

[101] Rawls, *A Theory of Justice*, p. 277.

for society. I have already raised doubts about the correctness of such claims; despite what Rawls and others assume, large economic incentive cannot easily be shown to perform such functions. Comparisons both within and across different societies suggest that much smaller incentives may be sufficient to assure that people will perform the necessary jobs in a competent manner.[102] If so, the distribution of rewards could be much less inegalitarian than Rawls seems to think is required.

Exactly the same may hold true with regard to the effects of progressive taxation on investment incentives. As Amy Gutmann points out, "The amount of investment currently undertaken by individuals is not well correlated with the degree of risk involved or with the expected rate of return. Rather, business economists report that there exist substantial random factors in the individual's investment decisions, as well as their actual returns."[103] In other words, it is simply not clear whether higher tax rates would have a strongly adverse influence on investments for the future. Further, as Gutmann also notes, the political structure of contemporary societies often encourages noneconomic incentives for wealthy persons to translate their personal economic accumulation into personal and political power. This quite obviously stands in the way of efficient capital-investment decisions.

Rawls believes that there must be highly unequal economic incentives in order to assure that competent people will fulfill the most demanding and important positions, that investments will be stimuated, and that efficiency will be maximized. It is because of this, I have suggested, that applications of the difference principle would be likely to result in a social minimum quite similar to what is currently found in capitalist societies like the United States and Great Britain. Rawls apparently accepts that contributions can be accurately determined, and that people's salaries and wages are proportionate to their productive contributions. If, as he assumes, people should be rewarded in proportion to their highly unequal contributions, then it is understandable that he sees very large economic inequalities as both necessary and just.

But if I am correct, i.e., if much less inequality than Rawls believes necessary (and that now exists in many societies) would still pro-

---

[102] Once again, Phelps Brown, *Inequality of Pay*, is especially relevant here. See also the excellent discussion in Amy Gutmann, *Liberal Equality* (Cambridge: Cambridge University Press, 1980), p. 134, and Lester C. Thurow, *Generating Inequality: Mechanisms of Distribution in the U.S. Economy* (New York: Basic Books, 1975).

[103] Gutmann, *Liberal Equality*, p. 135.

vide the needed incentives, then application of the difference principle might result in the provision of a very generous social minimum. Were it true—and it clearly is not—that *no* incentives at all were necessary, then the difference principle suggests that incomes and wealth would be distributed absolutely equally. In any case, the lower the incentives required for assuring competent job performances, efficiency, and investments for the future, the larger the social minimum will be.

Consequently, of course, the larger the social minimum, the greater the possibility that everyone would have an adequate level of the basic goods necessary for effective exercise of the fundamental rights to freedom and well-being. This means that Rawls's theory of justice—in contrast to those of Nozick and Gewirth—would be affected by my conclusion regarding incentives. Should it be possible to assure the major economic functions of a society with a less severe differential in rewards (as incentives), then there is a much better chance of being able to assure people's enjoyment of their generic rights.

I am not suggesting, however, that Rawls's difference principle—as it now stands—is the principle of economic distribution required for the just social order. Rather, I have tried to establish the possibility that Rawls's difference principle could—given certain incentive constraints—provide a generous minimum standard of living for everyone. Given this important conclusion, I intend to incorporate elements of Rawls's difference principle into my own suggested principles and policies for economic distribution in the following chapter.

NINE

The Realization of Freedom and Well-Being: Some Principles and Policies for a Just Social Order

My focus in the previous chapter was on the extent to which the application of various theories of justice would assure that all persons will have an adequate level of those basic goods required for effectively exercising their fundamental rights to freedom and well-being. I argued that justice in the distributive sphere has a higher moral priority and political practicability than arrangements for socialization and social control; unless the conditions for economic justice are first secured, there is little likelihood of either successful moral socialization or a system of legitimate legal authority.

It must be acknowledged, however, that this exclusive focus on distribution is subject to the Marxist objection that it ignores the hidden forces of the productive system that actually create and govern the pattern of distribution. Since goods and services must first be produced before they can be distributed, it seems obvious that distribution depends ultimately on the structure of production in an economy. The relations of production are viewed as casually fundamental, with the distributive relations being a consequence of them.[1]

Therefore, before I go on to specify several principles and policies of economic distribution and redistribution required for a just social order, I will first briefly consider some of the consequences of different productive arrangements with regard to the three requirements a productive system must ideally satisfy: a just distribution of social and economic benefits, a high degree of efficiency and economic growth, and conditions of work that foster people's identity formation and autonomous development. In the following

[1] For example, see Karl Marx, *Critique of the Gotha Programme* (Peking: Foreign Language Press, 1972). Nozick, too—as was seen in Chapter 2—warns about an exclusive concern with distribution and points to the crucial importance of attending to how things are produced, created, and acquired. See Robert Nozick, *Anarchy, State, and Utopia* (New York: Basic Books, 1974).

presentation, I will examine the two dominant kinds of economic arrangements in the contemporary Western world and will then suggest the sort of arrangements required for a just social order.

I

One type of economic arrangement, with which we are all familiar, is the capitalist economy found in, for example, the United States or Canada today. In such capitalist economies, it is a guiding assumption that private ownership of economic resources entitles the owners to whatever profit they are able to obtain. Maximization of profit is the main motive of the capitalist economic enterprise. Production, investment, price, and other economic decisions are made privately by those who own the means of production or by those who manage on their behalf. For those persons without ownership of the means of production, the major determinant of income is the pull they are able to exert in the marketplace where they sell their labor. Workers are highly dependent on the firm for economic benefits. It is, then, private property and the market that determine the allocation of resources and the living conditions of a society's citizens.

A second type of arrangement is the state-owned, one-party polity, centrally planned economy found in the Soviet-bloc countries. In contrast to capitalist societies, the economy is not governed by the pursuit of market profit on the part of separate private corporations. Instead, state policy is the prime economic motor. In such a Soviet-type economy, the state plays a dominant role in determining the distribution of income and of various goods and services. Since various sorts of state social insurance is provided, workers are far less dependent on the firm than in capitalist economies. With the elimination of the imperative of private profit maximization, production can theoretically be planned to meet the basic needs of the entire population.

An important question, then, is whether either of these two different sets of economic arrangements assures that everyone will have the basic goods necessary for exercising their rights to freedom and well-being. To answer this question, both the extent of social welfare services and the patterns of economic distribution found in these two sorts of economies must be examined. The latter is important because of the fact that the ability to acquire at least some of the required basic goods (e.g., food, shelter, and clothing) is usually tied to people's incomes. Further, of course, the granting of various civil and political rights is also of crucial importance as an element in our comparison.

Distribution

What, we might ask, are the actual consequences of the unequal ownership of property in capitalist societies? To begin with, corporate capitalism realizes huge profits and considerable political power. Further, those who own the means of production own and control tremendous wealth. Something less than 2 per cent of the population owns about 40 percent of all the wealth in societies like the United States and Great Britain.[2] Further, the very biggest incomes are derived mainly from property.[3] Wealth is, in fact, much more unevenly distributed than is income from wages and salaries. But this is not to say that income (in the form of wages and salaries for work) is in any way equally divided. In the United States, for example, the best paid one-fifth of the workers earn something like seven times what is earned by the bottom fifth.[4] Similar distributions of income can be found in other capitalist societies.[5]

Despite the great unevenness in the distribution of wealth, it is abundantly clear that it is income inequality rather than wealth inequality that accounts for most of the basic pattern of economic distribution in capitalist societies. With regard to the United Kingdom, for example, Phelps Brown states that "in the U.K. by 1973 income from employment was amounting to nearly 70 per cent of all personal income; income from self-employment made up another 10 per cent, and so did receipts from national insurance and other cash benefits; only 10 per cent of all personal income came from rent, dividends, and interest."[6] And Kuznets, surveying the distribution of the national income in Canada, the United States, France, Germany, Switzerland, and the United Kingdom, concludes that the proportion of "property income" is now below 20 per cent.[7] What matters most in capitalist societies, in Wolff's

[2] See, for example, S. J. Lampman, *The Share of Top Wealth-Holders in National Wealth: 1922–1956* (Princeton: Princeton University Press, 1962); and J. Westergaard and H. Ressler, *Class in a Capitalist Society* (London: Heinemann, 1975).

[3] Henry Phelps Brown, *The Inequality of Pay* (Oxford: Oxford University Press, 1977); and Lester C. Thurow, *The Zero-Sum Society* (New York: Penguin Books, 1981).

[4] Christopher Jencks et al., *Inequality: A Reassessment of the Effects of Family and Schooling in America* (New York: Basic Books, 1972), p. 213.

[5] Phelps Brown, *Inequality of Pay*.

[6] Ibid., p. 5.

[7] S. Kuznets, *Modern Economic Growth: Rate, Structure, and Spread* (New Haven: Yale University Press, 1966), p. 218.

words, is "how much your job pays, not how big your portfolio is or how much land you have inherited."[8]

These disparities in income and wealth between those at different points in the stratification hierarchy are considerable, as are the consequences of such disparities: differentials in health care, housing, educational attainment, diet and nutritional adequacy, and life expectancy.[9]

As long as there are large economic inequalities, the rich will always be able to outbid the poor for medical services (or at least to obtain the services of more highly trained and better-qualified physicians). Similarly with housing; the rich are able to outbid the poor for better housing. More importantly, the mere presence of a well-off group in a community dramatically increases the *price* of housing as the relatively disadvantaged must match their bids.[10] Large inequalities in wealth and income effect, then, the ability of

[8] Robert Paul Wolff, *Understanding Rawls* (Princeton: Princeton University Press, 1977), p. 197.

[9] In the United Kingdom, for example, men and women in the lowest occupational class have a two-times greater chance of dying before reaching retirement age than their professional counterparts in the highest occupational class. These class-related differences exist from birth onward. At birth and during the first month of life, the risk of death in families of unskilled workers is double that of professional families. During the next eleven months of a child's life this ratio widens even more. For the death of every child of professional parents, there are more than two among the children of skilled manual workers and more than three among the children of unskilled manual workers. Once children have passed beyond infancy, this class-linked gradient continues. This is especially pronounced in the case of accidents, the most important cause of death among children aged 1 to 14. Boys in the lowest class have a 10 times greater chance of dying from fire, falls, or drowning than those in the highest class. And the corresponding ratio of deaths of youthful pedestrians caused by motor vehicles is more than 7 to 1.

Material deprivation is also class related and obviously influences the physical development of young children. Nutritional deprivation has a clear effect on the physical growth of children: the lower the class origin, for example, the shorter the children and the later they reach maturity. These findings are reported in Peter Townsend and Nick Davidson, *Inequalities in Health: The Black Report* (London: Penguin, 1982). Individuals from poorer socioeconomic backgrounds are also disadvantaged in other ways that affect them adversely. See, for example, Paul DiMaggio, "Cultural Capital and School Success: The Impact of Status and Cultural Participation on the Grades of U.S. High School Students," *American Sociological Review* 47 (April 1982): 189–201.

[10] The best discussion of this phenomenon is found in Fred Hirsch, *Social Limits to Growth* (London: Routledge and Kegan Paul, 1977). See also Mark Kelman, "The Social Costs of Inequality," in Lewis A. Coser and Irving Howe, eds., *The New Conservatives: A Criticism from the Left* (New York: Quadrangle Books, 1974), pp. 151–64.

the disadvantaged to acquire such necessities as medical treatment, housing, and education.

Nor are these necessities made available by the government in such capitalist societies as the United States, Canada, Israel, Italy, or Japan. They fail to provide an adequate level of such social benefits and services as income maintenance (sickness and maternity benefits, family allowance, and the like), housing, education, and medical care. In fact, these countries are among the laggards in social security expenditures.[11] Thus, large portions of the population in capitalist societies lack either the economic means or the availability of state-provided benefits and services for assuring that they will have the necessary goods required for enjoying their rights to freedom and well-being.

What, then, about the second set of economic arrangements mentioned above: those found in a Soviet-type state that owns and controls the means of production? To begin with, income differences are considerably smaller in these countries than in advanced capitalist societies.[12] Yet if private ownership is done away with and the means of production nationalized, it might be expected that economic inequalities would disappear altogether. This, however, is not the case. While it may be true, as Marxists claim, that social inequalities are an inevitable consequence of private ownership in the means of production, such inequalities appear to be a consequence of various social experiments in the twentieth century as well. In fact, there is a striking similarity in the pay structures of capitalist and Soviet-type societies.[13] And, just as in capitalist societies, women are consistently paid less than men when they perform similar types of work.[14] As Shkaratan points out: "When socialism liquidates private property, it eliminates the consequences of private property—antagonistic classes—but it does

[11] See, International Labour Office, *The Cost of Social Security 1964–1967* (Geneva, 1972), Part II, Table 2; Unesco, *Statistical Yearbook 1970* (Paris, 1971), Table 2.19; and Christopher Hewitt, "The Effect of Political Democracy and Social Democracy on Equality in Industrial Societies: A Cross-National Comparison," *American Sociological Review* 42 (June 1977): 405–64.

[12] S. Jain, *Size Distribution of Income* (Washington, D.C.: World Bank, 1975); Shirley Cereseto, "Socialism, Capitalism and Inequality," *The Insurgent Sociologist* 11 (Spring 1982): 5–29.

[13] Phelps Brown, *Inequality of Pay*; Frank Parkin, *Class, Inequality, and Political Order* (London: Paladin Books, 1972).

[14] Michael Swafford, "Sex Differences in Soviet Earnings," *American Sociological Review* 43 (October 1978): 657–73.

not eliminate the original cause of social inequality: the division of labour into socially heterogeneous types."[15]

Thus, marked economic inequalities are found not only in capitalist economies but also in those various Soviet-type economies where there is state ownership of economic resources. Since there is no private propertied class of great wealth—as in the United States and Great Britain—the existing inequalities arise largely (but not entirely, as I will show shortly) from differences in the pay people receive for their work. Even when the inequalities arising from property have been swept away, those arising from work are considerable.

The Soviet-type societies of Eastern Europe do, however, provide a far wider range of welfare benefits than is the case in the West. These include income security, free and comprehensive health care for the whole population, free and compulsory ten-year education, and state-provided urban housing.[16] Although these are in principle distributed equally or in terms of need, the reality is otherwise. With medical care, for example, those at the top of the social pyramid often have privileged access to special medical treatment or treatment in a closed system of hospitals, clinics, and dispensaries.[17] They also receive preferential access to higher education, far better housing than that enjoyed by most people, the use of official cars, and special access to exclusive shops.[18]

But it is not only the inequality of state-provided benefits and services that constitutes a serious problem in Soviet-type societies. There is also the fact that the general level of such welfare benefits is low and they do not cover everyone. In the U.S.S.R., for example, almost two-thirds of the urban population lives in state-owned housing.[19] To a large extent, this means living in extremely overcrowded and unhealthy circumstances, without privacy or the basic amenities. With regard to coverage, there is no system of public assistance in the U.S.S.R. for those who are not entitled to basic income maintenance benefits (the "independent" workers, such as

[15] O. I. Shkaratan, "Sources of Social Differentiation of the Working Class in Soviet Society," *International Journal of Sociology* (Spring–Summer, 1973), p. 11.

[16] See, for example, Ramesh Mishra, *Society and Social Policy* (London: Macmillan, 1977).

[17] Mark G. Field, *Doctor and Patient in Soviet Russia* (Cambridge, Mass.: Harvard University Press, 1957), pp. 184–85; and Branko Horvat, *The Political Eeconomy of Socialism* (Oxford: Martin Robertson, 1982).

[18] Horvat, *Political Economy*, pp. 72–73; and André D. Sakharov, *My Country and the World* (New York: Knopf, 1975).

[19] *The Cost of Social Security, 1964–1967*.

the peasants, artisans, home workers, and the like) or for those with inadequate benefits.[20] Clearly, then, a large portion of the population is inadequately provided for. As we know, there are in Soviet-type societies today—just as in capitalist societies—a large number of persons who lack adequate food, housing, and medical care. In fact, using the Soviet authorities' own standard for a modest level of living, one Western writer estimates that one-third of urban households in the U.S.S.R. may be in poverty.[21]

No more than a capitalist economy, does a Soviet-type economy assure that everyone will have the necessary basic goods required for enjoyment of the rights to freedom and well-being. Even though virtually all major economic policies are centrally planned and even though there is a far wider range of social benefits than in capitalist societies, not everyone has an adequate amount of life's necessities. These inadequacies result from a combination of three sets of factors: a generally low level of social and economic benefits, class- and sex-linked income differentials, and a highly unequal distribution of certain crucial privileges. While it is generally true that money as such plays a less important role than it does in capitalist societies, such privileges of position as special medical care and better housing function to benefit those in positions of leadership. In any case, the combined effects of inadequate benefits, disparities in income—and what income can buy in the way of food, housing, travel, and special medical care—and an extremely unequal distribution of special privileges, are such that many persons do not have an adequate level of the required basic goods. Consequently, they lack the necessary preconditions for enjoying their generic rights.

In addition, of course, existing Soviet-type societies are generally reluctant to grant their citizens civil liberties of the kind that exist in the West: freedom of thought, speech, religion, assembly, and movement, as well as privacy.[22] Such societies are characterized by political and legal arrangements that are even less just and morally acceptable than those found in capitalist societies. These, too, adversely effect people's exercise of their fundamental rights. The power wielded by the political bureaucracy in the Soviet Union and Poland, for example, is much more clearly absolute than that

[20] Mishra, *Social Policy*, pp. 130, 134.

[21] Mervyn Matthews, *Class and Society in Soviet Russia* (London: Allen Lane, 1972), p. 88.

[22] Rudolf L. Tökés, *Dissent in the U.S.S.R.* (Baltimore: Johns Hopkins University Press, 1975).

possessed by the ruling group or groups in the United States or Great Britain.[23] Economic, power, and status inequalities have not withered away to the extent that many people hoped for and expected.

Production and Efficiency

Efficient production, growth, and investment mean a larger "economic pie," with the consequent increase in material and other benefits available for distribution. Both capitalist and Soviet-type societies, however, reveal a considerable amount of inefficiency in these matters. In the former, there is practically nothing to assure the sufficiency of aggregate demands, a stability of prices, or the absence of periodic slumps. This results from the fact that private ownership imposes severe constraints on social planning.[24] Except in times of war, there is no centralized planning of production and of resource allocation.[25] As a result of uncoordinated economic decisions, there is often business fluctuation, unemployment, inflation, and a tremendous waste of material resources. As a consequence, the rate of economic development is lower than it would be with more efficient planning.

In Soviet-type societies, on the other hand, central planning does (in theory) make possible rapid mobilization and reallocation of resources, and the balance between savings and investment can be secured in advance. In such societies, the top authorities decide what is to be produced and how resources are to be allocated. Inflation is easily controlled, and unemployment does not exist.[26]

But the rigidity of the planning apparatus itself prevents efficient coordination of planning activities.[27] There are serious problems of overcentralization and failures in coordination, with the result that production schedules and input allocations are endlessly reconsidered.[28] As Bauer points out: "Clumsiness and protraction of decision-making, poor coordination of participating activities, frequent changes in the plans, reallocations of investment limits and fading of responsibility for the effects of investment are well-known

---

[23] For a discussion of constraints on freedom in the United States, see Cereseto, "Socialism, Capitalism."

[24] Horvat, *Political Economy*, p. 197.

[25] Charles E. Lindblom, *Politics and Markets* (New York: Basic Books, 1977), p. 167.

[26] Horvat, *Political Economy*, p. 201.

[27] Lindblom, *Politics and Markets*, p. 293.

[28] Ibid., p. 325.

weaknesses of investment allocation under direct planning."[29] Much of this is, of course, a direct result of the fact that the state requires a huge and extremely cumbersome administrative apparatus in order to initiate and control economic activities.

In contrast, the autonomous firm in a capitalist economy is much more rationally organized and run. This generally makes for a relatively high level of microeconomic efficiency. But privately owned firms generate considerable macroeconomic waste due to a lack of coordination and planning at the national level. State ownership appears to be more efficient at the macroeconomic level because of central planning, but it generates great waste at the level of the firm because of the stifling effects of bureaucratic organization. Based on a detailed comparison of the two, Horvat concludes that neither of the systems has a clear net advantage.[30]

Whatever the differences in the various sources of inefficiency and waste in capitalist and Soviet-type economies, they are very similar as regards one particular source of waste. In both systems the potential productive efficiency of the economy is lowered because of a failure to maximally enhance the health, physical security, safety, and educational opportunities of the populace. A proper diet, adequate housing, and medical attention are not only necessary for reasons of justice but also help assure efficiency in the production sector. Similarly with education; there is a tremendous waste of talent when many persons are unable to acquire necessary skills and training because of their disadvantaged positions. If it is true, as seems evident, that a healthier and better-educated labor force is more efficient and productive, then we can conclude that both capitalist and Soviet-type economies fall far short of their potential.

Identity, Autonomy, and Meaningful Work

In addition to high levels of inefficiency and injustices in distribution, which appear to be inherent in both systems, capitalist and Soviet-type economic systems have another trait in common: a general absence of meaningful work. This has important consequences for people's identity formation and for their ability to lead autonomous lives.

Work, as I noted in Chapter 5, must be distinguished from labor.

---

[29] T. Bauer, "Investment Cycles in Planned Economies," *Acta Oeconomica* (1978), p. 246.

[30] Horvat, *Political Economy*, p. 209.

To labor is to be imprisoned in an activity whose outcome or product has no personal meaning for the individual performing it. Labor is usually accompanied by feelings of boredom, a lack of commitment, and an absence of personal involvement and satisfaction with the activity in which one is engaged. Adam Smith long ago provided a clear-cut example of labor, describing—in the opening pages of *The Wealth of Nations*—how pins are made in a factory: "One man draws out a wire, another straightens it, a third cuts it, a fourth points it," and so on through eighteen distinct operations.[31] "The man whose whole life is spent in performing a few simple operations," Smith recognized, "has no occasion to exert his understanding, or to exercise his invention in finding out expedients for removing difficulties which occur. He naturally loses, therefore, the habit of exertion."[32]

To work, i.e., to have meaningful work, by contrast, is to have opportunities for utilizing one's experience and understanding, for exercising initiative and inventiveness, for formulating aims, and for choosing the most appropriate means for achieving such aims. To work is to have the outcome or product of one's activity bear the stamp of one's particular capacities and individuality. Work involves interest, commitment, and satisfaction; it contributes to an expanding and enriched life. It contains the possibility of challenge, novelty, and personal satisfaction.[33] A commitment to work, I argued in Chapter 5, is one of the two major sources of the individual's personal *identity* (the other is love). A coherent, stable, personal identity–a sense of who one is—is to a large extent connected with the nature and quality of the jobs one performs.

In recent decades, as we know, most jobs have taken on the characteristics of labor. With capitalist and Soviet-type societies alike, more and more persons are employed to perform precisely specified activities. They are tied to a clock and to bureaucratic rules and regulations, and have few opportunities to exercise responsibility over what they do. When, as is increasingly the case

---

[31] Adam Smith, *An Inquiry in the Nature and Causes of the Wealth of Nations*, Edwin Cannan, ed., 2 vols. in 1 (Chicago: University of Chicago Press, Phoenix Books, 1976), 1: 8.

[32] Ibid., 2: 302–03.

[33] Marković states it nicely: "Work is the objectification of human powers: while shaping the confined object, man projects unto it his own consciousness, thoughts, desires, needs and imagination. Through it, he realizes the potential capacities of his being." M. Marković, *From Affluence to Praxis* (Ann Arbor: University of Michigan Press, 1974), p. 121.

in modern societies, employment is experienced as simply something that one must do to earn a living, there is little reason to expect that it can provide the necessary basis for identity formation.[34]

Aside from the adverse effects of labor (or the absence of meaningful work) on identity formation, the kinds of labor arrangements characteristic of capitalist and Soviet-type societies today are in conflict with the achievement and maintenance of individual *autonomy*. In my initial discussion of the rights to freedom and well-being in Chapter 2, I quoted Gewirth as saying that these two rights "have as their aim that each person have rational autonomy in the sense of being a self-controlling, self-developing agent who can relate to other persons on a basis of mutual respect and cooperation, in contrast to being a dependent, passive recipient of the agency of others."[35]

Having autonomy means being able to make decisions to achieve one's goals or aims and not simply responding to the wishes of others. It means being moved by reasons and conscious purposes, which are one's own, and not by external causes or the force of circumstances. Autonomous human beings take responsibility for their actions and attempt to rationally choose the best means of achieving their goals. This is not to say, of course, that autonomy involves a total independence from the influence of other persons or of particular social arrangements. Rather, an autonomous agent is a self-controlling and self-developing individual who relates to other persons on a basis of mutual respect and cooperation.

When, however, men and women are employed in the kinds of jobs analogous to Smith's pin-makers—on an assembly line, keypunching, typing, filing, or being a clerk on an automated checkout line—they are unable to act as autonomous agents. With increasing industrialization in the West and East alike, there are more and more people who perform these sorts of jobs.[36] In addition, there are many other kinds of jobs in bureaucratic settings, where people

[34] Interesting in this regard are the percentages of American workers who "would choose similar work again": University professors: 93%; Journalists: 82%; White-Collar (nonprofessionals): 43%; Skilled autoworkers and steelworkers: 16%." From R. L. Kahn, "The Work Module," in J. O'Toole, ed., *Work and Quality of Life* (Cambridge, Mass.: MIT Press, 1974), p. 204.

[35] Alan Gewirth, *Human Rights* (Chicago: University of Chicago Press, 1982), p. 5.

[36] See, for example, Harry Braverman, *Labor and Monopoly Capital: The Degradation of Work in the Twentieth Century* (New York: Monthly Review Press, 1974); and Studs Terkel, *Working* (New York: Avon Books, 1975).

labor under a hierarchical and authoritarian structure of authority that leaves little room for personal autonomy.

Whether it be in the factory or in the bureaucratic office, the employee plays little part in deciding what to do or how to do it; there is a fundamental break between the individual and his labor. Jobs are divided and subdivided in such a way that large numbers of persons perform only minute, repetitive, and meaningless fractions of the total work. Men and women in such situations are reduced to an instrument of their own existence. A wide discrepancy arises between such workers' actual crippled existence and the realization of their full potential for self-determination, self-realization, and emancipation from those internal and external forces that undermine their freedom and autonomy. This discrepancy between the actuality and potentiality of the human being is often described as alienation.[37]

Most importantly, this lack of autonomy in the job sphere carries over into people's lives more generally. To the extent that individuals labor solely at jobs involving mechanical and repetitive activities, they are made less capable of exercising individual judgments and coping adequately in more complex situations. They thereby lead less autonomous lives on the whole.[38]

Highly relevant in this regard is the research of Kohn and his associates concerning the effect of organizational structure on the worker and his personality.[39] Studying a representative group of employed men, they found a strong reciprocal relationship between what they call the substantive complexity of jobs and men's psychological functioning. By "substantive complexity" they mean the degree to which work, in its very nature, requires thought and independent judgment.[40] Substantively complex work requires making many decisions that must take into account poorly defined or apparently conflicting contingencies. Such substantive com-

[37] Horvat, Political Economy, p. 85; and Mihailo Marković, "Marxism as a Political Philosophy," pp. 94–112 in Marvin Richter, ed., Political Theory and Political Education (Princeton: Princeton University Press, 1980).

[38] Adina Schwartz, "Meaningful Work," Ethics 92 (July 1982): 634–46.

[39] Melvin L. Kohn, "Job Complexity and Adult Personality," in Neil J. Smelser and Erik H. Erikson, eds., Themes of Work and Love in Adulthood (London: Grant McIntyre, 1980), pp. 193–212; Melvin L. Kohn and Carmi Schooler, "Occupational Experience and Psychological Functioning: An Assessment of Reciprocal Effects," American Sociological Review 38 (1973): 97–118; Melvin L. Kohn and Carmi Schooler, "The Reciprocal Effects of the Substantive Complexity of Work and Intellectual Flexibility: A Longitudinal Assessment," American Journal of Sociology 84 (1978): 24–52.

[40] Kohn, "Job Complexity," p. 197.

plexity is at the heart of the experience of work; it gives meaning to the experience. The higher the degree of complexity, the higher the level of job satisfaction and occupational commitment, and the higher the valuation of self-direction and self-esteem.[41]

Further, men's "intellectual flexibility" is considerably affected by the substantive complexity of their work. That is, people's flexibility in coping with an intellectually demanding situation is very much influenced by the complexity of their jobs. "If two men of equivalent intellectual flexibility were to start their careers in jobs differing in substantive complexity," Kohn writes, "the man in the more complex job would be likely to outstrip the other in further intellectual growth."[42] This effect is likely to be compounded, it is shown, because someone's current intellectual flexibility has a significant effect on the future course of his career. When two men differ in intellectual flexibility because of differences in the substantive complexity of their first jobs, the substantive complexity of their second jobs is likely to vary directly with the created intellectual differences. This, in turn, may widen the gap in their intellectual capabilities and thus increase the difference between the substantive complexity of their third jobs, and so on. In short, small differences in the substantive complexity of two men's early jobs seem likely to lead to increasingly large differences in their intellectual development and in their subsequent careers. This reciprocal relationship between substantive complexity and intellectual flexibility operates in all social classes and for women as well.[43]

What is most interesting is that the greater degree of intellectual flexibility following from the structural complexity of work carries over to non-work-related activities as well. Men whose jobs involve complex tasks come to exercise their intellectual abilities not only on the job but also in their nonoccupational lives. They become more open to new experience, come to value self-direction more highly, and even come to engage in more intellectually demanding leisure time activities.[44] Individuals who are involved in substantively complex jobs come to view themselves as capable in doing other difficult and challenging tasks, and of being able to cope adequately with a variety of problems encountered in everyday life.

These results show that people employed in jobs that are low in substantive complexity are prevented from acting autonomously

[41] Ibid., p. 198.
[42] Ibid., p. 203.
[43] Ibid., p. 204.
[44] Ibid.

not only at work but also outside of the job situation. Routine, mechanical-type jobs hinder people from developing the intellectual flexibility and self-confidence that are necessary if they are to rationally frame, adjust, and pursue their own plans during the rest of their time.[45] Thus, the kinds of jobs that are increasingly characteristic of both capitalist and Soviet-type societies today have a negative effect on people's ability to lead autonomous lives.

It seems clear, then, that neither a capitalist nor a Soviet-type productive system will suffice for a just social order. Because of certain structural imperatives connected with the organization of labor, many people lack the kind of meaningful work necessary for identity formation and the development of autonomy. And due to weakness in efficiency and in policies for distribution, inherent in both systems, large numbers of persons lack the basic goods required to enjoy their generic rights to freedom and well-being.

As I noted earlier, ideally the productive system in a just social order would be characterized by a high degree of efficiency and economic growth, a just distribution of social and economic benefits, and conditions of work that foster identity formation and autonomous development. Needless to say, however, the simultaneous satisfaction of these demands presents a tremendous challenge. It might be the case, for example, that the degree of efficiency and economic growth necessary to provide the basic goods required for people to enjoy their generic rights is most easily attained by an increase in mechanization, centralization, and hierarchy. This would mean, of course, that efficiency and growth are achieved at the cost of depriving individuals of the working conditions that humans need to lead autonomous lives. On the other hand, it may be that securing the optimal working conditions for maximizing autonomy would so lower productivity and growth that people would lack the basic goods required for effective exercise of their rights. The problem, in short, is how to achieve an adequate rate of economic growth while, at the same time, creating conditions of work that allow for the development of autonomous human beings.

II

The Need for Market Socialism

To decide whether one sort of economic arrangement is superior or inferior to another, we must compare how well people in general

---

[45] Schwartz, "Meaningful Work."

fare in terms of the distribution of the necessary preconditions for action in different societies. We have seen that, today, neither the kind of economy found in capitalist societies like the United States nor the sort existing in Soviet-type societies is adequate for assuring everyone the basic goods necessary for exercising their generic rights to freedom and well-being.

In my view, a just social order requires a set of economic arrangements that is an amalgam of what is found in the two types of economies examined above. This necessitates an amalgam of plan and market, state control and individual initiative, centralization and decentralization, i.e., a socialist economy. To provide a detailed description of such an economy is beyond my powers and intentions. But I do want to briefly sketch out some of the characteristics of the socialist economy that I have in mind.[46]

To begin with, there must be a market in which social demands find expression. It is true, of course, that markets have many problems. Among other things, they generate inequalities, can be dominated by monopolies, and cannot satisfy the needs for public goods. Nevertheless, markets are necessary to avoid the "terrorization of the consumer" found in the Soviet-type economy, where legions of bureaucrats determine what people really need. In the U.S.S.R., for example, citizens must take it or leave it. With market socialism the willingness of customers to pay for eggs, shoes, hair ribbons, radios, jeans, or books will strongly determine what is produced.

At the same time, however, a just social order requires that there be social ownership of such natural resources as coal, oil, iron, and

---

[46] In the following discussion I draw on a number of different sources. Especially useful are Michael Albert and Robin Hahnel, *Socialism Today and Tomorrow* (Boston: South End Press, 1981); Rudolf Bahro, *The Alternative in Eastern Europe* (London: New Left Books, 1978); John P. Burkes, et al., eds., *Marxism and the Good Society* (New York: Cambridge University Press, 1981); Joseph Carens, *Equality, Moral Incentives and the Market* (Chicago: University of Chicago Press, 1981); Martin Carnoy and Derek Shearer, *Economic Democracy* (New York: Random House, 1980); Joshua Cohen and Joel Rogers, *On Democracy: Toward a Transformation of American Society* (New York: Penguin Books, 1983); Charles J. Erasmus, *In Search of the Common Good: Utopian Experiments Past and Future* (New York: Free Press, 1977); Neil Gilbert, *Capitalism and the Welfare State* (New Haven: Yale University Press, 1983); Jennifer L. Hochschild, *What's Fair? American Beliefs About Distributive Justice* (Cambridge, Mass.: Harvard University Press, 1981); Horvat, *Political Economy*; Lindblom, *Politics and Markets*; Marković, "Marxism"; Alec Nove, *The Economics of Feasible Socialism* (London: George Allen & Unwin, 1983); Alec Nove and D. M. Nuti, eds., *Socialist Economics* (Harmondsworth: Penguin, 1972); R. Selucky, *Marxism, Socialism and Freedom* (London: Macmillan, 1979); and David Schweickart, *Capitalism or Worker Control?* (New York: Praeger Publishers, 1980).

forests, and of the steel, transportation, and other large-scale industries. This will necessitate a greater amount of social planning than is found in contemporary capitalist societies. Major investment decisions involving electricity, oil, railroads, and the marketing abroad of principal products obviously need planning and coordination. But such planning should be avoided in the case of small-scale firms like clothing stores, restaurants, and the like.

Within a socialist economy, some enterprises will function most effectively on a large scale. A nationwide electricity network, for example, is cheaper and more efficient than a variety of smaller enterprises at the local level. With such a network, central planning is unavoidable; only those persons at the center know how much current is needed in one or another area and which particular power stations should be feeding into the national grid. The same goes for water, oil, steel, and railroads; all require centralized state planning in order to coordinate vastly complicated investment and production activities. But if the state-owned electricity grid, for instance, fails to supply power at a reasonable cost to its users, then other firms should be free to try to generate their own electricity.

Unless large-scale, state-owned enterprises are more efficient than other arrangements, smaller-scale enterprises are to be preferred. Generally speaking, the bigger the unit in which someone works, the more likely he or she is to feel remote from management decisions, alienated from what is being done, and engaged in meaningless labor. Other things being equal, therefore, smallness is to be preferred with regard to working conditions.[47] As noted above, however, some types of productive activities must almost inevitably be organized on a large-scale basis. To attempt to organize the production and distribution of electricity, for example, so as to assure small working units for everyone would obviously involve a prohibitive cost.

In addition to the *large-scale* centralized state corporations, a socialist economy will be characterized by *moderate-scale* state enterprises. They might be engaged in the manufacture of shoes, light bulbs, ashtrays, typewriters, or whatever. In these enterprises, employers will have far more voice in decision-making than in the large-scale ones. In fact, all individuals working in such firms will have the right to participate in decision-making. This requires "self-management."[48]

[47] Selucky, *Marxism, Socialism and Freedom*; Nove, *Economics of Feasible Socialism*.
[48] Horvat, *Political Economy*.

Organizations must be structured so as to eliminate hierarchy and competing bureaucracies by combining management and work by the same people. The intention here is to eliminate power-based hierarchy, which involves control, and to increase the autonomy of individual workers. But coordinating hierarchy is always required. In a self-managed socialist firm, all workers will participate in policy decisions. Once a policy decision is reached, it becomes a directive for the management. Thus, there are two fundamentally different spheres of activity or decision-making. In his book, *The Political Economy of Socialism*, Horvat describes them as follows:

> The first is concerned with value judgments, and consequently each individual counts as one in this sphere. In the second, technical decisions are made on the basis of technical competence and expertise. The decisions of the first sphere are policy directives; those of the second, technical directives. The former are based on political authority as exercised by all members of the organization; the latter, on professional authority specific to each member and growing out of the division of labor. Such an organization involves a clearly defined coordinating hierarchy but eliminates a power hierarchy.[49]

Enterprises must be divided into work units, groups small enough to make possible face-to-face interaction and informal communication. As far as possible, the decisions that affect the daily lives of workers are to be made at the level of the work unit. It is only when such decisions substantially affect the interests of other work units that they will be made at the level above the work unit.[50] Relevant here are decisions concerning work conditions, employment and dismissal, and distribution of the surplus.

Every enterprise faces, of course, the problem of efficient management and control; correct decisions must be taken and implemented in an efficient manner. But self-management does not, as noted above, require direct participation of all workers in every decision. The implementation of decisions—executive work and administration—is a matter of professional competence, not of democratic voting procedures. Those making such decisions are *responsible* for them, i.e., rights are to be matched by sanctions.[51] On the basis of their special abilities, experience, and familiarity

[49] Ibid., pp. 189–90.
[50] Ibid.
[51] Nove, *Economics of Feasible Socialism*.

with the work they do, managers will have a certain amount of discretionary authority. They must, at the same time, be evaluated as professionals, that is, on the basis of the adequacy of their technical performance.

Most important as regards adequacy are the over-all business results. Every worker in a socialist economy with social ownership will have a concern with such business results. This is because the personal income of every worker has two ingredients.[52] One (wages and salaries) is viewed as reflecting his own individual contribution to the work unit and firm; the other is the result of the collective efforts of everyone working in his firm (share in surplus or profit). Although a part of profits will always remain in the firm to be used for investment, a portion will be distributed among all the workers. Since, then, the worker is working for himself and not a boss and participates himself in work management, there are obvious incentives for everyone to work efficiently.[53] This need not assure that a particular firm will be commercially successful, however. Market fluctuations, new tariffs by a foreign country, and other factors outside the control of the workers may have an adverse effect on the firm's success. The same holds, of course, for firms organized along more traditional lines. In any case, self-management does not guarantee success. '

Nevertheless, the advantages of self-management are considerable. The available evidence suggests that in a self-managing group of workers, motivation, job satisfaction, work discipline, and production are increased; while absenteeism, the frequency of strikes, and the costs of supervision are lowered.[54] In short, incentives of participation, self-management, and profit-sharing combine to increase worker autonomy and provide economic efficiency.

In addition to self-management, moderate-scale state enterprises also require social planning. The activities of the different productive units must be coordinated in order to assure rational use of socially productive capital and to reduce uncertainty concerning

[52] Horvat, *Political Economy*.

[53] Ibid., p. 276.

[54] See, for example, Paul Blumberg, *Industrial Democracy: The Sociology of Participation* (New York: Schocken Books, 1969); J. Espinosa and A. Zimbalist, *Economic Democracy* (New York: Academic Press, 1978); Frank Lindenfeld and Joyce Rothschild-Whitt, eds., *Workplace Democracy and Social Change* (Boston: Porter Sargent, 1982); and Frank H. Stephen, ed., *The Performance of Labor-Managed Firms* (New York: St. Martin's Press, 1982).

investment.[55] "Central" planning, as found in the Soviet-type economies, implies control from above and destroys the autonomy of the firm. In contrast, "social" planning implies coordination based on economic interests. The aim, as Horvat notes, is to achieve "the desired *global* proportions . . . leaving each *individual* firm full autonomy—and responsibility—for decision making."[56] Such social planning assures a degree of efficiency not realized with central planning or the absence of coordinated planning as found in capitalist societies.

There must also be room in a socialist economy for *small-scale private enterprises*. Within limits (to be discussed shortly), individuals ought to be free to undertake economic activities outside the dominant socialist sector. If someone sees that there seems to be an unsatisfied market for roller skates, music boxes, poetry readings, or chocolate-chip cookies, then I see no reason why he or she shouldn't go ahead and produce privately for sale.

The problem, of course, is not with the individual enterpreneur or even with a small business run by three or four persons. Rather, it is the potential for becoming a large-scale privately owned enterprise that is the danger. What is morally offensive is the existence of people who exploit others, people with an unearned income arising simply from ownership of capital or land. To avoid this, limits are obviously necessary. Such limits must be decided democratically in light of people's experiences and preferences. The number of persons employed, the value of capital assets, the quantity of such small businesses, or a number of other factors might constitute the limits.[57]

In any case, the set of socialist economic arrangements found in the just social order will involve three different types of productive relations: large-scale centralized state corporations, moderate-scale enterprises with worker management, and small-scale private enterprises. What is most important, of course, is that the citizens be able to choose the types of cooperative and private initiatives they wish to have. After all, people differ greatly in the way they like to work. Some prefer working alone, some seek and welcome responsibility, still others like working in small teams, and so on. In addition, workers must be free to choose the nature of their work, if they so wish. Just as the market in the just social order enables

[55] Horvat, *Political Economy*; Nove, *Economics of Feasible Socialism*.
[56] Ibid. See also, Lindblom, *Politics and Markets*.
[57] This is suggested in Nove, *Economics of Feasible Socialism*.

citizens to register their preferences by spending their money one way rather than another, political democracy enables them to express their preferences as regards the organization of work.

People's effective exercise of their fundamental rights to freedom and well-being requires meaningful participation in political decision-making.[58] In a capitalist society, as we know, private property and class differentials in wealth make an equality of power impossible to realize. And in a Soviet-type society, the enormous concentration of power in the hands of bureaucrats works against an equality of political decision-making. In a socialist democracy, however, the selection of candidates for political office must be a prerogative of the voters, and not of the party apparatus or one or another power elite. Further, political campaigns must be financed out of communal funds so that political candidates will have direct access to the electorate. Finally, there must be the protection of such civil and political rights as: life, liberty, and security of person; freedom of thought and conscience; freedom of opinion and expression; freedom of peaceful assembly and association; and the right of information. This assurance of the equality of citizens follows from my earlier discussion of civil and political rights in Chapter 7. Such an equality is not only a demand of justice, but is likely to increase efficiency and growth by allowing for optional use of development potentials within the socialist society.

This, then, is a brief sketch of the sort of productive arrangements required for the realization of a just social order. Though only partial, I think that it suffices to show that such a nonexisting socialist economy would be superior to either a capitalist economy based on private ownership or a Soviet-type based on state ownership. There are several reasons for this: it is likely to be more efficient and thus will help assure a bigger "economic pie"; it will provide better opportunities for identity formation and autonomy as they relate to the work situation, and it is more just in terms of assuring the basic goods necessary for an effective exercise of the rights to freedom and well-being.

Although a just social order requires a socialist economy, I am not going to consider the kinds of structural transformations that might help existing societies move toward its realization. Instead of focusing on the various strategies that might speed a transition in that direction, I am going to discuss a number of required modifications and changes in *contemporary* advanced societies that will help secure some of the advantages that might better be realized

[58] Gewirth, *Reason and Morality*.

in a socialist economy. In other words, I am choosing for a "second-best" type of solution. In place of a complete restructuring of one or another contemporary advanced society, I am giving priority to a consideration of some alterations that appear to be both morally required and feasible in terms of their actual implementation in existing societies.

I might, of course, dream of a millennial world in which the state has withered away, where everyone works for the sheer pleasure of supporting the collective good, and where all bourgeois influences on the personality have been outgrown. But such a world strikes me as beyond the possibility of realization. Nor do I see any point in resorting to spaceship economics or behavioral engineering to support some utopian pipe dream.

I do, however, believe in the possibility of vastly improving the quality of life in our contemporary advanced societies. My concern in the remainder of this chapter is mainly with specifying some principles and policies of distribution and redistribution required to assure everyone the necessary preconditions for the enjoyment of their generic rights to freedom and well-being. This constitutes a rough portrayal of a better world, the virtues of which stand in sharp contrast to the vices of this one.

III

We do not yet have the required principles of economic distribution for a just social order. But we know that such principles must assure that all persons are enabled to effectively exercise their generic rights. As noted earlier, every human being is entitled both to those generic rights and to the necessary conditions for action. This means that all persons have rights to adequate food, shelter, health care, and the like. What is important about these entitlements is that they are logically prior to whatever people may be thought to be entitled to in terms of *existing* legal and nonlegal rules or agreements. How, then, are goods and services to be distributed in such a way that these entitlements are honored?

Some useful suggestions in this regard are provided by Marx in his *Critique of the Gotha Programma*, where he considers the transition from the lower stages of communism to the higher stages.[59] He is concerned with the problem of how society can pass from

[59] Marx, *Critique*. Further, I make use here of some provocative ideas from van der Veen. See Robert J. van der Veen, "From Contribution to Needs." Paper presented at the European Consortium for Political Research, Workshop on Regulative Political Theory, Aarhus, Denmark, April 1982.

an initial régime based on the principle of work contribution to the final stage of abundant wealth wherein each producer freely contributes according to his abilities and receives according to his needs. This is obviously a different problem than the one that concerns me here, since my specific focus is on economic distribution in contemporary Western societies. Nevertheless, there are some ideas that are directly relevant to my own concern with distribution in the just social order.

Marx argued that in the early stage of communism people will be rewarded according to contribution and in the final stage of abundance will receive in accord with their needs. He saw the defects of the so-called contribution principle and built in various remedies to correct them. He did so partly because he recognized that the right of producers under the contribution principle is *proportional* to their supply of labor. Thus, there is usually a portion of the product to which its producer is not entitled. While in a "bourgeois" society the aggregate of such residual products is the sum of the profits and forms the basis of capitalist accumulation, under communism the same surplus above earnings from labor is distributed on the basis of principles other than the "equal right of producers."

This is exactly the point of Marx's attack on the Lassallean slogan: that "the proceeds of labour belong undiminished with equal right to all members of society."[60] Here, of course, "equal right" refers to the principle of contribution. In response to this claim, Marx asks rhetorically: " 'To all members of society'? To those who do not work as well? What remains of the 'undiminished proceeds of labour'? Only to those members of society who work? What remains then of the 'equal right' of all members of society?"

With regard to the " 'undiminished' Lassallean 'proceeds of labour,' " Marx can be viewed as decomposing them into seven separate parts. The following long quotation is from Marx, while I have provided the itemization:

Let us take first of all the words "proceeds of labour" in the sense of the produce of labour; then the co-operative proceeds of labour are the *total social product*.

From this must now be deducted:

First, cover for the replacement of the means of production used up. [Item 1]

[60] Marx, *Critique*, p. 13.

Secondly, additional portion for expansion of production. [Item 2]

Thirdly, reserve or insurance funds against accidents, dislocations caused by natural calamities, etc. [Item 3]

These deductions from the "undiminished proceeds of labour" are an economic necessity and their magnitude is to be determined according to available means and forces, and partly by computation of probabilities, but they are in no way calculable by equity.

There remains the other part of the total product, intended to serve as means of consumption.

Before this is divided among individuals, there has to be deducted again, from it:

First, the general costs of administration not directly belonging to production. [Item 4]

This part will, from the outset, be very considerably restricted in comparison with present-day society and it diminishes in proportion as the new society develops.

Secondly, that which is intended for the common satisfaction of needs, such as schools, health services, etc. [Item 5]

From the outset this part grows considerably in comparison with present-day society and it grows in proportion as the new society develops.

Thirdly, funds for those unable to work, etc., in short, for what is included under so-called official poor relief today. [Item 6]

Only now do we come to the "distribution" which the programme, under Lassallean influence, alone has in view in its narrow fashion, namely, to that part of the means of consumption which is divided among the individual producers of the co-operative society. [Item 7]

The "undiminished proceeds of labour" have already become converted into the "diminished" proceeds, although what is withheld from the producer in his capacity as a private individual benefits him directly in his capacity as a member of society.[61]

What is most suggestive in this long citation from Marx is the stark contrast between Item 7, "that part of the means of consumption which is divided among the individual producers," and the rest of the items. The first four items in Marx's deductive scheme are all broadly concerned with the part of the proceeds of

[61] Ibid., pp. 13–14.

labor that relates specifically to production. Items 5 and 6, the common satisfaction of needs, and functions for those unable to work, etc., can be viewed as covering "common needs." Assuming that both the first set of items (1 through 4) and the second set (5 and 6) concern the meeting of social needs, without which production is not even possible, it is only Item 7, pertaining to personal consumption, that represents a concern with "private needs."

Although Marx never discusses the distinction in *Gotha*, he would surely agree that the meeting of common needs must have priority over the meeting of private needs. Thus, the funds for the first must take priority over the second. This leads, then, to the emergence of a two-tiered scheme for distribution. With this scheme, the priority of the public sector of the economy above the private sector is established.

The Distributional Principle for a Just Social Order:
A First Formulation

Translating this two-tiered scheme into the language of rights and obligations and applying it to the problem of assuring that everyone in society will have the necessary preconditions of action, suggests the following.

Given that my concern is with the realization of a just social order within existing advanced societies, I need not devote explicit attention to Marx's four items or steps regarding production. While this would be a serious omission for someone focusing on the features of a fully developed communist society, my own focus is quite different. I acknowledge, of course, the crucial importance of having a large portion of the proceeds of labor devoted to what is specified in Marx's four items—replacement of the means of production used up, expansion of production, a reserve of insurance funds, and covering the costs of administration. But I am assuming that existing resources will be used to satisfy these requirements—even if the so-called incentives (i.e., economic rewards) required for attracting investments are *less* than is now the case.

Once these requirements are indeed satisfied, a two-tiered scheme is necessary where everyone's entitlement to the generic rights to freedom and well-being has priority over the particular entitlements of individuals to receive differential economic rewards. In other words, the notion of individual entitlements (established by promises, agreements, and the like) and differential economic rewards come into play only *after* the basic rights of all societal members are realized.

Since all persons have the fundamental rights to freedom and well-being, they have a right to an adequate share of every distributable good whose enjoyment is a necessary condition of their being able to exercise these basic rights. Thus, as already noted, each and every person has a right to adequate food, clothing, shelter, medical care, and protection.

This obviously requires socialized medicine, collectively paid for, with access determined solely by medical need. And public housing—such as that found in Scandinavia and the Netherlands but not in the United States—must be provided for all who need it (and with subsidies if required). Since education is a necessary good for people to enjoy their basic rights to freedom and well-being in contemporary Western societies, everyone also has a right to an adequate education. Similarly with a job; everyone has a right to paid employment. When unable to work, he or she has a right to a minimum income. We can speak of at least some of these as basic *welfare rights* to which all persons are equally entitled.

The stipulation that every person has a right—legally specified as welfare rights—to an adequate level of all these goods and services does not mean that everyone has a right to an *equal* share of them. So long as everyone has the required preconditions for exercising their basic rights, it is not necessarily unjust that some persons may, for example, have more comfortable houses, more expensive clothing, better cuts of meat, more years of schooling, or more interesting jobs.

Nor does the fact that some people have adequate goods and still fail to successfully enjoy their rights to freedom and well-being mean that they have a right to a larger portion of necessary goods. And, of course, if some unusual persons manage to realize their basic rights despite the absence of an important good, this does not show that the good is unnecessary either for them or for other persons. That is, the success of extraordinary people to effectively exercise their rights to freedom and well-being in the absence of the good in question in no way demonstrates that the share viewed as necessary for people more generally is too large.

The point is that people have rights to distributable goods that are generally *necessary* for their being able to enjoy their basic rights. Although these goods are necessary, they may not always be sufficient and, therefore, will never provide an absolute guarantee that all persons will indeed be able to effectively exercise their basic

403

rights. (There is, in my view, no conceivable level of combination of distributable goods that could provide such a guarantee.) I will return to this issue in Section IV.

All of this might seem to suggest that the appropriate distributional principle for a just social order would be one of free provision of the necessary distributable goods and services to everyone who needs them. Such a principle would be consistent with Marx's statement that a part of the total product must be used "for the common satisfaction of needs, such as schools, health services, etc." and "for those unable to work, etc."[62] Indeed, the government ought to provide income security, comprehensive and free medical care, education, and public housing, according to nonmarket criteria. All of these constitute welfare rights to which everyone is entitled.

As already noted, however, such state provisions will not by themselves assure everyone of an *adequate* level of the necessary distributable goods. Not only do these not usually include food and clothing, but the less advantaged may lack the financial means for optimally utilizing some of these goods and services. The provision of public housing, for example, will not prove adequate unless all persons (or families) have the financial means to buy furniture, rugs, a stove and refrigerator, and other material goods associated with a decent housing situation. And even the state provision of comprehensive and free medical care will not give the poor equal access to physicians, clinics, hospitals, etc., unless they have a sufficient amount of money to pay for such things as baby-sitters and transportation.

I mentioned above that the distribution of economic goods and services requires a two-tiered scheme. It needs now to be pointed out that the first tier involves two separate steps. Step one requires—as guaranteed welfare rights—state provision of such goods and services as comprehensive and free medical care, education, public housing, and employment. Step two requires that the state redistribute wealth and income to assure that everyone is enabled to obtain an *adequate* level of the necessary goods and services.

Once these two stipulations have been met, we arrive at the second tier. Here the residual goods (presumably in the form of salaries and wages) are to be distributed in accordance with a principle somewhat akin to Rawls's difference principle. But while

[62] Ibid., p. 13.

Rawls's principle speaks of maximally benefitting the least-advantaged group within a society, the principle suggested here is somewhat different: *an unequal distribution of economic rewards is morally permissible only to the extent that it does not lead to concentrations of wealth that are demonstrably detrimental to the exercise of other people's rights.*

Thus, even if the conditions for the first tier are met, it must be assured that economic inequalities are not large enough to adversely effect the less advantaged in the exercise of their rights. There must, therefore, be assurance that economic inequalities will not lead, for example, to highly unequal power relationships among different groups or classes. Large inequalities in power that adversely affect people's effective exercise of their rights, especially their right to freedom, are not to be permitted.

Consider voting rights and political participation in this regard. In a just society the rich and poor alike will have identical voting rights. But if the rich are, by virtue of their greater wealth, better able to contribute directly or indirectly to the success of their preferred candidates, influence public opinion through their control of the media, and even affect the actions of public officials, there is an obvious inequality in people's right to participate in the political process.

Corporate executives, for example, have access to funds (including corporate assets), which can be made available for party, interest group, and electoral activity in pursuit of whatever objectives they themselves choose.[63] This is obviously important where running for public office in a country like the United States can cost millions of dollars.[64] LaPalombara notes that: "The cost of competing for public office in the United States has truly reached astronomical proportions. . . . For every presidentially aspiring haberdasher like Harry S Truman, there are several multimillionaires like John F. Kennedy or Averell Harriman. For less wealthy but well-heeled aspirants like Richard Nixon, enormously wealthy

[63] See, for example, Lindblom, *Politics and Markets*. Also important are a number of somewhat older studies: C. Wright Mills, *The Power Elite* (New York: Oxford University Press, 1956); Gabriel Kolko, *Wealth and Power in America* (New York: Praeger Publishers, 1962); G. William Domhoff, *Who Rules America?* (Englewood Cliffs, N.J.: Prentice-Hall, 1967); Henry W. Ehrmann, *Organized Business in France* (Princeton: Princeton University Press, 1967); Joseph LaPalombara, *Interest Groups in Italian Politics* (Princeton: Princeton University Press, 1964); and Stephen Blank, *Industry and Government in Britain* (Lexington, Mass.: D. C. Heath, 1973).

[64] C. Anderson, *Statecraft* (New York: Wiley, 1977).

backers stand ready to turn dollars into votes—sometimes by means that are flagrantly in violation of law."[65] Despite recent changes in the laws pertaining to campaign financing in the United States, standing for election is extremely expensive. In a just social order, the government would systematically assure public financing of competing political parties.

More generally in capitalist societies, business executives have enormous power to decide on a variety of issues—the allocation of resources to different lines of production, the allocation of the labor force to different occupations and work places, technologies, executive compensation, and the like—that are of monumental importance for people's exercise of the rights to freedom and well-being. As Lindblom points out, "Businessmen generally and corporate executives in particular take on a privileged role in government that is, it seems reasonable to say, unmatched by any leadership group other than government officials themselves."[66]

Businessmen are not the only persons, of course, who utilize their wealth and power in ways that would not be acceptable in a just social order. But whatever people's source of income, it is not the unequal distribution of economic benefits that is in itself objectionable. An unequal distribution becomes objectionable only when it leads to concentrations of wealth that are manifested in unequal power relations between classes or groups that adversely affect people's enjoyment of their fundamental rights.

The principle introduced above has, I believe, far less potential for negative consequences than Rawls's difference principle. For Rawls, it may be recalled, the difference principle is the *beginning* step with regard to economic distribution. Because he assumes that this principle requires large inequalities in distribution (as a matter of incentives), the necessary preconditions for the effective exercises of the rights to freedom and well-being would not be realized. That is, Rawls suggests no limits on economic rewards to prevent accumulations of wealth and income detrimental to other people's enjoyment of their rights.

With my principle, however, unequal distributions are not allowed to occur until the necessary preconditions have already been secured. In other words, the principle operates only *after* the necessary preconditions have been assured through the provision of

---

[65] Joseph LaPalombara, *Politics Within Nations* (Englewood Cliffs, N.J.: Prentice-Hall, 1974), pp. 486–87.

[66] Lindblom, *Politics and Markets*, p. 172.

basic goods and services and the redistribution of wealth and income so that everyone has an adequate level of the relevant goods and services. And even then, there are limitations on the extent of such unequal distributions. Whereas Rawls's scheme, as well as Gewirth's theory, permits economic inequalities of such a large magnitude that many people would be unable to enjoy their fundamental rights to either freedom or well-being, that possibility is minimized in the scheme presented here.

A comprehensive principle of distribution for a just social order would, then, take roughly the following form:

In a just social order, there must be (a) provision of such goods and services as free and comprehensive medical care and education, public housing, and guaranteed employment, as welfare rights; plus (b) a redistribution of wealth and income to assure that everyone is enabled to obtain an adequate level of these and other necessary goods and services; (c) any inequalities that remain once these stipulations have been met are permissible if and only if they do not lead to concentrations of wealth that are demonstrably detrimental to some people's effective exercise of their generic rights.

It is, as argued earlier, the government and its legal system that must establish and enforce the necessary mechanisms to ensure that this principle is implemented. Once the necessary preconditions for everyone's exercising his or her fundamental rights are assured, we come to that part of the distribution which Marx said is to be "divided among the individual producers of the co-operative society."[67] That part, as indicated in clause (c) of the above general principle, must be divided in such a way as not to prevent other persons from enjoying their rights to freedom and well-being.

I argued in Chapter 7 that the government in a just social order can assure the rights of all its citizens without violating the rights of any of them. Someone's right to freedom is not violated when he or she must, for example, pay taxes to satisfy the welfare rights of others. If the affluent are heavily taxed to help those who are starving or lack adequate housing or medical care, the former's right to freedom is not being violated.

Such taxation, as well as other mechanisms necessary for assuring the welfare rights of everyone, would indeed require certain restrictions on some people's exercise of their right to freedom. But it is not the case that *any* restriction on the exercise of freedom constitutes a "violation" of that right. People's right to freedom is

[67] Marx, *Critique*, p. 14.

relative to the requirement of agency on the part of each and every person. When the nonvoluntary payment of taxes is required to assure the necessary preconditions of agency for the needy, their welfare rights must take precedence over the unlimited freedom of the persons taxed to accumulate and use their money as they please.

Furthermore, these restrictions on the affluents' right to freedom do not constitute any loss of freedom to them as moral agents. Should those who now enjoy the necessary conditions for exercising their rights to freedom and well-being find themselves in serious need, they have a right to the required distributable goods. And, of course, these will be provided through the mechanism of levying higher taxes on those who are then more fortunate. The present *obligation* of the more affluent to help secure the welfare rights of others who lack the necessities for exercising their basic rights to freedom and well-being is, as pointed out in Chapter 7, the logical correlate of their own *right* for similar treatment should the need ever arise.

In a just social order, therefore, the redistribution of income is both morally required and permissible. It is required to assure that everyone will have the preconditions necessary for exercising their rights, and it is permissible since it can be implemented without violating anyone's rights. But such redistribution is not aimed, as with some egalitarian schemes, at achieving absolute equality. Rather, the distribution is intended to help assure that all persons have the necessary goods required for enjoying their basic rights.

IV

Entitlements, Freedom, and Problems of Paternalism

The distributional principle discussed above is justified by appeal to everyone's being entitled both to their generic rights to freedom and well-being and to the necessary preconditions for effectively exercising their rights. Precisely what level of housing, education, security, and the like, constitutes an adequate level is, of course, open to some debate. Consequently, it is not easy to specify how much redistribution of wealth and income would be required to assure an adequate level of welfare rights for everyone living in one or another contemporary society.

But even if we were able to be precise about what constituted an adequate level of the preconditions, to specify what redistribution is required, and to successfully implement various welfare policies and programs, we must recognize the arguments of those who say that this will not assure an improvement in the situation of everyone.

I am referring here to the claim that class- or income-linked inequalities in health status, education, and housing quality are in reality due to differences in various ideas and attitudes in the various social classes rather than to the lack of goods and services or economic means *per se*. Consider a simple example. Socioeconomic differences in such things as height and age of physical maturity among children are, in this view, due to the fact that the lower classes "choose" to spend their money on sweets and starchy foods rather than on fresh fruit and vegetables, on white bread rather than on the more nourishing brown breads, on soda pop rather than milk.

While it is undoubtedly true that the disadvantaged in most societies do consume less nutritional food and in general have a poorer diet than the better off, there is reason to believe that such differences can sometimes be eliminated with an improvement in the economic situation of the less fortunate. Recent findings from Sweden are striking in this respect. They reveal that there are today *no* socioeconomic differences in the height and age of maturity among children,[68] and, further, that income-related differences in the infant mortality rate appear to have been completely erased.[69] That such findings should emerge from Sweden is not at all surprising. Among Western societies, it has one of the highest levels of expenditures on social security and welfare services.[70]

But what works in Sweden may not work elsewhere. This is the claim frequently heard from Edward Banfield and others who emphasize the negative effects of the culture of poverty in the United States.[71] Such persons might grant that marked improvements for the poor in physical status and other aspects of their situation are indeed possible in societies other than the United States. After all, they would argue, the population of Sweden is quite homogeneous

---

[68] Gunilla Lindgren, "Height, Weight and Menarche in Swedish Urban School Children in Relation to Socio-Economic and Regional Differences," *Anals of Human Biology* 3 (1976): 501–28.

[69] S. Sjolin, "Infant Mortality in Sweden," in Helen M. Williams, ed., *Health Care of Mothers and Children in National Health Services* (Cambridge, Mass.: Ballinger, 1975).

[70] Christopher Hewitt, "The Effect of Political Democracy and Social Democracy on Equality in Industrial Societies: A Cross-National Comparison," *American Sociological Review* 42 (June 1977): 450–64; Harold L. Wilensky, *The Welfare State and Equality* (Berkeley: University of California Press, 1975).

[71] Edward C. Banfield, *The Unheavenly City* (Boston: Little, Brown & Co., 1968).

(despite the presence of "guest workers" from other countries) and there is no history of families being locked into poverty over several generations. In the United States, however, welfare expenditures as a way of improving the situation of the poor are often a waste of money. Banfield argues this position at great length in his book, *The Unheavenly City*.[72]

According to Banfield, policy considerations for alleviating poverty fail to give sufficient attention to class-related differences—especially those concerning people's orientation to the future. The higher the social class of the individual, says Banfield, the more distant the future he can imagine and discipline himself to make sacrifices for.[73] Banfield's focus is on the lower-class individual, whom he describes as follows:

> At the present-oriented end of the scale, the lower-class individual lives from moment to moment. . . . Impulse governs his behavior either because he cannot discipline himself to sacrifice a present for a future satisfaction or because he has no sense of the future. He is therefore radically improvident: whatever he cannot consume immediately he considers valueless. His bodily needs (especially for sex) and his taste for "action" take precedence over everything else—and certainly over work routine. . . . So long as the city contains a sizeable lower class, nothing basic can be done about its most serious problems. Good jobs may be offered to all, but some will remain chronically unemployed. Slums may be demolished, but if the housing that replaces them is occupied by the lower class, it will shortly be turned into new slums. Welfare persons will continue to live in squalor and misery. . . . The lower-class forms of all problems are at bottom a single problem: the existence of an outlook and style of life which is radically present-oriented and which therefore attaches no value to work, sacrifice, self-improvement, or service to family, friends, or community.[74]

Banfield certainly recognizes that the group composed of the poor is hardly homogeneous, and it does not seem that his description is intended to apply to all poor persons (what he terms lower-class persons). He would surely agree that there are large

[72] Ibid.
[73] Ibid., p. 47.
[74] Ibid., pp. 53, 62, 210–11.

numbers of poor persons (in fact, many more today than when Banfield published his book in 1968) who are poor through no fault of their own. This group includes the ill, the handicapped, those unable to find employment at all, and, of course, the children of such persons. Many of these individuals share middle-class aspirations, but lack the resources to escape poverty. Banfield's description does not apply to them at all. He might also agree that some of those who do possess the values and attitudes described would, if given the opportunity, alter their values and attitudes. Neither of these two groups, then, constitute the main focus of Banfield's attention. Instead, his remarks concern exclusively lower-class persons whose attitudes and values are both deeply ingrained and exceedingly difficult to change.[75]

It is difficult to know, of course, exactly how large this group is in the United States or other Western societies today. But whatever its size, it creates a serious problem for the application of the distributional principle that I advanced in the previous section. This problem concerns the right of persons captured in the culture of poverty to exercise their freedom by spending the money they receive in whatever way they choose.

Whether those with the attitudes described by Banfield are poor because of their own actions (and nonactions), as he claims, or are often the victims of various social forces beyond their control, as I tend to believe, it seems evident that there are many poor people who fail to use money income in the way that the state intends. With regard to providing money income to welfare recipients, Bowie points out the following: "Those who provide income assume that the recipients are wise and efficient in the use of money, namely, (a) that the recipient knows what he wants and needs, (b) that he will purchase things he genuinely needs before purchasing what he wants, and (c) that he will use his income so that he can maximize the utility of his purchases."[76] For many of the poor, as Bowie notes, these assumptions do not hold.

If we consider this in terms of the items constituting the necessary preconditions for enjoying the fundamental rights to freedom and well-being, we see that cash payments to the needy are involved with only some items. Medical care, housing, protection (i.e., the legal system, including the police), and education are provided in the form of goods and services in the just social order. But food,

---

[75] Norman E. Bowie, "Welfare and Freedom," *Ethics* 89 (April 1979): 263.
[76] Ibid., p. 264.

411

clothing, various consumer durables (stoves, refrigerators, television sets, etc.) would be purchased by those who need them with money provided through application of section (b) of the distribution principle discussed earlier. That is, the redistribution of wealth and income is intended partly to provide the needy with the funds required for obtaining an adequate level of those basic goods not made directly available in the form of goods and services.

If people are free to spend these funds as they choose, then some will certainly not spend them on the goods for which they are intended. Government studies in the United States have shown that probably no more than ten per cent of those receiving the income to purchase food with the necessary nutritional value (as established by the Department of Agriculture diet) do indeed receive an adequate diet.[77] Similarly with clothing: many persons who receive a clothing allowance do not spend it on clothing that is warm and serviceable. Whether it is their attitude and values, ignorance about what is required in the way of adequate food, clothing, and other necessities, or the psychological pressures created by advertising and various views of the good life, some poor people do not manage their money in a way that is to their own maximum benefit.

One need not agree fully with Banfield's analysis to see that the implementation of the distributional principle discussed in the preceding section would fail to assure that all persons have an adequate level of the preconditions necessary for effectively exercising their fundamental rights. Some people are simply not going to spend their cash income in a way that assures the necessary preconditions for themselves and their children.

The only way to make certain that such persons will have the necessary preconditions for exercising their rights to freedom and well-being is to provide them *directly* with the particular kinds of food, clothing, etc., that they ought to have, and to provide them with no money income at all. But this would obviously constitute an infringement on their freedom (the very freedom with which we are, in fact, concerned) that many persons would consider totally illegitimate. We might, of course, attempt to avoid this infringement by assuring that such persons are educated as to what they really need for their own (or their children's) physical welfare. Yet if Banfield's characterization is correct, if indeed values and

---

[77] U.S. Congress, Senate Select Committee on Nutrition and Human Needs, *Hunger and the Reform of Welfare: A Question of Adequacy*, 92 Cong., 2d sess., February 1972, pp. 26–31.

attitudes of these individuals are deeply ingrained and enormously resistent to change, then any attempts to educate or enlighten them may be exceedingly slow or even fruitless.

Any program that denies some poor persons the freedom to spend their welfare payments as they see fit will be, at the very least, highly paternalistic. Further, it will infringe people's freedom and will also have adverse effects on their dignity and self-respect. And, of course, it will have a negative influence on their views of the justice of the society in which they live. Thus, it would appear to be morally impermissible to refuse ("for their own good") to give cash payments to those persons who are seen as poor and irresponsible. Yet if they are unable to spend their cash payments in the appropriate way, then such payments are—as Banfield and others claim—a waste of money. Isn't it then unjust to tax people year after year in a vain attempt to provide the needy with certain basic necessities if some of them are unable to handle money in a responsible manner?

What does justice seem to require in this situation? One alternative is to simply accept that there are people who are, for whatever reasons, unable or unwilling to spend their welfare payments on things for which they are intended (e.g., nutritious food, warm and serviceable clothing). Allowing them to spend the money as they see fit does waste money and also harms them (or at least fails to benefit them in the ways intended), but it allows them to maintain whatever amount of dignity and self-respect they may have and avoids infringements on their freedom.

The other obvious alternative, as Bowie points out, is to avoid the adverse effects of mishandled money by having the state exercise massive social control over some of the poor.[78] In this case, the lower-class poor would become essentially wards of the state. In Bowie's words: "The monitoring of the life of the lower-class poor would not be dissimilar from the monitoring done on the inmates of prisons and asylums for the mentally ill."[79] Aside from such infringements on the freedom of those who are deemed irresponsible, there would be massive invasions of privacy and infringements of freedom involved even in the process of *identifying* such persons. There is the obvious danger, as Bowie also notes, of identifying the relevant persons on the basis of some particular

[78] Bowie, "Welfare and Freedom," pp. 267–68.
[79] Ibid., p. 267.

characteristic.[80] In the United States, for example, we can imagine that all poor persons who are, say, black might—for administrative purposes—be defined as that group of persons who ought not to receive cash payments.

There is, then, a dilemma. Either everyone entitled to cash payments will receive them, with the results that taxpayers' money will be wasted and that it will not actually help those who receive it, or draconian controls that infringe the freedom and privacy of many welfare recipients and adversely effect their dignity and self-respect will be required.

Although this is indeed a dilemma, the choice here seems obvious to me. Not only must we try to avoid imposing avoidable pain and suffering on the disadvantaged, but we must also be true to our own moral aspirations and commitments. Even though there is a price involved for the taxpayers and for the poor who mismanage whatever cash payments they receive, the continuation of such payments helps avoid (extra) psychological harms and provides at least the possibility that such cash payments may be used in ways that will indeed benefit the recipients. Further, the provision of welfare rights and money payments to the needy is done not only for their benefit but also for the benefit of those of us who do not require such assistance at the present time. Ideally, at least, it reaffirms those moral principles to which we lend our allegiance and support.

Nevertheless, the fact remains that even a just social order may be unable to assure that all persons will have an adequate level of the necessary preconditions for effective exercise of their fundamental rights to freedom and well-being. The best we can do is recognize this and work to educate those who are inclined to spend welfare monies in ways that are harmful to themselves, their children, the taxpayers, and, ultimately, to the moral standing of the society in which they live.

V

The Reduction of Economic Inequalities and Redistribution Through Taxation

It may be recalled that I said I was not going to consider what kinds of structural transformations might help achieve the economic arrangements most suitable for a completely realized just

[80] Ibid., p. 268.

social order. I will continue to ignore this difficult problem, but I do want to state my preference among *existing* economic arrangements. It seems clear to me that the best existing alternative to a capitalist or Soviet-type economy is that found in the Scandinavian countries. Denmark, Sweden, Norway, Finland, and Iceland are characterized by a mixed economy. Many of the economic arrangements are similar to those in a capitalist society like the United States, with the important difference that the state plays an extremely active role by utilizing policies for income differentials, tax schemes, transfer schemes, and transfer payments to help achieve its distributive aims.[81]

The governments of the above-named societies have been far more active than the governments of the United States, Canada, France, and Israel in reducing economic inequalities, providing widespread social benefits, and in general improving the position of the less advantaged. Recent evidence shows that the greater the involvement of the government in the economy, the less the extent of income inequality—at least in Western societies.[82] This relationship also seems to hold true with regard to unemployment. For example, the United States, a nation with low social welfare expenditures, has a relatively high rate of unemployment. Sweden, with one of the highest levels of such expenditures, has a far lower rate of unemployment.[83]

It is important to note that some of the countries mentioned above once had highly unequal income distributions.[84] In Sweden, for example, reductions in the inequality of earnings are largely a result of actions undertaken by the national organization of the manual workers' trade union. Such reductions have occurred in regard to both the average earnings among different industries and between the higher- and lower-paid within similar industries. This diminishing of wage differentials is due largely to "central framework agreements" negotiated with the national organization of employers, and not to market forces operating in the same direction.[85] These central framework agreements provide the basis for

---

[81] Cedrich Sanford, "The Taxation of Personal Wealth," pp. 102–21 in Aubrey Jones, ed., *Economics and Equality* (London: Philip Allan, 1976).

[82] Stephen Stack, "The Effect of Direct Government Involvement in the Economy on the Degree of Income Inequality: A Cross-National Study," *American Sociological Review* 43 (December 1978): 880–88.

[83] Ibid.

[84] See Hans F. Dahl, "Those Equal Folk," *Daedalus* 113 (Winter 1984): 93–107.

[85] Phelps Brown, *Inequality of Pay*, pp. 96–97.

collective bargaining at both plant and industry levels. Such bargaining is informed by two principles: an incomes policy based on wage increases at a level that will not adversely effect the international competitiveness of Swedish industry and a "solidaristic wages policy" designed to equalize wage differentials across various sectors. Through the same agreements, separate (lower) rates of pay for women have also been phased out. Thus, while a comparison of the pretax distribution of income in the United States and four European countries in 1935 showed Sweden as having the most unequal distribution, it now has the least unequal distribution of income.[86]

Although it is true that an increasing number of Scandinavians find the social welfare system too expensive, the evidence clearly indicates that the overwhelming majority are quite satisfied.[87] Perhaps relevant here is the fact that Scandinavians do not have to carry passports when traveling in any of the five Nordic countries. They can move across borders and have equal rights to work, to medical benefits, to social services, to social security, and to a pension in all countries.[88] Fundamentally, Anderson notes, "Nordic societies are based on private enterprise and the market economy, but the incentives that fuel the latter—inequalities in income, fortune, and power—are not given free reign there."[89]

All of this suggests that a greater economic equality could be achieved in the United States and other capitalist societies were there a strong commitment to doing so. If other highly industrialized societies with similar levels of economic development and technological requirements—for instance, Scandinavia and the Netherlands—can achieve greater economic equality without any serious damage to their economic functioning, then the United States, Canada, France, and other advanced societies are surely able to do the same.

This is not to deny that economic incentives are required to get people to perform certain kinds of work in a competent manner. Although it may sometimes be the case that noneconomic incentives (prestige, challenge, and the joy of accomplishment, for example) may be sufficient to encourage people to take on certain

[86] Hewitt, "The Effect of Political Democracy," p. 462.

[87] Dahl, "Those Equal Folk."

[88] Patricia Bliss McFate, "To See Everything in Another Light," Daedalus 113 (Winter 1984): 52.

[89] Bent Rold Anderson, "The Rationality and Irrationality of the Nordic Welfare State," Daedalus 113 (Winter 1984): 109.

jobs, I accept that—in today's world—pay differentials are probably the necessary incentives. But, as I indicated in the previous chapter, the differentials need not be *as large* as they frequently are in many contemporary societies.

It may be true—as Rawls's difference principle assumes—that inequality in economic rewards will elicit greater effort, a higher level of performance, or a greater contribution, and that this will, in turn, raise the over-all level of productivity so that there will be a surplus with which to raise the economic benefits for those in the lowest-paid jobs. Wolfe speaks of this as an "inequality surplus," which he defines as "the surplus income remaining after all the occupants of the roles of an unequally rewarded practice have been paid enough to draw them into several roles."[90] My claim is that smaller inequalities in pay would still prove sufficient for generating the necessary inequality surpluses.

Some persons might argue, of course, that there is something so fundamentally distinct about one or another contemporary Western society that larger income differentials are required to draw workers into various roles. In the case of the United States, for example, it could be that for reasons of tradition, convention, national character, or whatever, the rewards offered to people for acquiring certain qualifications "must" be more unequal than in, say, Sweden or the Netherlands. It is at least conceivable that with smaller economic differentials in the United States, there simply would not be enough people willing to undergo years of study or training and to take on certain jobs with heavy responsibilities.

But even if this were true, and I seriously doubt it, the question remains as to whether or not the differentials have to be as large as they now are in the United States. Although it is difficult to estimate exactly how much the existing earnings differentials could be reduced without eliminating the apparently necessary economic incentives, there is evidence to show that they can indeed be reduced.

I noted earlier in this chapter that the best paid quintile of workers in the United States earn approximately seven times what is earned by the bottom quintile. If, however, we distinguish between fully employed white males and the rest of full-time workers, we can learn something about the present over-all differentials. Inspection of Table 9.1, which compares the distribution of earnings for white males with that for "all other workers," i.e., for women and mi-

---

[90] Wolff, *Understanding Rawls*, p. 32.

Table 9.1
Distribution of Earnings in 1977

	Full-Time, Full-Year	
Quintiles	White Males (%)	All Other Workers (%)
1	7.7	1.8
2	13.9	7.2
3	18.2	15.8
4	23.5	27.0
5	36.7	48.2
Mean Earnings	$16,568	$5,843

SOURCE: U.S. Bureau of the Census, *Current Population Reports, Consumer Income 1977*, Series P-60, no. 118 (March 1979): 228.

norities, in the United States reveals two interesting patterns.[91] First, we see that the mean earnings of fully employed white males are about three times as high as those for the rest of the labor force. Second, and more importantly, the distribution of income among these white males is much more equal than for the rest of the work force. The differential of distribution is also less than for the working population as a whole. Whereas the earnings of the top quintile of all workers are (as already noted) seven times that of the bottom quintile, we see from Table 9.1 that the earnings gap for white males is much smaller than is the case within the category made up of women and minorities. The earnings of the top quintile of white male workers is five times as large as that of the bottom quintile. For the rest of the labor force, however, the same gap is twenty-seven to one—more than five times as large.

Fully employed male employees, as Thurow points out, come closer to the ideal of being able to fairly compete for a distribution of economic rewards than any other group in the United States.[92] They do not suffer from the handicaps of discrimination, lack of skills, or underemployment, as do women and minorities. If, as Table 9.1 shows, the work effect of white male workers is sustained by a reward structure with a five to one gap in earnings, then this is obviously sufficient for assuring that jobs will be filled by competent persons. Thurow's comments on this are very much to the point:

[91] This is taken from Lester C. Thurow, *The Zero-Sum Society* (New York: Penguin, 1980), p. 201.
[92] Ibid., p. 200.

Unless one believes that the culture in which women, minorities, and underemployed white males exist is different from the culture in which employed white males exist, there is every reason to believe that a reward structure that is capable of keeping white males on their economic toes is also capable of keeping other Americans on their economic toes. Inequalities greater than those that now occur in the earnings of fully employed white males are not necessary to keep the economy functioning. They are, in fact, counterproductive.[93]

It seems clear, then, that the present earnings gap of seven to one for the total working population of the United States can be reduced to a gap of five to one without eliminating the necessary economic incentives or weakening the economy. Whether it can be reduced still further without bringing about negative results is, of course, another question. But based on what we can witness in the Netherlands and Sweden, it appears that lesser differentials in pay and wages can serve both the fundamental purpose of production and reproduction of goods and services and generate inequality surpluses that can be distributed in such a way as to assure the necessary preconditions for everyone to be able to effectively exercise his or her rights to freedom and well-being.

Societies like the United States and France can come closer to realizing what a just social order requires, therefore, by following the Scandinavian countries in reducing the level of income differentials. What is crucial here is the adoption of income policies that will help assure all persons of an adequate level of distributable goods and services necessary for enjoying the fundamental rights.

None of this, to repeat a point made earlier, constitutes a claim that there ought to be absolute economic equality. Rather, I am pointing to the need for a reduction of existing income inequalities when it can be shown that this will help assure the necessary welfare rights for everyone. If, as in many Western societies today, the disadvantaged position of some segment of the population means that they lack the necessary preconditions for effectively exercising their rights, justice demands that they be provided with an adequate share of the required distributable benefits and goods.

A particularly acute problem today concerns the large number of "inactive" persons in many Western societies. In the Netherlands, for example, there are today (1984) around 850,000 unemployed (more than 15 per cent of the civilian working population),

[93] Ibid., p. 201.

about 460,000 disabled, 275,000 sick people (on an average working day), and 1.3 million people receiving an old-age pension. This total number represents a tremendous increase in the number of inactive people for whom economic benefits have to be provided. A clear indication of this is the ratio between active and inactive persons in the Netherlands. In 1970 there were seven active persons for each person who was inactive, while at the end of 1982 there were only three active persons for every inactive one.[94]

The presence of a large number of inactive persons in the Netherlands and other advanced societies raises a number of crucial problems. Judgments have to be made not only about (a) the distribution of income among those who are active (employed), but also about (b) the distribution of economic benefits within the group of inactive persons, and (c) the distribution of income and economic benefits between these two groups.[95] It is interesting in this regard that neither Rawls, Nozick, nor Gewirth gives attention to what justice requires with respect to these various sorts of inactive persons.

Given the enormous complexity of these problems, I can do no more here than suggest some rough guidelines for the distribution of income and economic benefits. To begin with, I have already said something about (a) above: the distribution of income among the active working population. In the case of the United States, there is good reason to believe that the present earnings gap between the top and bottom quintiles can be reduced from the present seven to one to at least five to one. Similar reductions may be both possible and required elsewhere.

As to (b), the distribution of economic benefits to the inactive population, a large number of persons in the United States and elsewhere lack an adequate level of those goods and services necessary for effectively exercising their rights to freedom and well-being. These goods, as already indicated, include economic benefits. Justice requires, therefore, that the inactive receive a social minimum that is adequate to provide for their basic needs. This must be higher than what exists in the United States (and many other societies) at the present time. Such a minimum must, of

---

[94] I draw here on the paper by Percy B. Lehning, "Cutting Lines We Dare Not Cross: Justice and Retrenchment in the Welfare State," p. 8. Prepared for the Conference on Futures of the Welfare State, Indiana University, Bloomington, Indiana, March, 1983.

[95] Ibid.

course, be realistically attainable and not so high that it will eliminate any incentive to take up work when the opportunity arises.

I suggested earlier that smaller inequalities in the distribution of income would increase the inequality surplus, i.e., the surplus income remaining after people are differentially rewarded on the basis of the various qualifications and abilities supposedly required for drawing them to different positions in the economy. Together with tax revenues, this enlarged inequality surplus constitutes the major source of funds to be used for providing the inactive with a reasonable social minimum.

Whether or not this social minimum would actually be high enough to provide an adequate level of the basic necessities for everyone is difficult to say in advance. But, in any case, the intent is to markedly improve the situation of those who are presently unemployed. At the same time, as noted above, the social minimum must not be so high that it eliminates incentives for working. How high, then, should this minimum be? This is not an easy question to answer. One reason is that we really don't know what degree of incentives (in the form of economic rewards) is required to make it worthwhile for people in general to keep on working or take on work if they are presently inactive. This concerns (c) in the above discussion: the distribution of income between the active and the inactive. Moreover, there is also the problem of (b), the differentials among various categories of persons within the group of inactive people.

In regard to the actual social minimum that ought to exist, Thurow suggests for the United States "a minimum floor that would provide a standard of living just half as large as that of the average American."[96] This is in line with the suggestion of Fuchs that the minimum be set at half of the median income.[97] My own preference is slightly different. In my view, the social minimum ought to be linked to the minimum wage level in the society. This level in the Netherlands today, for example, is set at about f24,000 (± $9,000).[98] I want to suggest that when an individual worker becomes inactive, for reasons of unemployment, sickness, disablement, or retirement, he or she ought to be entitled to a social minimum equal to 70 per cent of the level set for the minimum wage. This would be an amount of about f16,800 ($6,000) in the Netherlands. When,

[96] Thurow, Zero-Sum Society, p. 211.

[97] Victor R. Fuchs, "Redefining Poverty and Redistributing Income," Public Interest 8 (Summer 1967): 88–95.

[98] Sociaal en Cultureel Rapport ('s-Gravenhage: Staatsuitgeverij, 1982).

however, more than one person is dependent on the benefits received, the social minimum ought to be raised to the level of the minimum wage, in this case ƒ24,000.

With such a policy of entitlement to a guaranteed social minimum, no distinction need be made among the different reasons for an individual's being inactive. Further, of course, some persons—especially in the case of retirement—would receive higher amounts because of individual pension plans, insurance arrangements, and the like. The major point here is that the economic floor for an individual or a family ought to be calculated on the basis of the minimum (legal) income in the society in which one lives. Justice demands that everyone, whether they be active in the labor force or not, have a social minimum that will help assure the effective exercise of the rights to freedom and well-being. Movement toward a just social order, then, requires government policies to help achieve this end. It also requires certain tax policies directed at the redistribution of wealth and income.

Taxation

Even though a just social order demands that the government provide income security, comprehensive and free medical care, education, and public housing, we have already seen that such services are *not* egalitarian in their consequences. This is as true in the Soviet Union, where many people do supposedly have rights to these necessities, as it is in the United States. For everyone to be able to *obtain* the necessary distributable goods, there must be a more equal distribution of earnings and a large redistribution of economic benefits. Since the means of assuring that those now lacking the necessary preconditions for enjoying their basic rights— probably about 20 to 25 per cent of the population both in the United States and in the United Kingdom today—is through reducing economic disparities, I will now focus on the means for accomplishing this in terms of taxes on both income and wealth.

With regard to *income*, taxation is the main way of reducing disparities. Progressive taxation is, of course, intended to help accomplish this. Yet in the United States and Great Britain, for example, the reduction of income disparities is almost entirely in the direction of transfers of income from the upper to the middle groups. It is widely assumed in both societies that the wide gap between the middle- and lower-income groups is necessary in order to provide incentives for the middle group and to provide for faster growth of capital. Consequently, the lower half, and certainly the lower quarter, of the distribution has done no more than barely maintain its share of the total.[99] This holds both before and after taxes. Obviously, then, such progressive taxation schemes do little or nothing to improve the position of those who lack the ability to acquire the distributable goods necessary for enjoying their basic rights for freedom and well-being. Thus, a just social order requires a far more progressive (i.e., steeper) and fairer tax system than presently exists in many Western societies.

This points to the need for an immediate reform of the existing tax systems in some societies. Consider in this regard the system of so-called progressive taxes in the United States today. The intention of such a system is that it be fair. This requires both horizontal equity (that every person with the same income should pay the same tax) and vertical equity (that the tax rate should rise in accordance with whatever degree of equity the law has established). In reality, however, neither of these two demands is fully met.

Table 9.2 presents one estimate of the distribution of tax burdens in the United States.[100] Examining the vertical equity, it can be seen that the average tax rate rises from 16.8 per cent for the poorest 10 per cent of the population to 26.2 per cent for the richest 10 per cent. Although the tax rate is indeed progressive, the degree of increase is much less than one would expect given the large differences in the tax rate established for those with relatively low or extremely high incomes.

Furthermore, these figures reveal that the actual variance in tax rates meets the requirements of horizontal equity even less well than it does the vertical equity requirement. This can be seen by examining the second column, which presents the standard deviations around these mean values. Commenting on these, Thurow remarks that for those persons at the fifth decile with an average tax rate of 22.8 per cent and a standard deviation of 6.5, for instance, 68 per cent of the taxpayers in this income category would be included in an interval from 16.3 per cent (22.8 − 6.5) to 29.3 per cent (22.8 + 6.5).[101]

Not only is the difference between 16.3 per cent and 29.3 considerable, but 32 per cent of the taxpayers are excluded here: i.e., they either pay less than 16.3 per cent or more than 29.3 per cent.

[99] For Great Britain, see C. D. Harbury, "Equality versus Mobility," in Jones, *Economics and Equality*, p. 94.

[100] Taken from Thurow, *Zero-Sum Society*, p. 170.

[101] Ibid., p. 171.

Table 9.2
Variance in Tax Rates

Deciles of the Population	Mean Tax Rate (%)	Standard Deviation
1	16.8	30.1
2	18.6	14.6
3	21.6	19.6
4	22.6	8.8
5	22.8	6.5
6	22.7	5.5
7	22.7	6.6
8	23.1	5.9
9	23.2	5.4
10	26.2	10.2

SOURCE: Joseph A. Pechman and Benjamin A. Okner, *Who Bears The Tax Burden?* (Washington, D.C., 1974), p. 67.

Thurow shows that to include 99 per cent of all taxpayers, one would have to employ an interval of three standard deviations.[102] This means that among those who are in the fifth decile with an average tax rate of 22.8 per cent, the actual range is from 3.3 per cent to 42.3 per cent. "With such wide ranges needed to include most of the taxpayers," Thurow points out, "average tax rates mean very little. They do not tell us what the average person pays."[103]

As we know, this large degree of horizontal inequality in actual tax payments is due to various "loopholes" in the tax laws: special provisions such as tax breaks on long-term capital gains, depletion allowances, the interest on state and local bonds, and other advantages that benefit particular groups.[104] Such loopholes are of benefit largely to the very rich, and certainly not to wage-earners in general. Clearly, then, the tax system must be reformed to assure both horizontal and vertical equity in the payment of taxes.

Not surprisingly, "after-tax" incomes are far more unequal in the United States than elsewhere. Wiles, for example, reports that after-tax comparisons of income of persons at the 95th percentile line and at the 5th percentile line show a ratio of 3.0 for Sweden (i.e., those at the top receive three times more than those at the

[102] Ibid., p. 172.
[103] Ibid.
[104] See, for example, Leonard W. Weiss, *Economics and Society* (New York: Wiley, 1975), pp. 255–57.

bottom), 5.0 for the United Kingdom, 6.0 for Denmark, and, at the other extreme, 12.0 for Canada, and 12.7 for the United States.[105] I am suggesting that a just social order requires after-tax differences more like those found in Sweden than those now existing in the United States and Canada.

Turning now to the distribution and redistribution of personal *wealth*, there appears to have been a slight reduction of inequality in the United States and the United Kingdom. But, as with income, the share of the total in the top groups has fallen proportionately much more than in the groups just below them. Harrison reports that in the United Kingdom, while "the share of the top 1% has fallen quite substantially, groups just below the top 1% have increased their share of personal wealth so that, at least since 1936, most of the redistribution which has occurred has been within the top 20%."[106] Although those just below the top may have increased their share of total personal wealth, this again obviously does nothing at all for those who lack necessities. The required redistribution of wealth to provide an adequate share of distributable goods for those who now lack them demands more stringent implementation (and enforcement) of death duties, gift taxes, capital gains taxes, and the like, than is now the case.

Such wealth taxes have direct consequences for inheritance, the most important cause of inequality in the distribution of wealth.[107] Someone like Robert Nozick would, of course, object strenuously to such government interference in people's "right" to transfer their holdings. But neither Nozick nor anyone else has done very much to establish such a right. Recall what Nozick says in this regard.

His inductive definition of the entitlement theory is as follows:

(1) A person who acquires a holding in accordance with the principle of justice in acquisition is entitled to that holding.
(2) A person who acquires a holding in accordance with the principle of justice in transfer, from someone entitled to that holding, is entitled to that holding.
(3) No one is entitled to a holding except by (repeated) application of (1) and (2).[108]

---

[105] Peter Wiles, *Distribution of Income: East and West* (Amsterdam: North Holland, 1974), pp. ix, 48.

[106] Alan Harrison, "Trends Over Time in the Distribution of Wealth," in Jones, *Economics and Equality*, p. 84.

[107] Sanford, "Taxation," p. 118.

[108] Nozick, *Anarchy, State, and Utopia*, p. 151.

But, as noted in Chapter 2, Nozick never specifies the first two principles. There are no precise formulations of these principles and no arguments are offered in favor of them.

While Nozick points out that we lack a general theory of property,[109] this lack cannot possibly warrant his assumption that individual property rights must be full capitalist property rights.[110] Unless Nozick is able to establish, as he merely claims, that individual property rights are rights to control resources in all ways and to dispose of or transfer them as the owner sees fit, he has provided no basis for his complaints about government interference in the control and transfer of holdings.

As to the supposed injustice of wealth taxes, which would interfere with the "right" of people to pass on their advantage as they choose, it needs to be pointed out that Nozick merely *assumes* that inheritance is morally fundamental and an indispensable feature of private property. Yet, as David Lyons observes, moral rights to property are not necessarily inheritable.[111] Nozick discusses original acquisition as if it were inconceivable that one could acquire property that was not permanent and inheritable. But, remarks Lyons, "The idea of a right to property does not entail that it be inheritable. That is simply one possible form that property rights can take."[112]

In order to judge the moral defensibility of inheritance, it is necessary to locate property rights and all they entail within a broader moral theory concerning basic rights and the kinds of social institutions to which they give rise. If, as in the theory of justice defended in this volume, inheritance has the consequence of preventing some persons from exercising their (justifiable) rights to freedom and well-being, then rights to the inheritance of holdings (goods, property, money) are not morally defensible (or may, at least in some instances, be overridden). While the precise moral standing of inheritance requires more scrutiny than I am able to give it here, it is crystal clear that inheritance—as it now stands in most Western societies—contributes to concentrations of wealth and power that stand in the way of many people being able to enjoy their fundamental rights.

[109] Ibid., p. 171.

[110] Ibid., pp. 281–82.

[111] David Lyons, "The New Indian Claims and Original Rights to Land," *Social Theory and Practice* 4 (Fall 1977): 249–93.

[112] Ibid., p. 260. See also, C. C. Ryan, "Yours, Mine, and Ours: Property Rights and Individual Liberty," *Ethics* 87 (January 1977): 126–41.

Thus, there are, in my view, no serious moral prohibitions against imposing both wealth transfer taxes and taxes on the total stock of wealth. The former taxes are to be levied (progressively) when wealth passes from one person to another, by either gift or legacy. These taxes would, of course, be imposed irregularly, i.e., when holdings were transferred. Taxes on the stock of wealth, on the other hand, would be levied annually—as are income taxes. Such taxes are intended to gradually reduce the proportion of wealth held by the largest wealth-holders. Wealth taxes already exist in several European countries, where, generally, they can be paid from income in the form of supplementary taxes.[113] The intention in these countries (for example, Sweden, Norway, and the Netherlands) is that the combined income tax and wealth tax should not exceed a prescribed percentage of a taxpayer's income: 80% in the Netherlands, 90% in Norway.[114]

For those who might object to the levying of such heavy taxes on the rich among us, I would repeat my earlier conclusions about desert. There is no reason to believe that the richest people in societies like our own *deserve* the qualities or attributes that allow them to realize high incomes and accumulate extensive holdings. Aside from this, there is little reason to think that they are necessarily the most dedicated, the hardest working, or even the most talented. And while the kinds of tax arrangements proposed for a just social order would gradually reduce their economic advantages, they would continue to be comparatively well-off. In addition, of course, they would continue to receive relatively high "nonfinancial" benefits: interesting work, pleasant working conditions, prestige, and respect.

How much and how long people would have to be heavily taxed on their incomes and wealth would obviously differ from one society to another. The aim of such economic policies in the just social order, to repeat, is to redistribute a sufficient portion of income and wealth so that the necessary preconditions of action are available to *everyone*. This means that all persons must have an adequate level of those distributable goods—food, medical care, housing, etc.—to enjoy their generic rights to freedom and well-being. And, of course, these preconditions also include the establishment and maintenance of equal opportunities for everyone in the society.

[113] Sanford, "Taxation," pp. 112–13.
[114] Ibid.

VI

The Rectification of Injustices

In addition to overseeing the distribution of basic goods and services and the redistribution of wealth and income, the legal system in a just social order must concern itself with the *rectification* of earlier injustices. If the rights to freedom and well-being of certain groups of citizens have been systematically violated over a long period of time, then justice demands that these injustices be rectified, if at all possible. Past injustices should not simply be written off as unfortunate happenings that ought not to be allowed to recur. Instead, movement toward a more just society requires government-sponsored policies and programs that attempt to correct for the adverse effects of past injustices.

Since I have discussed various means of providing rectification at length elsewhere,[115] I will not elaborate further. But the point is, I believe, clear: when earlier injustices against women, blacks, or other minorities, have systematically disadvantaged members of these groups, they should now be compensated for the earlier wrongs committed against them.[116] A just social order requires, then, policies and programs (for example, preferential treatment) guided by the following principle:

If for generations many members of a group have encountered systematic violation of their rights to freedom and well-being, either initiated or allowed by the government, then it is morally required that the government institute policies and programs aimed at rectifying these earlier injustices and that it encourage (require?) the nongovernmental sector of the society to do the same.

VII

An Extended Distributional Principle for a Just Social Order

Earlier in the chapter I set forth a first formulation of the distributional principle necessary for helping to assure that everyone

[115] Derek L. Phillips, *Equality, Justice and Rectification* (London: Academic Press, 1979), Part III, "The Rectification of Injustices," pp. 249–318.

[116] Among the more important literature dealing with this are the following: Marshall Cohen, Thomas Nagel, and Thomas Scanlon, eds., *Equality and Preferential Treatment* (Princeton: Princeton University Press, 1977); Alan H. Goldman, *Justice and Reverse Discrimination* (Princeton: Princeton University Press, 1979); John C. Livingston, *Fair Game? Inequality and Affirmative Action* (San Francisco: W. H. Freeman & Co., 1979); and Barry R. Gross, *Discrimination in Reverse: Is Turnabout Fair Play?* (New York: New York University Press, 1978).

will be able to effectively exercise his or her generic rights to free-dom and well-being. Having now introduced rectification into the discussion, that first formulation needs to be extended. In revised form, the major principle of distribution now reads as follows:

In a just social order, there must be (a) welfare rights to the provision of such goods and services as free and comprehensive medical care and education, public housing, and guaranteed employment; plus *(b) a redistribution of wealth and income to assure that everyone is enabled to obtain an adequate level of these and other necessary goods and services;* and *(c) the implementation of rectification policies to rectify earlier systematic injustices. After these stipulations have been met, (d) any inequalities that remain in the distribution of income and wealth are permissible if and only if they do not lead to concentrations of wealth that are demonstrably detrimental to some people's exercise of their generic rights.*

Since the aim of distributive, redistributive, and rectification policies is not to reach an absolute equality of all economic benefits and distributable goods, such policies can be relaxed once it is assured that everyone's necessities have been provided for and that steps have been taken to rectify earlier injustices. After these conditions [clauses (a) through (c) above] have been satisfied, there is no moral objection to inequalities arising from people's entitlement with regard to wages and salaries—so long as such inequalities don't adversely affect other people's exercise of their rights. Clearly, then, these sorts of entitlements will play a *far less* determinative role in a just social order than in the theory defended by Nozick (or in the theories of Rawls and Gewirth, for that matter). Still, there would be some room for the influence of people's entitlements. They would function as follows.

Being entitled to something, I noted above, involves a claim, promise, or agreement. If, to put it crudely, the rules of the marketplace are such that some persons acquire more than others without violating either their basic rights or the law and other social rules, then this is in no way objectionable (so long, again, as the above conditions have been assured). Famous athletes or entertainers, for example, are entitled to their differentially high salaries if people voluntarily pay to see them perform. Similarly with the executive officers of large corporations, airline pilots, surgeons, and others with unusually large incomes; they are entitled to their larger economic rewards on the basis of having satisfied certain clearly defined conditions of their employment.

But, to repeat the point made in the previous chapter, such

persons cannot be said to *deserve* those particular abilities that allow them to obtain one or another sort of position. These are (to some admittedly unknown extent) heavily influenced by factors beyond the individual's control. People are, however, entitled to positions that they are able to fill on the basis of their supposed productivity or contributions. People involved in making assignments and appointments assume that different jobs require different sets of abilities if they are to be performed in a competent manner, and they assume further that individuals differ in the extent to which they possess the relevant abilities. Based on these two assumptions, it is usually inferred that some arrays of assignment to jobs will be more productive than others.[117] Given these mechanisms of job placement, one individual may be more entitled than others to a particular position because he or she is viewed as having more of the abilities relevant to productivity or contributions. Thus, those persons who occupy one or another position are entitled to that position even though they don't deserve the abilities that allow them to attain it. The same holds, of course, for the inequalities of reward associated with different jobs. Whatever the amount of wages and salaries connected with a particular job, it is to be seen as a matter of entitlement and not desert.

The upshot of all this is that people are entitled to whatever positions they are able to obtain on the basis of their (actual or expected) contributions and also to whatever economic rewards are associated with those positions. But these differential rewards are—in contrast to the views of Rawls, Nozick, and Gewirth alike—morally permissible only insofar as the various clauses of the distributional principle advanced earlier have been satisfied. Income and wealth may be distributed unequally only after it is assured that everyone's basic necessities have been provided for, that earlier injustices have been corrected, and that unequal distributions will not lead to concentrations of wealth that adversely affect people's effective exercise of their generic rights.

Even with these limitations on the extent of acceptable inequalities in wages and salaries, some persons will—as noted above—have more of various material goods than will others. Whether the distribution of wages and salaries is limited by a greater initial equality in economic rewards or by a highly progressive system of taxes, there will remain differences in the amount of people's in-

[117] Norman Daniels, "Merit and Meritocracy," *Philosophy and Public Affairs* 7 (Spring 1978): 209.

come and wealth. So long as the conditions stated earlier are fulfilled, this is not objectionable.

But I see no reason why the so-called right of inheritance should be allowed to continue. If a renowned opera star, for instance, is entitled to his or her exceptionally high earnings, then it is not morally impermissible for this person to provide expensive sorts of food, a large house, or rare books, for his or her spouse and children. Nor is it objectionable that vast amounts of knowledge and information are passed on to the latter, even though these are the result of the parent's privileged position. There is no justification, however, for the idea that the rich parent should also be entitled to pass on the vast wealth and holdings that he or she has accumulated.

Implementation of the Extended Distributional Principle

As I pointed out in earlier chapters, moral values or principles that can be rationally justified and defended are not only preferable morally but also sociologically. Rationally justifiable moral principles—and the social arrangements to which they give rise—are far more likely to gain consensus than are those that people accept or tolerate because of tradition, coercion, fear, ignorance, apathy, or feelings of powerlessness. Consistent with this view, I argued in Chapter 7 that a legitimate legal system commands more reliable conformity than does a system that is merely tolerated or blindly accepted. Exactly the same holds with regard to those distributive and redistributive measures required for assuring that everyone has the necessary preconditions for exercising his or her fundamental rights to freedom and well-being. A society in which such measures can be rationally justified will have greater stability than one where these measures are seen as either completely arbitrary or as simply the result of differentials in access to the corridors of power.

In societies (like many today) where some persons have large incomes and vast wealth, while others lack the basic necessities, there is frequently a high correlation between the extent of people's holdings and their social and political power. Simply because of their privileged positions and the extreme vulnerability of the least fortunate, the latter are subject to manipulation and exploitation. As we know, those persons who see themselves as the victims of such manipulation and exploitation will often react in ways that seriously threaten the stability of social relations: half-hearted commitments to their jobs, attempts to rip off the "system," crime, retreatism into drugs, and even revolution are well-known examples.

In a just social order, by contrast, income and wealth policies that gradually eliminate large disparities in economic holdings are intended to lessen the power of the rich and the vulnerability of the poor. If these policies are recognized as rationally justifiable, as required to assure or obtain justice, there will be far greater social stability than is the case in most societies today.

There is, of course, no existing society that could be accurately characterized as a just social order. But some come closer than others to realizing this ideal. Whatever the various shortcomings of one or another contemporary advanced society, however, there are certain modifications and changes that are both morally required and possible to bring about. I have considered these in terms of several policies and programs, which, if implemented, would improve the moral quality of the particular society concerned. Let me, then, briefly review the policies and programs that justice requires.

First, such state-provided benefits and services as free and comprehensive medical care, quality education, and decent public housing ought to be made available to all persons. These constitute welfare rights to which everyone is entitled.

Second, the government ought to provide income security in the form of a social minimum generous enough to assure that all persons will be enabled to obtain an adequate level of certain goods (for example, food and clothing) necessary for effective exercise of their generic rights. This social minimum, I suggested earlier, should be linked to the minimum legal wage level in the society. An "inactive" (i.e., unemployed, disabled, etc.) individual ought to be entitled to an income or level of economic benefits equal to 70 per cent of the minimum wage, and this should be raised to one hundred per cent when more than one person is dependent on the benefits received.

Third, there must be a reduction of existing inequalities in the structure of economic rewards for "active" (i.e., employed) persons. In the case of the United States, it is certainly possible to reduce the present seven-to-one earnings gap to a gap of five to one. This can be accomplished without eliminating the necessary incentives or weakening the economy. Evidence from other Western societies suggests that differentials in economic rewards can be reduced even further without negative results.

Fourth, many societies require a more progressive and equitable

432

system of personal income taxes than now exists. In the United States and Canada, for instance, the tax system is neither particularly progressive nor fair. As I pointed out earlier, the system in the U.S. is particularly unfair with regard to horizontal equity. Although in principle everyone with the same income is required to pay the same amount of taxes, various loopholes in the law allow many persons to escape the taxes imposed on others with the same incomes. Further, I believe that the extremely unequal "after-tax" income distributions in the United States and Canada can be reduced without adverse effects to anyone. Reforms of the present tax system are, therefore, necessary to assure a more progressive and fairer system of taxation.

Fifth, both wealth transfer taxes and taxes on the total stock of wealth are required in order to reduce huge concentrations of wealth and power, which interfere with some people's exercise of their fundamental rights. In the United States, where about 50 per cent of the great fortunes are gotten through inheritance, gift and inheritance taxes amount to a tax of only 0.2 per cent on net worth.[118] The current estate and gift tax system, Thurow points out, has practically no impact on the distribution of wealth.[119] Just as with income taxes, wealth taxes must be collected to finance government expenditures. There is simply no way of moving in the direction of a just social order without the income and wealth of some persons going down. Taxes are the most appropriate way of accomplishing this.

Sixth, high priority must be given to the rectification of systematic injustices committed against certain groups of citizens. Movement toward a more just society requires government-sponsored policies and programs that attempt to correct for the adverse effects of past injustices. Preferential treatment for blacks and women in the United States is a step in the right direction.

Seventh, it is important that the government try to help maximize the amount of work that is meaningful, creative, and intrinsically interesting. But this does not mean that people have a right to "work" as contrasted with "labor." There is, in my view, no right to meaningful work as such. The reason for this is quite obvious: there is no corresponding group of people with the possibility of meeting the obligation that would be the correlate of the so-called right to meaningful and creative work.[120]

[118] Thurow, *Zero-Sum Society*, p. 172.
[119] Ibid.
[120] Nor does anyone have a right to a particular sort of employment; there is no

Nevertheless, there are steps that should be taken to make jobs less monotonous and boring. Among other things, jobs ought to be upgraded to allow employees a way of transcending dead-end positions. Furthermore, the autonomy of people in the job-market can and should be increased. Important here, as shown earlier, is greater autonomy for work groups in industry and the introduction of self-management. Movement toward a just social order necessitates that careful attention be given to restructuring employment so that employees can participate in decisions concerning their conditions of work and their enterprise's policies.

Finally, more attention should be given to the rotation of jobs. More specifically, the "dirty work" in the society ought to be spread around. Perhaps the best way would be to require everyone during his or her working life to spend, say, two years on the kinds of jobs that are most boring, tiring, dirty, or otherwise undesirable. It is unjust that some persons—for whatever reasons—should spend their working life in such jobs.

The above policies and programs are feasible and capable of being realized in all of today's advanced societies. No vast transformations are required. What is required is that the government actively involve itself in meeting the demands outlined above. Only if these demands are met will all persons have an adequate level of the basic goods necessary for them to enjoy their fundamental rights to freedom and well-being. Only then will we have achieved the kind of social order that is both sociologically and morally required: what I have termed a *just social order*. It is, I believe, a vision worth pursuing.

---

group that could meet the obligation such a right would entail. Here in the Netherlands, for example, many university graduates insist that they have a right to employment in the subject they studied. Thus, sociology graduates often claim a right to employment as sociologists—whether or not any such positions are available. But the government cannot be expected to simply create jobs for those who want to practice a particular occupation or profession. Of course, there should be equal opportunities for access to training and education for *available* positions in the job sphere. For an interesting discussion of these matters, see Bengt Abrahamsson and Anders Broström, *The Rights of Labor* (London: Sage Publications, 1980).

BIBLIOGRAPHY

Abrahamsson, Bengt, and Broström, Anders. *The Rights of Labor*. London: Sage Publications, 1980.

Abrams, Natalie. "Problems in Defining Child Abuse and Neglect." In *Having Children: Philosophical and Legal Reflections on Parenthood*, edited by Onora O'Neill and William Ruddick. New York: Oxford University Press, 1979.

Adams, Virginia. "Behavioral Scientists Argue Guilt's Role." *New York Times*, 24 July 1979.

Albert, Michael, and Hahnel, Robin. *Socialism Today and Tomorrow*. Boston: South End Press, 1981.

Alexander, Jeffrey C. "Looking for Theory: 'Facts' and 'Values' in the Intellectual Legacy of the 1970s." *Theory and Society* 10 (1981): 279–92.

————. *Theoretical Logic in Sociology*. Vol. I. *Positivism, Presuppositions, and Current Controversies*. London: Routledge & Kegan Paul, 1982.

Alexander, Lawrence, and Bayles, Michael. "Hercules or Proteus? The Many Theses of Ronald Dworkin." *Social Theory and Practice* 5 (1980): 267–303.

Alston, William. "Emotion and Feeling." In *Encyclopedia of Philosophy*, vol. 2, edited by Paul Edwards. New York: Collier-Macmillan, 1979.

Alt, John. "Authority, Reason, and the Civilizing Process." *Theory and Society* 10 (1981): 387–405.

Alt, John, and Hearn, Frank. "The Cortland Conference on Narcissism." *Telos* 44 (1980): 49–58.

Andersen, Bent Rold. "The Rationality and Irrationality of the Nordic Welfare State." *Daedalus* 113 (1984): 109–40.

Anderson, C. *Statecraft*. New York: Wiley, 1977.

Anscombe, Elizabeth, "On the Source of Authority in the State." *Ratio* 20 (1978): 1–28.

Anthony, Dick, and Robbins, Thomas. "Spiritual Innovation and the Crisis of American Civil Religion." *Daedalus* 111 (1982): 215–34.

Apel, Karl-Otto, *Towards a Transformation of Philosophy*. London: Routledge & Kegan Paul, 1980.

Arendt, Hannah. "Thinking and Moral Considerations: A Lecture." *Social Research* 38 (1971). Quoted in James F. Childress, "Appeals to Conscience." *Ethics* 89 (1979): 315–35.

Arietti, S. *The Intrapsychic Self*. New York: Basic Books, 1967.

Aristotle. *Nicomachean Ethics*. Translated with an introduction and notes by Martin Ostwald. Indianapolis, Ind.: Bobbs-Merrill, 1962.

Arneson, Richard J. "What's Wrong with Exploitation?" *Ethics* (1981): 202–07.

Arnold, M. B., ed. *Feelings and Emotions: The Loyola Symposium*. New York: Academic Press, 1970.

Aronfreed, J. "Moral Development from the Standpoint of a General Psychological Theory." In *Moral Development and Behavior*, edited by T. Lickona. New York: Holt, 1976.

Austin, J. L. *The Province of Jurisprudence Determined*. 1832. London: Weidenfeld and Nicolson, 1968.

Ausubel, P. "Relationships Between Shame and Guilt in the Socializing Process." *Psychological Review* 62 (1955): 378–90.

Bahro, Rudolf. *The Alternative in Eastern Europe*. London: New Left Books, 1978.

Banfield, Edward C. *The Unheavenly City*. Boston: Little, Brown & Co., 1968.

Barlow, Robin; Brazer, Harvey E.; and Morgan, James N. *Economic Behavior of the Affluent*. Washington, D.C.: Brookings Institute, 1966.

Barry, Brian. *The Liberal Theory of Justice*. Oxford: Oxford University Press, 1973.

Bauer, T. "Investment Cycles in Planned Economics." *Acta Oeconomica* (1978): 243–60.

Baumrind, D. "Child Care Practices Anteceding Three Patterns of Preschool Behavior." *Genetic Psychological Monographs* 75 (1967): 43–88.

———. "Current Patterns of Parental Authority." *Developmental Psychology* 4 (1971): 1–101.

———. *Early Socialization and the Discipline Controversy*. Morristown, N.J.: General Learning Press, 1975.

Beals, Ralph; Hoijer, Harry; and Beals, Alan R. *An Introduction to Anthropology*. New York: Macmillan, 1977.

Becker, Lawrence C. "Economic Justice: Three Positions." *Ethics* 89 (1979): 385–93.

———. "The Neglect of Virtue." *Ethics* 85 (1975): 110–22.

———. *Property Rights*. London: Routledge & Kegan Paul, 1977.

Beitz, Charles R. "Bounded Morality: Justice and the State in World Politics." *International Organizations* 33 (1980): 405–24.

———. "Nonintervention and Communal Integrity." *Philosophy and Public Affairs* 9 (1980): 385–91.

Bell, Daniel. *The Coming of Post-Industrial Society*. New York: Basic Books, 1976.

———. *The Cultural Contradictions of Capitalism*. New York: Basic Books, 1976.

Bellah, Robert N. "Religion and Legitimation of the American Republic." In *In God We Trust: New Patterns of Religious Pluralism in America*, edited by Thomas Robbins and Dick Anthony. New Brunswick, N.J.: Transaction Books, 1981.

Benditt, Theodore M. *Law as Rule and Principle: Problems of Legal Philosophy*. London: Harvester Press, 1978.

Benn, S. I., and Mortimer, G. W., eds. *Rationality and the Social Sciences*. London: Routledge & Kegan Paul, 1976.

Bernstein, Richard I. *Praxis and Action*. Philadelphia: University of Pennsylvania Press, 1971.

Black, Donald J. *The Behavior of Law*. New York: Academic Press, 1976.

———. "The Boundaries of Legal Sociology." *Yale Law Journal* 81 (1972): 1086–100.

Blank, Stephen. *Industry and Government in Britain*. Lexington, Mass.: D. C. Heath, 1973.

Blumberg, Paul. *Industrial Democracy: The Sociology of Participation*. New York: Schocken Books, 1969.

Blustein, Jeffrey. "Child Rearing and Family Interests." In *Having Children: Philosophical and Legal Reflections on Parenthood*, edited by Onora O'Neill and William Ruddick. New York: Oxford University Press, 1979.

Bowie, Norman E. "Welfare and Freedom." *Ethics* 89 (1979): 254–68.

Braverman, Harry. *Labor and Monopoly Capital: The Degradation of Work in the Twentieth Century*. New York: Monthly Review Press, 1974.

Break, George F. "Income Taxes and Incentives to Work." *American Economic Review* 47 (1957): 529–49.

Brenner, Charles. *An Elementary Text of Psychoanalysis*. Garden City, N.Y.: Doubleday Anchor, 1955.

Broom, Leonard, and Cushing, Robert G. "A Modest Test of an Immodest Theory: The Functional Theory of Stratification." *American Sociological Review* 42 (1977): 157–69.

Buber, Martin. "Guilt and Guilt Feelings." In *The Knowledge of Man*, translated and edited by Maurice Friedman. New York: Harper & Row, 1965.

Buchanan, James M. *The Limits of Liberty*. Chicago: The University of Chicago Press, 1975.

Burkes, John P.; Crocker, Lawrence; and Legters, Lyman, eds. *Marxism and the Good Society*. New York: Cambridge University Press, 1981.

Cain, Maureen, and Hunt, Alan. *Marx and Engels on Law*. London: Academic Press, 1980.

Care, Norman S., and Landesman, Charles, eds. *Readings in the Theory of Action*. Bloomington: Indiana University Press, 1968.

Carrens, Joseph. *Equality, Moral Incentives and the Market*. Chicago: University of Chicago Press, 1981.

Carnoy, Martin, and Shearer, Derek. *Economic Democracy*. New York: Random House, 1980.

Cereseto, Shirley. "Socialism, Capitalism, and Inequality." *The Insurgent Sociologist* 11 (1982): 5–29.

Cicourel, Aaron. *Cognitive Sociology*. Harmondsworth: Penguin, 1973.

Cohen, Joshua, and Rogers, Joel. *On Democracy: Toward a Transformation of American Society*. New York: Penguin Books, 1983.

Cohen, Marshall; Nagel, Thomas; and Scanlon, Thomas, eds., *Equality and Preferential Treatment*. Princeton: Princeton University Press, 1977.

Collins, Hugh. *Marxism and Law*. New York: Oxford University Press, 1982.

Collins, Randall. *Conflict Sociology: Toward An Explanatory Science*. New York: Academic Press, 1975.

Cook, Karen S. "Expectations, Evaluations and Equity." *American Sociological Review* 40 (1975): 372–88.

Coser, Lewis A. "Durkheim's Conservatism and Its Implications for His Sociological Theory." In *Essays on Sociology and Philosophy*, edited by Kurt H. Wolff. New York: Harper & Row, 1964.

————. *The Functions of Social Conflict*. New York: Free Press, 1956.

Cowan, P.; Langer, J.; Heavenrich, J.; and Nathanson, M. "Social Learning and Piaget's Cognitive Theory of Moral Development." *Journal of Personality and Social Psychology* 11 (1969): 261–74.

Dahl, Hans F. "Those Equal Folk." *Daedalus* 113 (1984): 93–107.

Daniels, Norman. "Merit and Meritocracy." *Philosophy and Public Affairs* 7 (1978): 206–23.

Davis, Kingsley, and Moore, Wilbert E. "Some Principles of Stratification." *American Sociological Review* 10 (1945): 242–49.

Della Fave, L. Richard. "The Meek Shall Not Inherit the Earth." *American Sociological Review* 45 (1980): 955–71.

Dewey, John. *Art as Experience*. New York: Balch & Co., 1934.

DiMaggio, Paul. "Cultured Capital and School Success: The Impact of Status and Cultural Participation on the Grades of U.S. High School Students." *American Sociological Review* 47 (1982): 189–201.

Disco, Nil. "Critical Theory as Ideology of the New Class." *Theory and Society* 8 (1979): 139–214.

Domhoff, G. William. *Who Rules America?* Englewood Cliffs, N.J.: Prentice-Hall, 1967.

Donzelot, Jacques. *The Policing of Families*. New York: Pantheon, 1979.

Doppelt, Gerald. "Statism Without Foundations." *Philosophy and Public Affairs* 9 (1980): 398–403.

————. "Walzer's Theory of Morality in International Relations." *Philosophy and Public Affairs* 8 (1978): 3–26.

Durkheim, Émile. *The Division of Labor*. Translated by George Simpson. New York: Free Press, 1964.

————. *Essays on Morals and Education*. Edited with an introduction by W.S.F. Pickering. London: Routledge & Kegan Paul, 1979.

————. *Moral Education*. Translated by Everett K. Wilson and Herman Schnurer. New York: Free Press of Glencoe, 1966.

————. "Pragmatism and Sociology." In *Essays on Sociology and Philosophy*, edited by Kurt H. Wolff. New York: Harper Torchbooks, 1964.

————. *Sociology and Philosophy*. Translated by D. F. Pocock. Glencoe, Ill.: Free Press, 1953.

Dworkin, Ronald. "Dissent on Douglas." *The New York Review* 28, 19 February 1981.

———. "Liberalism." In *Public and Private Morality*, edited by Stuart Hampshire. Cambridge: Cambridge University Press, 1978.

———. "Philosophy, Morality, and Law—Observations Prompted by Professor Fuller's Novel Claim." *University of Pennsylvania Law Review* 113 (1965): 668–90.

———. *Taking Rights Seriously*. New impression with a Reply to Critics. London: Duckworth, 1978.

Ehrmann, Henry W. *Organized Business in France*. Princeton: Princeton University Press, 1967.

Ellul, Jacques. *The Technological Society*. New York: Vintage Books, 1964.

Elshtain, Jean Bethke. "The Self: Reborn, Undone, Transformed." *Telos* 44 (1980): 101–11.

Ely, John Hart. *Democracy and Distrust: A Theory of Judicial Review*. Cambridge, Mass.: Harvard University Press, 1980.

Erasmus, Charles I. *In Search of the Common Good: Utopian Experiments Past and Future*. New York: Free Press, 1977.

Erikson, Erik H. *Childhood and Society*. 2nd ed. New York: W. W. Norton, 1963.

Escalona, Sibylle. *The Roots of Individuality: Normal Patterns of Development in Infancy*. Chicago: Aldine Press, 1968.

Espinosa, J., and Zionbalist, A. *Economic Democracy*. New York: Academic Press, 1978.

Fallers, Lloyd A. *Law Without Precedent*. Chicago: University of Chicago Press, 1969.

Feinberg, Joel. *Doing and Deserving: Essays in the Theory of Responsibility*. Princeton: Princeton University Press, 1970.

Feur, Lewis, ed. *Marx and Engels: Basic Writings on Politics and Philosophy*. Garden City, N.Y.: Doubleday, 1969.

Field, Mark G. *Doctor and Patient in Soviet Russia*. Cambridge, Mass.: Harvard University Press, 1957.

Fishkin, James. *Tyranny and Legitimacy*. Baltimore: The Johns Hopkins Press, 1979.

Flanagan, Owen J., Jr. "Quinean Ethics." *Ethics* 93 (1982): 56–74.

Flathman, Richard. *The Practice of Rights*. Cambridge: Cambridge University Press, 1976.

Foot, Philippa, *Virtues and Vices and Other Essays in Moral Philosophy*. Berkeley: University of California Press, 1978.

Freud, Anna. "Child Observation and Prediction of Development—A Memorial Lecture in Honor of Ernst Kris." In *The Psychoanalytic Study of the Child*, vol. 13. New York: International Universities Press, 1958.

Freud, Sigmund. *The Basic Writings of Sigmund Freud*. New York: Modern Library, 1938.

———. *Civilization and Its Discontents*. Garden City: Doubleday, 1958.

———. *Collected Papers*. Edited by Ernest Jones. New York: Basic Books, 1959.

Freud, Sigmund. "The Ego and the Id." Stand. ed., vol. 19. London: Hogarth Press, 1923.

———. "Mourning and Melancholia." Stand. ed., vol. 14. London: Hogarth Press, 1917.

Fuchs, Victor R. "Redefining Poverty and Redistributing Income." *Public Interest* 8 (1967): 88–95.

Fuller, Lon L. *The Morality of Law*. New Haven: Yale University Press, 1969.

Fürer-Haimendorf, Christoph von. "The Sense of Sin in Cross-Cultural Perspective." *Man* 9 (1974): 539–56.

Galbraith, John Kenneth. *Economics and the Public Purpose*. London: André Deutsch, 1974.

Garbarino, J., and Bronfenbrenner, U. "The Socialization of Moral Judgment and Behavior in Cross-Cultural Perspective." In *Moral Development and Behavior*, edited by T. Lickona. New York: Holt, 1976.

Garfinkel, Harold. *Studies in Ethnomethodology*. Englewood Cliffs: Prentice-Hall, 1967.

Gaylin, Willard. *Feelings: Our Vital Signs*. New York: Harper & Row, 1979.

Geertz, Clifford. *The Interpretation of Cultures*. London: Hutchinson, 1975.

Gert, Bernard. *The Moral Rules*. New York: Harper Torchbooks, 1973.

Gewirth, Alan. *Human Rights: Essays on Justification and Applications*. Chicago: University of Chicago Press, 1982.

———. *Reason and Morality*. Chicago: University of Chicago Press, 1978.

Giddens, Anthony. "Agency, Institution and Time-Space Analysis." In *Advances in Social Theory and Methodology*, edited by K. Knorr-Centina and A. V. Cicourel. Boston: Routledge & Kegan Paul, 1981.

———. *Central Problems in Social Theory: Action, Structure and Contradiction in Social Analysis*. London: Macmillan, 1979.

———. "Four Myths in the History of Social Thought." *Economy and Society* 1 (1972): 358–72.

Gilbert, Neil. *Capitalism and the Welfare State*. New Haven: Yale University Press, 1983.

Gillespie, Norman C. "Abortion and Human Rights." *Ethics* 87 (1977): 237–43.

Gilligan, Carol. "Do the Social Sciences Have an Adequate Theory of Moral Development?" In *Social Science and Moral Inquiry*, edited by Norma Haan, Robert N. Bellah, Paul Rabinow, and William M. Sullivan. New York: Columbia University Press, 1983.

———. *In a Different Voice*. Cambridge, Mass.: Harvard University Press, 1982.

Gluckman, Max. *The Judicial Process Among the Barotse of Northern Rhodesia*. Manchester: Manchester University Press, 1967.

Goffman, Erving. *Interaction Ritual*. Garden City: Doubleday Anchor, 1967.

———. *The Presentation of Self in Everyday Life*. Garden City: Doubleday Anchor, 1959.

———. *Strategic Interaction*. Philadelphia: University of Pennsylvania Press, 1969.

Goldman, Alan H. *Justice and Reverse Discrimination*. Princeton: Princeton University Press, 1979.

Goodin, Robert E. *The Politics of Rational Man*. London: Wiley, 1976.

Gouldner, Alvin W. *The Coming Crisis of Western Sociology*. New York: Basic Books, 1970.

———. *The Dialectics of Ideology and Technology*. New York: Seabury Press, 1976.

Greenspan, Patricia S. "A Case of Mixed Feelings: Ambivalence and the Logic of Emotion." In *Explaining Emotions*, edited by Amélie Oksenberg Rorty. Berkeley: University of California Press, 1980.

Gross, Barry R. *Discrimination in Reverse: Is Turnabout Fair Play?* New York: New York University Press, 1978.

Gutmann, Amy. "Children, Paternalism, and Education." *Philosophy and Public Affairs* 9 (1980): 338–58.

———. *Liberal Equality*. Cambridge: Cambridge University Press, 1980.

Haan, Norma; Bellah, Robert N.; Rabinow, Paul; and Sullivan, William M., eds. *Social Sciences as Moral Inquiry*. New York: Columbia University Press, 1983.

Habermas, Jürgen. *Communication and the Evolution of Society*. Translated by Thomas McCarthy. Boston: Beacon Press, 1979.

———. *Knowledge and Human Interests*. Translated by Jeremy J. Shapiro. Boston: Beacon Press, 1978.

———. *Legitimation Crisis*. Translated by Thomas McCarthy. Boston: Beacon Press, 1975.

———. "A Postscript to *Knowledge and Human Interests*. *Philosophy of the Social Sciences* 3 (1973): 157–89.

———. "Some Distinctions in Universal Pragmatics." *Theory and Society* 3 (1976): 155–67.

———. *Theory and Practice*. Translated by John Viertel. Boston: Beacon Press, 1973.

———. *Toward a Rational Society*. Translated by Jeremy J. Shapiro. Boston: Beacon Press, 1970.

———. "Wahrheitstheorien." In *Wirklichkeit und Reflexion*, edited by H. Fahrenbach. Pfüllingen: Neske, 1973.

Hacker, Andrew. "Farewell to the Family?" *New York Review*, 18 March 1982.

Hale, Nathan. "Freud's Reflections on Work and Love." In *Themes of Work and Love*, edited by Neil J. Smelser and Erik Erikson. London: Grant McIntyre, 1980.

Harbury, C. D. "Equality versus Mobility." In *Economics and Equality*, edited by Aubrey Jones. London: Philip Allan, 1976.

Hare, R. D. *Psychopathology: Theory and Research*. New York: Wiley, 1970.

441

Hare, R. M. "Political Obligation." In *Social Ends and Political Means*, edited by Ted Honderich. London: Routledge & Kegan Paul, 1976.

Harrison, Alan. "Trends Over Time in the Distribution of Wealth." In *Economics and Equality*, edited by Aubrey Jones. London: Philip Allan, 1976.

Hart, H. L. A. "Are There Any Natural Rights?" *Philosophical Review* 64 (1955): 175–91.

———. *The Concept of Law*. Oxford: Clarendon Press, 1961.

———. "Positivism and the Separation of Law and Morals." In *The Philosophy of Law*, edited by Ronald Dworkin. Oxford: Oxford University Press, 1977.

Hayek, F. A. *Law, Legislation and Liberty*. Vol. 2. *The Mirage of Social Justice*. London: Routledge & Kegan Paul, 1976.

Held, Virginia. "Justification: Legal and Political." *Ethics* 86 (1975): 1–16.

Hendlin, Herbert. *The Age of Sensation*. New York: McGraw-Hill, 1975.

Henley, Kenneth. "The Authority to Educate." In *Having Children: Philosophical and Legal Reflections on Parenthood*, edited by Onora O'Neill and William Ruddick. New York: Oxford University Press, 1979.

Henry, Jules. *Culture Against Man*. New York: Knopf, 1963.

Hersh, Richard H.; Paolitto, Diana Pritchard; and Reimer, Joseph. *Promoting Moral Growth: From Piaget to Kohlberg*. New York: Longman, 1979.

Hewitt, Christopher. "The Effect of Political Democracy and Social Democracy on Equality in Industrial Societies: A Cross-National Comparison." *American Sociological Review* 42 (1977): 450–64.

Hirsch, Fred. *Social Limits to Growth*. London: Routledge & Kegan Paul, 1977.

Hirst, P. Q. *On Law and Ideology*. London: Macmillan, 1979.

Hobbes, Thomas. *Leviathan*. Edited with an introduction by Michael Oakeshot. New York: Oxford University Press, 1947.

Hochschild, Jennifer L. *What's Fair?: American Beliefs About Distributive Justice*. Cambridge, Mass.: Harvard University Press, 1981.

Hoffman, M. L. "Identifications and Conscience Development." *Child Development* 42 (1971): 1071–82.

———. "Moral Development." In *Carmichael's Manual of Child Development*, edited by P. H. Mussen. New York: Wiley, 1970.

Hollis, Martin, and Lukes, Steven, eds. *Rationality and Relativism*. Oxford: Basil Blackwell, 1982.

Hollis, Martin, and Nell, Edward. *Rational Economic Man*. Cambridge: Cambridge University Press, 1975.

Holmes, Oliver Wendell. "The Path of the Law." In *The Mind and Faith of Justice Holmes*, edited by Max Lerner. Boston: Little, Brown, 1943.

Homans, George. *Social Behavior: Its Elementary Forms*. New York: Harcourt, Brace & World, 1961.

Horvat, Branko. *The Political Economy of Socialism*. Oxford: Martin Robertson, 1982.

Huaco, George A. "The Functionalist Theory of Stratification: Two Decades of Controversy." *Inquiry* 9 (1966): 212–50.

Hull, David. *Critical Theory*. Berkeley: University of California Press, 1980.

International Labour Office. *The Cost of Social Security 1964–1967*. Geneva, 1972.

Isenberg, Arnold. "Natural Pride and Natural Shame." In *Explaining Emotions*, edited by Amélie Oksenberg Rorty. Berkeley: University of California Press, 1980.

Jacoby, Russell. "Narcissism and the Crisis of Capitalism." *Telos* 44 (1980): 58–65.

Jains, S. *Size Distribution of Income*. Washington, D.C.: World Bank, 1975.

Jasso, Guillermina, and Rossi, Peter H. "Distributive Justice and Earned Income." *American Sociological Review* 42 (1977): 639–51.

Jencks, Christopher; Smith, Marshall; Acland, Henry; Bane, Mary Jo; Cohen, David; Gintis, Herbert; Heyns, Barbara; and Michelson, Stephan. *Inequality: A Reassessment of the Effect of Family and Schooling in America*. New York: Basic Books, 1972.

Jenkins, Iredell. *Social Order and the Limits of Law*. Princeton: Princeton University Press, 1980.

Jouvenel, Bertrand de. *Sovereignty*. Chicago: University of Chicago Press, 1957.

Kahn, R. L. "The Work Module." In *Work and the Quality of Life*, edited by J. O'Toole. Cambridge, Mass.: MIT Press, 1974.

Kairys, David, ed. *The Politics of Law: A Progressive Critique*. New York: Pantheon Books, 1982.

Kaufman, Walter. *Without Guilt and Justice*. New York: Delta, 1975.

Kavolis, Vyatautas. "Logics of Selfhood and Modes of Order: Civilizational Structures for Individual Identities." In *Identity and Authority*, edited by Roland Robertson and Burkart Holzner. Oxford: Basil Blackwell, 1980.

Kelman, Mark. "The Social Costs of Inequality." In *The New Conservatives: A Critique from the Left*, edited by Lewis A. Coser and Irving Howe. New York: Quadrangle Books, 1974.

Kelsen, Hans. "Centralization and Decentralization." In *Authority and the Individual*. Cambridge, Mass.: Harvard University Press, 1937.

———. *Das Naturrecht in der Politischen Theorie*. Salzburg, 1963.

———. *The General Theory of Law and State*. New York: Russell and Russell, 1945.

———. "The Pure Theory of Law." *Law Quarterly Review* 50 (1934): 470–91.

———. *The Pure Theory of Law*. Berkeley: University of California Press, 1967.

———. *What is Justice?* Berkeley: University of California Press, 1957.

Kennedy, Donald. "Legal Education as Training for Hierarchy." In *The Politics of Law: A Progressive Critique*, edited by David Kairys. New York: Pantheon, 1982.

Kenney, Anthony. *Action, Emotion and Will*. London: Routledge & Kegan Paul, 1963.

Klein, Melanie. *Envy and Gratitude*. New York: Delta Books, 1977.

Kluckhohn, Clyde. "The Moral Order in the Expanding Society." In *City Invincible*, edited by C. H. Kraeling and R. M. Adams. Chicago: University of Chicago Press, 1960.

Kohlberg, Lawrence. "The Claim to Moral Adequacy of a Highest Stage of Moral Judgment." *Journal of Philosophy* 40 (1973): 639–45.

———. "Continuities in Childhood and Adult Moral Development Revisited." In *Lifespan Developmental Psychology*, edited by P. B. Baltes and L. R. Goulet. New York: Academic Press, 1973.

———. "From Is to Ought: How to Commit the Naturalistic Fallacy and Get Away With It in the Study of Moral Development." In *Cognitive Development and Epistemology*, edited by T. Mischel. New York: Academic Press, 1971.

———. "Justice as Reversibility." In *Philosophy, Politics and Society*. Fifth series, edited by Peter Laslett and James Fishkin. London: Basil Blackwell, 1979.

———. "Moral Development." In *International Encyclopedia of the Social Sciences*, vol. 10, edited by David L. Sills. New York: Free Press, 1968.

———. "Moral and Religious Education and the Public Schools: A Developmental View." In *Religion and Public Education*, edited by T. Sizer. Boston: Houghton Mifflin, 1967.

———. "Moral Stages and Moralization: The Cognitive-Developmental Approach." In *Moral Development and Behavior*, edited by T. Lickona, New York: Holt, 1976.

———. "Stage and Sequence: The Cognitive-Developmental Approach to Socialization." In *Handbook of Socialization: Theory and Research*, edited by David A. Goslin. Chicago: Rand McNally, 1969.

———. "Stages of Moral Development as a Basis for Moral Education." In *Moral Education*, edited by C. M. Beck, B. S. Crittenden, and E. V. Sullivan. New York: Newman Press, 1971.

Kohlberg, Stephen. "Max Weber's Types of Rationality: Cornerstones for the Analysis of Rationalization. Processes in History." *American Sociological Review* 85 (1980): 1145–79.

Kohn, Melvin L. "Job Complexity and Adult Personality." In *Themes of Work and Love in Adulthood*, edited by Neil J. Smelser and Erik H. Erikson. London: Grant McIntyre, 1980.

Kohn, Melvin L., and Schooler, Carmi. "Occupational Experience and Psychological Functioning: An Assessment of Reciprocal Effects." *American Sociological Review* 38 (1973): 97–118.

———. "The Reciprocal Effects of the Substantive Complexity of Work and Intellectual Flexibility: A Longitudinal Assessment." *American Journal of Sociology* 84 (1978): 24–52.

Kolko, Gabriel. *Wealth and Power in America*. New York: Praeger Publishers, 1962.

Kortian, Garbis. *Metacritique: The Philosophical Argument of Jürgen Habermas*. Cambridge: Cambridge University Press, 1980.

Kovel, Joel. "Narcissism and the Family." *Telos* 44 (1980): 88–100.

Krebs, Richard, and Kohlberg, Lawrence. "Moral Judgment and Ego Controls as Determinants of Resistance to Cheating." Unpublished manuscript. Harvard University, 1973.

Kristol, Irving. "About Equality." *Commentary* 54 (1972): 41–47.

Krygier, Martin. "Anthropological Approaches." In *Law and Social Control*, edited by Eugene Kamenka and Alice Erh-Soon Tay. London: Edward Arnold, 1980.

Kuhn, Thomas S. *The Structure of Scientific Revolutions*. Chicago: Chicago University Press, 1962.

Kuznets, S. *Modern Economic Growth: Rate Structure, and Spread*. New Haven: Yale University Press, 1966.

Lakatos, Imre, and Musgrave, Alan, eds. *Criticism and the Growth of Knowledge*. Cambridge: Cambridge University Press, 1970.

Lampman, S. J. *The Share of Top Wealth-Holders in the National Wealth: 1922–1956*. Princeton: Princeton University Press, 1962.

LaPalombara, Joseph. *Interest Groups in Italian Politics*. Princeton: Princeton University Press, 1964.

———. *Politics within Nations*. Englewood Cliffs, N.J.: Prentice-Hall, 1974.

Lasch, Christopher. *The Culture of Narcissism*. New York: W. W. Norton, 1978.

Lehning, Percy B. "Cutting Lines We Dare Not Cross: Justice and Retrenchment in the Welfare State." Paper presented at the Conference on Futures of the Welfare State, March 1983, Bloomington, Indiana.

Lindenfeld, Frank, and Rothschild-Whitt, Joyce, eds., *Workplace Democracy and Social Change*. Boston: Porter Sergeant, 1982.

Lindgren, Gunilla. "Height, Weight and Menarche in Swedish Urban School Children in Relation to Socio-Economic and Regional Differences." *Annals of Human Biology* 3 (1976): 501–28.

Lipset, Seymour Martin. *Political Man*. Garden City: Doubleday, 1960.

———. *The First New Nation*. New York: Doubleday Anchor, 1967.

Livingston, John C. *Fair Game? Inequality and Affirmative Action*. San Francisco: W. H. Freeman & Co., 1979.

Locke, John. *Two Treaties of Government*. Edited by Peter Laslett. 2nd ed. Cambridge: Cambridge University Press, 1970.

Louch, A. R. *Explanation and Human Action*. Berkeley: University of California Press, 1969.

Luban, David. "Just War and Human Rights." *Philosophy and Public Affairs* 9 (1980): 160–81.

———. "The Romance of the Nation-State." *Philosophy and Public Affairs* 9 (1980): 392–97.

Lynd, Helen Merrel. *On Shame and the Search for Identity*. New York: Harcourt, Brace and Company, 1958.

Lyons, David. "The New Indian Claims and Original Rights to Land." *Social Theory and Practice* 4 (Fall 1977): 249–93.

Macarov, David. *Incentives to Work*. San Francisco: Jossey-Bass, 1970.

McCord, W., and McCord, J. *The Psychopath: An Essay on the Criminal Mind*. New York: Van Nostrand, 1964.

McFate, Patricia Bliss. "To See Everything in Another Light." *Daedalus* 113 (1984): 29–60.

McIlwain, C. H. *The Growth of Political Thought in the West*. New York: Macmillan, 1932.

MacIntyre, Alasdair. *After Virtue*. London: Duckworth, 1981.

Mackie, John. "The Third Theory of Law." *Philosophy and Public Affairs* 7 (1977): 3–16.

Mandeville, B. *The Fable of the Bees*. 1724. Edited with an introduction by Philip Harth. London: Penguin, 1970.

Mann, Michael. "The Social Cohesion of Liberal Democracy." *American Sociological Review* 35 (1970): 423–39.

Marcuse, Herbert. *Reason and Revolution*. New York: Oxford University Press, 1941.

Marković, Mihailo. *From Affluence to Praxis*. Ann Arbor: University of Michigan Press, 1974.

———. "Marxism as a Political Philosophy." In *Political Theory and Political Education*, edited by Marvin Richter. Princeton: Princeton University Press, 1980.

Marx, Karl. *Critique of the Gotha Programme*. Peking: Foreign Language Press, 1972.

———. *The German Ideology*. New York: International Publishers, 1939.

Matthews, Mervyn. *Class and Society in Soviet Russia*. London: Allen Lane, 1972.

Mead, George Herbert. *Mind, Self, and Society*. Chicago: University of Chicago Press, 1934.

Melden, A. L. *Rights and Persons*. Oxford: Basil Blackwell, 1977.

Miller, Richard W. "Reason and Commitment in the Social Sciences." *Philosophy and Public Affairs* 8 (1979): 241–66.

Mills, C. Wright. *The Power Elite*. New York: Oxford University Press, 1956.

Mishra, Ramesh. *Society and Social Policy*. London: Macmillan, 1977.

Morris, Herbert, ed. *Guilt and Shame*. Belmont, Calif.: Wadsworth Publishing Company, 1971.

Mount, Ferdinand. *The Subversive Family: An Alternative History of Love and Marriage*. London: Cage, 1982.

Murphy, J. M., and Gilligan, Carol. "Moral Development in Late Adolescence and Adulthood: A Critique and Reconstruction of Kohlberg's Theory." *Human Development* 23 (1980): 77–104.

446

Nisbet, Robert. *The Twilight of Authority.* New York: Oxford University Press, 1975.

Nonet, Philippe, and Selznick, Philip. *Law and Society in Transition.* New York: Harper Torchbooks, 1978.

Nove, Alec, and Nuti, D. M., eds. *Socialist Economics.* Harmondsworth: Penguin, 1972.

Nove, Alec. *The Economics of Feasible Socialism.* London: George Allen & Unwin, 1983.

Nozick, Robert. *Anarchy, State, and Utopia.* New York: Basic Books, 1974.

O'Connor, James. *The Corporation and the State.* New York: St. Martin's Press, 1974.

———. *The Fiscal Crisis of the State.* New York: St. Martin's Press, 1973.

O'Neill, Onora, and Ruddick, William, eds. *Having Children: Philosophical and Legal Reflections on Parenthood.* New York: Oxford University Press, 1979.

Parkin, Frank. *Class, Inequality and Political Order.* London: Paladin Books, 1972.

———. *Marxism and Class Theory.* London: Tavistock Publications, 1979.

Parsons, Talcott. *Essays in Sociological Theory: Pure and Applied.* Glencoe, Ill.: Free Press, 1949.

———. "The Law and Social Control." In *Law and Sociology: Explanatory Essays,* edited by William M. Evans. New York: Free Press, 1962.

———. *Social Systems and the Evolution of Action Theory.* New York: Free Press, 1977.

Parsons, Talcott, and Bales, R. F. *Family: Socialization and Interaction Process.* London: Routledge & Kegan Paul, 1956.

Parsons, Talcott, and Shils, Edward, eds. *Toward a General Theory of Action.* Cambridge, Mass.: Harvard University Press, 1951.

Parsons, Talcott; Shils, Edward; Naegele, Kaspar D.; and Pitts, Jesse R., eds. *Theories of Society.* Vol. I. New York: Free Press, 1961.

Paul, Jeffrey, ed. *Reading Nozick.* Oxford: Basil Blackwell, 1981.

Pechman, Joseph A., and Okner, Benjamin A. *Who Bears the Tax Burden?* Washington, D.C.: The Brookings Institute, 1974.

Peirce, Charles S. *Collected Papers.* Vol. 5. Edited by V. C. Hartshorne and P. Weiss. Cambridge, Mass.: Harvard University Press, 1934.

Pen, Jan. *Income Distribution.* London: Allen Lane, The Penguin Press, 1971.

Peters, Richard S. "A Reply to Kohlberg," *Phi Delta Kappa* 56 (1975): 78.

Pettit, Philip. "Habermas on Truth and Justice." In *Marx and Marxism,* edited by C. H. R. Parkinson. Brighton: Harvester Press, forthcoming.

Phelps Brown, Henry. *The Inequality of Pay.* Oxford: Oxford University Press, 1977.

Phillips, Derek L. *Equality, Justice and Rectification.* London: Academic Press, 1979.

———. *Knowledge from What?* Chicago: Rand McNally, 1971.

Phillips, Derek L. *Wittgenstein and Scientific Knowledge*. London: Macmillan, 1977.

Piaget, Jean. *The Moral Judgment of the Child*. 1932. New York: Free Press, 1965.

———. *The Origins of Intelligence in Children*. New York: International Universities Press, 1952.

———. *Six Psychological Studies*. New York: Random House, 1967.

Piers, Gerhart, and Singer, Milton S. *Shame and Guilt: A Psychoanalytic and a Cultural Study*. Springfield, Ill.: Charles C. Thomas, 1953.

Pitkin, Hannah. "Obligation and Consent." In *Philosophy, Politics and Society*. Fourth series, edited by Peter Laslett, W. G. Runciman, and Quentin Skinner. Oxford: Basil Blackwell, 1972.

———. *Wittgenstein and Justice*. Berkeley: University of California Press, 1975.

Postema, Gerald J. "Bentham and Dworkin on Positivism and Adjudication." *Social Theory and Practice* 5 (1980): 347–76.

Quine, W. V. *From a Logical Point of View*. Cambridge, Mass.: Harvard University Press, 1953.

Rawls, John. "Kantian Constructivism in Moral Theory." *The Journal of Philosophy* 77 (1980): 515–72.

———. "Legal Obligations and the Duty of Fair Play." In *Law and Philosophy*, edited by Sidney Hook. New York: New York University Press, 1964.

———. *A Theory of Justice*. Cambridge, Mass.: Harvard University Press, 1971.

Raz, Joseph. *The Authority of Law: Essays on Law and Morality*. Oxford: Clarendon Press, 1979.

Regis, Edward, Jr. *Gewirth's Ethical Rationalism: Critical Essays with a Reply by Alan Gewirth*. Chicago: University of Chicago Press, 1984.

Rieff, Philip. *Fellow Teachers*. New York: Harper & Row, 1973.

———. *The Triumph of the Therapeutic*. New York: Harper & Row, 1966.

Riesman, David; Glazer, Nathan; and Denny, Reuel. *The Lonely Crowd*. Garden City, N.Y.: Doubleday Anchor, 1956.

Rogow, Arnold A. *The Dying of the Light*. New York: Putman's, 1975.

Rorty, Amélie Oksenberg. "Agent Regret." In *Explaining Emotions*, edited by Amélie Oksenberg Rorty. Berkeley: University of California Press, 1980.

Rorty, Amélie Oksenberg, ed. *Explaining Emotions*. Berkeley: University of California Press, 1980.

Rorty, Richard. *Philosophy and the Mirror of Nature*. Oxford: Basil Blackwell, 1980.

Rose, Gilbert J. "Some Misuses of Analysis as a Way of Life." *International Review of Psychoanalysis* 1 (1974): 509–15.

Rothman, G. R. "The Influence of Moral Reasoning on Behavior Choices." *Child Development* 47 (1976): 399–406.

Rousseau, J. J. *The Social Contract.* Translated by G. D. H. Cole. New York: Dutton, 1950.

Ruddick, William. "Parents and Life Prospects." In *Having Children: Philosophical and Legal Reflections on Parenthood*, edited by Onora O'Neill and William Ruddick. New York: Oxford University Press, 1979.

Ryan, C. C. "Yours, Mine, and Ours: Property Rights and Individual Liberty." *Ethics* 87 (1977): 126–41.

Sakharov, André D. *My Country and the World.* New York: Knopf, 1975.

Sanford, Cedrich. "The Taxation of Personal Wealth." In *Economics and Equality*, edited by Aubrey Jones. London: Philip Allan, 1976.

Schaar, John. "Legitimacy in the Modern State." In *Power and Community*, edited by Philip Green and Sanford Levinson. New York: Vintage Books, 1970.

Schoeman, Ferdinand. "Rights of Children, Rights of Parents, and the Moral Basis of the Family." *Ethics* 91 (1980): 6–19.

Schwartz, Adina. "Meaningful Work." *Ethics* 92 (1982): 634–46.

Schweickart, David. *Capitalism or Worker Control?* New York: Praeger Publishers, 1980.

Sears, R. R.; Maccoby, E. E.; and Levin, H. *Patterns of Child Rearing.* New York: Harper Brothers, 1957.

Selman, R. L. "The Relation of Role-Taking to the Development of Moral Judgment in Children." *Child Development* 42 (1971): 79–91.

Selucky, R. *Marxism, Socialism and Freedom.* London: Macmillan, 1979.

Sellars, Willifred. *Science, Perception and Reality.* London: Routledge & Kegan Paul, 1963.

Shkaratan, O. I. "Sources of Social Differentiation of the Working Class in Soviet Society." *International Journal of Sociology* (1973): 10–26.

Simmons, A. John. *Moral Principles and Political Obligations.* Princeton: Princeton University Press, 1979.

Singer, Peter. "The Right to be Rich or Poor." *The New York Review of Books*, 6 March 1975.

Sjolin, S. "Infant Mortality in Sweden." In *Health Care of Mothers and Children in National Health Services*, edited by Helen M. Williams. Cambridge, Mass.: Ballinger, 1975.

Skillen, Anthony. *Ruling Illusions: Philosophy and the Social Order.* Hussocks, Sussex: Harvester Press, 1977.

Skolnick, Arlene. *The Intimate Environment: Exploring Marriage and the Family.* Boston: Little, Brown, 1973.

Smelser, Neil J. "Issues in the Study of Work and Love." In *Themes of Work and Love in Adulthood*, edited by Neil J. Smelser and Erik Erikson. London: Grant McIntyre, 1980.

Smith, Adam. *An Inquiry into the Nature and Causes of the Wealth of Nations.* 2 vols. in 1. Edited by Edwin Canna. Chicago: University of Chicago Press, 1976.

Sociaal en Cultureel Rapport. 's-Gravenhage: Staatsuitgeverij, 1982.

Solomon, Robert C. "Emotions and Choice." In *Explaining Emotions*, edited by Amélie Oksenberg Rorty. Berkeley: University of California Press, 1980.

———. *The Passions*. Garden City, N.Y.: Anchor Press, 1977.

Soltan, Karol Edward. "Empirical Studies of Distributive Justice." *Ethics* 92 (1982): 673–91.

Sousa, Ronald de. "The Rationality of Emotions." In *Explaining Emotions*, edited by Amélie Oksenberg Rorty. Berkeley: University of California Press, 1980.

Spencer, Herbert. *The Man Versus the State*. Ohio: Caxton, 1960.

Spiro, Manfred. "Social Systems, Personality, and Functional Analysis." In *Studying Personality Cross-Culturally*. Evanston, Ill.: Row, Petersen, 1961.

Stack, Stephen. "The Effect of Direct Government Involvement in the Economy on the Degree of Income Inequality: A Cross-National Study." *American Sociological Review* 43 (1978): 880–88.

Stanley, Manfred. *The Technological Conscience*. New York: Free Press, 1978.

Staub, Ervin. "Helping a Distressed Person: Social, Personality, and Stimulus Determinants." In *Advances in Experimental Social Psychology*, vol. 7, edited by L. Berkowitz. New York: Academic Press, 1974.

———. *Positive Social Behavior and Morality*. Vol. 2. New York: Academic Press, 1979.

Stephen, Frank H., ed. *The Performance of Labor-Managed Firms*. New York: St. Martin's Press, 1982.

Strauss, Anselm, ed. *The Social Psychology of George Herbert Mead*. Chicago: University of Chicago Press, 1958.

Sullivan, William. *Restructuring Public Philosophy*. Berkeley: University of California Press, 1982.

Swafford, Michael. "Sex Differences in Soviet Earnings." *American Sociological Review* 43 (1978): 657–73.

Swidler, Ann. "Love and Adulthood in American Culture." In *Themes of Work and Love*, edited by Neil J. Smelser and Erik Erikson. London: Grant McIntyre, 1980.

Taylor, Charles. "Neutrality in Political Science." In *Philosophy, Politics and Society*. Third series, edited by Peter Laslett and W. G. Runciman. Oxford: Basil Blackwell, 1969.

Terkel, Studs. *Working*. New York: Avon Books, 1975.

Thurow, Lester C. *Generating Inequality: Mechanisms of Distribution in the U.S. Economy*. New York: Basic Books, 1975.

———. *The Zero-Sum Society*. New York: Penguin Books, 1981.

Tipton, Stephen M. "The Moral Logic of Alternative Religion." *Daedalus* 111 (1982): 185–213.

Tökés, Rudolf L. *Dissent in the U.S.S.R.* Baltimore: Johns Hopkins University Press, 1975.

Toulmin, Stephen. *Human Understanding*. Vol. I. Oxford: Clarendon Press, 1970.

Touraine, Alain. *The Post-Industrial Society*. Translated by Leonard F. X. Mayhew. New York: Random House, 1972.

Townsend, Peter, and Davidson, Nick. *Inequalities in Health: The Black Report*. London: Penguin, 1982.

Turiel, Elliot. "Developmental Processes in the Child's Moral Thinking." In *Trends and Issues in Developmental Psychology*, edited by P. Mussen, E. J. Langer, and M. Covington. New York: Holt, 1969.

————. "An Experimental Test of the Sequentiality of Developmental Stages in the Child's Moral Judgments." *Journal of Personality and Social Psychology* 3 (1966): 611–18.

Tushnet, Mark. "Corporations and Free Speech." In *The Politics of Law: A Progressive Critique*, edited by David Kairys. New York: Pantheon, 1982.

UNESCO. *Statistical Yearbook 1970*. Paris, 1971.

Unger, Robert Mangabeira. "The Critical Legal Studies Movement." *Harvard Law Journal* 96 (1983): 561–75.

"United Nations Declaration of the Rights of the Child." Resolution 1386 (XIV). Published in the *Official Records of the General Assembly, Fourteenth Session, Supplement No. 16*, 1960.

U.S. Bureau of the Census. *Current Population Reports, Consumer Income 1977*, Series 8–60, no. 118, March 1979.

Veen, Robert J. van der. "From Contributions to Needs." Paper presented at the European Consortium for Political Research, April 1982, at Aarhus, Denmark.

Wald, Michael. "State Intervention on Behalf of 'Neglected' Children: A Search for Realistic Standards." *Stanford Law Review* 27 (1974–75): 985–1040.

Wallace, James D. *Virtues and Vices*. Ithaca, N.Y.: Cornell University Press, 1978.

Walzer, Michael. *Just and Unjust Wars*. New York: Basic Books, 1977.

————. "The Moral Standing of States: A Response to Four Critics." *Philosophy and Public Affairs* 9 (1980): 209–29.

————. *Spheres of Justice*. New York: Basic Books, 1983.

Weber, Max. *Basic Concepts in Sociology*. New York: Citadel Press, 1962.

————. "The Concept of Legitimate Order." In *Theories of Society*, vol. I, edited by Talcott Parsons, Edward Shils, Kaspar D. Naegele, and Jesse R. Pitts. New York: Free Press, 1961.

————. *Economy and Society*. Translated by Guenther Roth and Claus Wittich. 3 vols. New York: Bedminster Press, 1968.

————. *General Economic History*. Translated by Frank H. Knight. New York: Collier Books, 1966.

————. *The Methodology of the Social Sciences*. Translated by Edward A. Shils and Harry A. Finch. Glencoe, Ill.: Free Press, 1949.

————. " 'Objectivity' in Social Science and Social Policy." In *Philosophy of the Social Sciences*, edited by Maurice Nathanson. New York: Random House, 1963.

———. *On Law and Economy in Society*. Translated by Max Rheinstein. Cambridge, Mass.: Harvard University Press, 1954.

———. *The Theory of Social and Economic Organization*. Translated by A. M. Henderson and Talcott Parsons. New York: Oxford University Press, 1947.

Weiss, Leonard W. *Economics and Society*. New York: Wiley, 1975.

Westergaard, J., and Ressler, H. *Class in a Capitalist Society*. London: Heinemann, 1975.

Wheelis, Allen. *The Moralist*. New York: Basic Books, 1973.

———. *The Quest for Identity*. New York: W. W. Norton, 1958.

Wilensky, Harold L. *The Welfare State and Equality*. Berkeley: University of California Press, 1975.

Wiles, Peter. *Distribution of Income: East and West*. Amsterdam: North Holland, 1974.

Williams, Bernard. *Problems of the Self*. Cambridge: Cambridge University Press, 1973.

Wilson, Bryan A., ed. *Rationality*. New York: Harper Torchbooks, 1970.

Wittgenstein, Ludwig. *Zettel*. Oxford: Basil Blackwell, 1967.

Wolfe, Alan. *The Limits of Legitimacy*. New York: Free Press, 1977.

Wolff, Robert Paul. *Understanding Rawls*. Princeton: Princeton University Press, 1973.

Wrong, Dennis. "The Oversocialized Conception of Man in Modern Sociology." In *Sociological Theory*, edited by Lewis A. Coser and Bernard Rosenberg. 4th ed. New York: Macmillan, 1976.

———. *Power: Its Forms, Bases, and Uses*. New York: Harper & Row, 1979.

Zimmerman, David. "The Force of Hypothetical Commitment." *Ethics* 93 (1983): 467–83.

Zimmerman, D. H., and Wieder, D. L. "Ethnomethodology and the Problem of Order." In *Understanding Everyday Life*, edited by Jack Douglas. London: Routledge & Kegan Paul, 1972.

INDEX

Library of Congress Cataloging-in-Publication Data

Phillips, Derek L.
Toward a just social order.

Bibliography: p.
Includes index.
1. Social justice. 2. Social norms. 3. Moral conditions. I. Title.

HM216.P53 1986   303.3'72   85-43303
ISBN 0-691-09422-5   ISBN 0-691-02834-6 (pbk.)